SIMORGH

SIMORGH

PORTRAITS ON MY MIND

Abbas Milani

TRANSLATED FROM THE PERSIAN BY

Mahasti Afshar

MAGE PUBLISHERS

This book is part of a series of Iranian Studies publications made possible by the Hamid and Christina Moghadam Program in Iranian Studies at Stanford University.

Mage Publishers Inc.
www.mage.com

Library of Congress Cataloging-in-Publication Data
Available at the Library of Congress

First hardcover edition
ISBN: 978-1-949445-87-9

Visit Mage online: www.mage.com
Email: as@mage.com

CONTENTS

PART 2

To H.S.

PREFACE

Simorgh: Portraits on My Mind, was originally published in Persian in two volumes in August 2022 and April 2023. Each volume was titled *Si Chehreh* (Thirty Portraits) after Attar's *Conference of the Birds,* an allegorical quest for enlightenment where thirty birds survive a fraught journey in search of Simorgh only to realize that the legendary bird is none other than themselves. The sixty portraits are presented in Parts 1 and 2 in this one-volume English edition.

Simorgh is a collection of memories and encounters with individuals I have known – friends, acquaintances, and colleagues. I based my selection not only on their significance in my life, but the light they shed on developments in Iran in the past nearly half century.

None of the portraits in *Simorgh* is a biography of the personalities presented here, but a brief and condensed sketch highlighting only certain aspects of their life. None of them draw upon research. They are a narrative genre at the intersection of short essays and even shorter stories. What I do vouch to the reader is that no element in any of the segments is fictitious. I have presented material that to my mind and recollection is entirely factual. Recognizing that memory is nonetheless flawed and selfish and at times even self-deluding, I have striven to be deliberative and steer clear of facile urges, running every memory through the filter of doubt before committing it to writing.

Tom Stoppard wrote one of his most brilliant plays, *Rozencrantz and Guildenstern Are Dead*, about two "secondary" characters in Shakespeare. But in historical accounts, the distinction between the secondary and the primary is often dependent on the raconteurs of the period and the horizon of knowledge at that time. In reality, the wider and the deeper that horizon, the more fluid the boundary appears between the secondary and the primary. Several of the personalities in *Simorgh* were notable actors on the political stage though not always in the foreground, while several others were like the chorus in Greek tragedy; they did not play a leading role but provided the connective tissue in the body of the drama. Each of the sixty portraits may thus be thought of as a kind of historical short story. I have not supplied any dates of birth or death or included any photographs, for as we know, these are beside the point in a short story, even of the historical kind.

Each of the portraits, while standing on its own, is part of a unified goal, which is to offer, to the best of my ability, some help in elucidating and transcending the nightmare of recent Iranian history. Every historical account – and in my view, every study and genuine piece of research – deconstructs reality in the precise meaning of that term and attempts to tease out both the complexity of seemingly simple events and the simplicity of what is considered complex. *Simorgh* will be a success only if it tempts the reader into thinking that, at least in some instances, their unassailable – ergo, clichéd – perceptions of the "other" deserve to be revisited, whether the "other" be the deputy director of SAVAK or an intellectual who has spent a lifetime fighting dictatorship as their conscience dictated. Such reevaluations are, I believe, a necessary step toward achieving a collective understanding and critique that will help us overcome this nightmare.

They say we are all a product of our memories. Historical transformations are on the one hand driven and shaped by economic and political structures and the conduct of leaders, and on the other, by the struggles and vicissitudes of contemporaneous individuals who, quiet or confrontational, expansive or insular, corral those transformations and determine their outcome. Over the past twenty-five years, I have penned four books on Iranian personalities who have carried a singular weight in history. I began in 2000 with *The Persian Sphinx: Amir Abbas Hoveyda and the Riddle of the Iranian Revolution*, followed in 2008 by the two-volume *Eminent Persians* where a hundred and fifty figures were selected for their leading-edge contributions to the cultural, economic, and/or political domains under the Shah. *The Shah*, a biography of Mohammad Reza Pahlavi, came next. *Simorgh* is the latest addition to this collection.

The premise of Simorgh, which portrays sixty individuals in more or less the order in which I came to know them, is that instead of searching for a demonic design behind the terror that engulfed them all we should look at how our own thinking and decisions as Iranians helped bring it about. Such a dispassionate reckoning is, I believe, a prerequisite for ridding ourselves of the nightmare of our recent history and moving ahead bright-eyed and self-aware.

Abbas Milani

TRANSLATOR'S NOTE

I learned so much from translating *Simorgh*, and not just facts and words I did not know before. My brain is now rewired with a more humanized attitude in judging others, excepting brutes that terrorize and torture and who act as if the end justifies the means no matter the human cost.

In the translation and review process, I was backed by a dream team, the author himself and Mage Publishers. I owe Abbas Milani and Mohammad Batmanglij endless thanks for their meticulous and incisive observations and suggestions throughout. Any remaining faults are mine alone.

An array of Persian terms has been retained and shown in italics, followed by their meaning in English. Kinship terms such as *daie* (maternal uncle) appear in italics only at first mention for a particular individual, e.g., *Daie* Jalal. Words such as *comrades* that appear in quotation marks in the original, often for ironic emphasis, have also been italicized. Some terms that are lost in translation may be found in the Glossary on page 453.

As for transliteration, I have not used diacritic marks for vowels except an occasional "ā" for the long "a" in Persian. In the case of consonants, "q" stands for the Persian letter "qāf" (as in "Mosaddeq") and "gh" for the Persian "ghain" (as in "Ghaffari"), except where the name of a living public figure is spelled differently (as in "Moghadam"). The letter "ayn" has for the most part been dropped (e.g., "Jafar" and "Sanaan,") but retained in a few instances (as in "Sa'di" and "Sa'adati").

Finally, in terms of style and vocabulary, I have tried to stay as close to the original as possible without being obsessive. This has meant occasional additions or omissions of words or phrases to render the whole legible in English while remaining true to the author's intention and voice. A handful of Persian terms have also been elaborated and supplementary information provided to further identify the persons named or to date events.

Mahasti Afshar

PART 1

Zinat Shadman

My mother was a lionhearted rebel born at a time and place that wanted its women chickenhearted and submissive. In intelligence and smarts, prudence and diplomacy, she was at least equal to those among her four brothers who rose to be parliamentarians and ministers and senators and leaders in Iran. I have often thought that if she had lived in England in the second half of the twentieth century, for instance, she might have very likely become a crack stateswoman like Margaret Thatcher. At the same time, when I think back, I believe she never felt envious or bitter about the fact that she abided as a "housewife" with only a sixth-grade education – home-schooled, no less. On her birth certificate she is named Zinat al-Sadat Shadman Valavi. We, her five children, and some of her nephews and nieces, called her Zizi *Jan*. She almost always went by her maiden name Shadman – not Milani. Her sense of independence and pride in her brothers' achievements kept her from changing her name to her husband's. Her free spirit did not lie merely in her choice of name. She was financially independent as well.

Her father, *Seyyed* Abu Torab, was a *rawzeh-khan*, a reciter of Shia elegies in ritual ceremonies. He was also believed to be blessed, which is why he was chosen to wed our grandmother, whom we called *Khanom Bozorg* (Grande Dame) as she exceeded all other members of the family in grace and gravitas. My mother's financial independence was a credit to Khanom Bozorg's personal resources. A spirit of independence was evident in my mother's political ethos as well as her comportment. She was close to her older brother *Seyyed* Fakhreddin. His dismissal as deputy administrator of the Imam Reza Endowment – allegedly due to his disagreements with the Shah – coincided more or less with the rise of Ayatollah Khomeini. I remember how one day my mother, who always went about unveiled except at *rawzeh-khani* gatherings or the bazaar, pulled on a chador and took me along to the Grand Bazaar in Tehran. She exchanged a few words with the proprietor of a stall and bought a little something too. But her actual target was an audiotape that she quickly grabbed from him and hid under her veil. She also managed, obstacles notwithstanding, to borrow a cassette player from a relative, and when Seyyed Fakhreddin came to our house, he and my mother listened to the tape. It was a hawkish speech by Ayatollah Khomeini. Every day from then on, the two exchanged political news in supposedly cryptic and covert ways but whose drift was not hidden even from me as a young child. My mother's tone in criticizing the Shah grew harsher by the day. The fact that the Shah's land reform law of 1962 had divested my father of his share of village acreage near Kouch-Esfahan fueled her anger. On the cusp of the Islamic revolution, however, sensing the danger that lurked in the air not just for the country but her brothers, she had changed her mind and was no longer in favor of it.

My mother's daily life was another reflection of her independence. She shunned housework and cooking – except on Fridays when she made *chelokabab* – leaving the house about the same time as my father and returning a little earlier than he did. She mostly went to her brother Jalal's home where Khanom Bozorg held sway; sometimes she also ran errands and went shopping. Of course, our home was attuned to my father's sleeping, eating, and resting habits. When he took an afternoon siesta, silence ruled the house. Yet it was my mother who ruled supreme at home, as my sister Farzaneh also observed in her own writings, giving examples from all over Iran.

It was sometime in the late 1950s that my mother decided to get a driver's license. I knew of no other woman in her circle and generation who entertained such a thought. My mother took a private instructor and ventured out to practice two or three times a week in the nearby hills – the same hills that now lie in the city center, Tehran having widely expanded since then. She always took one of us kids along and we watched her driving from the back seat with great trepidation. My mother had no talent for learning how to drive. She took a test a couple of times in Tehran and failed. It was finally decided that she would take a test in Qazvin where my maternal *daie* (uncle) Kamal had some clout. On the day of the test, it was my lot to occupy the back seat. Even as a ten-year-old I could tell that my mother's jerky stops and starts in the middle of the street were no sign of her competence. At the end of the test, the poor examiner turned to my mother and said, "Mrs. Shadman, I've been ordered to award you a driver license, and I will, but if you love your precious boy, he nodded at me – don't drive." My mother got her license but never drove again.

My mother's willpower was no less tenacious than her spirit of independence. One summer day, I was sitting next to her as she was using a new Singer sewing machine she had just bought. The old Singer operated mechanically and was part of her dowry. The new model was electrically powered and mounted on a table; its wheel turned by pressing the foot on a wood plank that functioned like a gas pedal. Holding the edge of the fabric with both hands, my mother gently fed the cloth through as the needle scurried up and down at great speed. She was completely focused on the needle and the cloth, while I looked on, spellbound by her skill and the machine's performance. Suddenly, I watched aghast as the needle pierced the nail of her left index finger. The machine stopped at once. Terrified and in tears, I said, "Shall I call someone?" "No, no need," she replied calmly and somewhat testily, and quietly removed the needle from the machine with her uninjured hand. It was like a scene from a horror movie. The needle had punctured the nail and gone right through her finger. She pulled the needle out and then stopped the bleeding with a handkerchief. In those fleeting moments that felt like a lifetime, I marked my mother's every move with a mixture of dread and admiration at such a display of steely sang-froid.

I witnessed another example of her willpower later on. During the entire year that I was locked up at the *Joint Committee*, the headquarters of a counterinsurgency task force, and at Evin, I never saw my mother. My family was given visiting rights forty days after my arrest, but only my father came. My mother had said, "They had no damn right to arrest my son. He hasn't done anything. I refuse to visit him in a prison cell." And she kept to her word.

On the day I was released, I went straight to my parents' house. I knocked. Father opened the door. Both of us broke down instantly and cried uncontrollably. Moments later, he called out in a quavering voice, "Zinat *Khanom*, your son has arrived." My mother stepped out of the hallway into the yard, sobbing aloud, and hugged me so tight it was as if she had been waiting for that moment all her life.

I witnessed her steadfast willpower and impressive defiance even when old age and a stroke had transformed her into an invalid. My mother used to smoke for as long I can remember. Sometimes two or three packs of Homa a day. At the start of the Iran–Iraq war in the fall of 1980, all goods were rationed, and some items grew scarce. Naturally, Homa was not easy to find; nor did cigarette rationing meet my mother's consumption. Of course, societal corruption offered a way out. In those days my friend Farhad Ardalan used to say frequently and in jest, "Perhaps the only solution to the current abomination is the sweeping rot palpable in the system."

Everything could be had in the free – or the black and gray – market, including Homa. One day, I went to my mother's house. She asked, "Abbas, dear, did you pick up any cigarettes?" I apologized: "I forgot." She reacted somewhat apprehensively, "I've run out of cigarettes. I forgot to tell you yesterday." I said, "I'll pick up a pack from the grocer around the corner." I knew from experience that *Hāj Aqa Ba-Taqva* (the Pious Haji) also dealt in the black and gray market. Thanks to his corruption, I usually managed to acquire some scarce goods for my parents.

When I reached the grocery store, the owner was busy. Waiting until the coast was clear, I greeted him and said, "I forgot to pick up cigarettes for my mother; she smokes Homa, you know. If you could let me have a pack now, I'll pay you back tomorrow." He pouted, placed a pack on the counter and said, "Here! But tell Mrs. Shadman there's been a revolution. It's not like old times where she could always issue sundry commands." The tenor of his words caught me off guard. I didn't know what commands my mother might have issued in the past. I said nothing except thanks. But I returned the same unopened pack to him the following day.

When I came home, I handed the pack to my mother. She praised Haji for his sense of gratitude, saying he was not like "those others." I did not know that my next words were to turn my mother's life upside down. I related what Haji had said. Although the stroke had bent my mother's face a little out of shape and it was difficult to read her expressions, she grew visibly upset. Enraged and defiant, she said, "Return the pack to him tomorrow!" Then, as if wishing to round off her declaration with a simple finale, declared, "I will not smoke anymore," and added: "We had yet to be shat on by an asshole crow." She quit a forty-year habit on the spot, and never smoked again.

My mother was an inexhaustible repository of stories and aphorisms and verses – though it was Mehdi Bazargan, a distant relative of my mother who first popularized "asshole crow." Zizi Jan also wrote poetry. Her poems were of little substance, however, not a mark of her talent for poetry but of her aspirations. In later years, I often asked myself, on those occasions when she read her poems to Seyyed Fakhreddin, which I know she did, how did he, a Sa'di connoisseur and a Shakespeare buff, respond to his dear sister?

Proverbs that were not standard *ladies'* fare also used to roll off my mother's tongue. On a trip to the U.S., when she noticed how I'd come home late and leave early, she dropped a hint with: "Abbas *Jan*, a windblown ass doesn't collect dirt," meaning I was too lazy to achieve much. Another time in my childhood, my mother was hosting a Hazrat-e Fatemeh *sofreh*, a ceremonial "meal." All the female members of the family including Khanom Bozorg were there. A professional elegist recited woeful tales of trials and tribulations, then got her fee and left. It was now time for singing and drumming. My mother beat the *tonbak* and at times sang popular tunes with a backup chorus of women – unbridled and iconoclastic poems in the genre of Obeid and Iraj Mirza, including perhaps some of their original verses. That time when she called the twitting Haji a crow with a cracked derrière, she finished with a biting: "Son-of-a-bitch, what temerity!" Some of mother's anger that day was because she resented being the object of pity. In her mind, Haji had taunted *Mrs. Shadman* with a mix of animus and, indeed, pity.

My mother was a very generous woman. She helped people out without thinking of them as piteous, including hosting wedding parties for needy relatives. Most of the family counted her among those women regarded as dependable matchmakers, and reputable. They said her matchmaking was "auspicious," that the unions she created lasted and had a bright future. My father – *Aqa Jan* – though not superstitious, nevertheless believed that my mother's countenance was auspicious. For that reason, he made sure to look at her every day before leaving the house.

On Nowruz, too, my mother's face was the first that my father wanted to see. In turn, my mother believed in the auspiciousness of some of her relatives and friends – some for their esoteric power to help achieve her dreams, others her prayers.

A number of those mystically *favored* souls regularly visited my mother even at the height of her infirmity. Most days, my mother doled out something to them, and those handouts were at the root of tensions between her and my father. Aqa Jan did not subscribe to the notions of *nazr*, religious vows, or the *nazar-kardeh*, mystically blessed souls, and owing to his love of money, could not resign himself to people taking cash from my mother or, in his words, "shafting" her.

He resorted to countless ploys to prevent my mother from making such payouts. On one visit while we were together, he urged my mother: "Zinat, if you have any money to spare, give it to this one," meaning me. He uttered "this one" in such a tone as if I were the neediest person on earth. In those days, I was a member of the Faculty of Law and Political Science at the University of Tehran. My mother would never bow under pressure from my father, and that day was no exception. "I'll spend my money exactly as I please; it's none of your business," she said. Of course, my father didn't agree that it was none of his business.

One day, I was in the classroom when the assistant of the Political Science Department rushed in. Such a scene was unprecedented. "Your father is on the phone," she gasped, "and wants to talk to you urgently." I ran to the office. "Your mother has fallen ill," I heard my father say, his voice trembling. "Get yourself to the hospital!" When I reached the American Hospital – which was renamed after the revolution – my mother was lying in bed in the emergency room. The doctor had not yet arrived. My father was sitting outside the door, distraught and apprehensive. Extremely frugal though he was in all affairs, when it came to my mother's medical care – and, of course, his children's education – he never thought twice about expenditures.

My mother seemed to be unconscious and a nurse was standing next to the bed. As I sat next to my mother and kissed her hand, she grabbed one of my fingers and pressed it. I thought to myself that perhaps she had recognized me and was not completely comatose. The moment the nurse left the room, my mother opened her eyes mischievously and, with a child-like tenderness, said, "Don't worry, child. Mahmoud acted crazy again; I had to punish him." When we returned home that night, she told me how my father had spotted one of her visitors outside the house and given them a piece of his mind. My mother had then pretended to fall into a coma in order to punish him. Evidently, in a patriarchal world, even a woman who is financially independent must fight myriad battles, even feign a medical crisis, to maintain her independence.

Despite all the protest and kerfuffle, my mother loved my father very dearly. Whenever she heard us children gripe, she would say, "Mahmoud has his batty moments, but for you, he's been a perfect father. He's not such a bad husband to me either." Perhaps the worst scourge of entrenched patriarchy for women like my mother is that it invariably lowers their expectations of life. For a woman as intelligent and capable as she was, being content that my father was "not such a bad husband" encapsulates something of that internalized patriarchy.

Mahmoud Milani

My father, *Aqa Jan*, came close to marrying *Mashrouteh* (Constitution). Mashrouteh *Khanom* was his cousin on his father's side. In those days, genetics was not on anyone's radar, and it was held that the betrothal of paternal cousins was sanctified in heaven. Mashrouteh was one of three sisters. The second girl was called *Jomhouri* (Republic), and the third "*Iran*." My grandfather and his brother were business partners in Rasht. They operated a trading company there and in Baku – or, as my father called it, Badkubeh. Both were staunch advocates of constitutionalism. According to my father, they had also met *Mirza* Kuckak Khan Jangali, the revolutionary leader and later president of the short-lived Gilan Socialist Soviet Republic in northern Iran.

My father's uncle was very keen on his children's education, especially his daughters'. Around that time, he had even sent off Mashrouteh Khanom to Russia to study medicine. It's been said that she was the first gynecologist in Iran. Nevertheless, as best I remember, no one addressed her as Dr. Mashrouteh Milani. The root cause may have been the ethos of a patriarchal society. Or perhaps it was because she did not practice for very long. For reasons that never became clear to me – curiosity in such affairs, especially by children, was frowned upon – they "gave" her to another cousin. The usage of that term in such transactions speaks to a key feature of these exchanges. At any rate, even if Mashrouteh had practiced medicine post-marriage, she would have likely been known more as an exemplary mother than a trailblazing doctor.

My father had in many ways adopted the mindset of his father and uncle. Like them, he became a merchant. He imported paper and crystal from Eastern Europe and steel beams from England. Also like them, he was devoted to educating his children, whether a son or a daughter. His dream was that all five children would study medicine. Despite being frugal in almost every other instance, he was generous when it came to his children's education. As one can tell from the photographs of Baku, my grandfather and his brother were both stylish, as was my father. His attachment to English designer tweed suits and Parisian Sulka ties, and shirts with detachable starched collars, persisted up to the onset of the revolution. Afterwards, he retired his swanky attire and certainly the silk ties that had become a stand-in for *Christians*, and more often than not wore an old, almost frayed suit. The first time I grumbled about it, I was supposed to take him to visit my friend who was a renowned orthopedic surgeon in Tehran; it was he who operated on Khamenei when there was an attempt on his life. The sleeve of my father's jacket was tattered, but he was upset by my respectful complaint. He shut me down and said he would not go to see a doctor at all. It took many apologies and pleadings from me, and my mother's mediation, for him to agree to go. My father always loved doctors' visits and he trusted my friend and had great confidence in him. His reluctance that day meant my protest had genuinely offended him; either that or he had deliberately overreacted to deter me from such meddling ever again. The next time I broached his frayed sleeve in a more deferential and somewhat imploring tone, he said, with a chuckle: "Dear son, who's going to point a *tiliscope* at my sleeve?" I couldn't tell whether he had mispronounced telescope on purpose to make me laugh.

After his father died, taking care of his mother and brother and sister fell on my father's shoulders. Though his brother Taqi went to Paris with my father's support and became an accomplished and renowned surgeon – and for years served as the director of the National Bank Hospital, which ranked among the best in those days – my father never attended college himself. Nevertheless, for years he served as the Chamber of Commerce delegate on the board of the Merchants' Bank Hospital, which along with the National Bank and the Soviet Hospital, was among the best in Tehran at the time. The National and Merchants' Bank hospitals were both close to the Grand Bazaar, which was considered the economic pulse of the country. At the point when I was leaving Iran post-revolution, all the top hospitals in the capital were located in northern Tehran instead and most of their shareholders were American-educated doctors. In any event, after my grandfather's death, his family did not inherit any of his wealth. It was rumored that some relatives had pocketed his assets by devious means. Another story goes that before he passed, the trading company he had run with his brother had gone bankrupt.

Years later when I traveled to the Republic of Azarbaijan on behalf of Stanford University, I decided to visit the state archives in Baku to see if I could find any trace of my grandfather's past activities. I assumed that since the Bolsheviks' secretive bureaucratic apparatus had been dismantled, accessing the archives of the newly liberated republic would be a breeze. I called the archives and asked to schedule a visit. It appeared that the woman who answered the phone had never received such a request before. She said she would have to transfer me to the director of the archives, and she did. He, too, had misgivings and asked suspiciously, "Why do you want to visit the archives?" After repeating the same explanation that had surprised and alarmed the woman, I said I merely wished to review my family's records and added that I was not even certain such records had survived. I did not tell him that I had read in a book that Baku had suffered widespread damage and destruction in the first two or three years of the October Revolution when the Bolsheviks fought to "liberate" Azarbaijan and annex it to the Soviet Union. The director of the archives listened carefully before replying: "I need to consult with my superior. Stay on the line if you wish." I stayed on. His response after a few minutes was that Stanford University must send a formal letter to the embassy of Azarbaijan in Washington and describe the research in detail. Should the embassy approve, they would forward the request to the Azarbaijan Ministry of Foreign Affairs and should the ministry approve my plan, I would be granted permission to visit the archives. I told him I would be leaving Baku in a few days and declined, for the archives' promise wasn't worth the trouble. Perhaps it was better for the ultimate fate of my grandfather and his brother's firm to remain ambiguous. In ambiguity, each can savor their own version of the past and familial blissfulness will remain undisturbed.

My father had learned not only the art of the deal from his constitutionalist father and uncle; he had also acquired misgivings about mullahs. Emulating his father and uncle's beautiful calligraphy, his handwriting was superb. He scripted his letters in the cursive ornamental style known as *nastaaliq-e shekasteh*. For me, each one of them was like a beautiful work of art – even before Zendehroudi introduced the aesthetic capacity of Persian calligraphy to the general public as an element of modern Iranian art. My father began a letter at the center of the page and, when addressing one of his children, usually started with: "Dear light of my eye." The script then flowed down to the bottom of the page and from there to the blank margin on the right and then up to the top of the page. He did not sign his personal letters in the same exquisite and hard to copy style as his signature on bank checks and promissory notes and official documents. In his letters – at least the ones he wrote me – he never failed to urge me to study, and to switch from political science to medicine. One time, he earnestly offered to cover my costs, even though I was already teaching at the law school, if I were willing to transfer to medical school. Ever since childhood when he used to take me along to the bazaar, his constant mantra was the superiority of medicine over all other disciplines.

Years later, when I returned to Iran after graduation, he would gripe about my chosen field, especially as I had not thrived financially and had to occasionally ask my parents for help and borrow money from my brothers or sister. Yet it took just one phone call for the bitterness of all his complaints to transform into a lasting sense of gratification and comfort in me. One day, he rang my home in the U.S. Overseas calls were both difficult and costly in those days. "Yesterday, I went to the bazaar. Several of my friends praised your latest book," he said, adding: "I know you didn't listen to me, but I wanted you to know that I no longer have any doubt that you chose the right path." He then said, "I called to let you know I'm proud of you." I was over the moon, unaware that this was the last time I would hear his voice. My father passed away a week later; he had developed heart disease since his forties. Perhaps for my father, who had absorbed constitutionalism through the teachings of his father and uncle, the strain of living in a country where the constitutional order had been dismantled doubled the stress on his heart.

Even as a child, I found my father's attitude toward mullahs to be extremely interesting and a rarity. Whenever his eyes fell on a mullah, he'd say, "See that thick neck, Abbas Jan?" and add, giggling: "You should wet your hand and hit him right on the neck." After the revolution, I saw the euphoria of mischief in his eyes the day I took him to an office building for some business. I drove the car over the sidewalk up close to the entrance. My father had just been discharged from the hospital. A car had hit him on a rainy night and knocked him into the gutter. His legs were in a cast for several months and for some time afterwards he had to walk on crutches. Passersby marked his distressed state, and nobody fussed when I pulled onto the sidewalk; but while I stood there waiting for him, I got an earful of expletives aimed at my mother and sister – not that they were around. When my father exited the building hobbling on his crutches, he had a triumphant smile on his face. "I finally rode a mullah piggy-back!" he said. "I was having a tough time getting down the stairs with these crutches. A mullah walked up to me and said, 'That is such a burden, father!' He spoke loudly so everyone could hear. I replied in an even louder voice, 'Perchance a merciful holy man like you may lighten it.' He had no other option. I came down the stairs on his back."

I witnessed that aspect of his character most summers in Qazvin as well. My maternal uncle *Daie* Kamal carried a lot of weight in Qazvin during my childhood. For ten nights every year during the month of *Muharram*, he would sponsor elegiac sermons in his particularly handsome and large mansion, which as I recall was adjacent to the seminary. Carpets were spread in the square outdoors for the mourners.

On the tenth night, *Ashura*, which commemorates the martyrdom of Imam Hossein, *Seyyed* Javad Zabihi – a Quran reciter with a notable voice whose corpse turned up with a slit throat after the revolution – was usually the last to climb the pulpit, and extract many tears from the assembled throng. On such a night, the house and the square would fill up with more mourners than ever. We trekked to Qazvin for those *rawzeh-khani*s every year. My father would only come for the finale, if at all, and clearly not to mourn. All the mourners sat on the floor except a few among the town grandees and VIPs who sat on chairs close to where Daie Kamal stood as the mourning host. My father also sat there in a suit and tie, but with mischief squarely on his mind. Knowing that many of the special guests, and the mullahs, were opium buffs, he would yawn incessantly, as yawning reportedly makes hungover addicts even more hung over. My mother, who was more of a believer and whose faith and support for the clergy grew stronger with age, frequently argued with my father on his critical comments about the clergy's attitude toward financial matters. She would warn him, "Don't say those things. They'll say you've become a Sheikhi" – a radical Shia sect. I did not know what *Sheikhi* meant when I was a child, except that to my mother to be called one was clearly a perilous and damning indictment.

When I was growing up, my father was considered wealthy. He bought a large parcel of land from Malek o-Shoara Bahar on an eponymous street, where he built a mansion, designed by an Armenian architect apparently. It's not clear why he declined to implement some of the architect's suggested features, such that the façade looked unfinished. There was a large balcony on the second floor, for example, topped by a handsome concrete canopy. But my father had not erected the supporting pillars intended to secure the deck.

Not only did the balcony fail in its purpose as a summer-
time entertainment and rest area, but it was also dangerous.
It's possible that my father preferred the unfinished façade
because he didn't want the house to look ostentatious.

Nevertheless, when television came to Iran in 1958, my
father bought a large TV set within the first few days. It took
up as much space as a closet. At the time, television was more
popular and fantastical than any peep show. The mullahs
issued a fatwa against it. Some people attributed that to their
animosity toward music and modernity. Others thought the
mullahs had decreed a ban because television was imported
to Iran by the industrialist Habib Sabet, a Baha'i. Naturally,
neither Aqa Jan nor most of the public paid any attention to
the edict. Within the first few weeks after the advent of television in Iran, our living room turned into a virtual theatre.
Neighborhood kids and some adults came by our house
to look at this novel Western offering at six o'clock sharp
when the evening programs started. It was only a four-hour
schedule but none of the guests stayed to the end. I heard
from the filmmaker Ebrahim Golestan that when Shiraz was
powered with electricity in 1928 and his parents' home was
among the first to be wired, his friends would come to his
house in the early evening to witness the wonder of flipping
the switch and watching the room light up.

My father used to carefully shave every morning; that
was before a beard turned into one of the prerequisites of
doing business post-revolution. To get a haircut, he went to
a famous salon called Diyarmand. It was on the second floor
of a large building on Shahabad Avenue. Men and women
shared the same space. The salon occupied an enormous hall
decked out with numerous styling chairs. The entire wall on
one side was one big mirror. On the other side, large windows
offered a view of the hustle and bustle of the street. My father

only visited the salon after closing hours. Mr. Diyarmand himself trimmed my father's thinning hair. He always dressed in a stylish white jacket, a comb and scissors poking out of his pocket. Having spent the day at the bazaar with my father, the Diyarmand evenings bored me. It meant staring out the window for half an hour watching the comings and goings and the street vendors. It also meant no movie that night. Occasionally, my reward for spending the day at my father's workplace was a trip to the cinema before returning home. Some Fridays, we could persuade him, who also liked movies, to take some of us children to see a film. We mostly picked shows we knew drew large crowds – *Trapeze* at the Moulin Rouge and *The Bridge Over the River Kwai* at Cinema Rex. We knew long lines and random brawls and skirmishes were inevitable in the crush to reach the box office. My father bought tickets on the black market at the door.

One night when we hit the street after I'd spent a trying half hour at Diyarmand Salon with a movie itch, my father stopped at a fruit juice stand. Pepsi-Cola had recently arrived in Iran, also by Habib Sabet who in 1955 had bought the rights to bottle it in Tehran. A fatwa was issued against that as well. Regardless, the soda as well as the factory on Eisenhower Avenue were very popular. The plant had turned into a sort of tourist attraction for the populace in Tehran. People would visit it like a museum, which in one sense, it was – a showcase of new industry, of an emerging culture of production and consumption. Pepsi ads were on view in every shop and grocery store on Shahabad Avenue. Kerosene lanterns hanging high on poles and bare light bulbs dangling from ceilings cast a magical and cinematic halo about the storefronts. I was holding my father's hand as we walked in. The shopkeeper stood behind the counter. My father said in a raised voice so he could hear: "Sir, a bottle of Pepsi." The

shopkeeper pulled one out of a huge pail brimming with ice
and Pepsi bottles by the counter and popped the cap in a
theatrical move that he might have learned from the swash-
buckling film star Beyk Imanverdi. A picture of a beautiful
woman standing on a shore with a Pepsi in hand and a smile
on her lips hung on the wall behind him. The shopkeeper
handed the bottle and the cap to my father. Some caps came
with a token underneath the cork, though our cap did not
have one. My father handed me the chilled bottle. Full of
excitement, I promptly put it to my mouth and can still taste
the wondrous flavor of Pepsi on my tongue today. When I
read how Proust recovered childhood memories after tasting a
madeleine cake dipped in tea, I no longer felt so embarrassed
that one of the most lasting memories of my childhood was
my urgent desire to swallow a whole bottle of Pepsi-Cola on
Shahabad Avenue. For I was a rookie – we had never been
allowed to eat or drink anything on the street – and didn't
know the protocol for sipping carbonated soda. I had barely
slugged half the bottle when part of what I had consumed
shot out of my nose. The shopkeeper said to my father, "Tell
Aqazadeh – your son – he must drink slowly." *Aqazadeh*
had not yet become the derogatory term it is in Iran today
where it almost uniquely refers to the pampered children of
the mullahs. My father said nothing, of course, and perhaps
out of embarrassment, I no longer had the urge to drink the
rest. I handed the bottle back to my father. He drank what
little remained and handed five cents, *qerans*, the price for a
bottle, to the shopkeeper. That night we had great fun even
though we didn't go to the movies.

As far as I know, madeleines were not around in the Iran
of my childhood, but another of my most abiding and pleasant
memories is connected with my father and ice cream. My
father used to go on business trips, regularly for the purpose

of releasing goods that for some reason had become stuck in customs; it could be Khorramshahr or Tabriz, or Jolfa. On one such trip to Tabriz, my father who knew my passion for ice cream took me to Café Shahgoli (now El Goli), a striking and well-designed building at the center of a magnificent lake. My father ordered me an ice cream. As I ate it, the stillness of the water, the glory of the trees around us, and the love in my father's eyes turned that ice cream into the most delicious in my life, and that moment into an experience akin, or even superior to, the promised paradise. What could surpass a heaven whose twin is not the dread of hell?

Another trip that I went on with my father took place in winter. A heavy snow was falling. My father was asleep in the train cabin. I knew since childhood that sleep was important to my father – his after-lunch siesta was inviolable. He was also extra circumspect about his nighttime rest. In the last thirty or forty years of his life, he took a 10 mg. Valium every night. It's as if by taking vitamin C and a good dose of uninterrupted sleep at night, he had an intuition of today's medical guidelines and findings. Or perhaps it was owing to his constant contact with doctors. Today, we are told that sleep is even more important to overall health and longevity than our genes and diet; my father prioritized his sleep instinctively. Long before Linus Pauling published his famous book on the miracle of vitamin C, my father used to drink a glass of fresh lemon juice every day, right after rising from his siesta. In the summer, he bought enough fresh lemons to last him for a year and hired several souls who were experts in squeezing fruit juice. They stored the juice in large, green canteens, and sealed them with paste to keep the air out. On that trip, I knew better than to let my fidgeting disturb my father's sleep. So, I left the cabin. The train's headlights lit up the landscape that lay blanketed in snow. As far as the eye could see, there was snow and white-clad trees. When a section of the carriage came into view as the train turned a corner, the scene of a magnificent iron steed sweeping through the heart of that splendored nature was hypnotic to behold. I felt beyond exhilarated. In Westerns, railways were always an icon of modernity; for me in that moment, they were an icon of beauty and serenity. I also saw the other side of modernity on that trip, in Jolfa. My father bribed every one of the customs agents, from the doorman to the director. I was astonished at his expertise in that enterprise. I also felt shame.

My father's economic position turned upside down not long afterwards. He was among the merchants during the period when the center of trade and distribution of goods, as well as types of entrepreneurs, was repositioned. The economic engine moved from the Grand Bazaar and its stalls and warehouses to modern firms and corporations uptown. Some merchants – such as the Lajeverdis and Khosrowshahis – understood the nature of the dynamic and aligned with it, creating a new class of industry. Other bazaar tradesmen and investors did not fall in line, and their ventures stagnated as a result. Large contingents of entrepreneurs who had ties with the National Front, the Liberation Movement, or the Islamic Coalition Party joined the opposition to the regime, and in the Shah's last years turned into supporters of Ayatollah Khomeini. The Asgaroladis, Hajtarkhanis, and Zarifs were of that breed. My father's constitutionalism and his inherent conservatism prevented him from joining that group politically. In the 1960s, my father went bankrupt. For a while, he was also jailed for nonfulfillment of promissory notes. But he started up a new business right from inside prison, then, and operating for a while under the name of a man who worked in our house. Eventually, he started doing business in his own name. Meanwhile, he had become a certified accountant and earned some income through that channel as well. To advance his business, he was also willing to feign being a practicing Muslim and, despite not taking the pilgrimage to Mecca, designated himself *Haji*. He even grew a beard. But the constitutionalism that he had inherited from his father and uncle was deeply embedded in his mind.

After I immigrated to the U.S., none of my siblings were left in Iran. Two of my brothers, Mohsen and Hossein, and my sister Farzaneh used to travel to Iran as best their lives and work allowed and sometimes stayed with my parents for several months. When my mother passed away, my brother Hasan tried to bring my father to America. But Aqa Jan never agreed. He knew the ways and means of living in Iran to the core and would have felt torn from his roots, though perhaps closer to his constitutionalist ideal.

Jalal Shadman

When I was a child, my mother used to say, "*Aqa* Jalal eats *paludeh* – noodled sorbet – with the Shah." She sometimes called him *Miz-Dādāsh*, reserving *Aqa Dādāsh* for her older brother Fakhreddin Shadman. We called him *Daie* Jalal. When I was older and researching the Shah's life, I did not find any record of him eating *paludeh* with Daie Jalal. I'm not even sure the Shah liked *paludeh*. But it became clear to me that Jalal Shadman was one of his most loyal, lasting, and trusted allies. He last served as president of the Pahlavi Foundation – for several months right before the revolution; he had served on its board since its inception. Even before the Pahlavi Foundation was established, he was head of the Royal Estates for years. He was a Majlis representative and a senator for several terms and one of the permanent and effective members of the Senate leadership. I believe his real power was always greater than his distinct positions. That said, it's fortunate that he did not land in jail even for a day after the revolution.

Being a Shadman and an *aqazadeh* – as in the child of a cleric – was certainly not the reason he was spared. His brother Zia left Iran before the revolution and his other brother, Kamal, a two-term Majlis deputy from Qazvin, was imprisoned and only released after he had "donated" his beautiful historic mansion to the town's new and newly powerful imam Jomeh, the Friday prayer leader. His mansion, with its grand halls and exquisite sash windows and alcoves is thought to have been a royal residence when Qazvin became the Safavid capital in the mid-sixteenth century. But after the revolution, a feudal system of sorts had emerged whereby every locale that was assigned a Friday prayer leader cum Khomeini representative functioned like a capital city in its own right. Post-revolution, Daie Jalal remained in his old house in Tehran on Shadman Avenue off the Old Shemiran Road and dressed in one of the same suits that he wore during his glory days, put on an elegant tie, and walked around town looking respectable and undaunted.

He visited my mother, by then bedridden due to a stroke, every day. The first night after the victory of the revolution, the whole city seemed to have caught the infectious fever of "grab and hold" the agents of the ancien régime. Activists on the left and right, and sometimes even the centrists, fanned this flame. When I visited my mother that night, Daie Jalal's daughter Zahra Shadman was also there. She was a learned and industrious lady who had earned a doctoral degree in library science in France. Together with her friend and colleague Pouri Soltani, she had made an enormous contribution to librarianship and information management in Iran. When she was laid off post-revolution – owing to her name and relations, I believe – she undertook an extended collaboration with the literary scholar Hossein-Ali Heravi who seemed to have lost his eyesight, and with due effort helped publish his four-volume commentary on Hafez.

In the chaotic days following the revolution, Zahra devoted herself more than anything to taking care of "her dear father." Her brothers and sister were then living in the

West. In fulfilling her mission, Zahra was, like the heroes of legend, uncompromising. Time and again, I heard Daie Jalal say, "I feel ashamed; I don't know how to thank Zahra." For my part, I feel Zahra's heart was filled with boundless love and that due gratitude resides in the heart.

That night at my mother's house, Zahra seemed nervous. "Father is alone. I should hurry back," she said. We had walked out to the yard as I didn't want my mother to hear us and worry. "The city is a bit crazy," I told Zahra. "If you're worried about Uncle, why don't you both come over to our house, at least for tonight?" She thanked me and said she would tell her father but that she doubted he would agree to shelter elsewhere. She obviously knew her father better than I did, as half an hour later she called: "Father said to thank *Mirza* Abbas and to tell him I haven't done anything wrong to leave my home and go into hiding." He clearly understood Iran's situation and his own predicament much better than I did.

I eventually solved the puzzle of Daie Jalal's relative immunity from the madness of *revolutionary rage*. It turned out that the man who had served as his driver before the revolution was related to an influential cleric. That cleric had executed a writ of amnesty at the driver's request stating that Jalal Shadman came from a clerical family and was a man of faith and hence, despite the positions he occupied in the old regime, was granted amnesty. Nevertheless, they dragged Daie Jalal to court and forced him to pay back all the income he had earned as a lawmaker and senator. They then left him no option but to "donate" – to whom I do not know – a major portion of his land including his primary residence, the same house that his son Ali, my cousin and childhood friend, had once lived in and which was later rented to a school. It's apparently easier to curb *revolutionary rage* than *revolutionary greed*.

A wealthy merchant who had backed Khomeini and thus acquired much clout after the revolution, increasing his wealth exponentially through myriad stunts, had a hand in that. Alongside commerce, *Haji* was also in the business of buying bad debts. His name was Hāj Ali Hāj-Tarkhani. The year I returned to the U.S., I heard from one of the expropriated industrialists that Hāj-Tarkhani had offered to "buy" one of Daie Jalal's houses a few days before the official order to seize his properties was issued. I read later in one of the Islamic regime's own newspapers that when in 1961 Teymour Bakhtiar, chief of the intelligence and security agency SAVAK, left Iran having lost the Shah's trust, he had assigned power of attorney to the same "devout" merchant. Evidently, once Bakhtiar's star dimmed under the Shah and his properties were seized, Hāj-Tarkhani managed to swipe a large share of General Bakhtiar's wealth. On that occasion, someone had purged the bad guy but it was Haji who profited from it. In the case of Daie Jalal, Haji and his associates were both embodiments of the bad and the buyers of bad debts. Nonetheless, he did not accept Haji's proposal. He knew the mettle of Hāj-Tarkhani from of yore, and rather better than I did.

I used to see a lot of Daie Jalal in the chaotic aftermath of the revolution. Sometimes I visited him at his home, other times at my mother's. On several occasions, I suggested that he write his memoir or record himself on audiotape. I heard from Zahra that she, too, had repeatedly suggested the same to her father. Apparently, he never agreed. If he had, it would have surely been an extraordinary record of the Shah's lifetime. He was among the rare souls who had seen the Shah when he was at his weakest politically, especially in the Mosaddeq era, and also when he was at the height of his power. He had been the Shah's financial confidant. He knew the political elite and was familiar with the ins and outs of their lives.

Powerful individuals, from Mirashrafi and Hossein Ala to Sharif-Emami and Massoudi were among his friends. Master musicians such as Marziyeh and Jalil Shahnaz participated in many of the receptions he hosted at home. When I was doing research for my books on Hoveyda, the Shah, and other eminent Persians, I had conversations with many notables of that period. There was hardly anyone who did not know Jalal Shadman. Nor did I ever hear anyone speak of him disparagingly. No doubt they did not take my being his nephew into consideration, for they did not hesitate to criticize his brothers. Some of the most successful industrialists and entrepreneurs of the time were also his intimate friends. He was particularly close to the Soudavars, who played a stellar role in industrial development during that period. I have never heard anyone say, nor read anywhere, that Jalal Shadman's name has ever been smeared by corruption or bribery.

I once asked what had made him enter politics. "I used to work at the Ministry of Finance when Abdolhossein Hazhir was the budget director," he replied. "Reza Shah had requested a budget cut of several percentage points owing to the loss of state revenue in the foreign exchange markets. The day Hazhir was to present the revised budget at the court, he told me to join him. 'Reza Shah is going to ask for details, and you know them better than me,' he said. I was going to see Reza Shah for the first time.

"We were standing in an office with the budget sheets scattered all over the table. Reza Shah arrived on the dot. Without further ado, he said, 'Let's start.' Hazhir began to talk. Reza Shah sometimes asked a question that I'd answer. At one point, Hazhir said we had also cut back student scholarships by a fraction. Reza Shah was furious. He banged on the table and said, 'Students are the future of the country! You are not to slash their scholarships!' Finally, he said to go

ahead and prepare the new budget estimate. When we were
leaving, Reza Shah turned to Hazhir and said, 'The next time
you come, bring this blindy along with you.'" Daie Jalal wore
dark glasses most of his life. He had a disease in one eye since
he was young, hence the tinted spectacles. I never found out
nor asked about the exact nature of his affliction.

In his youth, Daie Jalal's life inclined more toward literature than politics. He had written a play called *Yousef va
Zoleikha* (Joseph and Zoleikha) and given production rights
to a director with a grand name, Arbab Aflatoon Shahrokh
(Regal Master Plato). Prior to that, he had followed in his
father's footsteps and dressed as a seminarian. But his rebel
spirit and literary gifts, his curious mind and love of fun,
did not let him wear that garb for long. He tossed away his
robe and turban and outfitted himself in a suit. His photographs from those days show a very handsome and suave
man. He had a reputation as a ladies' man as well. Not even
being married made him resist those siren calls. According to
my mother, he spent most evenings at *Loghanteh*, a modern
café-restaurant in Tehran that was all the rage. His wife Mehri
Ferdows was regarded by the family as a kind and forbearing
woman. Right from the start of their marriage, she had to
share a house with her authoritative mother-in-law, but I never
heard of any squabbling between her and *Khanom Bozorg*.
Sometimes I even listened with curiosity to adults whispering
that, in the rising tensions between Daie Jalal and his wife
in which Khanom Bozorg played referee, she would back
Mehri *Khanom*. A few members of the Ferdows family were
apparently Baha'i. I never found out which ones. But that
was not an *issue* for anyone in those days; nor would Daie
Jalal tolerate anyone poking their nose around his private life.

Years later when Houri Moghadam – the mother
of Hamid – read me parts of her memoir and showed me

pictures of her cultural and philanthropic activities – such as an exhibition of Iranian women's clothing in pre-Islamic times – Mehri Khanom played a major and conspicuous role in those undertakings. But as a child, I only knew her as Daie Jalal's kindhearted wife and Ali's loving mother.

Daie Jalal and Mehri Khanom's home had a special attraction for me as a kid. Ali, the third of their five children, was my best friend. The two of us used to share all our juvenile romantic secrets and family gossip. A passion for soccer also strengthened our bond. Ali always came top of the class, while I was consistently an average student, but even my parents' occasional jabs at my laziness by pointing out Ali's example never dented my love for him. Every one of Daie Jalal and Mehri Khanom's children pursued higher education. Ali earned a Ph.D. in electrical engineering and was a prominent member of one of the top institutions in electronics research in the U.S. His brother Mohammad obtained a Ph.D. in economics and after a period of teaching in Iran went to the U.S. where for years he held a high-ranking position at the World Bank. His sister Fatemeh, too, had a doctoral degree in econometrics; she applied herself to teaching and research in England and Belgium. And Ahmad, who was the youngest, was employed as a doyen of statistics in a large insurance company in the U.S. Absent the revolution, I believe we would have all stayed in Iran.

One day, my mother took me along to visit Daie Jalal and Khanom Bozorg. Daie Jalal's house was where members of the family gathered every afternoon. Some were into politics, others were writers; some sought advice, others employment. They would come together and sit around and chat. Important topics were discussed in whispers. On rare occasions, someone would go into Uncle's office for more weighty talks. There was always tea and other beverages and pumpkin seeds to crack

and fruits to eat. Close to nine in the evening, everyone knew
they must leave. Not only the guests, but even Daie Jalal's
children observed his strict schedule as well.

But that day, my uncle had just returned from a trip to
Europe. He described the London Underground and the resto-
ration of Berlin with eloquence and delightful touches. At the
time, I only knew him as a politician who ate *paludeh* with
the Shah and had no clue about his *Joseph and Zoleikha* soul.
He was saying how, everywhere you looked, there was a lively
bustle. People were on double time. They had built something
like a city inside London's guts. Everybody stood in line and
with no pushing or shoving got to ride trains that arrived on
time. For me, as a seven- or eight-year-old, his stories were
more irresistible than any magic act. He had also brought
me a gift. Nearly twenty years later when he came to visit his
two sons who were studying in the U.S., he also came to see
me and my brother in San Francisco. The same curiosity and
passion that colored his description of postwar Europe was
also on display during the days he spent with us. Early each
morning, he would haul all of us along on a sightseeing expedition. At the crack of dawn on day one, we reached the city
center in San Francisco and found ourselves alone on a street
with the sweeper trucks that had only just rolled out. He was
also eager to treat us at the city's best restaurants, knowing
we never hit those spots on a student budget. Every time my
brother Hasan offered to pay, Daie Jalal would say, laughing,
"*Mirza* Hasan, quit that already!" He had a special bond with
Hasan. When Hasan returned to Iran and became executive
director of Arvandan Foundry, they grew even closer.

Three years before hearing the story of his trip to Europe,
I had seen Daie Jalal in a different scene that was yet another
feature of his life story. It was around noon. He rushed into
our yard out of breath and said something to my mother.

Moments later, his driver and a friend hauled large boxes of the Shah's photographs inside our house and hid them in the kitchen in a cistern that had never seen water. It was a turbulent day in the summer of 1953. The driver returned the next day and carried off the photographs. Daie Jalal was among the string of figures blacklisted by Mosaddeq's government and were to be discharged from service in the future owing either to their affiliation with the court or their alleged corruption. On 19 August, the tide turned in the Shah's favor and Daie Jalal remained faithful to him till the end and achieved greater stature in the process. He was never boastful in his glory days, though, nor did he display any meekness or despair in the wake of his fall from power. He comported himself like a sturdy cypress and did not bend and is honored in memory even though he might not have had *paludeh* with the Shah.

Zia Shadman

When I was a child, *Daie* Zia often used to come to our house on a Friday. Friday was when my mother prepared *chelokabab* and Uncle Zia loved his sister's kababs. His love of *pudding*, apparently a token of his trip to Europe, and the scramble to find the ingredients and prepare it on time kept our household very busy in the lead-up to his visit. For the boys, the greatest attraction of his visit was that he played soccer with us in the yard. We had chalked a goalpost on two facing walls, and the game was our number one pastime. Some days, we also invited our neighbor's son and daughter and set up a match of sorts. We were obsessed with the rivalry between Taj and Shahin, Real Madrid and Barcelona, but playing with Daie Zia was a whole other ballgame. At the time, he was the lead broadcaster of soccer matches on the radio. For us, playing with the person whose voice announced Taj or Shahin goals live was an honor and the ultimate thrill. It was also dangerous. Daie Zia sometimes overlooked our age and height and his shots on goal were not compatible with our game and the size of the playing field or my small stature as a goalkeeper.

The yard also sported a basketball ring. Mostly for my older brother Hossein, who played for his high school

team. Daie Zia, who sometimes played on Iran's national
basketball team, floated a ball in the yard as well, though
he likely considered it below him to play with a greenhorn
like my brother. Plus, he had met the Shah on account of
basketball when Iran's national team had visited the royal
court for an audience. I later learned from Sadreddin Elahi
who had joined the team as a reporter at the 1948 Summer
Olympics, that when the Shah learned that the Basketball
Federation lacked the budget to send the national team to
London, he instantly offered to cover their expenses out of his
own pocket. The team went to London and returned empty-
handed, but sometime later, Daie Zia was appointed head of
the federation.

Our older maternal uncle *Seyyed* Fakhreddin was
not happy with his younger brother kicking balls around.
Evidently, he had once asked him to use an alias as a radio
broadcaster, saying such "tomfoolery" did not become the
Shadman name. In fact, these same tomfooleries were the first
steps in Daie Zia's political ascendance. It did not take long
before the house adjacent to ours turned into his stomping
ground. The newly formed Progressive Circle rented that
building from the Goharis for their headquarters. I don't
have particularly fond memories of the Gohari household
from my younger days. They had a servant who looked
like Hedayat's decrepit man, an old opium addict who is a
metaphor for moribund tradition. At our house, they called
him *lulu* (boogeyman) to scare us children. Later, when I was
writing *The Persian Sphinx: Amir Abbas Hoveyda and the
Riddle of the Revolution*, I learned that the Americans set up
the Progressive Circle as a boogeyman to frighten both the
National Front, which refused to collaborate with the Shah,
and the Shah, whose hunger for power was growing by the
day. In time, the Circle became the Iran Novin (New Iran)

Party and Daie Zia was elected to parliament representing Jiroft, the capital of Kerman province. To the best of my knowledge, this was the first family crisis fomented by Daie Zia's political ambitions. Until then, the Jiroft deputy had been Daie Jalal, a confidant of the Shah and a longtime head of the Royal Estates. In the political wheeling and dealing to replace old-school statesmen with technocrats, they seated Daie Jalal's younger brother in his place without telling him. In any event, neither brother had ever lived in Jiroft, not even for a day. Not long after, the Shah appointed Daie Jalal to the Senate and, as far as I know, the tempest subsided.

Earlier on, tensions had simmered within the family in regard to Daie Zia's marriage. My mother, who was involved in the formal courtship process and prenuptial agreements and wedding arrangements, was caught in the crossfire. What I remember most vividly from the ceremony was the presence of Elaheh, the famous singer, and the grandeur of the bride's house. The bride was Sima Abhari. The Abharis were among Tehran's old monied families. Abhari Arcade was one of the most modern in Tehran and was located in the heart of Lalehzar, itself the epitome of new urban lifestyle and architecture in the Reza Shah era. The Abhari house is said to have once been a *Loghanteh*, the ritzy eatery with poolside seating. As a child, the only thing I knew about Loghanteh was that it was a hangout of the rich and the nighttime playground of dapper dudes in bowties. When my mother spoke of a Loghanteh habitué, she meant someone who was spirited and flirty, well off and propertied. Apparently, my father had also treated my mother at Loghanteh when they were engaged. The first *Loghanteh* opened in 1906 on Bab-e Homayoun near the Golestan Palace and then branched out; the third one faced Meidan-e Baharestan. Whether or not it's true that the Abhari house was an ex-*Loghanteh,* its door opened onto a street in Baharestan Square. It had a splendid garden and a large pool and towering trees and lush green hedges.

Other memories of that wedding party have also stayed with me. One was sighting a distant relative who was rumored to have a soft spot for young boys, owing to which we were warned to stay away from him. *Haji Aqa* was clenching his nose with his left hand and lugging in booze with his right, sloshed. I also saw him wobble and nearly fall.

In time, Daie Zia became the mayor of Tehran, which even in those days was a lucrative or, as we might say today, high-margin business. I heard that Seyyed Fakhreddin had carped about it: "Zia has become the head of the hood." My Aunt Batoul, who was not a fan of my mother's, nor of her boasting about her brothers, would often swipe at her in her faintly Gilaki accent: "Zinat *Khanom*, people are saying *Aqa* Zia repaves the streets to get kickbacks from contractors." And my mother, who never gave an inch in a war of words, would shoot back: "People should keep their trap shut!" But Aunt Batoul was right. People were, in fact, saying things to that effect, but neither Daie Zia nor his friend Amir Abbas Hoveyda, who had become a minister, paid any attention. Once Hoveyda became prime minister, Daie Zia's rank was elevated by the day. In 1975, when I returned to Iran after an eleven-year absence, he had become the premier's executive deputy. As was customary in the family, he hosted a welcome party for me at his home. When I had first left Iran, he was living in a simple house on Shadman Avenue close to Daie Jalal. My welcome party was held in his new home in the posh Evin neighborhood across from the newly built Hilton Hotel. I did not see much of him afterwards. I had started my university job and anti-regime political activity.

One day, a distant relative of my mother's passed away in Qazvin. He had spent a lifetime burning through his father's

legendary inheritance with his opium habit. I was to take my
mother to the funeral. As luck would have it, I sat facing
Daie Zia in the men's hall. As always, he was dressed in a
designer suit. His shoes were polished and shined, and his
calves sheathed in knee-high socks. Glancing at my unpolished
footwear and wrinkled socks, he said sarcastically, "*Mirza*
Abbas, that's exactly how professors should dress these days,"
speaking in a loud voice so others could hear. Out of respect
for my mother, and perhaps political prudence, I said nothing
and merely grinned.

A few months passed. One day my mother said Daie
Zia wanted to see me at the prime minister's office. I went
to see him. He was seated behind a large desk in a large
room. Frowning, he said, "I don't want to know exactly what
you're up to, but I've heard you're active." He didn't name
his source. Later, I found out he was friends with the deputy
director of SAVAK Parviz Sabeti. He continued: "I thought I
should ask you to come here for Zinat's sake and to warn
you." It is possible he really meant to save me out of love, but
he sounded more like a master addressing a mutinous serf.
"Don't be naïve and throw away your life. Know that if they
arrest you, I won't help you and won't be able to." I replied
coldly and of course falsely that I wouldn't, and made my
exit. In reality, contrary to Daie Zia's posturing, the Shah's
regime was neither a *Reich* nor lasted a thousand years. But
he was right that my opposition to the Shah stemmed largely
from naïveté and would not end well, neither for Iran nor
for me. I was arrested a few months later, and he kept his
promise not to help. Nor did I expect otherwise. In a sense,
he was right. When speaking with Parviz Sabeti at the Joint
Committee on the day I was arrested, when I pointed out that
Zia Shadman was a minister and deputy premier to illustrate
my pique with the system, Sabeti replied, "You're right. We

did not approve of his ministerial appointment but our hands were tied, for he's friends with the prime minister." Given that reaction, to expect Daie Zia's help would have of course been the ultimate conceit, and unfair.

After being released from prison, I ran into him only a couple of times, and only at family gatherings – cold and loveless encounters, and tense. The revolution came to pass and fortunately he left Iran before the roundups started. He settled first in Paris and then in Montreal in Canada. When a group of Iranians invited me to give a talk in Montreal, I heard from my sister Farzaneh before I left that Daie Zia had said, "If Abbas comes to town and doesn't stay with me, it will be a scandal." It was decided I would stay at his house. He hosted a large reception for me, too, and as he lived alone did all the cooking himself. Life as an exile had morphed him into a good cook. He owned a sumptuous house. His children, all of whom were successful and had families of their own, had moved away. His wife had effectively branched out on an independent life of her own. While politically ascendant, Daie Zia had been no laggard in extramarital antics. It was now Sima *Khanom*'s turn, as it were. Surrounded by great artefacts and exquisite Persian carpets, Daie Zia was a solitary man whose main wealth was memories of his long-lost chutzpah. He passed away sometime later, alone on a hospital bed. I heard that he had inscribed in a large and beautiful script at the door – he practiced calligraphy during his years of exile – "If you come to visit and I'm asleep, wake me up." When I heard the news, I thought that if my mother had been alive, she would have no doubt shed great tears of sorrow at her brother's lonely fate.

Hasan Lebaschi

In legends, reports of a hero's fame and fiber and their exploits precede their appearance in the narrative. Hence we are already familiar with their persona before they get in on the action. For my generation that was just getting to know the Confederation of Iranian Students in the mid-1960s, an organization that had been formed only a few years before, Hasan Lebaschi's name came wrapped in legend. He was reportedly a founding member of the Confederation. Whenever he presided over a meeting, we knew the meeting carried special weight. A lot of tension was also to be expected. It was said that the cachet of his presence was that everybody respected him, which prevented tension from turning into turbulence. Rumor had it that he had met Mosaddeq, and naturally, Mosaddeq was a pillar of our legend-rich history.

The first time I saw him up close was in Berkeley, at a party at the home of Ardavan Davaran, a graduate student in comparative literature at the time and later my brother-in-law. A friend had arrived from Iran and Ardavan had organized the event in his honor. Lebaschi, a fellow guest, was sociable and lively. Most of the discussions centered on politics. We left the party together by chance. Or perhaps by his design. When we were alone outside, he said, "Why don't we get

41

together next week and talk about these issues a bit more?" I accepted eagerly. My political urges were intensifying by the day, so naturally the invitation to hang out with an icon was not to be spurned.

We arranged to meet the following week at a restaurant that happened to be the favorite watering hole of Iranian college students. Lebaschi arrived at the appointed hour, I a little earlier. He was wearing a tie, which to our generation of students was a token of *bourgeois excess*. For us, feigning poverty and moral piety and abstaining from alcohol and drugs was part and parcel, or even the prerequisite, of our revolutionary ethos. Lebaschi was not into those disingenuous affectations. Both on that day and at our following meetups he ordered beer. He even fixed our rendezvous at three in the afternoon. For those of us who were swept away by the revolutionary tide, the proper thing was to meet at six in the morning and in a remote location no less – a further sign of our *proletarian* struggle in service to the masses. Lebaschi did not put up with that kind of revolutionary posturing either.

He said, "You must know that I work with the National Front of Iran." I did. In fact, I assumed he was one of their principal leaders abroad. He went on: "From the discussions the other night, it occurred to me we have a lot in common. If you like, we can meet once a week and talk. If everything goes well, then you can collaborate with us officially." I was politically savvy enough by then to realize he had invited me to a *howzeh-ye emtehani*, a sort of trial novitiate cell. After a while, the organization would decide whether I fitted the profile or not. When I read Le Carré, years later, I realized that both counterintelligence agencies and revolutionary organizations followed the same principle in their selection and testing and recruitment process. The similarity was probably inevitable. An individual is summoned to an undercover organization whose work is fraught with danger and whose survival depends on no one betraying its secrets. Furthermore, both types of organization consider themselves a sort of assembly of *experts*. I accepted Lebaschi's invitation to the novitiate cell.

In those days – and for years to come – the hot topic at the Confederation was the *Asiatic mode of production* and whether or not Iran was a feudal society. Many members of the National Front, including Lebaschi, believed that Iran represented the Asiatic mode of production. The idea had originally been advanced by Marx. He had said that not every society passes through the ubiquitous stages that he had assigned to history – primitive communism, slavery, feudalism, capitalism, socialism, and, finally, the awaited utopia of communism. Water scarcity in some societies (such as Iran) engendered a *despotic* state, he wrote, and made it impossible for powerful classes and feudalism to form and generate the later stages. It is quite odd that when it came to Iran and societies with an Asiatic mode of production, Marx who usually applied scholarly methods in exploring capitalism and its rise in the West advanced doctrines based on slapdash studies and deficient knowledge. Of course, Stalin who preferred a simple global strategy over plans that were more complex or that involved exceptions, had decreed that the Asiatic mode of production was not an element of Marxism. Stalinist members of the Confederation also unequivocally regarded his decree as gospel truth, which is why my first *howzeh* homework with Lebaschi was to read an essay by a National Front theorist on the Asiatic mode of production.

When I mull over those discussions today, I realize how very alien they were to Iran. It seems those abstract arguments were chiefly a mechanism for denying the reality of Iranian society, or else a theoretical veneer to hide our ignorance of that reality, or our resistance to it. The Shah had dismantled feudalism, yet we were engaged in a battle royal over whether Iran was a feudal society or not. When I became a Maoist, I found that Maoism too denied the Asiatic mode of production in Iran and per the dictate of the Leader's fatwa clung onto the vague and indistinct "semi-feudal, semi-colonial" notion instead. It is as if we, the revolutionaries, were prepared to entertain any discourse, no matter how abstract, to deny the reality that the Shah had demolished the scourge of the feudal system in his White Revolution. My test with Lebaschi started off on that same abstract discussion.

The following week, we held our session on time, at the same place. Before, when he said, "Same place next week," I asked, a little surprised, "Isn't it a problem to be seen here? This place swarms with Iranian students." At the time, concerns about informants hung like a cloud over all political activities. Lebaschi laughed. "No way will anyone think I'm doing organizational work here!" He led the session; my duty was to follow. After briefly commenting on current events, he asked if I had read the essay. I said that I had, and we began. As we talked, he realized that I had also read the *Siyasatnameh* (Book of Governance), which was cited in the essay, and that I had a different take on it than the essayist. I had also read up on Marx and the Asiatic mode of production in college, ideas that didn't square with the author's hard and fast narrative either. Lebaschi said, perhaps playfully, or perhaps seriously, "You were only supposed to read the essay for today's discussion." Perhaps the choice of the term "novitiate cell" for our private session, which also applied to the Confederation's public meetings, was because in both situations we were expected to echo what we heard and do as we were told by our superiors!

A couple of weeks later, he brought along an issue of the National Front newspaper to the *howzeh*. "A friend has written an article about the Shah and OPEC, Organization of the Petroleum Exporting Countries. Translate it into English," he said. The anonymous author, as I later found out, was Ahmad Salamatian, a National Front leader in Europe. Post-revolution, he, too, like Lebaschi, was appointed deputy to Karim Sanjabi, minister of foreign affairs in Bazargan's *transitional* government, and a while later had little option, also like Lebaschi, but to flee Iran. These days, Salamatian runs a small bookstore in Paris and sometimes writes commentaries on the political situation in Iran.

Salamatian's long essay was in effect a critique and disavowal of the Shah's constructive role in OPEC. At the time, the Shah was playing a more prominent role at OPEC in which he called for an increase in the price of oil. He confronted and challenged member oil companies as well as the consortium that had monopolized the Iranian oil industry since Mosaddeq's fall. The Shah's struggle for autonomy contradicted the claim made by the National Front and the Confederation that he was a "lackey of imperialism" and an opponent of Iran's independence. The essay argued that the Shah's face-off against oil companies and Western countries was a mock battle scripted and directed by the *Master,* the U.S. I translated the essay – which took up an entire issue of the periodical and was in fact more like a supplement – and believe it was published in the English edition of the same newspaper soon after. But Lebaschi and I gradually realized that our paths were diverging from that of the National Front. Not just because I was critical of the crux of the essay's rationale, but like many students of that generation, both of us were seeking a movement even more revolutionary. The National Front was progressively seduced by the People's

Fadaiyan Guerrillas, *Cherik-ha-ye Fadaie-ye Khalq*, and had
practically morphed into their agent in the Confederation. But
the "revolution" or "doctrine" that I sought was at a remove
from their position. Lebaschi, too, passed up the Front's new
guerrilla rhetoric, but he never left them and never quit being
a moderate. He used to say, "I'm *Aqa*'s son." Aqa was of
course Mosaddeq, and so the distance between Lebaschi and
the Confederation grew by the day.

While Lebaschi was in essence a pragmatist, the
Confederation grew more ideological and factional as time
went by. Once I had delved into Aristotle and learned about
his concept of "prudence," I recognized that Lebaschi was a
man of moderation and practical wisdom in the Aristotelian
sense. He opposed every form of extremism. His prudence
was not a cover for opportunism, but an urge to find the
common denominator between people and political currents.
While he mainly favored unity, advocates of factionalism had
the upper hand at the Confederation at the time. Each group
seemingly perceived itself as representing the absolute truth,
and other factions as varied grades of evil. Inevitably, the
distance between them and Lebaschi grew wider by the day.
His honesty was not out of naïveté but sprang from his sense
of honor and his disdain for the ideological rhetoric of the
pure and the *absolute*. He reportedly had a hand in conceiving
one of the Confederation's most successful anti-Shah political
stunts. The University of California was scheduled to award
the Shah an honorary doctorate on Commencement day at
a ceremony held in a large outdoor stadium in Los Angeles.
As the degree was being conferred upon the Shah, a small
aircraft appeared above the stadium. A banner with large
and legible writing fluttered in the air: "Need a fix, see the
Shah." The aircraft flew around the stadium twice before a
police helicopter came and chased it away. "I was given credit

for that stunt," Lebaschi used to say, laughing, "but I didn't have much to do with it. A few days before the ceremony, an American guy had contacted the Association of Iranian Students in Los Angeles and said, 'How about doing something like that? We'll arrange everything.'" He added: "I never found out whether he belonged to a radical American group or if he was part of some other intrigue."

I heard from my friend Parviz Shokat, a Confederation activist like Lebaschi, how on one occasion, at the height of clashes between Iranian leftist groups who invariably accused one another of opportunism or revisionism or affinity with the Shah's regime and other political blasphemies, Lebaschi had asked Parviz, "What are they squabbling over?" Parviz had replied, "The first group says the revolution should begin in the countryside, eventually besieging the cities; the second group says the revolution should be ignited in the cities first." Lebaschi had asked, "Why doesn't one group start from the rural areas and the other from the cities?" I don't think he was being facetious. It was simply a reflection of his pragmatism.

It wasn't only the student groups' ideology and self-centeredness that was at odds with his ethos. Not long after he had gone back to Iran and become deputy minister of foreign affairs, he had enough of the newfangled bigotry and returned to the U.S.

The last time I saw him was three years before he died. I learned he was suffering from depression and some memory loss. I found it hard to imagine that mirthful face shrouded by melancholy; to look at him would be even more painful. I was very keen to visit him. He did not go out much, I was told. Nonetheless, gracious as ever, he agreed to have dinner with me and Shokat and another friend, Faramarz Pakzad. Outwardly, he was with us all night. He laughed and joked and recounted old memories. But there were moments when

every trace of emotion and curiosity and joie de vivre seemed
to vanish from his eyes. He would stare into space, void of any
emotion. What was going on inside him in those moments,
I wondered. Then, as if lit by an inner spark, he would in
an instant return from that eternity – that *no-placeness*, to
cite the poet Esmail Khoie – and be with us again. When I
heard the news of his passing, I told myself that perhaps he
was relieved from profound suffering. More poignantly, I
consoled myself that legendary heroes remain alive in story
and memory even after death.

Mehdi Khanbaba Tehrani

I had heard about him before we met. The congress of the Confederation of Iranian Students had just ended. A friend – more precisely, a *comrade* – had just returned from the meeting. For us enthusiasts, her standing was like that of a *haji* fresh back from Mecca. Short of offering her a sacrificial lamb, we hung on to her every word and observation with the same fervor as religious zealots.

A battle royal had broken out at the Confederation among the *revolutionaries*, *liquidationists*, *revisionists*, and *representatives of the national bourgeoisie*. Naturally, given that, as Sa'di says, "everyone presumes their own intellect to be supreme," each believed they were *revolutionary* and righteous, and the others *heretical* and *deviant*.

According to the comrade, "Mehdi Khanbaba was leaning against a wall and taking a puff nonstop with his long cigarette holder." She enunciated "long cigarette holder" as if it epitomized the moral depravities and delinquencies of the bourgeoisie and went on to say: "A group of his greenhorns were coiled around him." Knowing the *heretics'* acolytes were greenhorns, while *our* followers were *revolutionary youth*, I asked, "Which tribe does this Mehdi hail from?" "Khanbaba

49

is one of the leaders of the liquidationists," she replied – in a tone that packed an earful, meaning, "What a jerk! You call yourself a revolutionary and you don't know the name of this *enemy of the people*?" Later on, when I learned a little more about Mehdi's life, I realized that in fact that same long cigarette holder was a token of his immunity to the revolutionaries' mostly duplicitous protocols and procedures; he considered his private life *private* and did not brand the appetite for worldly pleasures *immoral*. Oddly enough, both Mehdi's revolutionary rivals as well as SAVAK and the cultural commissars of the Islamic regime wielded certain aspects of his private life as weapons against him, and still do, referring disparagingly to his long cigarette holder or his visit to a nudist lakefront.

The first time I saw Mehdi was around thirty years after the episode where I'd first learned his name. He had come to Berkeley. A few years had passed since the revolution. The hostile and heretical factions of our student days had turned into a benighted, frustrated fellowship tapped out by the newfangled dictatorship in Iran. That night, the same comrade who thirty years ago had ridiculed Mehdi's long cigarette holder was among the guests at a celebration held in honor of *Aqa* Mehdi's arrival. As usual with such *parafactional* parties, everyone had gathered at Parviz Shokat's small but beautiful hilltop home in Berkeley. When I walked in, I recognized Mehdi from his photographs. He was sitting alone at a large table in the middle of the dining room. The distant lights of San Francisco and the famed Golden Gate Bridge were visible through the large window behind him. Mehdi had a phone to his ear. Others looked on in silence, lost in awe and admiration. Mehdi was giving a radio interview to Hossein Mohri – whose friendship I, too, was fortunate to gain later – editorializing the state of affairs in Iran. Literally the epicenter of all news from Iran, he was always eloquent and artful, on top of the latest developments and clued into most *behind the scenes* drifts. As well, he often punctuated his accounts with witty asides rarely found elsewhere. Commenting on the Tudeh Party's decision to support the Islamic regime, for instance, he had once quipped, "Kianouri rode a streetcar named Desire whose driver was *Ruhollah* (Spirit of God)." It is due to his vast reserves of information and savory speech that when Iranian media had just started to operate abroad, he was a regular guest on channels with the largest audiences.

That night, Mehdi seemed to be scanning every move of every guest in that gathering with his sharp and penetrating gaze. He made eye contact with everyone, including a newcomer like me, the look establishing that he knew who you were and what you did. That focus, I think, was rooted in his smarts as a public speaker and master of ceremonies and not in the protocols of a political activist who is constantly on the lookout for the police and spies; nor were his visual audits issued from fear but from an interest in every single person in a crowd. Sometimes, too, with a hand or eye gesture or a certain expression in his always expressive face, he would distance himself from what he had just said, or perhaps even mock himself.

In all the time I knew him, Mehdi was a *professional revolutionary* in the exact Leninist sense of the term – someone whose thoughts and concerns and work and leisure is devoted to revolution and nothing else. Even after he renounced the Leninist model and declared the *death of Marxism* and grew more in favor of reform and change through *civil society*, he remained a professional revolutionary. At the same time, he never took himself too seriously. His performance as a speaker is consistently more gripping than any seasoned raconteur's, but like a director or actor in a Bertolt Brecht production, he uses myriad ploys to create a *distancing effect* with those watching and listening. He craves his audience's attention and knows untold ways in which to retain it, but he also wants to make them aware that this is a *performance*, one version of reality, his version, perhaps more credible than all others, but one version alone; reality and life are someplace else out there. I have no doubt that if Mehdi were to describe the party at Parviz Shokat's house that evening, he would paint a more colorful picture than mine. He would relate the guests' idiosyncrasies – including mine as one late to the party – charmingly, tenderly, and eagle-eyed. He would be at the center of his story but would no doubt parody himself as well. He knows that a gag works best when the speaker sticks a needle into themselves even as they thrust an awl into others.

A few years passed before the day I visited Mehdi at his home in Frankfurt. That visit produced a slight froideur between me and my brother Hossein. I was in Europe on a lecture tour at the time and Hossein was a surgeon and the CEO of a hospital in Brussels. He kindly took a ten-day vacation and drove me around from city to city in his very comfortable car. He, too, like many political activists past and present in Iran (and perhaps Germany) had heard countless stories about Mehdi's hospitality. An unrepentant devotee of grilled meat despite his heart condition, Hossein knew that any visitor who turned up at Mehdi's around noon would be treated to his famous *chelokabab*. Paying a visit to Mehdi had been a long-established *must* among all Iranian literary and political luminaries who traveled to Frankfurt. He once said, smiling, "I prepared so many kababs at home that my daughter announced she'd refuse to stop by anymore because the place smells of nothing but!" Hossein wanted me to reschedule our rendezvous with Mehdi so that we could be his lunch guests and taste his dish. He asked me several times to call and reschedule, but I did not indulge his request (and my own strong urge) to taste Aqa Mehdi's *chelokabab*. A few years later, I shared that story with Mehdi while on another visit. By then, my brother Hossein had died of a heart attack. Mehdi himself had only recently been discharged from the hospital. The charcoal grill had been removed. Mehdi remonstrated me for not having brought my brother along on that bygone day and graciously prepared kababs for two on a cooktop. He talked about his father's *chelokabab* stall, and as always, he spun his story into a piece of theatre and an inventive and charming monologue.

Mehdi Khanbaba Tehrani is no longer a political activist but an institution, the sign and symbol of a notable slice of the history of the Iranian leftist movement over the past few decades. His role was not restricted to Iranian leftism, though. In the 1960s and 1970s, he had a close relationship with German radical groups. On one occasion, I found myself sitting in an airport lobby next to Joschka Fischer, the former foreign minister of Germany, as we waited for a car to take us to a conference. I had a Persian book in my hands. Fischer asked, "Are you Iranian?" I answered affirmatively. "Do you know Khanbaba Tehrani?" he said. "Everybody knows him," I replied. He went on: "We had many adventures during our student days." I learned afterwards that, back then, he had taken refuge in Mehdi's house for some time, or perhaps Mehdi in his. Once on a walk with Mehdi in Frankfurt, we passed a large bookstore. He pointed to it and said, "This Fischer who's now a big deal worked here for a while."

During the same period, Mehdi was friends with Qashqa'i chiefs and, earlier, with the poet Forugh Farrokhzad and her brothers. He had met Zhou Enlai, the renowned Chinese premier and had photographed Mao's momentous *historic*

swim in the Yangtze. At the same time, just when he joined
the Tudeh Youth Organization at the age of eighteen – he
said his uncle had mentored him on the party's cells and
ideology since he was twelve – he drew up a party charter for
a group of pro-Shah roughnecks who planned to assassinate
the famously abrasive journalist Amir Mokhtar Karimpour
Shirazi and blame the Tudeh Party for his assassination.
Ebrahim Golestan has penned a version of his life story in a
brilliant book, *Mokhtar dar Rouzgar* (Mokhtar in His Times).
Like Golestan, Mokhtar was also once a supporter of the
Tudeh Party.

Mehdi played a decisive role in forming numerous other
political organizations as well. A charismatic figure, he lent
significant weight to the shaping of the Confederation of
Iranian Students, the Revolutionary Organization of the
Tudeh Party, the *cadres* (liquidationists – according to the
comrade who scorned Mehdi and his cigarette holder), the
Democratic Front, and the National Council of Resistance.

He founded several publications and journals, though for
the most part he either did not join these enterprises or if he
did, his membership was short-lived. It may be that his unruly
and individualistic spirit conflicted with the nature of organizational activity, or that, as he put it, he could not stand it
when organizations diverged from their original mission. At
the same time, he never quit trying to help build new ones.

It seems to me that nobody's life reflects the peaks and
troughs of at least three generations of leftist Iranian militants
as much as his does. Yet his personality is unique. The breadth
of his skills and the slants and secret depths of his activities
are beyond comparison. Portraying him is hard given that he
has personally recounted the most winning and captivating
stories of his life. In chronicling each event, he digresses again
and again. Laurence Sterne's *Tristram Shandy* is considered

one of the most outstanding novels in history, its chief stylistic feature being a digression-within-digression format. Mehdi's accounts are akin to *Tristram Shandy*. They're work and play in concert; they're both fascinating and also highlight pivotal moments in history from his perspective. His extensive conversation with the historian Hamid Shokat, for instance, opened a new chapter in the study of the Left and the history of the Confederation. He later divulged some of what was unsaid in that dialogue when interviewed by Habib Lajevardi, director of the Iranian Oral History Project at Harvard. In many of these exchanges, he openly shares the movement's most heavily guarded secrets. He states candidly and ingloriously that, in attacking the Iranian embassy in Switzerland, they stole some embassy letterhead and faked a report on one asserting that SAVAK operated a wide network to spy on Iranian students in Europe and the U.S. That fake letter caused a lot of trouble for the Shah's regime. Mehdi is like Goethe's protagonist in *Faust* where an evil deed is justified if it is well intended. Almost all his stories are spiced with a sharp and biting humor. Anyone hearing his delightful and witty inuendoes about this or that person might wonder, thinking of Saʿdi's "gossip that comes around goes around," what Mehdi's parody of that person would be like. His portrayal of a certain landowner's sexually abusive posture toward a *peasant*'s young son is as clear and cutting and bitter as any Luis Buñuel movie. His description of a meeting to announce the establishment of the Democratic Front, and by his account, Ayatollah Taleqani's wreckful role in that meeting, has the precision of a scholarly study and the playfulness of a burlesque.

Mehdi is not given to brevity, nor does he fall prey to verbosity. He can contextualize a trivial and simple event across the vast and complex canvas of history. Even his name, in whose selection he played no part, aligns with the nature of popular ideas in an important period of his life. "Mehdi" is in tune with the then assumption by all leftist intellectuals, especially partisans of Lenin and Stalin and Mao, that they were in varying degrees the "Mahdi" or Savior of the masses. The leftist Mehdi is the secular version of the Shia Mahdi, who himself is a variant of the Zoroastrian Sushiyans and the Greek Prometheus. They all assume to be the teacher, savior, guide, and *daddy* of the masses who are presumed to be minors in need of a *warden* and *guardian*. Interestingly, though his given name is cognate with millenarian Marxist thought, Mehdi never seemed to take that equivalence seriously.

We find another contradiction in Mehdi as well. Almost all his life, he has personified collective thinking and doctrines that denigrated individualism and upgraded uniformity or conformity. Yet Mehdi Khanbaba Tehrani always projected his own brand of individualism, at times with a long cigarette holder, while he also rose to be the symbol and a singular institution of anti-individualism.

Parviz Kalantari

Parviz Kalantari was a skillful artist and a seductive writer. But his greatest talent and most distinguished trait was his humanity. He was a rare personality whose modesty and erudition were on a par with his altruism and creativity.

What fused the two sides of his endearing character was his contagious love of people and of Iran. There were no rough edges, it seemed, no festering bitterness, no toxic hatred in his genial manner and generous spirit that nonetheless hid an inner anguish. He wept easily. Out of joy or grief. When I was leaving Iran, it was he who graciously drove me to the airport. He came to fetch me at two in the morning. It was raining. The moment I got into the car, we both broke down and sobbed. Afterwards, he made a beautiful painting of that night and sent it to me as a gift.

The first time I saw him weep, or more precisely, the first time we wept together, we had traveled to his parents' home in Taleqan with our families. It was nighttime and the sky was starlit, the silence of the village broken only by a dog's intermittent barking. Mohammad, the husband of Parviz's sister Shahla and a gifted architect, was grilling lamb fries with our mutual friend Ardavan. Vodka, tomatoes, and cucumbers

were laid out on a table by the grill. Parviz's parents and the
other guests were waiting inside their spartan rustic house.
Taleqan was very different then from what I hear about it
from friends today. While chatting and swilling and taking
a bite of the fries – a first for me as I had never tasted them
before – Parviz relived memories of his political activities as
a youth. He had become a member of the Tudeh Party, like
his father who was still a Tudeh'i at seventy and seemed never
to have risen to his feet from the opium brazier since 1953
and the party's defeat. It is as if Akhavan Saless had penned
Winter, in which he portrays a man frozen stiff in the face
of that defeat, with *Aqa Joon* in mind. Aqa Joon was an
extremely amiable soul. To him, Ehsan Tabari, theoretician
of the Tudeh Party, was still the epitome of intellectuality.
One day I was having a discussion in the same house with
a friend who claimed the mantle of a dervish and who had
opened the first hamburger joint in the style of MacDonald's
called *MacAli*. He was defending his mystical ways, and I was
stuffing dialectical materialism down his throat. After a while,
Aqa Joon turned to me and muttered under his breath, 'Leave
him alone, man. Even Comrade Tabari himself couldn't bring
him around.'

Parviz no longer had any illusions about Tabari, of
course. But that night under Taleqan's starry sky, perhaps
affected by the grandeur of Alamout, the shadow of whose
presence loomed over the village, he conjured up his politically active days: "We brimmed with good intentions and an
extraordinary sense of mission." He could have been echoing
the ninety-year-old Ebrahim Golestan whom I once heard
say, "The yearning to have an impact, and the passion to
engage, was never as strong in me as in my activist days in
the Tudeh Party." That night, one could see tears welling in
Parviz's eyes in the glimmer of the glowing coal in the brazier.

Then he added, with a profound sadness, "Where did all that honesty go? Why have people become so venal?" We who were standing close by and witnessed his tears knew he was speaking of those times, and of these times too, and also of the weariness of his own life. But true to form, he segued to a hilarious story moments later and made everyone laugh. He told us about how one day, just when their school headmaster was ranting and raving at the students for engaging in political activities, his teacher walked up to the pool in the school yard, pressed his palms down on the ledge and performed a handstand like a crack gymnast. When Parviz published his memoirs, his exquisite and humorous vignettes included an anecdote about that athletic teacher as well.

Parviz is among those to whom I owe my appreciation of old Tehran and sundry corners of Iran because of his love and intimate knowledge of the land, unaffected by the hubbub of modernization and development and economic growth. He had once said accurately, "I am the painter of the soil of this land." That was in reference to his famous paintings of earthen houses. But he was a painter of the soil of Iran in a larger sense as well. Iran and her natural landscape, her towns and tribal areas, her crumbling mosques and derelict villages, were the warp and weft of all his paintings, his illustrations for Khanlari's *History of Iran* and his artwork for the United Nations stamp included.

Yet Parviz was not hostile or opposed to modernization. In art, I believe he was in fact one of the forerunners of a genuine modernity in Iran. He was well acquainted with the ideas and techniques of Western modernism. But he believed that over and above any elements derived from the West, it was native materials and designs and colors, tribal costumes and Kashan carpets and rural earthen houses, that provided the requisite and inimitable basis for a modernism (and modernity) rooted in Iran.

One day, a few months after I had returned to Iran, he announced, "Come, let me show you Old Tehran," by which he meant the historic district of Oudlajan. A taxi dropped us off close to Shams ul-Emareh. We first stopped at a tea house with a rich past. I don't know if that erstwhile hangout is still standing or if it's been replaced by a mosque or a mall. Parviz ordered tea. I realized he had brought me here not only to imbibe the look and feel of the tea house but to also coach this Johnny-come-lately-from-the-West on proper etiquette. Perhaps one of the most embarrassing outcomes of having lived in the West for eleven years, and the fact that prior to leaving Iran at age sixteen I had grown up in an area confined to the then *uptown* neighborhood of Takht-e Jamshid and Malek o-Shoara Bahar avenues, was my unfamiliarity with such sites of societal life. At the time I came back, we activists saw ourselves not just as the deputies of the *masses*, but of course as their *leaders*. Yet each day that passed after my return, I sensed more keenly how alienated I was from the masses. That day, too, it felt like I was a tourist on a visit with Parviz as my guide. I had seldom frequented tea houses in the past. I did not know their rituals. I did not know the difference in such a venue between hospitality and *t'arof* – a civil formality not meant to be taken literally.

A little earlier during the same period, I drove toward Ardabil in the northwest to pick up my wife Fereshteh and a group of her friends who had gone on a trip to Mount Sabalan. I had just gotten my hands on the latest Peugeot 504, which was metallic no less. It was my graduation *allo-cation*. To induce educated Iranians living abroad to return home, the Shah's regime had ruled that each of them could buy a *foreign* car without paying customs duty. Some sold their right to others and bought a domestic Paykan instead, with money to spare. I had come into the latest model Peugeot thanks to my father's affection and funding. Driving along the foot of Mount Sabalan, I stopped in a small town whose name I did not know to refresh myself and have some tea. Pulling up right in front of a delightful tea house, I got out and walked in. A man whom I presumed to be the proprietor was seated at a wooden desk by the door with a bowl full of coins in front of him. I said hello and found an empty table. Presently, a young, dark-skinned, wretched-looking man set down a glass of tea before me. Either I was exhausted or the tea was particularly well brewed, or perhaps it tasted better because I was in the company of the proletariat. One of Mao's edicts was, after all, "join the masses."

Feeling suitably refreshed and having mingled with the common people, I went to the man at the desk by the door to pay the bill. Using a clumsy idiom in which respect and admiration and affected familiarity with the ethos of the masses must have been all too obvious, I asked, "How much may I offer?" Without a moment's hesitation, the man at the desk replied, "Not to worry, Doctor. The service was not worthy of you." I should have understood what he meant by *Doctor*, but of course I didn't. Feeling a little antsy and unsure and buoyed by the heroic masses' hospitality, I said, "You are too kind. Allow me to pay for the two teas that I had." In a tone somewhat different from the first *t'arof* – a tone whose finer shades of meaning escaped this "Western comeback guy" – he repeated, "As I said, Doctor, it was not worthy of you. How could I put a price on two glasses of tea?" My third attempt must have been even clumsier than the first two. Anyway, at that point I had little doubt that I had just witnessed the hospitality of hard-working Azarbaijani compatriots near Mount Sabalan. Had I been a character in a Chekhov play,

I would have certainly congratulated myself that they knew I was a freedom fighter on their behalf. I wasn't. I offered a thank-you and left the tea house. Nor did the owner, I think out of a mixture of pity and mercy, chase after me to say, "Learn the meaning of *t'arof*, asshole!"

I hadn't shared that story with Parviz, but I guessed he took me to a tea house so I would learn the current protocols in a country that was different from the Iran of eleven years ago. After the tea house, he took me to Oudlajan. That, too, was a different kind of revelation for me. Later on, when I got to know his oeuvre and stylistic versatility I realized that our visit to Oudlajan was also a gateway to some of his artwork. He knew the old districts of Tehran well. He remembered all the exquisite antique doors and their weighty and well-designed knockers. The interlocking buildings that had become textile workshops drew his attention with envy and admiration. Even the narrow, stinking gutters that ran the length of some streets and smelled of rot did not diminish the beauty of the houses and the neighborhood for Parviz, or his enchantment with what he saw. Shortly after that wondrous visit to Old Tehran, I went to see Iraj Kalantari, Parviz's brother. A noted architect in Iran, he had designed his brother's house, which was superb and a brilliant reflection of Parviz's character. We talked about my tour of Old Tehran. He asked if I had read *Shekar-e Talkh* (The Bitter Sweet), which I hadn't. He then asked if I'd heard of its author Jafar Shahri who was born in the Oudlajan neighborhood and explored Tehran's social history. Before I could respond, he said, perhaps as a consolation, that apparently no one had. I had not heard of him either. I read *Shekar-e Talkh* and was wholly taken by the extraordinary figure that was Jafar Shahri. And after reading many of his works, I ended up writing an article on him.

But the wonders of that trip to old Tehran were not limited to the charms of Oudlajan and the exceptional quality of that tea house. At the end of our tour, we reached a square and Parviz announced, "I need a new pair of reading glasses; my eyesight has diminished a little." I assumed we were on our way to see an optician, but we weren't. He led us to a street vendor hawking an assortment of spectacles on the sidewalk. Parviz tried on some of the glasses on display. I said, quizzically, "Parviz *Jan*, this is not the right place to buy glasses." He replied, laughing, "Why not?" After testing a few, he picked a pair for his weakened eyes and, without bothering to haggle much, bought them. It's remarkable to think that one of the country's most highly acclaimed artists, who had a deep grasp of traditional and modern art and aesthetics worldwide, saw the world through a lens he had found on a street corner.

Rahman Hatefi

He was as if lifted from a nineteenth-century Russian novel. At times, he evoked Chernyshevsky's *What Is to Be Done?* or one of Dostoevsky's protagonists. His unflinching organizational discipline recalled Nechayev and his *Catechism of a Revolutionary*, a treatise that is said to have been at the root of Lenin's thinking about the Communist Party. Rahman's willingness to be sacrificed in the interest of the Tudeh Party and its Navid Organization, and to sacrifice others on their behalf knew no bounds.

I met him and some of his close friends in the first week of my return to Iran after completing my studies in America. They were all Fereshteh's old friends; she and I had married a short time after returning to Iran. It is through her I knew that Rahman and his friends were Tudeh'i. I did not know the scope of their activities. For us in Mao's camp – we who had learned to distinguish the road to *revolution* from the dungeon of *revisionism*, and, by literally revolting against the Tudeh Party, thought we had become *revolutionaries* – Rahman and his group were *heretics*. He and his friends assessed me and my thoughts in like manner. But our ideological differences lost their edge because of our friendship and mutual opposition to the Shah, and perhaps most importantly, because of Rahman's cheerful and friendly spirit, and his brains and breadth of knowledge. A sort of tacit agreement held between us from the start. When we were together, we would not discuss China and the Soviet Union, which were at logger-heads at the time. It didn't matter that we tagged the USSR *social imperialist* in deference to China while they, echoing Russian theorists like Mikhail Suslov, branded the Chinese leaders illiterate and power-hungry peasants, and us, duped children. The amity and warmth of intimate huddles and the presumption of unity in a shared struggle was enough to sustain the form and flow of our friendship.

Back then, Rahman was effectively the editor of *Kayhan* (Universe) newspaper. Amir Taheri was chief editor nomi-nally, and doubtless ranked higher than Rahman in the newsroom hierarchy. But everyone knew that the daily grind of publishing *Kayhan*, which in those days had the highest circulation in the country unlike its current state of ignominy, was in Rahman's hands. He was the darling of the newspaper's co-founder Mostafa Mesbah-zadeh. When I interviewed Mesbah-zadeh for my book *Eminent Persians*, I asked about his relationship with Rahman and how it was that even after his arrest and the revelation of his closeness to Houshang Teezabi – a top-level Tudeh'i who whenever Rahman mentioned his eyes would fill with tears – SAVAK allowed him to occupy such a sensitive position at *Kayhan*. Of course, in our then conspiracy-mongering minds, Rahman's presence at *Kayhan* was part of a "Shah and the regime" ploy: they wanted to scare the Americans with USSR's influ-ence in Iran; and we had several blatantly anti-American and implicitly pro-USSR *Kayhan* headlines to back up our claim. Some of my like-minded friends went even further. They fabri-cated whole plots out of their ideological delusions, saying the regime wanted the Tudeh'is to be strong as an antidote to revolutionary Marxism, which we were manifestations of, naturally! I found Mesbah-zadeh's viewpoint to be more rational. He said, "I loved Rahman like a son. Plus, I knew the newspaper couldn't run without him. I vouched for him personally." That said, if one scans *Kayhan*'s headlines, especially in the few months leading up to the revolution, I believe Rahman's position and considerable influence in hyping the role of the Tudeh Party and discounting the menace of the impending dictatorship is clear. I remember one outsized *Kayhan* headline gave a quote from Khomeini in bold type: "Marxists Have the Freedom to Express Themselves." Below, in small letters, it read something like: "of course, within the framework of Islam." That night, I saw Rahman at our usual get-together. A few of us fell into a discussion about the *Kayhan* headline. We said the crucial and key phrase was *within the framework of Islam*, which basically meant forget about freedom. I asked in protest, "Why make 'freedom' the main headline?" Rahman's response was emphatic and, in my opinion, delusional. He said that with freedom as the main headline, Ayatollah Khomeini would have no choice but to respect that feature of his statement in the future. I knew that was a misguided fallacy. I did not know whether he truly believed that argument or if he was merely applying and echoing the party line.

In any event, one reason hanging out with the group was a joy despite lurking ideological tensions was Rahman's full grasp of current events and any stories cooking behind the scenes and on the margins. I expect that by dint of his organizational discipline, he reserved many of the most significant *marginalia* for Tudeh Party publications. Articulate and eloquent, he was also closely acquainted with many writers. He regularly infused humor into his accounts and never abandoned his *revolutionary optimism* even when relating the darkest news.

When the revolution happened, those lurking tensions ignited into sparks of endless disagreement among us regarding the course of events. Our fellowship ended when the poet and playwright Saeed Soltanpour was killed. I knew he was close friends with Rahman. In addition, he and I had also been cellmates for about six months. Soltanpour came across to me as a courageous and resolute man, albeit a hot-tempered and revolution-struck militant. To me, his art criticism was a second-hand (or third- by way of Tabari) derivative of Zhdanov's doctrine under Stalin. All the same, I was deeply saddened by his execution; I also took it as a warning that the political climate in the country was worsening. One night, I was a guest at the house of Fardin Modaressi, a mutual friend of Rahman and mine. Naturally, the conversation pivoted to news of Soltanpour's execution. In words reeking of self-entitled revolutionary militancy, Rahman said, "Saeed was a victim of immature guerrilla tactics. Such murders are inevitable in pursuit of revolution, and necessary and justified." We got into an argument. After a while some friends asked us to change the subject. The vodka brewed by our Armenian neighbor brought a cheerful finale to the drama. But after that night, I did not see Rahman more than once or twice again.

Once the regime had cut almost every group down to size with the Islamic sword of mercy aided by the Tudeh Party, time finally caught up with the party itself. Rahman was arrested along with almost all the party leaders. When I heard about the lamentable fate of those individuals, I was not surprised to learn that both Rahman and our friend Fardin Modaressi were among those who did not capitulate and were killed. I even heard a story that to escape torture

Rahman had chewed through his own vein. They say every revolution devours its own children. Rahman Hatefi was a genuinely decent and lovable individual who, for a while, had a hand in the devouring due to his unwavering faith in the party, and in the end was himself devoured.

Fardin Modaressi and
Niyaz Yaqub-shahi

Niyaz was in love and her beloved Fardin, who met a
tragic and, according to *comrades*, epic end, cherished
that love. For Niyaz, no barrier or hurdle, whether an offshoot
of class or religious bias or an outcrop of dictatorship and
oppression, could thwart her love or dispel it. And nothing
ever did.

Fardin, whose birth name was Fatemeh, was the
grandchild of a mullah called Modaress; perhaps even the
grandchild of the famous *Seyyed* Hasan Modaress. Her
father, who was once a cleric, was housebound ever since
I first met him. His clothing was always the same – a long
shirt and baggy trousers in white linen. Everyone called him
Aqa. Fardin's mother's sobriquet was *Khanom*. They lived
in a lovely but not luxurious estate in Shemiran. Khanom
ruled the household. Her governing style was quiet and of
the breed of innate power. A slight twitch in the corner of
an eye sufficed for her wish to be executed. A free-spirited
and fearless warrior, Fardin was nonetheless mindful of her
parents and, as far as I could tell, respected her father and
heeded her mother. At the same time, she walked her own
path and did as she pleased.

When our friendship began – she attended the same high school and college as Fereshteh – I knew her to be a fan of the Tudeh Party. It was by accident that I discovered the extent of her role in it. I was at her house to help her move. She had boxed up everything in advance. As I was hauling off the boxes, one fell over and its contents spilled out. Copies of the newspaper *Navid* (Glad Tidings) an organ of the Tudeh Party's clandestine operations, and some party records and internal pamphlets spilled across the floor. Both Fardin and I panicked. It felt like I had barged into an off-limits room unawares. Neither she nor I said anything. She came over to me calmly and without saying a word helped retrieve the scattered papers and pack them back in the box. After the revolution, I read that she had traveled to East Germany during the same period and had met with the party leaders, including Maryam Firouz.

When I first knew her, she and her brother who later became a linguist were living on the second floor of the family home. To reach their quarters, one had to pass through the main living room. Aqa and Khanom were the silent and always gracious and respectful observers of all the comings and goings. They greeted every visitor cordially except for Niyaz, neither whose coming nor whose going gave them any pleasure. One of most touching stories about Niyaz and Fardin reflects that parental disapproval.

One night when it was snowing heavily, Niyaz, who lived in the working class district in southern Tehran, was pining for his beloved. As he later recounted, "I yearned to see Fardin with all my body and soul." He somehow managed to get himself to Shemiran in the north, and climbed over the wall. Then with much difficulty, and quietly so as not to awaken Aqa and Khanom, he hauled himself onto the second-floor balcony by Fardin's window. Niyaz tapped on the glass softly. With a sweet smile that never left her lips, Fardin recalled, "I woke up rattled. I turned on the light. I could see Niyaz standing in the falling snow. I wanted to laugh and felt delirious and scared, all at the same time. Should Aqa and Khanom come in and see Niyaz on the balcony, they would have a heart attack!" I never asked how that night ended, or how long Niyaz stayed. All I know is that Aqa and Khanom never found out about his visit. They prohibited Fardin from marrying Niyaz and she, despite all the respect she felt for her parents, refused to acquiesce. Fardin was a maven of finer things and recognized the value of Niyaz's pure and guileless love. Nor would she cave in to pressure.

Later, after seeing *The Dead*, John Huston's brilliant adaptation of the last story in James Joyce's *Dubliners*, I thought of the final scene as a tragic variant of Niyaz and Fardin's tryst in the snow and their unrequited love. In Joyce's story, on hearing that his beloved will be leaving the city the next day, the seventeen-year-old Micheal Furey sneaks out into the icy Irish snow and standing outside her window while sick with consumption and a cold, sings a love song until dawn to say goodbye, and not long after her departure, dies. In the story, it was the force of nature and the beloved's departure, along with Michael's illness, that forged the fate of a love unrequited, and in the case of Niyaz and Fardin, political dictatorship.

Fardin was always upbeat and cheerful. She had studied accounting and worked at the National Iranian Oil Company. I heard she was diligent, competent, and hard-working. She was well liked and held in high regard by her co-workers. Her humane and ever-kind persona was not a party dictate; it was rooted in her warm and sunny nature. At the same time, in both party discipline and fidelity to her ideals, she was of the same steely breed as the longstanding "Great Leader of the international proletariat." Nor was her faith in the party a political front or a mere fad; I believe it lay in the depths of her yearning for social justice. When she was arrested along with other party members and leaders, and despite seeing almost all those leaders and Islam-backers such as Ehsan Tabari turn into collaborators, Fardin stood by her convictions and faith in the party to death. Her fellow warrior and principal role model in the party – and perhaps her closest friend in all the world – was Rahman Hatefi who also gave up his life for the party; both have become tools for the Tudeh Party propaganda whose leaders, unable to withstand the regime's tortures and threats, buckled under pressure, and confessed to myriad felonies and crimes, including spying for Big Brother. In a note written by one of Fardin's cellmates, I read that every time she was dragged away to be interrogated, she agonized about her stamina and told her cellmate, "Wish me luck that I can hold out in my resistance and in saying no." She held out and was executed.

During the period in which she was regularly tortured, her daughter Nazli who was just a year old lived in the cell with her. No words can fully capture the inhumanity of those interrogators and the regime that they represented. Even if one took to lamenting those acts in writing 'not for a moment, nor even a lifetime,' as Beyhaqi put it, one would not be able to communicate the agony and torment that was inflicted upon prisoners like Fardin. The pen breaks not just when it comes to describing love, but depravity too.

After some time, Nazli was released from prison. But even once she was free, religious curbs and constraints still beset Niyaz, now as her father. I learned indirectly that Fardin's family who were against their marriage from the start, took the little girl under their wing and effectively denied the father custody rights. My guess is that if Niyaz wanted, he could have won custody through the courts given their inherent misogyny and the entrenched patriarchy. Perhaps he was thinking of his daughter's best interests and felt that protestation defied the purpose.

Years had gone by since then, when one day I was at a conference in some city in the U.S. After the session ended, I was approached by a young woman. Something in her face looked familiar; I did not know what. "I'm Nazli Yaqub-shahi," she said. "I told my father you were giving a talk. He said to definitely go and say hello." I broke into tears for the sorrow that had been laid on Niyaz and Nazli and Fardin, and the heavy price that despotism and bigotry had made them pay. Niyaz wrote poetry, most of it romantic. One of his collected works is even titled *Romanticisms*. Reading each of his poems, nobody other than Fardin springs to my mind as the gospel and grounds of his love and its sublime expression. When I read these lines – *The light of your face and form poured forth / The sweep of my mirror eyes / Weaving you in white alone / It was your infinite rainbows / Braiding all the colors into one* – I can only think of the time he had stood on Fardin's balcony in the snow. Pure poetry springs from the heart, and from the time I knew Niyaz, his heart was awash and brimming with the love of Fardin. Apparently, other than publishing his poetry, he had also collaborated with the poet Ahmad Shamlou on a few projects. He was also a translator. But Niyaz's greatest art was himself. There was not an ounce of fakery in his soul. He did not take himself too seriously. In every laugh and lark, he poked fun at himself as well. Mischief was in his nature. One hot summer afternoon in Tehran, we were lolling around on the floor in Fardin's old room after a heavy and somnolent lunch, chatting away. Each of us was sharing their hopes and dreams with a mixture of seriousness and jest. Niyaz who was wide awake said, buzzed and playful,

"I wish I were invisible and had a feather in my hand and could creep up to anyone I wanted and rub it on their ear or nose or face and watch them react." Not to miff anyone, just to tease. Later, when I saw Shakespeare's *Midsummer Night's Dream* and delighted in Puck and his pranks, I was reminded of Niyaz who was our very own mischievous Puck, but also full of love and charm.

While his eyes were often laden with deep sorrow, humor was his default mode. He even related the story of his arrest and torture under the Shah as a hilarious event. Niyaz was a native of Mashhad. In high school, he was classmates with some who were later involved in founding the People's Fadaiyan Guerrillas. That close association and intimate contact, and the reality that Niyaz's head was "full of *crazy* ideas," was enough to get him arrested. The interrogation was all threats and tongue-lashing and beating on the part of the interrogator, and on the part of Niyaz, all denial of contact with, or knowledge of, the guerrilla organization. The interrogator suddenly changed his tone. "If you really had no contact, then swear that you're telling the truth." Eyeing the Shah's picture above the interrogator's head, Niyaz said, "I swear on the tuft of His Majesty that I am not in contact with the guerrillas now and wasn't then." Before he could finish the sentence, a hard slap landed on his face. "You son-of-a-bitch! How dare you, an unclean Marxist, swear on His Majesty's tuft!"

Ahmad Qoreishi

While new money and ostentation with the requisite obnoxious bluster was endemic among most bigwigs in the last years of the Shah's reign, Ahmad Qoreishi was the opposite – a winsome image of modesty and abstinence from any display of wealth or power. Although Khaf, one of the oldest cities in Iran, was among his family's landholdings in Khorasan, his nobility did not derive from blood and turf, but from his humanity and generosity. His loyalty to friends knew no limits and, based on my own experience, he never sacrificed a friend on the altar of political or financial expediency. That is why his circle of friends was so wide. In whatever task he undertook, however important, it was as if he made as much effort to accomplish the task as to hide his own role in it. He stepped into the political arena only once, and that was when he accepted a prominent position in the Rastakhiz (Resurrection) Party when it was formed in 1975. I never knew the reason for that uncharacteristic decision. Perhaps because a number of his friends were among Rastakhiz theoreticians. In exile, he was key to securing funding for *Iranshenasi* for years. Yet his name was never mentioned in the journal or even heard in that connection. He hosted an assortment of friends in sundry receptions and one of his unique qualities was that, in each case, every participant felt they were closest to him in the throng.

His receptions, both at the time and in exile, had many features in common. In Tehran, his garden estate across Sa'dabad Palace was so large that when *Aqa* – his father – came to visit, he could perform his morning equestrian routine in the grounds. In exile in the U.S., there was no room at his property for Aqa to ride horseback. His property was of moderate size and in a semi-affluent town. In neither home was there any sign of affected luxury. In my experience, the food was always Persian and Qoreishi himself had a hand in preparing a variety of dishes, and capably so. The guests ranged from ambassadors and ministers and regular colleagues to close and distant relatives. My friendship with Ahmad Qoreishi began at work.

When we met, it took less than twenty minutes for him to hire me as a faculty member in the Department of Economics and Political Science at the then National University of Iran. Only later did he broach my appointment at a faculty meeting, as was legally and customarily required, and their vote of approval was duly registered. He enjoyed a special status and esteem among departmental faculty members. His office was a large room with a panoramic view of Tehran through a picture window. It often happened that I would enter his office and find him standing there, gazing at the view with his hands behind his back. I always felt that, beneath his beaming smile and animated manner lurked a kind of angst, even a touch of melancholy. One always had the sense, too, that in every interaction he knew more about the subject than he would let on. He was as attached to poetry and literature as to politics and economics.

That day I had gone to visit him together with my friend Khashayar Javaherian. After the initial small talk, made even more delightful by his strong Mashhadi accent, the moment he heard I had a Ph.D. from the U.S. he said, "The next term begins next week; that is when you should start." He called his assistant, who I think went by Ms. Ebrahimi, and said, "Miss, add three courses to the curriculum for *So and So*." They also assigned me an office the same day. I have no doubt that no other department chair dared make such summary decisions in those days without getting clearance from the security apparatus. I did not know about his close friendship with SAVAK's Parviz Sabeti at the time, though Qoreishi's chutzpah did not rest on that relationship – or other relationships – but in his self-confidence and the willingness to take the blame for any decision that might turn out to be flawed.

Though the students kept their distance from any faculty they viewed as close to the regime, they displayed a special respect and affection for Qoreishi due to his brass and forthright behavior. I heard them say on many an occasion, "Dr. Qoreishi is different from the rest. He is really principled." He secured visiting rights for one student whose brother was in prison and arranged for others to buy a Peykan out of turn. I was also the object of his munificence. He even enjoyed great popularity and acceptance among the faculty, which was an eclectic mix of individuals with different backgrounds and beliefs – from a minister to a cousin of the Queen, to an aristocratic Marxist, to technocrats who aspired to a ministerial portfolio and the modernization of Iran. He got along with all his colleagues and was close friends with a number of them. Without having illusions about anybody, he nonetheless treated each individual with respect.

One of his close friends was Professor Akbar. Like Qoreishi, Akbar hailed from a wealthy landowning family. He had been educated in England and considered himself a Marxist; he had also studied Freud. His suits were still tailored at London's Savile Row. He was kind to the students that he liked (mainly studious girls) and treated others harshly for their illiteracy, giving them low grades and occasionally offering Freudian interpretations of their conduct. Every now and then, students complained about Akbar to Qoreishi, who prevented the issue from escalating into a crisis with a combination of savoir faire and humor. When the revolution happened, not only Ahmad Qoreishi but Akbar as well no longer had a place at the university. Years later, I visited Qoreishi in his adopted hometown in the U.S. I asked for news of Akbar. He laughed. "As a matter of fact, I had a letter from him a few days ago. He's still living with his mother. Most of their properties in Tehran and Rasht have been confiscated; only a garage near their home on Istanbul Avenue was spared." Akbar had written: "I sit at the counter in the garage every day, I read Hegel, issue receipts, and collect cash." I heard from a student that in all the years Akbar taught at the university he never drew a salary. When I joined the Faculty of Law post-revolution, I shared an office with Mohammad Razavi who also counted among the major landowners in Kerman. I was aware that he, too, rather than take a salary, donated it to a noble soul whose job was to clean the offices and provide services for the professors. I, of course, invariably depended upon my monthly salary.

Although my hiring took less than half an hour, I did not receive my first paycheck until ten months later. The reason for the delay was seemingly the meanness of the then National University chancellor, Dr. Abbas Safavian. While he was said to be a competent physician, he was not particularly good at running a university. The campaign against Qoreishi seems to have started with Dr. Safavian's appointment as chancellor. At the time, Qoreishi had been earmarked for the chancellor's post. He was Prime Minister Hoveyda's candidate. The final decision rested with the Shah, of course. Qoreishi had been told by Hoveyda's office to be prepared the next day in official *salam* attire for an audience with the Shah, where he would be appointed chancellor. But Asadollah Alam, the court minister, had been lying in wait, scheming. In the morning, Hoveyda's office informed Qoreishi of an aberration. Alam's might had defeated Hoveyda and it was Dr. Safavian who was given an audience. Later, when I read about the Shah's cancer and learned that Dr. Safavian was on the medical team that treated him from the outset, I reckoned it was not only Alam's power and his rivalry with Hoveyda that had kept Qoreishi waiting at home that morning dressed for *salam*.

With that, Dr. Safavian saw Qoreishi as a rival from the moment he began his tenure as chancellor, and provoked discord; the delay in paying my salary was a backlash in that same conflict. Such mean-spiritedness and his gratuitously harsh treatment of students meant that Dr. Safavian's leadership was short-lived. When I was released from prison a year later, Ahmad Qoreishi had been named the new National University chancellor.

A few days after my release, I made an appointment to see him in his new office. My hope was to resume teaching. I later learned that the minute he heard about my arrest, he had called Sabeti and asked about my status. In those days, if a friend or colleague was sent to prison for political reasons, hardly anyone dared to hint at a relationship or friendship with that person before SAVAK. Manuchehr Ganji, a colleague of mine in the same department, had assembled a group of professors to serve as advisers to the Queen and had also

invited me to join the group. On the eve of my arrest, in his
own account, he called the Queen and the Shah and apologized for having been deceived by my facade. Ganji's brand
of caution was the standard currency of the day, and understandable. Qoreishi's loyalty and compassion were rare and
laudable. A few weeks into my arrest, he had stepped in so I
could meet with my father in SAVAK's Joint Committee holding
pen. I was now resorting to him in the hope of rejoining the
university.

I was sitting in the waiting room when the door to
Qoreishi's office opened and a man that I had known in prison
as the Joint Committee deputy, Hossein-zadeh, stepped out.
He was accompanied by a woman. I felt unnerved. Should I
greet him or not? He walked up to me and introduced his wife
without telling her where he knew me from. "Are you here to
visit your friend?" he asked. There was a kind of power play
even in the tone of his question, meaning, "I know Qoreishi is
close to you." I said, "Yes." He wasn't inclined to carry on a
conversation either. As he left the waiting room, Ms. Ebrahimi
showed me to Qoreishi's office. "I had met that gentleman
in prison," I said, still feeling nervous. He laughed and said,
"Well, yes." After the revolution, I heard Hossein-zadeh was
selling rugs in Washington under a pseudonym.

I pitched my request to Qoreishi. Right away, he
called Sabeti. Given his urging and pledge to vouch for me
personally, I knew that Sabeti's reaction had been negative.
Qoreishi's graciousness and personal guarantee on my behalf
were especially remarkable given, as he must have known,
that I had once abused his friendship in the past.

In those years, even if you had money, buying a
Peykan wasn't easy. You had to wait your turn to get your
car, sometimes for several months. One day I was talking
to Parviz Vaez-zadeh who was my go-between at the

organization – thirty or so active members and a couple of dozen sympathizers who claimed to represent the working class and to be leading the revolution – about how Qoreishi had intervened on behalf of some students to buy a Peykan. He immediately said, "See if you can get hold of a Peykan for the organization." One day when Qoreishi was alone, I told him I have a needy friend who wanted to buy a Peykan to earn his living. I asked if help was possible. He picked up the phone and spoke with one of the Khayyami brothers who owned the company and asked if they might provide a Peykan for *So and So* out of turn. He used the fake name I had given him, the one Vaez-Zadeh was using then. The following week, Vaez-zadeh drove up to see me in his new Peykan. Neither at the time nor afterwards when he must have learned that I had bought the Peykan for the organization did Qoreishi ask me about the particulars of my friend. Worst of all, neither the organization nor I had questioned the fact that should the details of the affair ever become known to SAVAK – which they did – it would have consequences for Qoreishi whose only offence was compassion. We believed our goal was *sacred* and that any *profane* act on its behalf was thereby sanctified. In exile, when I tried to say something about that affair by way of an apology and an explanation – or justification – Qoreishi listened, then gave me a friendly pat on the back and said, "Forget it, man."

Hamid Enayat

The first thing one noticed about him was his glasses. With their wide frames and thick lenses they looked larger than his face, as if a token of someone who wished to be known above all by the way they saw the world. He was short. One might have spotted the red patch on his face later on, but even then, it was his piercing and incisive gaze, his eyes often awash with warmth and mischief, that most drew attention. He was among the few professors who was also admired as an intellectual. Most departmental faculty behaved akin to employees of a corporation named the Faculty of Law, either out of fear of persecution or because of the nature and limitations of their knowledge. They started to work the moment they entered the campus, and the moment they left, they lowered the blinds of thinking and reasoning and scholarly research. Neither their offices nor their living quarters betrayed any signs of intellectual passion or pain – books, art, journals, posters. Their homes might as well have belonged to an employee of the bureau of records management.

Hamid Enayat was at once a learned professor devoted to teaching and a prolific and authoritative intellectual. His career and commitment were a symbiosis of thinking and research. His translations set a benchmark for accuracy and integrity and mastery of both the original and the translated language. They were always clear and fluent. When it came to most other faculty, their books, if they wrote any, were published by the university press in small print runs and exclusively served the courses they taught. Most were no more than pamphlets that comprised essentially the same outdated and repeated sermons they served up in the classroom. Students were instructed to regurgitate the professors' effusions at exam time *verbatim et literatim*.

A major segment of the faculty followed, and still follows, what the renowned Brazilian philosopher Paulo Freire called the *banking concept* of education. In such a paradigm, professors consider themselves *custodians* of the asset that is knowledge, and regularly grant shares of that asset to students whose duty is to receive and deposit the shares in their mental accounts. Enayat's pedagogy – and indeed that of all genuine teachers – was the direct opposite. He urged students to think, and he taught them the ways and means of critical thinking. The woman he married shared that same emancipated mindset. I only saw her a few times. She is highly educated and a skillful editor. When I saw her in Oxford after Enayat had passed, she was cataloguing her husband's writings.

Enayat took another road less traveled by public intellectuals as well, and successfully so. Looked at in one way, Iranian intellectuals in that era may be divided into three groups. One group fought the Shah; a second group had stopped fighting but still snubbed him and the regime; while a third group had concluded that the opposition was misguided and that collaboration with the Shah was the right path to saving and helping Iran. Enayat did not fit into any of those three groups. He neither tussled head on with the regime, nor stayed out of it, nor was he considered an establishment intellectual. He did not mind collaborating with the regime on his terms and within a framework that he himself determined. He lived honorably and with dignity and played an influential and enduring role in educating generations of academically oriented Iranians.

The first time I saw him was a few days after I had returned home from the U.S. I had just received my doctorate degree and was very eager to teach in Iran. I went to see him with my friend Khashayar Javaherian who taught biochemistry at the University of Tehran. Enayat chaired the political science department. He understood from Khashayar's veiled remarks that, like him, I had been an activist during my student years. He explained the hiring process. "The application will be submitted to the group," he said. "If they accept it, hiring can proceed." He added that he did not expect any problems "unless they reject it," meaning SAVAK whose approval was a prerequisite in faculty hiring. When we remember that even at the height of the Shah's *authoritarianism*, professors were entitled to select their colleagues per the standard of academic freedom and that SAVAK's role was limited to rejecting some of them, and compare that pattern with the current conditions where "faculty and students" are by and large allocated by special quotas, we can better grasp the catastrophic ambit of the educational system in the country today. At any rate, because I wanted to start working as soon as possible and thought my hiring may not be approved unless Ahmad Qoreishi pressed for it, I accepted the offer to start at the National University rather than sweat out the University of Tehran process. In addition, both Enayat and Khashayar insisted that to teach at the National University now would make it easier to transfer to the University of Tehran later.

I had been teaching at the National University for only a few months when I got a call from Hamid Enayat; he invited me to lunch in the faculty dining hall at the University of Tehran. I waited for him by the entrance. When we walked in, it seemed everybody knew him. Most said nothing but their stealthy glances and whisperings with companions or colleagues showed they were pleased by the presence of one of the university's most distinguished professors. After we had sat down and chatted for a while about things in general, Enayat said he was taking a sabbatical and asked me to teach his courses in his absence. I accepted eagerly. I knew he had in the meantime been making inquiries about my classes among some of his former students who were now taking my graduate course. When one of those students who had told me about this learned about Enayat's invitation, he advised me to decline it. "Enayat's courses are the weightiest at the law school," he said, "and he's heard your courses here are popular. This is an outright land mine." I found his comment odd. It sounded conspiratorial. Or maybe he was convinced I couldn't handle Enayat's courses. In any event, I did not take his concerns seriously. I met with Enayat two or three more times in his office to get his advice on the curriculum and the students. He was clearly trying his best to make sure I would be successful.

During the first term, I felt nervous and uneasy in class. Right from day one, the students, missing him and likely feeling unhappy or unlucky that he had been substituted by a stranger, raised a host of tricky questions both to express their discontent and to assess or expose the limits of my knowledge. Before starting my work in Iran, I had taught a few classes in the U.S. I had also read some literature on *scientific sociology*, which at the time was a euphemism for Marxism. Based on such limited experience and knowledge, I offered veiled but at the same time revealing answers so they would know I was *familial* and *accommodating*. Enayat's counsel had prepared me for such a day. He warned me that the students would test me on the very first day. "If you cave in, you're finished."

A few months after that experience, Enayat who had returned once his sabbatical was over invited me to the faculty dining hall again. He said the Ministry of Foreign Affairs had established a special training school for diplomats. Mahmoud Foroughi was the president, and Enayat was responsible for the curriculum. "I'm free to invite anyone I consider suited to teach at the school, and there will be no censorship in class." He asked me to teach a course on U.S. politics and one on political sociology. It was decided that I would offer one of the two courses in English to help improve the future diplomats' proficiency in that language. He reiterated that he himself would be teaching Western political philosophy and had assigned the courses on Marxism and the Soviet Union to Enayatollah Reza. I knew Reza was one of the leaders of the Tudeh Party and had spent years in Russia, that venerated living utopia of socialism, before coming back to Iran. Reportedly, it was his brother Professor Fazlollah Reza, president of the University of Tehran, who had orchestrated his return. Enayatollah Reza had translated Berdyaev's *The Origin of Russian Communism*, a singular book that traced the origins of Leninist Bolshevism back to Orthodox Russian Christianity. Few understood the essence of Russian Marxism as keenly as Enayatollah Reza, which is perhaps why few endured as many indignities and personal attacks by Soviet rhapsodists as he did.

When it came time to teaching at the law school for a second year, I was arrested. After I was released, even Qoreishi's weight was not enough to restore my position at the National University where he once headed the political science department. At the turn of the revolution, though, the new chair of political science at the University of Tehran, Abdolmajid Abolhamd, contacted me and said, "You can join our faculty of law full time." Enayat was still an influential voice in their political science group. Though I had been a political prisoner and previously dismissed as a faculty member, and despite a prohibition against new hirings, the first post-revolution chancellor of the University of Tehran, Mohammad Maleki, and his deputy, Ali Sabbaghian, had the goodwill to approve my appointment, and I got busy teaching.

In the early months after the revolution, having served time as a political prisoner was an asset. All such prisoners were entitled to resume their former jobs; they were even told their salary for the duration of their prison term would be reimbursed in full, not a penny less. That turned out to be a fleeting promise. Soon enough, they manipulated and distorted the definition of *political prisoner* in such a way that only Islamist "insiders" fitted the bill. It didn't matter that in the years prior to the revolution, the great majority of political prisoners were "outsiders."

Through Enayat, during that same period, I met his brother Mahmoud, editor-in-chief of *Negin* (Signet). I published a few articles in his magazine, and meanwhile came to know Hamid's unique sense of humor and insight into history. He used to say, "I know the mullahs inside out." Enayat knew that what was coming was a singular iteration of despotism in political thought, an even more taxing version of Plato's *Republic* and the dictatorship of the *benevolent* philosopher king. Once in a while, he would point out a certain Shia *hadith*, canonical vignettes and edicts of worshipful figures in Islam, that he found bizarre. The article I eventually wrote on *Usul-e Kafi* (Sufficient Principles), Abu Jafar Kolayni's 10th century collection of hadith, and the texture of his thoughts, grew out of my conversations with Enayat at the time, and I am indebted to him for that. He once said, "According to one hadith, eating one slice of honeydew melon cleanses the faithful of their daily transgressions. Another proclaimed that 'shedding one teardrop for the martyrs of Karbala absolves all sins.' He added: "It's a good thing the faithful aren't into reading these stories because that would unleash a pandemonium of vice!" Enayat did not live to see the pandemonium unleashed by the new generation in Iran with their digital access to such hadith. Perhaps it is because of his very insight into the core of *Velayat-e Faqih* (Guardianship of the [Islamic] Jurist), the current theocratic system of governance in Iran that, a few months after the revolution, he applied for an unpaid sabbatical and time away from the campus.

His application had to be approved by the political science department. For reasons that were never clear to me, Abolhamd who then chaired the department was vehemently against approving it. Was it jealousy because Enayat had been offered a position at Oxford? Was it because he wished to maintain the department's standing by holding on to one of its most distinguished professors? I never found out. In any event, I and most of the faculty felt that Enayat's request was in compliance with university regulations and his rights. His application was thereby approved. But Enayat's appointment at Oxford did not last long. Within two years, he died of a sudden heart attack, leaving a deep void in Oxford's Iranian studies program. At a time when, given his erudition and perspicacity and familiarity with Western political philosophy as well as Islam, along with his mastery of the varied dimensions of Shia thought and the ethos of the clergy could have served as a nonpareil guide to understanding Iran, he passed away, and even his prolific and widely read oeuvre cannot make up for his absence. He left the world at the height of his intellectual prowess. The novelist Houshang Golshiri used to lament the premature death of writers. Enayat's end was the premature death of a distinguished teacher, researcher, and champion of freedom.

Reza Baraheni

The last time I saw Reza Baraheni he was in a nursing home in Toronto.* It was through friends I learned that he had been moved there. I had seen him several times in exile. The last couple of times was also in Toronto when his occasional lapses of memory and blank stare that echoed the void inside his head had worried me. I used to see a lot more of him in Iran. Both of us were then teaching at the University of Tehran, I in political science and he in English literature. His department was for a long while led by Ardavan Davaran, an old friend and my brother-in-law at the time. That was when Baraheni and I became friends.

I had seen him once or twice at meetings of the Confederation of Iranian Students when I was in college. He was one of the Shah's noted foes. There was a problem, which is that most of us in the Confederation were Stalinists and he leaned Trotskyite. For reasons that were not clear, at least not to me but which I accepted – for in our sect Stalin's pronouncements were the gospel truth – *they*, the

---

* This essay was written two years before the passing of Reza Baraheni in 2022.

Trotskyites, were more nefarious than *class enemies*. When
I later translated Kolakowski's *Main Currents of Marxism*
into Persian, I concluded that the feud between Stalin and
Trotsky was in fact a phantom battle, but back in time, in
deference to Stalin's fatwa, we considered Trotsky and *them*,
his acolytes, more corrupt than any *corrupt bourgeois*. On
occasion, some of us would even go to the Trotskyites' bookstore in Berkeley and steal books. The justification was that
stealing from the enemy was a de facto hallowed and *revolutionary* act. I never participated in that revolutionary act,
not because I doubted its sanctity; I didn't participate because
I was scared. That said, Reza Baraheni was too high-profile
to be wholly *cancelled*; nor had he ever officially joined a
Trotskyite group. It is because of his celebrity that he was
invited to testify before a U.S. Congressional committee in the
early 1970s. From a historical perspective, the choice of individuals selected to testify before such committees reflects the
persuasions and preferences prevalent among various factions
in the U.S. government at a particular time. The highly exaggerated claim that Iran had one hundred thousand political
prisoners stemmed from Baraheni's testimony in Congress.
Having been imprisoned in Iran while a professor lent him
special credibility. He eventually wrote a book in English
produced by a leading publishing house whose theme was
summed up in its title, *The Crowned Cannibals*.

Baraheni had learned English chiefly in Iran, and in
Turkey where he earned his doctorate. His mastery of the
English language was another reason for his success in the
U.S. and the singular impact of his testimony in Congress.
Moreover, in *The Crowned Cannibals* and in interviews, he
talked of outlandish forms of torture that as far as I know
have never been described by anyone before or since. Among
other acts, he claimed that his interrogator had tried to violate

him while he hung upside down from an electric ceiling fan. When I saw Parviz Sabeti the first night I was jailed at the Joint Committee he mentioned Baraheni jokingly and said, "You should tell your friend if we were able to perform such acts, we'd start a circus."

In the aftermath of Baraheni's testimony, Amnesty International repeated the figure of a hundred thousand political prisoners citing the U.S. Congressional hearing, and from then on, the anti-Shah opposition repeated the false allegation citing Amnesty International, which being a highly reputable agency, gave credence to the story. It was the historian Roham Alvandi, then a young and diligent scholar, who traced the trail of that exaggerated figure as part of an interesting research project and found its source in Baraheni's testimony.

Half a century after that incident, I was on my way to visit him in the nursing home. It turned out that gaining access to the place was not easy. When I arrived with a friend who knew Baraheni well, the security guard stopped us. "Who are you here to visit and what are your names?" she asked, then checked the flickering computer screen before her and said, "The gentleman is indeed our guest, but you're not listed as authorized visitors; visitation is conditional on his family's authorization." "What, is this a prison?" I said, taken aback. The woman sitting at the reception desk quipped with a mixture of tart contempt and official protocol, "The rules are in the guest's best interests, lest a con artist attempt to exploit his predicament." Her words translated into: "What rock have you been living under that you don't know what's going on in the world and in establishments like this? And you think you are entitled, to boot?!"

Security then called Sanaz, Baraheni's wife. Years ago, her marriage to Baraheni had caused a quite a stir, for the year before she had been crowned "Queen of Tourism." At

the time – and to this day – both secular revolutionaries and
religious puritans considered *Dokhtar-e Shayesteh* (Miss Iran)
and such pageantry to be symbols and examples of *corruption*, *Westoxification*, and the *objectification of women*.
Luckily, Sanaz picked up the phone and when she heard my
friend's name and mine, she gave her consent. We were led to
a room down a long hallway lined with identical doors. It is
said that the architecture of prisons, hospitals, and asylums
(and even some large city squares) is designed to facilitate
the greatest level of surveillance and control with a minimum
of effort. The long hallway and the corner office for nurses
and security guards reflected that selfsame panoptic principle.
There were two beds in the room, both empty. Baraheni's
name was inscribed on one. No books or writing materials
were anywhere in sight. A few moments later, a nurse entered,
accompanied by a different guard. "The person you have
come to visit has been taken to the TV room," she announced
before leading us to a sorry purgatory, a place that evoked
Gilgamesh's land of the dead and Homer's Hades.

In not too small a room, seven infirmed individuals, each
seated on a wheelchair, were staring at a TV screen. I thought
of Parviz Kimiavi's film *The Mongols*. Reza Baraheni was
dressed in a black sweatsuit. You could tell his hair and beard
had been trimmed that day as strands of white hair still clung
here and there to the front and shoulders of his jumper. I
said hello and held his hands in mine, pressing them. I also
kissed his cheek. He threw me a glance devoid of recognition
but smiled. "Yes. Yes," he said. I had no doubt that he had
not recognized either me or my friend. But then something
happened that eclipsed the tension and melancholy of that
first moment of an agonizing visit.

An old woman who sat staring at the television next to
Reza suddenly grabbed my hand and cried out in English,

"Johnny, you finally came! You finally came, Johnny!" At this, the nurse who had guided us to that abyss took a couple of steps forward and pulled my hand away from the old woman's, firmly, but not forcefully. "Your Johnny will come for sure," she told the woman genially, "but this gentleman is not Johnny." Then she whispered in my ear, "Johnny is her son. It's been two or three years since he paid her a visit. It's not even certain he's alive." I had a lump in my throat because of Johnny's lonesome mother and even more because of my dear friend Baraheni, for all that remained of his past bluster, his provocative and brilliant wisecracks and incisive gaze, was a vacant look and a heavy silence. The *Infernal Times* of Mr. Baraheni, though he had lamented a different protagonist in his book thus titled.

Only a few months had passed since the revolution when Baraheni called me at home one afternoon. Hollywood had just released a blockbuster movie, and he knew I loved films. "I've gotten a hold of a copy of *Batman*," he said. "Come over, let's watch it together." In those days most movie theaters had been torched by revolutionary fanatics and video players for watching widely smuggled movies were prized objects. They were expensive and not available in every household. A mutual friend of ours who was the son of a venerable scholar of Persian literature and also favored by the Islamic regime had even turned the upper floor of his parents' home into a sort of cinemathèque. He screened a movie every week, after which we would discuss the film and eat slices of cucumber and parsley just before leaving – a precaution to shield us from the street patrol and spare ourselves and our friend's family from the trouble that would follow should our breath smelt of arak and wine. So, it was only natural that, despite a heavy snowfall, my wife Fereshteh and I eagerly accepted Reza's invitation that evening and headed to his house.

He gave us a warm welcome, then left Fereshteh with Sanaz saying, "I need to take care of some business with Abbas." He led me to his office, which was packed with books, with a desk and chair the middle of the room. He shut the door behind us. "I've written a new poem and would like to read it to you," he said. I cheered him on. "Because it's long," he said, "I've taped it." Reaching for a large audiotape player on his desk, he pressed the start button. It was a recital of *Esmael*, in Baraheni's resonant voice, in remembrance of the poet Esmael Shahroudi, a friend who had recently passed. Perhaps the reason he wanted me to hear the poem before publishing it was that I had once run into him and Esmael at Doc's shop. Doc was a former dentist who had abandoned dentistry and set up a small eatery whose kababs were very popular. It was a hangout of the literati. I sometimes used to go by with Ardavan and the filmmaker Dariush Mehrjui who was a friend of ours since college days. Saedi was a regular there, and one time we had also run into Baraheni and Shahroudi. That night in his office, Baraheni left the room after starting the tape and closed the door behind him. I sat on the floor near the wall-mounted heater. Knowing the exact duration of the recording, he came back a minute or two before the ending. When it had stopped, he asked for my opinion. I had neither expertise in poetry (and still don't) nor had read Baraheni's poems closely. I shared with him whatever came to mind, which wasn't much. Mehrjui was the other link between Baraheni and me. Baraheni was very eager for Mehrjui to make a film of his historical novel *The Infernal Times of Mr. Ayaz*, a story that had intrigued him since those days. Dariush would not oblige, nor was Baraheni's book on Ayaz ever published in Iran owing to the exigencies of censorship. But his Esmael was published as a stand-alone book a few years later.

It is said that Caravaggio's moving painting of the moment Ishmael is about to be sacrificed by his father Abraham is one of the most spectacular and earliest signs of modernity and the thinking behind it. In Caravaggio's depiction, Ishmael gapes at his father not in consent and submission but in rage and rebellion. Was Baraheni's Esmael with its haunting images of young boys sent to the frontlines in the Iran-Iraq war, the same Baraheni who had earlier written *Masculine History* as a critique of patriarchy in Iranian history, in effect an attack against the patriarchal child-killers that had gained power in Iran in the name of revolution and had put a thousand Esmaels to death? It was to get away from those killings and purges that, despite his initial efforts to fit into the new Islamic university, Baraheni, too, had no option but to flee abroad.

He never found a full-time job in the U.S. or Canada that lived up to his talents or, more importantly, to his expectations. I once called him when I learned about an academic opening in the U.S. He was not interested in teaching Persian literature anymore, he said. "I want to teach my own thoughts." Such an opportunity never came up. If the monster of dictatorship had not spread its sinister shadow across Iran and Baraheni had stayed home, would he be staring at a television screen in purgatory in Tehran just as he was in that nursing home in Toronto? A noted European critic and staunch fan of his had said Baraheni ought to come to the West because he is an international writer. For a writer like Baraheni, before being international one must be Iranian, and Baraheni was truly an Iranian writer. In the last two decades of his life, he had grown increasingly conscious of the Azarbaijani facet of his identity within the multiethnic Iranian landscape. His views were at times infuriating. But was the calamity that Baraheni came to suffer – that desolate and dire isolation in his eyes, his loneliness next to a mother longing for her lost son – part of the price that Iran paid for the *Abrahamic revolution*? Or perhaps it was a share of the punishment that our ideologically driven generation had to suffer for our exaggerations.

Reza Bateni

"I had just returned from England," said Bateni. "I got hired at the Faculty of Literature and started translating a book on linguistics. I ran into difficulties finding the right semantic equivalents for some words. Lotfali Souratgar who headed the department was known to one and all for his mastery of English and Persian." Years later, I heard the same Souratgar described by Ebrahim Golestan, who said his translation of a contract for oil exploration was full of so many errors that signing it was postponed and they had to have it retranslated with Foad Rohani's help and oversight. "I made an appointment and went to see Souratgar," Bateni continued. "'What's the Persian equivalent for such and such a term?' I asked. 'There isn't one,' Souratgar replied, smiling sweetly as he spoke. I couldn't be sure if he knew the meaning of the English term. I asked about another term. Again, he said, 'There isn't one.' As I mouthed a third term, he asked without suggesting an equivalent, 'What do you need these for, young man?' 'To translate a scientific study in linguistics,' I replied, to which he said, 'That's not how we translate things over here. We either scrape or scrap.'" It's possible no one wised up to all the scraping and scrapping that had occurred in literary or even scientific texts over the years, at least not for a long time. But according to Golestan's account, when it came to the oil company contract where they went over everything with a fine-tooth comb, Souratgar's style did not pass muster.

It did not pass muster for Reza Bateni either. When he got to the scraping and scrapping in his story, he howled with laughter. At parties, his laughter was usually the loudest and the merriest. His simplicity and amiability and his casual reaction to everyday issues were the exact opposite of his exactitude and rigor and fussiness when it came to things scientific. The first time I saw him was when he had come to Berkeley on sabbatical. I was a student and assistant to a British professor who taught Persian literature, a reactionary and fanatical recent convert to Islam named Hamed Algar. It was he who gave me a copy of Ayatollah Khomeini's book on Islamic government at around the time it was published in Najaf. I did not take the book seriously for I thought, in error, that its ideas had no place in Iran, certainly not sixty years after the hanging of Sheikh Fazlollah and the demise of his concept of a Sharia-based political order.

I came to know Abdolhadi Haeri around the same time. He was writing his doctoral dissertation at McGill University in Canada while on sabbatical at Berkeley. His dissertation, titled *The Role of the Ulema in Constitutionalism*, was later translated and published in Persian as *Shiism and Constitutionalism in Iran*. He and Bateni were both extremely likeable people; both were opposed to the Shah, and both were academic types. Of clerical lineage, Haeri had a deep-rooted attachment to Islam, while Bateni was a freethinker in the mold of Enlightenment intellectuals. Our three-way friendship at Berkeley, then a center of anti-Shah student activities, and our differing fates in the years following the revolution is a small window into the whys and wherefores of the tragedy known as the Islamic revolution.

Ever since Berkeley, Bateni was particularly drawn to Noam Chomsky's writings on linguistics. In those days – and I think even today – Chomsky's fame rested more on his political views than on his leading theories in his field of expertise; some ranked him as high as "a Newton of linguistics." To us anti-Shah students, he was known as a progressive and anti-imperialist thinker. We prized his anti-war stance and willingness to sign petitions against the Shah. But Bateni appreciated his scholarship above all else. That said, like Chomsky, he never used his commitment to linguistics as an excuse to avoid politics or evade taking a clear position on freedom. Needless to say, the university never fired Chomsky on account of his political views. Bateni would not hesitate to express his views openly, even though he knew he was dealing with a regime that planned to shut down all institutions of higher education for two years in order to Islamize the university system and had put a bunch of ambitious and immoral self-styled professors and moronic and insolent students in charge of purging "undesirable" faculty and students. And he paid the price – expulsion from the university in the prime of his career as an eminent linguist.

Another side of his humanity is apparent in the fact that he was married to Shahin Nafarabadi. At the time, scores of male intellectuals treated their spouses chiefly as a *wife*, a *mother*, and a *cook* rather than a like-minded partner and soulmate; some of these men occasionally looked for a fellowship of heart and mind in another, *intellectual*, woman. The age-old dualism of *saint* and *slut* turns on a million games men play to justify their relationship with what they regard as one or other type of woman. Shahin, a well-educated woman, was Bateni's partner and soulmate and always insisted on her rights, even at the cost of a contentious argument, and Reza was a proponent of gender equality to the core.

A group of us, all of whom taught at the University of Tehran, had formed a discussion group. In those days, as authoritarian control over public spaces intensified, people increasingly sought the company of trusted friends in the safety of private circles. In our get-togethers with Bateni and Shahin, Haideh Daragahi, professor of psychology, and Fereshteh Shahpar and Azar Nafisi, of English literature, constituted one such *circle*. According to one Western thinker, the appeal of these gatherings was that they were free from the hegemonic ideas of consumer capitalism and accommodated a pluralism of views. In one of those get-togethers, we hashed out the question of forced hijab for female professors. Fereshteh, Haideh, and Azar decided not to submit to the mandate, even though they knew they would likely be expelled. Reza Bateni backed their decision unequivocally. "One must take the rightful step," he said, "even if it doesn't deliver in the short term." He never preached what he did not practice. When the calamity of the *cultural revolution* engulfed the University of Tehran (and other educational institutions), he openly defended his and other professors' rights and was consequently expelled. Even his popularity among a wide spectrum of students could not forestall his being *purged*.

Another one of these circles comprised a group of professors from the universities of Tehran and Sharif. One was a physicist who was interested in philosophy and the other a mathematician who was into literary criticism. My friend Farhad Ardalan who is a top-notch physicist invited me to that circle. Kamran Fani and Bahaeddin Khorramshahi, both literary figures, were also among the regulars. Reza Bateni, too. Anyone who had a question or article or problem on their mind had the opportunity to present and discuss it. The meetings were either held in a classroom at the University of Tehran or at Sharif University. Bateni sometimes likened our efforts, especially when trying to hash out the situation in Iran, to attempting to twist the wind into a knot. He said it was like playing chess with a monkey. One could carefully plan sixteen moves ahead, but your rival might just up and swallow the rook.

After Bateni was purged from the university, the altruistic and scientific ventures he pursued were a mirror image of his great nature. He complained about being out of work but did not succumb to mental paralysis; he joked about it and, most importantly, challenged it. After accepting an offer from a publisher who was an expert in picking a gem of a scholar like him, he diligently set to work. The publisher lamented the paucity of reliable English–Persian dictionaries and knew Bateni was the one who could tackle that monumental task. Furthermore, Bateni had learned from Souratgar's *scraping and scrapping* how desperately such a dictionary was needed. Unlike most know-all intellectuals, Bateni knew he could not undertake the task alone and assembled a team of experts for the job. His method exemplified his approach to all matters. As a first step, they collected notes from all extant Persian–English dictionaries. Then, after comparing entries and consulting other sources such as the *Oxford English Dictionary*, he would rely on his and his collaborators' respective mastery of Persian and English to select the closest equivalents. When the project had just started, he would sometimes read us eccentric definitions from assorted lexicons and end on a peal of laughter and a dig at Souratgar.

For a linguist like him who did not believe that language is static and used to say that speech and the sense of words and synonyms are all dynamic and hinge on developments in history and society, editing a dictionary must have been doubly challenging. Aside from producing that ground-breaking tome, he also wrote and translated many works on linguistics. He countered the bitterness of the times, and the heavy weight of despotism in Iran, with the antidote of scholarly ventures, continuous creativity, and a rebellious spirit. The fruits of his labor have rendered generations indebted to his erudition, dedication, and pursuit of liberty.

Manuchehr Safa

When I left Iran, certain people and places always lurked in the back of my mind, and I missed them. Manuchehr Safa was one such person and the Faculty of Law and Political Science one such place. Manuchehr Safa was for me that ever-vigilant conscience that I believe resides watchfully behind every writer's mind. We measure every word or phrase, and every critique or comment we write, against that conscience and ask ourselves, if it were to read this line or opinion, what would it say?

I came to know him at the Social Sciences Research Center. When my efforts to return to teaching at a university after imprisonment failed, I was told there was no objection to my being employed at research centers. I was readily hired, and it was decided I would write a book on psychoanalysis and history. It was probably not clear to me at the time, but developing that book turned out to be part of the process of stepping away from the Stalinist–Leninist version of Marxism. The process of that exit usually involves covering several *territories*. The effort to synthesize Marx and Freud – as in the case of Norman Brown and Herbert Marcuse and Wilhelm Reich, for instance – is one such territory, and translating Gramsci's works is another. I managed to cover both in a short time. Of course, I did not share that information with the director of the research center. After I was hired, he took me to a room in which there were multiple desks and he assigned one to me. I plunged into work. Barely a week had gone by when the same director rushed into my office. "Collect your stuff and leave; they called from SAVAK asking, 'Who gave you permission to hire *So and So?*'" It was Thursday. I went home feeling despondent, and on Monday once more resorted to Ahmad Qoreishi. He called Parviz Sabeti and was told "There's been a mistake. Tell him to return to his job." When I tried to go back, however, the wary director said, "It's inappropriate for you to return until we receive a written permission from SAVAK."

Two weeks later, it was deemed appropriate for me to return. The same director led me to a spacious room that until then was Manuchehr Safa's monopoly. I received a warm and hearty welcome. From day one of arriving at the center, I learned that Safa and Anvar Khamei – once a prominent theorist of the Tudeh Party, now its critic – were its most notable and esteemed researchers. The writer Eslam Kazemieh and lexicographer Dariush Ashuri were also among those on the payroll. I had read a few articles and short stories by Safa who published humorous pieces under the penname "Q. Davood." In my view, they are among the masterpieces of satire in modern Persian. In any event, the more I was in Manuchehr Safa's company, the more I appreciated not only his humor and erudition, but also his humility and nobility of spirit. The headache that SAVAK had caused me in my temporary discharge from the center, and the fact that Sabeti had called the director to reiterate that they had no objection to my employment, had convinced the director that my rightful place was next to Safa, not in my original multi-desk room. In all establishments everywhere, the room size and the presence or absence of windows and the direction they face is all part of the power play; the research center was no exception.

Contrary to other high-profile intellectuals who took advantage of their status and rarely showed up to work, Manuchehr Safa was extremely self-disciplined and very punctual. His desk was always well organized and he worked nonstop. When others occasionally stopped by to chat and share political gossip he would ask them to leave, politely but firmly. With me, too, his exchanges were initially confined to the topics we were working on. It was obvious that like any cultured person, he had read some Freud. The noted twentieth-century thinker Leszek Kołakowski once said that given Freud's discovery of a new continent in modern thought, one could not consider oneself to be modern without being familiar with him. Manuchehr Safa's modernity had a profound and genuine depth. Thus, his research at the center was closely tied to it. He was busy writing a book on totalitarianism, which is the bastard child of modernity. His pithiness and precision in that book, published on the cusp of the revolution, are astounding: it is as if he had anticipated the unfolding developments. The effort to establish a form of totalitarianism in Iran under the banner of Islam failed, not for lack of trying but because civil society, always an obstacle and the bane of totalitarianism, was more resistant and stronger than what the plotters had hoped or envisaged. My writings, too, appeared serially in *Negin* right before the magazine was banned for having published Saiidi Sirjani's brilliant articles about Sheikh-e Sanaan and his ravishment by *Ghodrat Khanom* (Lady Power) who was taken to be a brazen parody of Ayatollah Khomeini.

Being officemates with Safa gradually turned into being members of the same *dowreh*, a regular private get-together or "circle." An American researcher once observed that, in

1950s Iran, a *dowreh* was a proxy for a political party. In the 1970s (and the following decades) *dowreh*s in Iran were a safe haven, removed from the toxic cultural and political currents swirling around. It was during that period that I had the good fortune to meet Afat Shariati, Safa's learned wife and fellow activist. A high school teacher and advocate of women's rights, she also published articles in *Elm o Zendegi* (Science and Life), a magazine published by the democratic socialist politician Khalil Maleki and his followers. The couple lived in an apartment, or to quote the rueful words of the literary scholar Badi'ozzaman Forouzanfar in one of his essays, in a small, *rented home*. Another member of our circle was Safa's brother Fereydoun who, he used to say, "is much funnier than me," though his own sense of humor was second to none. Their sister Pari was also a humorist and a writer and also a first-class graphic artist. She and her husband were in charge of designing posters for Rudaki Hall. Both were staples of our *dowreh*. We would congregate once or twice a month at the home of one of the members, have a glass of wine or vodka and a light dinner, and discuss the news or, for the most part, listen to hilarious anecdotes by the Safas. We were all angst-ridden about what was happening in Iran. Having spent years behind bars under the Shah owing to his association with Maleki, Safa was duly alarmed by the trajectory of current events and envisioned a very bleak outcome. He and his brother and sister's perspective varied from the rampant mutterings and gossip one otherwise heard in those days.

It was a few months before the revolution and the summer heat in Tehran had not yet abated. Fereydoun joined the group one evening, drenched in sweat and a little late. He poured himself something to drink and said, "I had an interesting experience today. I was stuck behind red lights in my rickety Jhian, soaked from head to toe. A large black

Cadillac pulled up next to me. Its tinted windows were closed – clearly, its air conditioning must have been working well. I stepped out of my car and approached the Cadillac. I tapped on the driver-side window and the man at the wheel wound it down." Fereydoun then editorialized: "If it weren't for the revolutionary climate and the *oppressive* owner of the Cadillac weren't afraid of the *oppressed* driver of the Jhian, he would certainly not have lowered the window." He went on: "As soon as the window was open, I said, 'It is such a thrill to see such a car with such an air conditioning system. Hopefully, I'll have one like it someday.' The owner breathed a sigh of relief, said thanks, and as the light turned green, drove off." Fereydoun continued: "For sure he must have expected to be read the riot act." Pari added, "For sure he must have also checked the bodywork afterwards to make sure you hadn't scratched the metallic paint in rage." I had read in Nietzsche that the foremost catalyst in politics and revolution is resentment, a theory that Fereydoun appeared to be distilling in his short and humorous anecdote.

Safa said nothing but just kept laughing. He was sparing and selective in his speech. There was a modesty about him that was remarkable. Throughout my life, I have observed two types of modesty in people. I have seen the cheap and duplicitous – or, in the precise sense of the term, counterfeit – type at the time we were all *revolutionary* and our leader Mao had said one must show modesty before the masses. Later on, in shame and distress, I learned how disingenuous those words were, and how arrogant Mao was vis-à-vis the multitudes. His personal physician had once diagnosed him with gonorrhea and advised him to avoid sexual intercourse with the young women he was always surrounded by. Our modest leader had responded, "They would be delighted to catch gonorrhea from me." When that physician's book came out in

English, I introduced it on BBC Persian – Reza Farrokhfal was
the editor of the cultural segment in those days – and before
discussing it, I apologized to the Iranian people for my past
role in translating a couple of books by that *modest leader*.

The second type of modesty is authentic. It projects
neither arrogance nor duplicity, but arising from empathy,
it also elicits empathy. Safa's modesty was of that variety. It
had a unique characteristic as well. His habitual pose was to
compress himself, as it were, lest he take up too much space.
His hands were always glued to his side. He dressed simply
and properly. In every photo of him that I have seen, he looks
like a passenger on the back seat of a car doing his best to
make the most room for the two people flanking him. He was
equally modest when it came to his research.

Our first joint project was to respond to Najaf
Daryabandari's critique of Arthur Koestler in *Naqd-e Agah*
(Informed Review.) A praise-cum-blame. *Naqd-e Agah* was
a periodical that launched after the revolution and like other
independent liberal ventures in those days met with speedy
success, gaining a stellar spot in the constellation of democratic media as soon as its first issues rolled off the press. One
wonders, regretfully, whether we might be facing a different
Iran today if the likes of *Naqd-e Agah* had survived. On the
other hand, from a historical perspective, one could perhaps
surmise with optimism (or realism) that those very ravages
and the nature of the power that could not tolerate the likes
of *Naqd-e Agah* might have prepared the grounds for an even
brighter and more accommodating prospect in Iran.

In any event, Daryabandari himself was on the editorial board of the periodical, as were Houshang Golshiri, the
translator and critic Bagher Parham, and Hossein Hossein-
khani, one of the founders of the umbrella company Agah
Publishing. Late one night, Bagher Parham called and said

he had urgent business to discuss. As he lived nearby, he was at my door a few minutes later. "Daryabandari's article on Koestler has ignited a firestorm," he said. "They've found a lot of faults with it." He said he wanted to ask me on behalf of the editorial board to write a response to the article for the next issue. I had read the article, which presented a litany of quasi-Stalinist views about Koestler and kindred intellectuals. I told Parham I'd think about it and would let him know the next day.

Knowing the article called for a serious response, I had no doubt I could pen the best possible rebuttal with the help of Safa, someone who had spent a lifetime combating native Stalinism. I discussed the *Naqd-e Agah* proposal with him the next day. Safa agreed but was emphatic that he would merely *collaborate* with me. "I don't want to be named co-author," he insisted. I knew that he published his exquisite humorous stories – as well as numerous pieces in tracts connected to Maleki – either under a pseudonym or anonymously. I suggested we discuss the question of authorship later. We immediately set to work preparing for the task. I updated Parham. He set a deadline saying it absolutely had to appear in the next issue; and we obliged. On the first day, we each prepared a list of points that needed to be addressed. An outline then emerged from our combined lists, and each of us committed to writing up certain sections. Once our respective pieces were ready and integrated, Safa did the final editing.

In those days, Fereshteh and I and Houshang Golshiri and his wife Farzaneh Taheri, a translator, and Azar Nafisi and her husband Bijan, had formed a literary *dowreh*. If any of us had written something new, the group would read it and give feedback. I did not share the article that I had co-authored with Safa with the group. Not only was it a joint effort but Golshiri was on the editorial board of *Naqd-e Agah*; I did not want him to see it before the full board had had a chance to read it. My discretion was a moot point. As soon as the article reached the board, Daryabandari had a meltdown. It may be that Parham had asked me to write it not on behalf of the *editorial board* as he said, but on behalf of select members.

Before we submitted the article, Safa finally agreed to us picking a pseudonym for him, his initial insistence that only I sign it being out of the question as it had not been a solo effort. One night, after imbibing a fair quantity of alcohol and juggling his long list of humorous names, we chose "Faramarz Tabrizi." I had told Parham that the name of the co-author of the article, Faramarz Tabrizi, was a pseudonym. He had no clue about Safa's identity and I had said nothing. I heard that Daryabandari's initial objection to our piece was that *Naqd-e Agah* had not published anything under a pseudonym before and should not do so now. Other members had offered the defense that the lead author's name was real. I never discovered if he ever found out Faramarz Tabrizi's true identity. Next, he objected to the length of our response, which exceeded that of his original article. He finally agreed to publish our piece on condition that it appear together with a rebuttal that he would write; we said in that case we would reserve the right to counter his rebuttal in the following issue, and we did. Our second article was published along with his final response in the last issue of *Naqd-e Agah* before the magazine shut down. The editorial board had by then become fractured even as the pressure of censorship had been rising by the day. As a collection, those four articles form an interesting discussion about the nature of Marxism and its relationship with democracy and the place of Stalinism across that landscape.

I heard from Parham and Golshiri that the tone of the draft version of Daryabandari's rebuttal was even harsher than the one that was eventually published. He, who thanks to his brilliant translations deservedly lived in a rather luxurious mansion, had called the two of us who lived in rental apartments the *bourgeoisie's houseboys*. Daryabandari had served as editor-in-chief of the Franklin publishing house – an endeavor supported by the US government – where he had overseen truly invaluable cultural initiatives; now, knowingly or inadvertently, he had labeled Safa and me American agents. Regardless, and despite such tastelessness, the quartet of articles was a respectable achievement for all three of us and for *Naqd-e Agah*. If the late Khalil Maleki had a soul, he would surely be pleased after reading them and the defense that his friend and fellow activist Safa and I had put up on behalf of social democracy.

I hadn't met Daryabandari before these articles were written. A few weeks had passed since their publication when he invited me and some other guests to his home; I believe they were all *Naqd-e Agah* affiliates. Golshiri and I went together. I was curious to get a look at him and his house, which I had heard about from its architect, my friend Iraj Kalantari. Needless to say, Faramarz Tabrizi (Safa) was not invited. If he had been, my guess is he would not have showed up.

The building was extremely handsome and well presented. The exquisite scent of Persian cuisine greeted us upon arrival and Daryabandari was keen to stress that he had cooked every dish himself. Later, when he published his impressive cookbook, I learned about the scope of his culinary skills. My presence at the dinner injected tension in the air. I think everyone had heard about the serious polemic between us, though they feigned ignorance. Daryabandari never said a word either and did not break his silence until several years later.

The next time I saw him was in America. He had come to California. A visit with the author and dramatist Sadeq Chubak was arranged. The relationship between these two was strained because both had had feelings, at separate times, for the short story writer Mahshid Amirshahi. Chubak invited a few people to his house that night, me included. A little whiskey and vodka helped ease the tension. Chubak served a southern Iranian dish in addition to what his wife Qodsi *Khanom* had prepared. When Daryabandari returned to Iran and published the story of his visit to Chubak's house, he claimed that Chubak "had invited *So and So*", meaning me, to peeve him because he thought there was bad blood between us, though there wasn't.

The publication of the final two parts of that fourfold interchange of articles was delayed. According to Hossein-khani, the magazine was stuck in the censorship bureau; there was disagreement among the censors over whether to allow or ban its publication. I grew worried. I was very eager to see our response to Daryabandari's critique and rebuttal published. One day, Hossein-khani rang to say something had come up and that he wanted to tell me about it in person. I went to see him. "Abdolkarim Soroush has called *Naqd-e Agah*," he said, referring to the highly engaged religious intellectual who served on the Cultural Revolution Committee. "He's asked for a meeting with you and Faramarz Tabrizi." I was surprised and a little apprehensive. "What does he want with us?" "He's read your article," Hossein-khani replied. "He wants to discuss it with you." "Where did he see the article?" I asked. "Have you given him a copy?" He chuckled. "There is a committee at the Ministry of Islamic Guidance that has the last word on important issues whenever the thought police can't reach a consensus. The *Naqd-e Agah* stalemate has reached that committee, and Soroush is a member." Knowing that *Faramarz Tabrizi* would certainly have no interest in meeting with Soroush, I asked Hossein-khani, "Am I obliged to go, and would my going impact the fate of *Naqd-e Agah*?" "I don't know about the impact," he replied, "but no, there's no obligation." When I told Safa about it, he laughed. "Even Orwell wouldn't have dreamed up such a scenario." I did not go to see Soroush. That issue of *Naqd-e Agah* came out, but the increasing exigencies of the censors and attacks by even some *progressive* intellectuals and regime *ideologues* hastened the magazine's closure shortly afterwards.

In time, the same pressures that forced *Naqd-e Agah* to shut down also drove Safa from the research center. As an upshot of the *cultural revolution*, I, too, was suspended for a year from the university. Safa, who was dependent on his monthly salary and on Afat Shariati's two-bit retirement income, had no choice but to give up his apartment. Fortunately, a friend who had fought alongside Safa and his wife since the time of Maleki and the Third National Front had gotten rich thanks to his architectural firm and he let Safa and Afat live on the top floor of his residence. To make a living, I signed a contract with the gracious Hossein-khani, owner of Agah Publishing, to translate a three-volume book titled the *Main Currents of Marxism* into Persian; he would advance me a monthly fee almost equal to my university salary – which was about eight thousand tomans at the time. Contrary to the standard practice of a large segment of Iranian publishers past and present who take every opportunity to avoid paying writers and translators, Hossein-khani remitted my fee every month with no need for a reminder. One time, he even drove to my home late in the evening lest the check be delivered late.

When the translation of the first volume was complete, I suggested to Hossein-khani that we ask Manuchehr Safa to edit it. I had read several of his translations. They were accurate and cogent and clear. I had to implore Safa before he agreed to edit that volume. He did not take on the next two. In fact, the second and third volumes met with a strange fate that, incidentally, was not unrelated to the surviving roots of Stalinism in Iran.

One day when Safa and I were busy writing our second critique of Daryabandari, I told him that given Daryabandari's outstanding translations of works by liberal thinkers such as Isaiah Berlin, I found his obsession with Stalinist thought and what he wrote about Koestler perplexing. He smiled. "Once Tudeh'i thought enters the bloodstream, it may fall into a temporary coma, but it will never leave." Once the thought of a cherished friend and colleague and mentor like Manuchehr Safa enters the mind, it does not retreat, not even temporarily.

Eskandar Shahrokhi

His name was *Eskandar* (Alexander), most inappropriate given his insatiable love affair with Iran and Iranian studies. I know of no other country where people gleefully and proudly name their children after conquerors that had sacked their land in the past, from Alexander and Genghis to Mohammad and Ali.

Eskandar worked at the Institute for the Intellectual Development of Children and Young Adults, *Kanoon-e Parvaresh-e Fekri-ye Koodakan va No-javanan*, known simply as the Kanoon, one of the wonder institutions of the Shah's era. He was related to the Shah. His kinship plus his erudition was why nobody bothered him at work. He would show up late and leave early and spend his time in the office reading literature that he was fond of. There were a number of intellectuals at the Kanoon who had been rejected everywhere else due to SAVAK's strictures and were only employable at the institute. Kanoon was headed by Lili Amir-Arjomand. Everyone called her *Khanom*. She was friends with the Queen. As such, Kanoon was one of several institutions under the Queen's patronage and enjoyed relative freedom in its operations. Some artists and intellectuals who therefore found work at the Kanoon appreciated it as a dependable shoestring

source of subsistence. Some engaged in serious and conse-
quential activities while some, like Eskandar, did not even
pretend to work.

He was a native of Babol. His father was a close relative
of Reza Shah, which is why the Shahrokhis enjoyed a privi-
leged position in his birthplace. Eskandar was an outlier in
the family. They had homes in both Babol and Deraz Kola,
an incredibly picturesque village; in my experience, Eskandar
enjoyed a special cachet in both. His educational sophistication and reserve, and his patent remove from the political
order, had, as far as I could see, earned him popularity among
both communities.

Eskandar and his father did not see eye to eye. They
clashed both politically and in their lifestyle. He loved his
mother very dearly and it was she who mediated between father
and son. Eskandar was a friend and close associate of many
intellectuals and dissidents in the Shah's time. He knew many
of them since high school or college. His favorite professor at
university was Gholam-Hossein Sadiqi, a noted social scien-
tist and a notably loyal friend of Mosaddeq. Eskandar would
sometimes recite some of Sadiqi's class lectures by heart. But
he never joined any political organization. He admired the
dissidents' courage but could not stand the naïveté of their
thinking, while he treated some intellectuals' affectations of
radicalism as a source of fun and amusement. The prolific
writer, translator, and literary critic Mohammad-Ali Sepanlou
and his *proletarian* charade occupied a place of honor in the
roster of satire he spun about them. Still, he defended their
right to protest the status quo.

His father, like many others of his generation, considered
those who opposed the Shah to be immature and unreal-
istically demanding, and even lackeys of foreign powers.
Mohammad-Zaman Pahlevan, a Tudeh Party officer and a

relative of Reza Shah who had thrown all caution to the wind and returned to Iran following years of drifting in the *camp of socialism*, was a friend of both father and son. He might have admired the son's erudition and the father's tolerance, though some of the tension between father and son was rooted in the father's animosity toward anyone who was anti-Shah.

Though filicide and patriarchy are said to be woven into the fabric of Iran's storied history, with thirst for power as the connecting thread in those conflicts, in this case the tension also stemmed from the fact that the son was a habitué of the opium demi-monde; the father begrudged his addiction and considered it beneath the family. Both Eskandar's father and mother had a particular fondness for me and Fereshteh and our son Hamid, for in so far as we were not partial to opium, they believed and hoped that our friendship with Eskandar would lead him to the right path, but it did not.

Eskandar was Fereshteh's colleague at the Kanoon. They both worked under a director who the instant I met him reminded me of the character of Victor in *Dr. Zhivago* – the kind of shrewd and amorphous individuals who at every opportunity try to wheel and deal with those in power to advance their personal goals, and who smugly assume that *national* and *revolutionary* goals match their own aspirations. Ironically, while opportunistic by reason of self-interest, such individuals sometimes serve the common good as well. But Eskandar's persona was more like that of Zhivago himself. Like him, he was a romantic, but absent his fighting spirit. I found out fairly quickly that Eskandar was in fact in love with my wife Fereshteh and that Fereshteh relished the attention. To echo Milan Kundera, she was the kind of woman for whom a single person's love and attention did not suffice. Eskandar was sophisticated and choosy. He had a host of male friends but I never saw him with a woman. At any rate, I don't believe the mutual attraction between him and Fereshteh went beyond desire and longing. Eskandar's moral principles would never have allowed him to take steps to gratify that urge. At least that's what I thought and believed. After reading Albert Camus's "The Adulterous Woman" and reflecting on the relationship between Eskandar and Fereshteh, I came to the conclusion that the line between desire and gratification basically springs from a kind of self-deluding sense of *honor* and *manhood*. In Camus's story, a couple is traveling. They stop at a hotel. When the man is asleep in bed, the woman sneaks out and experiences such excitement by indulging in the beauty of the desert from atop a fort that she has an orgasm. Had she climaxed with a man, would she have been more, or less *adulterous*? In each case, the woman finds at least some gratification in the *other*. How could one assert that she has no right to enjoy the lure of the desert?

Whatever the case, Eskandar poured a liberal portion of that secret love on my son Hamid. The love and attention he showered on him was no less genuine than my own rapport with my son. Freud might have said his paternalizing Hamid was a proxy for romancing Fereshteh. The subconscious finds a thousand ways to satisfy repressed emotions. He played soccer with Hamid one on one at our house or in a nearby park. He used to say, laughing, "If I lose, Hamid gets upset and says, 'You didn't play for real!' And if I win, he cries because he lost." He read him books for hours and told him stories from the *Shahnameh* (Book of Kings) in sort of dramatized recitals. I heard him yell at Hamid only once.

We had all gone to his parents' house in Babol. After a few phone calls, he asked me to drive him to the house of a *friend*. I had taken him there in the past and knew the homeowner was an architect by profession. I had heard from Eskandar that in many instances when the architect was commissioned to design a house, the client would pull him aside and tell him under his breath that he must include a room that is discreetly sited and well ventilated, intended for *relaxation*. The architect, who was likewise prone to relaxation, would not openly let on that he'd caught the client's drift. I did not let on, either, that I knew why Eskandar wanted me to take him to a certain friend's house.

Hamid also came along and sat in the back. Eskandar sat next to me. His face lost color by the minute. He sweated more and more profusely and kept fiddling with the edge of his jacket. He was not in the mood to talk. I don't remember what Hamid said that caused Eskandar to suddenly explode. In fact, he exploded even before Hamid spoke. But to my utter surprise, this time he took his jitters out on Hamid. He yelled at him. I did not react. He had spent hours and weeks with my son lovingly, and that love granted him certain inalienable rights, one of which was the right to a one-off misplaced and unfair yelling.

When we reached his friend's apartment in Babolsar, he asked that we pick him up in half an hour. I knew his father monitored our moves in and out of the house. I also knew that half an hour would not do the job. We went back to pick up Eskandar an hour later. I rang. It took a few minutes before he opened the door. He walked out looking bright and even animated. Instead of taking the front seat, he sat next to Hamid in the back and they carried on talking all the way. I reckoned from my son's roaring laughter that no trace of the dressing-down the hour before had settled in his heart and soul. The difference between Eskandar's demeanor on the outgoing versus the return trip was something of a revelation to me. I had met drug addicts before. I had also noted the symptoms of withdrawal from watching movies. Witnessing the despair of an elegant individual like Eskandar allowed me to grasp the full sweep of his addiction.

When I felt close enough to Eskandar to ask him why he had turned to opium – I had heard him say opium is a cure for every pain except the pain of addiction – he quipped, "Abbas dear, you have no idea what an inimitable circle the vicarious fellowship of the brazier constitutes. It's manifest Paradise. Everyone is free to speak and fabricate whatever tales they want, and no one has the energy or urge to question even the most ludicrous claims." He went on: "One day we were unwinding around the opium brazier with a bunch of former Tudeh'is in Babol." I knew that, during World War II, that city had been a center of Tudeh Party operations under the protection of *Big Brother*, which had occupied Mazandaran, and it was now home to a coterie of opium buffs who had been educated and groomed as Tudeh'is. Eskandar had bonded with that group. In describing their gatherings, he continued: "One fellow declaimed, his cheeks flushed, 'When Comrade Stalin was on his way to the Tehran Conference, once they got to the Kandovan Tunnel they realized a rockslide was blocking the Comrade's vehicle from passing through. He was in a particular hurry because, per his Bolshevik discipline, he certainly did not want to be late. I was the expedition pathfinder. I loaded Comrade Stalin on my back and trekking a trail I knew, transported him from one side of the mountain to the other side. The snow was up to my knees. But the excitement of carrying Comrade Stalin on my back would let me dread neither snow nor rain.'" Eskandar added, chuckling: "In that educated and jail-hardened circle, not a single soul questioned any detail of that totally mythical though rather meaningful story. Except, when he finished talking, another former Tudeh'i held out the opium pipe and said, 'Comrade, have another pod to relieve your fatigue,' and the still Stalinist comrade replied, 'Not now.'" I also learned from Eskandar that opium smokers never say, "I don't want any," or "I've had enough." They only say, "Not now."

A few years passed and we went into exile and Fereshteh and I divorced. Eskandar had stayed behind. One day a friend called from Iran. "I have bad news" – which always travels faster than good news; I've never found out why. He went on: "I wanted you to know that Eskandar passed away." I couldn't breathe. The more I heard about the whys and wherefores of his death, the deeper my grief and anguish. I heard both his family's version and his wife's. When his wife called, she didn't even give her name. "I'm Eskandar's wife," is all she said.

After the revolution, Eskandar eventually married a girl from Babol. Even in the dark days of wholesale expropriations, and although the Shahrokhis' kinship with the royal family was well known, their properties were not seized, something that speaks to their exceptional popularity. I do not know to what extent Eskandar's marriage was from loneliness, or fear of ageing, or wanting a child, or a combination of all those factors. What role did Fereshteh's leaving Iran play in him getting married? I did not hear from anyone that the union was out of love. They had children, but after some time the whole set-up fell apart. Eskandar's opium addiction did not ebb. Given the ever-more miserable nature of the times, it was probably even swelled. According to one account, after much futile effort the wife sought out the *Sepāh*, the Islamic Revolutionary Guard Corps to take him away. But according to her account, the Guard arrested him by accident. At the time, the Guard had set up camps at some distance from cities to force addicts to quit, without any assistance or medication. I had read that the Nazis in Germany and the communists in the Soviet Union and China also availed themselves of

that type of *cure*. For Eskandar who had been an addict for
thirty years, such a cure was as good as a death sentence.
I don't know how many days or hours he lasted in that
camp before his heart stopped. Who is accountable for the
untimely end of that urbane and decent man? Is it life, which
according to *Kalileh o Demneh* (Kalileh and Demneh) – one
of Shahrokhi's favorite books many of whose fables he knew
by heart – bends toward mendacity? The Guard and its
barbaric crusade against addiction? Eskandar's weary wife,
if it is indeed true that she entrusted her husband to them?
Shahrokhi's own fragile soul that could not bear the weight of
the hardships and opted for a mortal pill worse than the pain?
Whoever the perpetrator, it is Iran that lost an enlightened
and patriotic son, and his family and children and friends who
lost the gift of his bountiful presence.

Azar Nafisi

Years before writing a highly acclaimed book about reading *Lolita* in Tehran, she was part of a small circle of friends where we would get together one night a week to read Persian literature. Houshang Golshiri was the group's éminence grise. We read Hafez and Rumi and Attar's *Tazkarat ol-Olia* (Memorial of the Saints) and Sohravardi. Having selected parts of a particular text to study, someone would lead the discussion based on their research. Each session began with a ritual that Golshiri referred to as "purging tensions" from the group's children. One adult was designated to play and run around with the kids to get them ready to sleep. Azar, who had studied in England and the States as an adolescent and was teaching English literature at the University of Tehran, was especially keen on reading classical Persian literature to gain a better mastery of the language. After a while, our friendship within the larger group evolved.

Both she and her husband Bijan, whom I'd first met at a high school in the U.S., were active in the Confederation of Iranian Students. Like many Confederation activists, when SAVAK closed shop a few months prior to the revolution they returned to Iran. Azar had written her doctoral dissertation on proletarian American literature, but even at the height of left-mania in the Confederation, she was, in her own words, more of a "hippie" than a lefty. After their return to Iran, neither she nor Bijan felt any temptation to lead the Iranian proletariat. Bijan worked as an engineer at the construction company of his brother-in-law – who was an extremely proper man – and Azar as a professor.

The first book that Azar gave me after one of our meetings was *The Master and Margarita*. It was a present for my birthday. Once I got home, I picked it up and spent the whole night reading Bulgakov's exquisite novel. When I saw Azar a couple of days later, I told her that if I were discharged from the university, I would translate the book. Not long after, I was suspended from teaching for a year and started translating *The Master and Margarita*.

The second book that Azar gave me was a present for another birthday, this time a masterpiece by Nabokov called *Ardor*, a title that like more or less every word off the pen of that great wordsmith has a myriad nuanced meanings. For various reasons, my reaction to that gift upset Azar. She said I had failed to appreciate the book and her gesture. But that incident did not stop our collegiality and mutual empathy from developing further. At the time, Agah Publishing had produced a hundred-page book of mine in Persian called *Malro va Jahanbini-ye Trajik* (Malraux and the Tragic Vision). I had for a long time been reflecting on the tragic vision – which in the West can be intimated from Pascal to Marx, Nietzsche, and Malraux – and talked about its instances in Persian literature with Azar. In the process of those exchanges, we decided to co-author a book about Sadeq Hedayat. We picked the format as well. We would write a book in the form of two parallel texts. Each page would display two separate but related blocks of text. In one, Azar would discuss an excerpt of Hedayat's work from the viewpoint of its literary techniques, precedents, and innovations, while in the other I would parse the same excerpt with respect to its formative and philosophical underpinnings. We met regularly at Epicure to try and polish these paired iterations to perfection.

Before the revolution, Epicure was probably the best restaurant in Tehran and had an adjacent bakery-cum-café. It had reportedly been financed by a family whose source of wealth was their gas company, Butan Gaz – one of the founder's children was an activist in the Confederation. Epicure did not last long, though. When the revolution happened, the eatery was labeled *taghuti* (idolatrous). Apparently, the arbiters of correctness had found the name "Epicure" objectionable; they said it was Westernized. I doubt anyone knew its actual meaning. When forty years later I searched online for Epicure, I found a list of current "Luxury Restaurants" in Tehran, each more *idolatrous* and *Westernized* than the other. Only two had Iranian names. Everything about that list was phony. Write-ups for all of them were provided by a gentleman named *Mester* [sic] *Tester* who had duly become rich and famous.

The name and *idolatrous* ambience of Epicure caused the restaurant to be shut down for good, but not the café, which reopened sometime later. When you walked in, the spacious restaurant area was to the left, unchanged, but covered in dust and void of occupants. Some tables were shrouded under dust sheets. If I had summoned Khaqani's alarm call "Oh, lesson-wise heart!" to take the reins of my mind, that scene would have "wisened me to the lesson" of the calamity that was taking control of society by the day. But Azar and I were simply happy that the café was open and we could work on the Hedayat book in solitude.

One time, when Azar and I were the only patrons at
the café, our small table covered in coffee cups and cookies
and books and notepads, the man who had served us earlier
rushed up in a frenzy. "I don't think you're husband and
wife." I don't know how he had guessed – from the vigor of
our exchanges and the absence of long silences? From the
books and papers? "The Guard is on its way!" he exclaimed.
"If you sit together, they'll give you a hard time." He rushed
Azar out the back door, and I left through the front. When I
stepped outside, I broke into tears, for myself and for Azar
and for all Iranians whose basic human rights were being
trampled underfoot by the boneheaded dogmatism of a bunch
of male chauvinists and misogynistic philanderers. In time,
Azar published her writings on Hedayat in Iran and I, who
had left the country by then, wrote an article on Hedayat and
the tragic vision.

After leaving Iran, Azar and I used to occasionally
exchange letters, mostly expressions of grievance. I knew that
a long time after being purged from the university – and her
expulsion was due to her courageous resistance to the forced
hijab – she had returned to teaching at Allameh University.
For reasons that I never discovered, she and Golshiri had a
falling out, at least for a while. She was determined to stay
in Iran, innumerable challenges notwithstanding; she was
attached to her teaching. But perhaps more than anything,
the reason she stayed was her love for her father and her
complex and emotional relationship with her mother.

In Tehran, Azar lived with her husband and child on the
second floor of a three-story building on Fereshteh Avenue.
The Islamic Comité headquarters was across the street inside
an expropriated property. Azar's mother Nezhat Nafisi lived
on the ground floor. Azar's father Ahmad, who for some
time had famously served as Tehran's mayor, had divorced

her mother and was living separately with his new girlfriend more or less clandestinely in dread of the regime – for whom hunting down the "idolators" was both a source of revenue and a badge of their revolutionary mantle – and out of fear of Nezhat *Khanom*. Ahmad Nafisi had been mayor at the time of the stormy Congress of the Movement of Free Men and Women in August 1963; the event had been designed to celebrate the Shah's White Revolution, which had ushered a new political era in Iran and populated the government with young technocrats. Nafisi's star was then on the rise. Word on the street was that he might be appointed prime minister. But come November, he was suddenly removed from office, plunging headlong from the height of fame and power to the mire of prison and allegations of fraud. He and Azar always contended that the charges against him were politically motivated, a pretext to upend his expected premiership. At any rate, he spent some time in jail. A few years after his release, he built a house on Fereshteh Avenue for himself and his wife and two children, Azar and her younger brother Mohammad. But he himself moved in with his then wife Shahran Tabari and rented the third floor to a newcomer from the West named Babak Ahmadi.

Azar's mother felt bitter and lonesome. She was an affectionate woman, but in any relationship the price for her affection was a steady repayment of gratitude for that affection. She took umbrage at the hardship resulting from the Shah's fall and being abandonment by her husband, and was blunt and, at times, coarse. Azar was attached to her but also weary of her opinions and constant interference. By contrast, I found Nezhat Khanom's conversation engaging. She was full of often interesting stories about the past, frequently seasoned with quips about the cretinism of people like me and her daughter and son-in-law who had opposed the Shah. The

immorality of her ex, Ahmad Nafisi, whom she claimed owed
his rise in the world to her wisdom and grace, was another
subject of her effusions. It was natural that such tongue-lash-
ings affected me and even Bijan less than they did Azar given
all the history between the two. When in her second book,
Things I've been Silent About, Azar courageously disclosed
that she had been abused by one of her relatives as a child, new
intersections of that history and the tensions between mother
and daughter became clear to me.

The first time the subject of her mother was brought up
was by me, unknowingly and unwittingly. One evening we
were chatting at Azar's house after dinner. I don't know why
or how the conversation led to the Shah's era and the first
women to be elected to parliament. Out of my then sense of
entitlement, I scoffed, "Do you remember how one of the three
freshly elected female reps declared, 'His Majesty wiped out
the *sendeh-ye roqiyyat?*'" I didn't tell them that I hadn't known
the meaning of *roqiyyat* (female slavery) when I'd first heard
it, only that I'd had a laugh at the mispronunciation of the
homophone *send-e* (bill) vs. *sendeh* (turd) when compounded
with "wiping out." That evening, the rest of the company
had a laugh, too, but not Azar. "That parliamentarian was
my mother," she said. "She was nervous, otherwise she would
have pronounced it correctly." I felt embarrassed for having
bruised her feelings, and ashamed that she did not belabor the
point but readily accepted my apology. I also realized we had
just dodged a potential catastrophe. There were times when
Azar's mother would take the stairs up and walk right into
her daughter and son-in-law's apartment unannounced. Had
she happened on the scene as I was telling that dumb joke, all
hell would have broken loose. I would have been added to her
blacklist of the damned, and she would have jumped down
her daughter's throat for entertaining such an impudent guest.

In time, Azar and her family also left Iran and came abroad. I think she did not want to leave before her father had left. Sometime later, her *Reading Lolita in Tehran*, a book about teaching Western literature to girls in the privacy of her home, became a bestseller in the U.S. No book by any Iranian writer had ever met such success outside Iran and none has since.

I saw her only once in recent years. And that was during a trip to Washington. We had dinner together with Bijan. I had heard that she was upset with me because she thought I had concurred with Iranians who had criticized her book and alleged that it had been supported by neoconservative U.S. interests. Of course, she did not bring up the subject that night. Nor did I. We had our memories of Tehran to share, and that was enough.

Ayatollah Taleqani

E ven before I met him in prison, all of us anti-Shah students in the Confederation – from followers of the National Front and the Liberation Movement to freshly baptized Maoists to seasoned Tudeh'is and Marxist and religious guerrillas – considered Ayatollah Taleqani a legend in resistance. I do not know when he was first incarcerated. Once, when he asked my opinion about some issue, I said, "*Hāj Aqa*, you were a political prisoner before I was even born." Gently, or perhaps sarcastically, he replied, "I asked for your opinion as an academic, not as a political prisoner." From the very first day I stepped into the *aqayan*'s – mullahs' – cell block, I knew he was different from other clerics.

Had anyone paid attention at the onset of the revolution, his distance from the dominant sweep of the religious mindset would have been even more conspicuous. In his convictions, he was heir to Ayatollah Naini, who had tried unsuccessfully to make Shiism compatible with modernity and democracy; it is Naini who issued a fatwa to dispatch Sheikh Fazlollah Nuri, who had denounced constitutionalism and promoted governance by Sharia. Right before the 1979 revolution, which was effectively the death of the struggle for constitutionalism, and the stupefying ascendancy of individuals of

135

the ilk of Sheikh Fazlollah, Taleqani reissued Naini's *Tanbih al-Umma wa Tanzih al-Milla* (Admonition of the Faithful and Refinement of the Nation) with a new foreword. Politically, he was affiliated with the National Front and Mosaddeq, but his tragic life bespeaks his unshakable devotion simultaneously to Mosaddeq and Ayatollah Khomeini. An even more irreconcilable conflict was his belief in democracy and national sovereignty on the one hand, and the agenda to impose religion (any religion, especially Shiism of the Sheikh Fazlollah kind) and theocracy on society on the other, a clash that in the Qajar period had led to the feud between Nuri and the constitutionalists.

In the aqayans' cell block, only the mullahs were excused from dressing in prison garb. I never found out whether the clergy's special privilege was the outcome of the dynamics of the policy we called *Jimmycracy* – improvements to prisoners' creature comforts that resulted from Jimmy Carter's election to office – or whether it sprang from a certain approach by SAVAK and the Shah's regime toward the clergy. Anyway, the first day we arrived at the prison, those mullahs were the only inmates who were attired differently from the rest, while all other famous political prisoners in the block – from Saeed Soltanpour and Mohsen Yalfani to Asadollah Asgaroladi and the once zealot Islamist revolutionary turned democracy advocate Kazem Bojnurdi – wore prison duds.

Another dramatic effect of Jimmycracy was that prisoners were given the option to buy a television set for their block. The TV for the mullahs' block was purchased by Asgaroladi. He had been involved in the 1965 assassination of Prime Minister Hasan-Ali Mansur, and his brother was a well-known bazaar merchant. After the revolution, the brothers became the two richest men in the country. Had I known then that thirty years later I would cover Mansur's assassination in

The Persian Sphinx, I would have asked Asgaroladi hundreds of questions during our time in prison. If life were like a Kieślowski movie, I might have found an opportunity to pen yet a variant narrative of the past. In any event, in that unrepeatable history, *Haji* bought the largest television set I'd ever seen for the block, but the mullahs had no interest in watching anything other than news. Except for Ayatollah Taleqani, of course, and then only sporadically.

From the very first days of my transfer to Evin in 1977, Taleqani decided that we would sometimes walk around the yard for half an hour or so. Taking a walk is the inmates' chief distraction and exercise. It is as if by reprising small steps they wish to disrupt the tedious repetition of time in detention. Plus, who you walk with is a political choice of sorts. In a situation where most of the mullahs considered the rest of us "unclean," Taleqani's choice had a special import. A few days after our arrival, I began to better understand Taleqani's choices.

It was customary that when an inmate was released, other prisoners would line up by the door to say goodbye. A mullah who had been locked up recently was being discharged that day. I can't be certain but I believe it was Khoeiniha, one of the masterminds behind the American embassy hostage-taking, the same guy who later on turned critical of the status quo for a while when he was purged from power. Everyone, the devout and the turbaned, erstwhile and current leftists, lined up. When the departing mullah approached a believer, he would "embrace" and kiss his cheeks; when he came to a "non-believer," he would hold out a finger and offer a virtual handshake, remotely and reluctantly, as if he were handling a piece of filth. When he came to Taleqani, he was naturally performing the embrace, but Taleqani, speaking so those standing by could hear said, "You embrace the prison guards; why don't you treat your cellmates the same way?" That moment was an augury, as it were, of the inferno that was flickering on the horizon.

Taleqani's consultation with me was an even more portentous warning. A pity I lacked sufficient awareness to grasp the full import of our conversation and its link with the future of Iran. Taleqani used to wear a white, two-piece outfit whenever he came out to the yard. Sometimes while walking about, he would stop and gracefully, as if he did not want others to see him in a "non-clerical" pose, stretch for a spell. One day he said, "SAVAK has recently made a proposition to the *gentlemen*." He went on: "They have said they will release us provided we pledge to attack the Marxists as strongly as we have attacked the regime." That was less than three years before the revolution; the Shah's regime believed that the left posed the greatest threat to it while also believing the system to be eminently stable. Releasing disaffected mullahs who had a considerable capacity to combat communism was considered the right strategy. Years later, when I interviewed Parviz Sabeti in preparation for my book *The Shah*, I asked him about the particulars of that proposal. He did not deny the move but attributed the initiative to another SAVAK director. In consulting with me, Taleqani asked, "In your opinion, should this proposition be accepted?" Then, without waiting for my answer, he added: "Some of the gentlemen say we should accept their condition; and some are opposed." The timing of that conversation is important when assessing the scope and significance of SAVAK's proposal.

Although it was Asgaroladi who had acquired the television, no *devout* confrère ever came to the TV room except one or two members of the Mojahedin group, and then only on the sly. One rainy afternoon when I was walking with Taleqani in the hallway instead of in the yard, I noticed that whenever we reached that room, he would take a peek for a few seconds through the small porthole in the door. I said, "Hāj Aqa, let's go inside and watch the program if you like." "Not a good idea," he replied. "The gentlemen disapprove." When I took a peek, it was Googoosh performing a song.

Sometime later, I witnessed another facet of the *miracle* of Googoosh. Saeed Soltanpour, who owed a great deal of his notoriety to repeatedly mimicking Zhdanov's pronouncements on "a style of art, a style of thinking" and berating the "banality" of bourgeois culture in television programming, was watching the Googoosh broadcast. Lest the gods of his "style of thinking" assume he had succumbed to banality, he said aloud, "Googoosh's performance has a distinctive theatrical feature; she is the only female singer who knows what to do with her hands on stage!" In other words, he who supports the right "style of art" has not succumbed to banality but is engaged in studying Iranian theater.

All the red lines and proscriptions and prohibitions fell by the wayside, and all the inmates – the holy, the Marxist, and the simply frustrated – assembled to watch TV the day Hoveyda's resignation headlined the evening news. After thirteen years as prime minister, his continuity in that position was thought to be a token of stability in the country. Naturally, following the broadcast, a lengthy discussion ensued as to the significance of such a shift in government. Each person fell into analyzing its roots and import from their personal perspective. At the same time, they all agreed on one point: Iran was primed for transformative change. Of course, on that particular evening, had anyone told the mullahs that in about two years they would have absolute control over the nation, body and soul, and would claim absolute sovereignty and guardianship as their divine right, the mullahs would have doubtlessly questioned that person's sanity. It is interesting that Taleqani's consultation with me about SAVAK's offer took place after that "eventful development."

I said in reply to him, "Given that criticizing Marxists has in any case been an essential component of your record, and even one of your chief goals, to make such a pledge would not be colluding with the regime but taking advantage of an opportunity." I advised that "being released without collusion or unethical conduct makes more sense than being locked up." He listened to me with the patience that was his hallmark. "Right," he said. "Some of the gentlemen are of the exact same opinion as you." But then he added: "My situation is somewhat different. To put pressure on me, they've also arrested my daughter. It's not right for me to go free and for her to stay behind."

His daughter was Azam Taleqani. When we launched the first large conference on Iran at Stanford University some twenty-seven years later, Azam was invited to speak, along with the poet Simin Behbahani, Shahla Lahiji, a publisher, and Shirin Ebadi, lawyer and future Nobel Laureate. After Abdolkarim Soroush's lecture on religion and democracy at the conference, Taleqani, Behbahani, and Lahiji delivered harsh criticisms of some of Soroush's positions on the forced hijab. All three were adamantly pro-choice in regard to covering the head.

Back to Evin, Taleqani declined to make a pledge to SAVAK. Some of the other mullahs, including Mahdavi Kani who became an interim prime minister in 1981, gave their word and were released. Taleqani was to be freed in November 1978 on the eve of the revolution. Although I have not seen and do not have reliable data, I do believe that besides other indicators, the number of votes cast for him in the first free election in early 1980 suggests that he was the most popular cleric after Ayatollah Khomeini. However,

it gradually became clear that, despite supporting the revolution, he would not be able to get along with those who
upsurged in its wake. Every day, one noted the increasing
humiliations that his fellow warrior and old friend Mehdi
Bazargan suffered as the first post-revolution prime minister.
They arrested Taleqani's son on the charge of membership of
an opposition group, and Mohammad Reza Sa'adati, one of
the leaders of the Mojahedin, on the charge of spying for the
Soviet Union. Taleqani, who was known to the Mojahedin
as "Father Taleqani," had insisted repeatedly that "Sa'adati's
case is not one of espionage." The reality is that Sa'adati had
planned to hand over one of SAVAK's most sensitive secret
files relating to the arrest of General Moqrebi, the highest-ranking Soviet spy in Iran, to the Soviet counterespionage
agency (and evidently obtain a list of American spies in Iran
in return). Certainly, Sa'adati's execution – and any capital
punishment on any charge – is in my opinion state barbarism,
but according to every indicator known to me, and despite
Taleqani's insistence, Sa'adati had been engaged in espionage.

In the end, Taleqani was unable to withstand the crush of
different pressures and the debilitating sense of embitterment.
They said he died of a heart attack. Some conjectured he had
been *given* a heart attack. My feeling is he died of heartbreak.
One of the last pictures of him at the Assembly of Experts
convened to draft a new constitution is the very image of death
by such a cause. He is sitting on the floor, his back against the
console table around which the assembly's executive board
would sit. A walking stick lies by his side. His drooping head
rests in one hand. As if to say, I am sorry that the upshot of
my struggles for democracy should be this assembly and this
constitution. As if he was aware and regretful that, even though
a torchbearer for a Naini, he had become a road paver for a
Sheikh Fazlollah.

Mohsen Yalfani

The first time I saw him, I didn't recognize him. I had read one of his works in my student days. As members of the cultural committee of the Iranian Student Association at Berkeley, we were getting ready to stage his *Amuzegaran* (Teachers). The play was to be directed by Manijeh Mohamedi, who later became a professional theater director. We had chosen that work because we were looking for a *progressive* text, but nothing too political. As activists, we thought of ourselves as shepherds and wardens of sheep and did not want the flock to take fright and bolt at an overly political work. Moreover, our student group was ostensibly not an official member of the Confederation of Iranian Students; we wanted to maintain the semblance of a student union. That said, I think everyone, from SAVAK to the Iranian students at Cal Berkeley, were aware of the political substance of our activities and that our *charade* amounted to nothing more than sophomoric diversions. *Stealth* was a feature of the *revolutionary* game in our student days – a game that was to have truly dire and bloody consequences later on. The fact that SAVAK had banned *Teachers* after a few performances in Tehran in 1970 where Saeed Soltanpour had directed the play was enough for us to establish its progressive pedigree.

As was customary in student productions, the program had to include a poetry recital. Following the same calculations and considerations, we chose a poem by Forugh Farrokhzad that while political was not considered radical. If staging a long play with amateur actors was tough, our tangle with Forugh's poem was a challenge of a different nature. The female student who was supposed to recite it refused to read the verse "I hold the green grain to my breast." As a leftist, she insisted the phrase was unbecoming of a progressive cultural agenda. It didn't matter that in the next line Forugh refers to "suckling" the green grain, leaving no doubt that her goal is not a utilitarian exploitation of a woman's breast. It didn't matter either that we were at Berkeley, which at the time was the center of the sexual revolution and the movement for social justice. We were "revolutionary" and from our revolutionary viewpoint feigning puritanism was as vital as it was to a Muslim fanatic. That same student later married another activist and they left for Iran at the onset of the 1979 revolution. Her husband was hanged in the course of the bloody 1982 uprising in Amol by Sarbedaran, members of the Maoist Union of Iranian Communists, while she herself fortunately escaped death with the help of human traffickers. But the day I got into the SAVAK minibus following a six-month lockup at the Joint Committee, I did not know the tall man inside was Mohsen Yalfani, the author of *Teachers*.

When it was decided to bus our group to Evin in spring 1977, we were ordered to cover our eyes with a blindfold, a standard procedure. They said we could only remove the shades after we had boarded the minibus. When I climbed in, someone was already sitting there. I said hello, and was responded to, sort of. He wore a warm but long-suffering expression. Tall and clearly uncomfortable in that cramped space, he kept quiet but his discomfort was obvious by the way he fidgeted and kept adjusting his position. Not one word came out of him throughout the trip. When I came to know Yalfani better later on and read more of his works, I could see that the style and tone of his writing were in sync with his bearing and languid locomotion. The stillness and serenity and grace that were always apparent in his movements are discernible in the fabric and narrative structure of his work as well. But what lurks in the subtext of his placid, at times languorous, and always slogan-free writings is a raging and rebellious consciousness, mindset, and underlying message. Behind the narrator and his narratives, a rare, justice-hungry, and searching soul looms tall like a stalwart cypress.

As was customary, soon after we arrived at the mullahs' block at Evin, the inmates came out to greet us and to explain the rules and regulations that pertained to the area or which they expected us to observe. Our trial had been public and the *brothers* and *comrades* did not know how they were supposed to deal with us. The welcome party was both to show kindliness and respect and to recite the diktat of the mullahs' cell block. In any event, each detainee introduced themselves, which is how I found out that my nameless minibus companion was Mohsen Yalfani. In the course of over forty-five years since then, my respect for him has soared higher every day. Whether at the height of fame as a member of the Iranian Writers' Association secretariat post-revolution, or when in dire straits in exile, I never observed anything in his manner and speech other than modesty coupled with dignity, reserve with transparency, plus a commitment both to the theater and freedom of thought. He never thought of himself as a liberating mountain-chained Prometheus or boasted thus to the *masses*, nor would he let misfortune dent his elegant and steadfast demeanor. He did not take the sudden post-revolution celebrity of political prisoners too seriously nor the indifference, or even the calumny and hostility, exhibited toward those same prisoners soon after. The initial attacks against the Left came from the nascent Islamic regime and the opposition, particularly the monarchists, gradually joined the chorus of disapproval.

Attar's saying "Seem as you are" and "Be as you seem" might well be Yalfani's guiding principle, warning him not to take flattery or rejection to heart, for both are overblown. He overcomes obstacles and brooks adversities with the dispassion of a gently flowing stream. I used to hear indirectly about the mortal pain and grief that had befallen him. I was never close enough to feel I could give him a call and ask after him. When he accepted our invitation and came to Stanford University in late 2022 to give a talk and supervise a play reading of his *Diaspora: A Tale of Transcendence*, I spent a few days with him in town. One day, our conversation led to his experiences in exile. I knew he had spent years driving a taxi and wanted to ask him about it but held back out of discretion. He noted the curiosity in my eyes. Without my asking, he said, "A lot of people think driving a taxi in Paris is tough. As a matter of fact, it provides a lot of opportunity to read, and for reflection." Listening to him, I wondered how many passengers had hitched a ride with him unaware of being in the company of one of the most decent and free-spirited artists and human beings that ever lived.

Neither in prison nor on any of the occasions I saw him abroad did I ever hear him malign anyone. I never heard him praise anyone excessively either. He always saves a few jabs for himself and instead of sticking the needle into anyone will express his views about others and their shortcomings lucidly and candidly in the gentlest way possible. It is said that art is, above all, a lesson in empathy; it shows us the way and the need to have empathy for others. Artists can put themselves in other people's shoes and see and paint the world through the eyes of the "other." The need for such empathy is naturally twice as important in the theater, and Yalfani's capacity for it truly knows no end. At the same time, he is selective in choosing his collaborators and the company he keeps. His work in exile is laudable, both for his continuous involvement in creative work and for his efforts to cultivate a more democratic language and stance in cultural and political exchanges.

He wrote several new plays in France and has published a series of illuminating articles in various journals. He had a hand in initiating and managing at least two serious cultural magazines. Several of his plays have been translated into French and staged, yet he modestly and constantly bemoans his lack of productivity and praises others for their *important* works. Every time I hear someone knock those who opposed the Shah and snipe that they handed over the country to the mullahs then went abroad to have fun, I think of Yalfani's painful yet ever-principled life. I ask myself whether these pundits might change their mind if they spent a little time with him and learned something about the ups and downs of his life? Not only in his creative output, but also in the conduct of his life, Yalfani is one of our eminent teachers.

Mohammad-Reza Jafari

The term *adab* is defined in *Dehkhoda* in a long litany that includes "literacy, knowledge . . . art . . . know-how, sociability . . . common sense . . . decorum, respect . . . gratitude . . . wonder . . . cultural refinement . . . mental agility . . . civility . . . and rectitude." Mohammad-Reza Jafari is a man who embodies *adab* in all those senses, and his *adab* (and the cultural legacy of three generations of Jafaris) is a glowing and ever-inspiring lodestar in the practices and intricacies and culture and ethos of the publishing industry in Iran and of the Persian language.

Like more or less every Iranian, I had heard of Amir Kabir Publishing before I met him, and I had seen and read some of their books. His father Abdolrahim Jafari revolutionized the concept of publishing in Iran when he founded Amir Kabir and made books available to the new social strata that were emerging within the growing Iranian population. He pioneered the production and timely distribution of well-designed textbooks across the country with the help of Homayoun Sanatizadeh's Offset Printing Company. On the cusp of the revolution, Amir Kabir was the largest publishing house in the Middle East, yet in the years preceding the revolution, it was inconceivable for many who opposed the

regime, including anti-Shah students like us, that a venture
that enormous and successful could exist absent some monkey
business. In those days, we were entranced by Marxist mottos,
specifically in the simplified versions redacted by Mao. The
ardor and aspiration in those slogans clouded our knowledge
and awareness of the Marxist principle that, at its outset,
capitalism is the most progressive force in history. We considered ourselves Marxists; ergo, we transcended Hegel. In fact,
we were just as idealistic as Hegel who had once said, "This
is my interpretation of reality and if reality does not corre-
spond with my interpretation, too bad for reality." Likewise,
we who thought of ourselves as materialists, considered the
stuff of our imagination more concrete than objective and
material reality. We also held that Iran was semi-feudal and
that even if capitalism were to arrive, it would be sort of
deformed and dysfunctional. In our worldview, anyone who
had a *job* in Iran was suspect, unless their work was *revolutionary*. In truth, what was suspect was our mindset and its
doctrinaire disposition. When I did some research on Amir
Kabir Publishing to write about Abdolrahim Jafari for my
Eminent Persians book, I was both astonished at the breadth
of that undeniably worthy enterprise and mortified by the
truly bizarre obtuseness of our minds.

My first close encounter with an Amir Kabir book was
when I was assistant to a university professor who taught
Persian literature. Sadeq Hedayat's *Blind Owl* was naturally
one of the course's source materials. The copy that I was using
was part of a very attractive edition of Hedayat's collected
works produced by Amir Kabir. In the modern world,
publishing the collected works of one of the most important
writers of that country generally enhances the publisher's
reputation and brings it fame and riches. But after the revolution, when the ownership of Amir Kabir was donated to

the Islamic Development Organization, that same edition of Hedayat's collected works was cited among a litany of charges drummed up against the publishing house and its founder Abdolrahim Jafari. It was a little earlier, on the eve of the revolution, that I first came to know his son Mohammad-Reza Jafari.

I had translated Karl Kautsky's *Foundations of Christianity* into Persian. It was my first step in parting with Stalinism and Maoism. Every sect in our religion ranked Kautsky among *heretics* and deviant *revisionists*. My next step in that process of separation came when I translated Antonio Gramsci's *State and Civil Society*. I read later that my translation, *Dolat va Jameh'e-ye Madani,* found a wide audience among those seeking to abandon Leninist–Stalinist dogma. Back then, I sent a sample of the Kautsky translation, *Bonyadha-ye Massihiyat*, to Mohammad-Reza Jafari via a friend and went to meet him at his office a short time later. He agreed to publish my translation but added something to the effect that his father had to sign the contract, which he did. I believe that statement had more to do with his *adab* and respect for his father, for at the time, Amir Kabir was effectively run by Mohammad-Reza, at least in so far as selecting which titles to publish, but formalizing a contract was his father's domain. From that first encounter, his composure and respectful demeanor and intellectual curiosity and notable erudition pointed to his *adab*. Even after the expropriation of Amir Kabir and Abdolrahim Jafari's incarceration, his son did not abandon their business enterprise. It is as if books and words and paper were ingrained in the Jafaris, body and soul. While making every effort to save his father from prison and pain, it did not take long before he founded his own company, *Nashr-e No* (New Publishing).

When I finished translating *The Master and Margarita* (*Morshed va Margarita*) in 1982, Nashr-e No and Mohammad-Reza Jafari were the only publisher and press that I called on. Forty years since the first edition of that translation, I have no doubt that no publisher other than Nashr-e No and no editor other than Mohammad-Reza would have done that book justice. Close to the fortieth anniversary of that publication, Jafari came across a new English translation of *The Master and Margarita*. That version was reportedly not only closer to the original than all others but also included notes by the translators that diligently parsed and analyzed many of the obscure and seminal points in the book. With astonishing determination and keen insight and dedication, he set about comparing this new edition with my original translation and dedicated more than a year to the task. He not only embodied *literacy* and *mental agility* and *civility*; he also recognized the importance of Bulgakov's work and would leave no stone unturned to produce the best version of it in Persian.

This attitude was evident even in our first exploratory meeting over the publication of my translation of *The Master and Margarita*. I met him in a small house where the newly founded Nashr-e No was headquartered. He showed enormous interest in the book. After he himself edited the text with great care and perspicacity, I suggested we invite Houshang Golshiri to also look it over. Jafari agreed wholeheartedly and without hesitation. I learned only later that in those days he was facing a plethora of challenges under back-breaking financial constraints. Yet he never talked about those difficulties, at least not to me, even as he fulfilled his contracts with authors and translators. It was as if he shouldered the burden of the labor so laborers who penned works for Nashr-e No could more easily devote themselves to elevating the mind and consciousness and creativity. In all those years, I never saw him treat an author or translator other than with *respect* and *gratitude*. I did not see him resort to untold schemes – as some publishers do – to violate an author's rights, or when remitting author's or translation royalties, behave as if he were doling out charity from some imperial purse. His *decorum* and *rectitude* precluded such abusive behavior.

In that same period, I came to know another facet of Mohammad-Reza Jafari's ethos and his Nashr-e No. Zahra Shadman was a colleague of Pouri Soltani, with whom she collaborated in building the foundation of modern librarianship in Iran. After the revolution, she was shown the door merely because she was the daughter of *Seyyed* Jalal Shadman – *Daie* Jalal, as we called him in the family. I don't know if she needed work for the money. I had no doubt she needed intellectual and professional stimulation. A society with a thoughtful leadership would certainly not have wasted her research and analytical skills and her passion to serve. Fortunately, Nashr-e No stepped in like thoughtful leaders in the civil society sector do, and had the foresight to have Zahra Shadman partner with Hossein-Ali Heravi – who had effectively lost his eyesight by then – and the result was the four-volume commentary on Hafez's lyric poetry written by Heravi in collaboration with Zahra Shadman. I recently read in one of the late Shahrokh Meskoob's collection of notes that Mohammad-Reza Jafari's father had told him, "We reprint *Sahifa-ye Sajjadia*, Imam Zainul Abideen's book of prayers, every year and dispatch it to Qom and Mashhad and we use the profits to publish books that we like." No doubt the Hafez commentary, *Sharh-e Ghazalha-ye Hafez,* was not quite as profitable.

Rather than agonize over making quick money from Nashr-e No, Jafari was perhaps more concerned with Iran's cultural heritage. For that reason, about two or three years before the revolution he placed rather extensive resources at the disposal of Gholam-Hossein Saedi to publish *Alefba*, which was the finest of all literary and intellectual journals during those years. It is also possible that because the Jafaris understood Iranian culture (they still do) and because he was given to *adab*, and still is, he knew that new generations of Iranians were going to be drawn to reading classical Persian literature again.

Descartes said, "I think, therefore I am," and Camus, "I rebel, therefore I am." Based on a worldview that holds the courage to think and provoke thinking as the axiom of modernity, Mohammad-Reza Jafari might have said: "I am an *adab*-defined publisher, therefore I am."

Aslan Aslanian

In the *gentlemen's* cell block at Evin where the future leaders of the Islamic revolution and many famous self-appointed representatives of the proletariat were locked up, he was the only actual worker. The cell block's moniker did not owe itself to SAVAK's respect for the detainees, most of whom were well-known. The *aqayan*, or "gentlemen," signified the incarcerated mullahs who at Evin and every other prison at the time constituted a minority but who in less than three years would become the sovereigns of Iran. Aslan was not a mullah, but a truck driver. Prior to that he was, as he put it, a "taxi driver." He also wrote poetry and was acquainted with some leftist intellectuals. In those days, a working-class pedigree was a priceless asset in leftist circles.

One day, Aslan had paid a visit to some *engaged* intellectuals committed to the theater. As bad luck would have it, at the hour of his visit SAVAK agents raided the building, which was used by a drama group for rehearsals. SAVAK claimed it was one of the venues where the People's Fadaiyan Guerrillas conducted clandestine operations. At the time of the raid, the actors were rehearsing Maxim Gorky's *The Petty Bourgeois*. Saeed Soltanpour, Nasser Rahmaninejad, and Mohsen Yalfani were detained on the spot and charged as sympathizers or

155

supporters of leftist dissidents. But Aslanian's only offense was his poor timing in visiting friends at the drama group. He was arrested and received a three-year jail sentence; I don't know exactly why. Was it SAVAK's intransigence and idiocy or had he been possessed by the spirit of Generale Della Rovere, the main protagonist in a brilliant 1959 film by Rossellini with Vittorio De Sica in the lead role. The film is about a petty thief who is picked up by the Nazis knowing he is not involved in politics. They propose that to escape punishment, he impersonate the Italian Resistance leader General Della Rovere and get his fellow inmates to capitulate. But having experienced the prisoners' sympathy and support, he so thoroughly self-identifies as the general that he maintains the act all the way to the gallows and refuses to urge the prisoners to acquiesce.

It was a few days after our arrival at the mullahs' cell block that Aslan approached me in the prison yard. He introduced himself as a *chauffeur* and a *poet*. In his attitude and even his stride, he was different from other political prisoners, all of whom seemed to be cast in the same mold. He flung his arms about. His legs moved wide apart when he walked, like a truck driver who's just made it back home after a long haul and needs to loosen and stretch his stiff muscles. Diction matching demeanor, he spoke like a truck driver too. Political prisoners reaching for a refinement peculiar to revolutionaries considered coarse language taboo; Stalin whose vulgar tirades were reportedly the staple of his speech all his life might have been an exception. But Aslan didn't give a hoot about that righteous creed. He spoke in a footloose riot of bitter humor that epitomized his punishing life. He called me *Dash* (Bro) Abbas. From our very first encounter, taboo terms and topics were the garnish of his conversation.

As was customary in prison, he started by talking mostly about his *file* and asking about mine, though given that my trial (and that of ten others) had been public, SAVAK's and the newspapers' version of that file was common knowledge. In relating his own story, he was not eager to paint himself a hero, as was standard practice. He said without rancor that he had a spell of bad luck and that it did not behoove him, "when they arrested me," to forget *manliness* and *camaraderie* and abandon the *comrades*. When in time he became famous because the celebrated classical vocalist Mohammad-Reza Shajarian sang one of his poems, the *comrades* claimed him as an early member of the People's Fadaiyan. I found out early on in our exchanges that among the engaged comrades in the drama group, he was most attached to Mohsen Yalfani, which speaks to his fine taste. His affection for me was seeded elsewhere.

Knowing I had studied in America and had been a university professor in Tehran before my arrest, he was curious about the world that he imagined I came from. Right off the bat, he felt I was someone he could confide in. Perhaps that motivated him to pick me as a friend.

One day we were resting in the pleasant shade of a wall in the mullahs' block waiting for our turn to play volleyball. The mullahs and leftist intellectuals used to take their meals separately. The mullahs considered us *unclean*, of course, and even in those days acted as a class apart from us *non-Muslims*, except when it came to volleyball although that, too, was apparently taboo for some. Aslan suddenly said, "You must have noticed that I'm the only one who has a spoonful of honey in the mornings." I hadn't noticed. Though canvassing and parsing and discussing the slightest feature of every prisoner's carriage – including what they chewed at the communal meal – was one of the leftists' regular pastimes (or maladies), I did not indulge in such talk. In the standard vocabulary of the day, such probing and *enjoining virtue* was exercised under the banner of *ideological struggles* and *constructive criticism*. In any event, I had never noticed Aslan's spoonful of honey. "I have a nocturnal spermatorrhea problem," he said, "and Doc has prescribed honey." I was sure I'd misheard him and so asked, "*What* problem?" Thinking I didn't know what nocturnal spermatorrhea meant, he elaborated in plainer terms. I thought if Federico Fellini ever filmed such a dialogue, viewers would believe it was fantasy. Not knowing what I should do, or say, I responded awkwardly: "O wow! I didn't know honey had such properties." It was perhaps the stupidest possible reaction, more out of desperation than reflection. I never found out and nor asked how he had managed to confront the very stiff prison doctor with his wet dreams earnestly enough to get him to prescribe him honey. It was easier to digest why the comrades had not censured him. Aslan was an actual worker and no doubt a proletarian nocturnal problem was more digestible than petty bourgeois bellyaches.

When he realized that his confessed involuntary emissions hadn't turned me off, he felt even more at ease. A few days later, when we were resting in the shade again waiting to play volleyball, he said, "Dash Abbas, I have a question. If I, for instance, like the way that lad plays," and he glanced over at a young man, "would that be very wrong?" That query was much weirder than his honey habit. Among political prisoners, any hint at such urges and fantasies was an affront and unforgivable transgression. Political prisoners expected to be at least safe from the curse of being raped by cellmates. As far as I knew, the only inmate who had reportedly had illicit intentions toward a cellmate at the time was a devout

Muslim who for a while after the revolution became minister of guidance.

After a short pause, I replied, "Dash Aslan, you're free to fancy; I don't think anyone will object so long as you don't bother him." I even unloaded some Freud on him – how everyone entertains such thoughts at some point in their life and is attracted to others of the same sex. As if he had been licensed to retain his emotions while also feeling antsy, he said, "Dash Abbas, if the *comrades* get so much as a whiff of this, they'll rip me apart." I said nothing to the comrades and nobody ripped him apart. For one, he was proletarian; he also lived simply and honestly and did not give in to his temptations.

Aslan's prison chats were not restricted to honey and wet dreams, of course. He sometimes talked about his doleful past and sometimes about what "twenty years of chauffeuring" had taught him. "Being a cabbie is the best way to get to know people." Years later, when I was researching U.S. government records for my book on the Shah, I came across a report that said taxi drivers in Tehran and their outlook on the state of the country was one of the most accurate barometers of public opinion in Iran. Some of Aslan's other discoveries were of a different nature. Long years of driving trucks and taxis had taught him two things, he said. "Don't ever trust anyone who trims his mustache in a straight and neat line. They're all pimps." For years afterwards, whenever I saw a musta-chioed man, I'd fixate on his upper lip. I was never able to determine the accuracy or otherwise of that part of his – as he put it – *chauffeurial wisdom*.

Fact-checking item two of this wisdom was even more difficult. "Everyone whose eyebrows tilt sharply down has a good singing voice." I never asked him how he had come to that conclusion; had he tested every person with sharply down-tilting eyebrows? Regardless, in the years since, whenever I encounter someone with a good singing voice, I involuntarily check their temples. I even asked the iconic singer Shajarian about our mutual friend's theory. He laughed and said, "I doubt there's a connection."

I was released a few months ahead of Aslan. My parents were ageing fast and I visited them regularly. One day, the phone rang when I was at their house. Luckily, I picked it up myself. Without any preamble, the caller said, "If I may, I'd like to speak to Mister Abbas." Had my father answered the phone, he would have no doubt quipped testily, "You mean *Doctor*?" And then he would have asked, "And you are?" And if the name was unfamiliar, he would have ordinarily asked, "What do you want?" Had Aslan disclosed he had just been discharged from prison, my father would have likely slammed the phone down hard and not even told me about the call. Parviz Kalantari told a story about the time he was active in the Tudeh Party. One day he went to a comrade's house to attend an organizational meeting. The code name was "The storks are flying today." He knocked, feeling a little jittery. As with every covert meeting, he told the fellow who opened the door that the storks were flying that day. The guy slapped him hard across the face. "The storks can go fuck themselves, and you should be ashamed of trying to get my son into trouble!" If my father heard Aslan was just discharged from prison, he would have thought he wanted to get me in trouble.

Though Aslan said nothing about flying storks, I recognized his voice and greeted him warmly and gleefully. We arranged to meet. He had told me about the truck drivers' hangout. "There's arak with stone-oven baked potatoes and delicious pickled herbs." We agreed to meet at the tavern near Qazvin Gate.

The tavern was huge. Steaming potatoes and aromatic pickles and the brew lent it all an inviting air. After greetings and a couple of shots and some small talk, he said he wanted to buy a truck. "I also want to publish my poems," he said. It was obvious he didn't have enough to buy a truck. He had just been freed after three years behind bars. Worried I might hurt his feelings, I said, "I don't have a penny to my name but I have a brother who may be able to loan you the money." He expressed his consent with, "Dash Abbas, love you!"

My brother Hasan was the director general of a large shipyard called Arvandan on the Persian Gulf. When I talked to him, he immediately agreed to loan Aslan the money. My brother's business was booming in those days. He was always traveling, the company's prospects getting brighter by the day. They were short of both engineers and blue-collar workers and recruited staff and laborers from South Korea and Pakistan. Less than three years later, Saddam's invading army dismantled the entire inventory of Arvandan's shipbuilding equipment and hauled it away to Iraq.

Aslan bought his truck, and in time his business grew so lucrative he bought a second truck. He personally hit the road less and less frequently. A selection of his poetry titled *Shabahang* (Evening Song) was published, and he married in a tremendous hurry. Once the revolutionary fervor abated, that matrimonial pledge – like countless political ones – fell apart. I heard his wife and children emigrated. He stayed put, with his poetry and fame and his two trucks.

He owed his fame above all to Shajarian. Shajarian sang Aslan's "*. . . the brother soaked in blood . . .*" on a day when the revolution was at fever pitch. They said that initiative came from another virtuoso, the celebrated tar player Mohammad-Reza Lotfi. The story went that Aslan had composed it in memory of the founder and theoretician of the People's Fedaiyan Guerillas Amir-Parviz Pouyan; the word *pouyan* (searching) appears in the poem. Shajarian's tune and Aslan's lyrics gradually became one of the Guerrillas' favorite songs. In the new biography they crafted for Aslan, he had been their comrade from the start. But if what I heard from him in prison and later from fellow inmates like Nasser Rahmaninejad is true, that story is nothing but a myth. The thrust of the poem did not dovetail with Shajarian's other earlier or later songs either, but merely echoed the revolutionary fervor and fever of the times: *It is nighttime and the land is umbrous / Sitting in the dark alone is unholy / Hand me my rifle so I can hunt my way.* Aslan himself never sought the way of the rifle.

As revolutionary passions ebbed and the Fadaiyan's popularity unraveled overnight, so did the fame of "Brother is Restless." Adding insult to injury, Shajarian later petitioned the despotic rulers in a brilliant and mutinous chant to "Set Down Your Rifle." I had no more news of Aslan either at the height of his celebrity or during his forced seclusion. It was in exile when I read in an article that he had passed. It said that he had died on 17 November 2018 in Karaj, alone.

Gholam-Hossein Saedi

He could not bear the pain of exile. Or maybe pain itself. In Iran, he was always on the road. From the villages of Azarbaijan to the hovels of the Persian Gulf, he knew every locale firsthand. He had devoted many a journey to each. Sometimes with people like Samad Behrangi and Reza Baraheni, sometimes with Al Ahmad and Mehrjui. He had close ties to many *natives* everywhere as well. That said, even among them, he was as if an outsider. He was also melancholic. Though a psychiatrist by profession, to grapple with that extra burden he resorted chiefly to work or alcohol. The source of depression is said to be at times internal and at others external – chemical and physical disorders or social imbalances and delinquencies. Saedi suffered from both types. One time in Paris, I heard him say, "This being my métier, I know what afflicts me." He knew grief. His choice remedy was self-destructive, intentionally or unwittingly. At the height of the AIDS epidemic, the renowned American critic Susan Sontag wrote an illuminating book titled AIDS *and Its Metaphors*. She writes that in nineteenth-century Europe, tuberculosis as well as alcohol and opium abuse became signifiers of intellectualism; the greater the abuse, the higher the abuser's prestige. In the twentieth century, a variant of that malady was also prevalent in Iran. Both at home and as an immigrant abroad, Saedi used alcohol as a cure for the grief that pained his heart, and perhaps as an emblem of intellectualism. Furthermore, to feel a social *exile* was considered a prerequisite by thought leaders in Iran. Alienation nourished their struggle and affirmed their status. Saedi, especially in the last years of his life, felt exilic both at home and in France where the added geographic, cultural, and linguistic otherness plunged him into despondency and a profound melancholy. It was as if he had shut out himself and the world.

When living in Paris, he called the Persian language his homeland and bona fide sanctuary, wholeheartedly and with pride. Like many diaspora intellectuals, he carried on grounded in the hope that he would eventually go back, and perhaps worried that if he learned French or English his homecoming might be delayed, or that others may question his aspiration and zeal to return. Of course, while living in Iran and later as an expatriate, his other means of confronting grief was creative work. Like Chekhov and Bulgakov, Khaled Hosseini and Nawal Saadawi, he virtually abandoned medicine and pursued a literary career. The number of individuals who in recent history chose a similar path and prioritized the pen over the scalpel is not negligible. I don't know why. Even when Saedi used to practice medicine, he was more at the service of art. Writing was his vocation, medicine his avocation. He had set up a clinic in southern Tehran close to the red-light district, *Shahr-e No* (New Town). He treated the patients, most of whom were poor, free of charge, working with his brother who was also a doctor; he also turned the clinic into an intellectual hub. I have seen and read several reports to the effect that some of the literary community's most important decisions, including to establish *Kanoon-e Nevisandegan*, the

Iranian Writers' Association, were made in that clinic. But the meetings, according to Parviz Sabeti, became Saedi's Achilles heel. Apparently SAVAK outfitted the clinic with audio surveillance devices and recorded and studied all the medical, literary, and on occasion romantic, exchanges that took place there.

If Sabeti's account of events is true, the whole episode is a window into both the toxic political climate in Iran at the time and the naïveté of people like Saedi. Equally, it is as if SAVAK did not recognize the sanctioned privacy of a doctor's clinic, and a psychiatrist at that. To remain au fait with the goings-on, and more importantly, to collect evidence or audio recordings that could be used against dissidents, it knew no bounds. I have no doubt that the current security apparatus has wholly outdone SAVAK in every respect. That said, such disgraceful acts of the kind in which Saedi paid the price can never be whitewashed. Those intellectuals who used to congregate in Saedi's clinic are also partly to blame. How was it possible to write plays and stories and poems about SAVAK's despotism and omnipresence but not suspect that it would be spying on and surveilling such a focal hub of well-known anti-Shah intellectuals?

According to Sabeti, what helped them break Saedi at the time of his arrest and compelled him to give a television interview-cum-confession was an audiotape of a meetup and sexual intercourse he had had at his clinic. "I identified the woman who was the wife of one of Saedi's friends by name," said Sabeti with pride, "so he would know that we had recognized the voice." He added: "Consequently, there was no need for torture and threats." Saedi submitted to that interview and I believe that decision altered the course of his life. It seems he spent the rest of his days repenting the confession. He belonged to the same circle and convictions as the likes of

Samad Behrangi and Behrouz Dehqani and carried the burden
of what he perceived as his weakness to the end of his life.

It was about two or three years after that affair when
he came to our house one night at around eleven o'clock,
totally plastered. I had met him numerous times at the home
of Dariush Mehrjui and his wife Faryar Javaherian, both old
friends from my student days. That night, Saedi and Mehrjui
had been to a party and he had asked Mehrjui to drop him
off at our place. His unexpected visit was a welcome event, of
course. We walked to a tavern down the street. He did most of
the talking, bad-mouthing SAVAK. "They want to destroy us.
We mustn't let them. We have to *karate* them." For years, "to
karate something" was his catchphrase. "We have to stand up
to those sons of bitches and keep doing what we do." I never
found out if his words were meant as self-consolation or if he
had come by to sympathize and share my woes and boost my
morale. I had not given a TV interview but was among a group
that was tried publicly in 1977. The comrades had expected
us to act before a public tribunal like Khosrow Golsorkhi had
done back in 1974, proclaiming Karbala and Imam Hossein
and Hazrat-e Ali and Marx and Lenin's proletariat as the political backbone of their *revolution*, and like him, stick to their
guns all the way to the gallows. I had not followed suit at
the trial and was pardoned by royal decree a year later and
released. Whatever Saedi's motivation, his night visit while
drunk doubled my respect for him.

I later learned that to assuage his pain, he had chosen
another path as well. Before they heaped such torments upon
him, he was one of the most cherished intellectuals of the
time, known for his progressiveness and free spirit. Mehrjui's
Gāv (The Cow), which was assuredly his masterpiece and still
is, was above all indebted to Saedi's writing on which the film
was based. When Saedi traveled to the U.S., the Confederation

celebrated him as a national hero. His fame and popularity were such that at one point a longstanding resident of Berkeley wedded Saedi's sister to establish a closer and more intimate relationship with him, the first such instance of what Milan Kundera later came to call venereal fame. But none of it alleviated Saedi's pain while living in Iran. As the revolution took shape, he began collaborating with some leftist groups. He wrote articles for their publications under a pseudonym. It did not take long before that journal gained fame for its polished pieces. The author's identity was not known. Nor was there any shortage of whisperings about authorship. One point was clear: this was a consummate writer, not a fanatical communist. When the Islamic regime's round-up and execution of the opposition began, Saedi had no choice but to take refuge in a safe house and go underground. Was that publication's evanescent stardom worth the price he paid? Clearly, in the sense that he was not bound by any material *obligation* to write, and the *choice* to do so was his alone, no one else is to blame. But it is also true that he was bound by a tacit and unspoken obligation that emanated from the pain and stress that he had internalized for years. His choice was also rooted in one of the challenges that *progressive* intellectuals faced in Iran during that era. It was a rare intellectual who was willing to carry on and stay within their artistic and mental space. One moved to issue a (mostly simplistic) political manifesto about the theater and called anyone who dismissed it *cheap* and *compromising*, while another considered his children's story a tool for disseminating *revolutionary rage*. What a cursed fate that Saedi, one of the most brilliant writers of the time, should have been driven, for a superficial and short-lived reward, to forgo writing stories and plays and travelogues as he had long done so brilliantly, and instead pen articles that preached to the choir in a publication with a limited readership, and as a result be forced to go into hiding, wear a wig, be inundated with a thousand and one dreads and dangers, and eventually flee Iran to take refuge in a bigger prison that he forged for himself abroad. He managed the pain of exile by resorting to vodka and regret and depression and reclusiveness, but also notably, by applying himself to creative work.

A few years prior to the revolution, Amir Kabir Publishing had provided him with an office and funding to launch *Alefba* (Alphabet) in Tehran. I believe the six issues that he published between 1973-1977 were among the most enriching literary and social journals while also having the widest circulation in Iran. Bahram Beyzaie, Ahmad Mahmoud, Houshang Golshiri, Mostafa Rahimi, Simin Daneshvar, and Shahrnoush Parsipour all contributed to it. Bahaeddin Khorramshahi and Kamran Fani assisted him in running the publication. I had been released from prison at around the same time and had produced a Persian translation of *Foundations of Christianity* by Karl Kautsky – the selfsame man that the *comrades*, channeling Lenin, called "Kautsky the Heretic" – which was published by Amir Kabir. I used to go to the publishing house to check the galley proofs where I would sometimes run into Saedi. He was no doubt one of the most hard-working writers of the time. Had the revolution not happened, had Amir Kabir not been expropriated and *donated* to the Islamists, had Saedi remained in Iran and continued to publish *Alefba*, what kind of Iran would we have today, and Saedi what kind of life?

He relaunched *Alefba* in exile and published seven issues in Paris between 1982-1986. He also wrote plays. But none of that relieved his pain. His death was perhaps more than anything due to grief, or even suicidal. Perhaps the comrades' simplification and utilitarianism that turned one of the greatest travel writers of Iran into a pamphleteer, plus SAVAK's stunts that pressured him to give a televised confession, and perhaps his innate depression were all complicit in forging his mournful fate. But what pulled the trigger of his steady descent into a virtual suicide was a regime that could not accommodate a free spirit and creative writer like him, a polity that considered Iran its divinely ordained fiefdom and felt entitled to decide who had a right to live in the country and in its blindness denied that right to someone like Saedi whose existence, it seems, was conceivable in Iran alone.

Mostafa Rahimi

Had he only written that one letter about the reason for his opposition to the Islamic Republic, his name would in all likelihood have still gone down in history. That letter was just one moment, and perhaps the essence, of his bounteous life, an exhalation of his integrity and courage rather than an isolated or incidental gasp. When discussing the revolution, many choose to point to the Shah's misstep in arranging for the 7 January 1978 publication of the infamous op-ed "Iran: Red and Black Colonialism" in *Ettelaat* (News) by Farhad Nikukhah under a pseudonym, which alluded to Ayatollah Khomeini's Indian lineage. Focusing on that blunder and misbegotten article distracts us from paying attention to Mostafa Rahimi's equally important missive.

It might be comforting to brush off our collective error in ignoring Rahimi's thoughtful and prescient letter. It helps to forget how we got swept up without thinking in the hysteria stirred up by Nikukhah's, and how those rivulets of protest cascaded into a revolutionary flood. The greater the notoriety of the *Ettelaat* article, the more we can sustain the self-deluding narrative that we did not know, or had not been warned. The Cassandra of that era was Mostafa Rahimi.

171

Others, including Gholam-Hossein Sadiqi, Shapur Bakhtiar, Hossein Mohri, and Mahshid Amirshahi played a similar role. They put their reputations on the line in the faint hope of stemming the flood, which they could not.

Two weeks before the instigator of the flood Khomeini returned to Iran – despite the fact that in the preceding months, especially during the days he was living in Paris, he spoke of democracy and a republic and, to "deceive and dissimulate," as he himself put it, never referred to the concept of *Velayat-e faqih*, Guardianship of the [Islamic] Jurist – Mostafa Rahimi unscrambled the pretender's game plan in a letter addressed to Khomeini titled "Why I Am Opposed to an Islamic Republic" that would explode like a bomb. While owing to delusion or ignorance, the majority of intellectuals thought it possible to fuse the notion of a republic, which is grounded on the sovereignty of the people, with an Islamic state, which claims divine sovereignty, Mostafa Rahimi thought otherwise. Aware of the incongruity of these two terms (and the irreconcilable differences between the principles of democracy or a republic and the dominion of religious ideology), and after a lifetime spent studying the constitution and law in detail, he had the courage and the audacity to risk a mortifying backlash by putting his name to the letter and that appeared on 15 January 1979 in *Ayandegan* (Futurists), one of the newspapers with the widest readership at the time. Publishing that letter may be one reason why *Ayandegan* was the first target and casualty of the attacks against the freedom of the press.

Virtually every argument against dictatorship by proponents of secular democracy can be found in that letter. Nowadays, former supporters and even agents of the Islamic regime also criticize the system and at times behave as if such judgments had never occurred to anyone before. But the nub of all those critiques can be found in Rahimi's letter. He elucidated the shortcomings and intransigent contradictions of the concept of an "Islamic" republic with the pithiness of a poet, the keen eye of a legal expert, and the daring of a rebel. It is as if he, a fan of Camus, had like him turned the axiom of modernity that "I think, therefore I am" into "I rebel, therefore I am." He even anticipated the likes of the Shia political theorist and member of the Assembly of Experts Mesbah Yazdi who said, "What have people got to do with anything?" Saeedi Sirjani had as a storyteller portrayed the fate of those who were consumed by love for *Qodrat Khanom* (Lady Power) in his exquisite *Sheikh-e Sanaan* (The Ascetic of Sanaan); Rahimi outlined that same fate in incisive detail from the viewpoint of a legal expert. The unhappy end of these two brave writers is the joyless story of the Iranian revolution.

In the euphoric and slogan-filled, mindless and thought-less atmosphere of those days, which is characteristic of all revolutions, scores of people refused to take these warnings seriously. Instead, in the lead-up to the impending regime, Ayatollah Khomeini mobs, with the moral support of count-less leftist and liberal fellow travelers – especially Tudeh'is and Maoists miffed by Rahimi's criticism of Stalinism and Marxism – vilified him viciously. I kept hearing about those attacks from different sources. I had never met Rahimi but I had read some of his writings. On reading his interpretation of the 1968 student movement in France, I had been moved to say, as demanded by my dogmatism, *Now ain't he just a "lefty petty bourgeois" ministering to the bourgeoisie?!* He had called his book *Nim-negāh* (A Half Peek) because one of the book's key chapters had been censured at the time. That said, I also realized that whoever had written that book was eminently learned and a freethinker. I was not the only one to pay him such homage. Before the revolution, Rahimi was one of the most esteemed and well-liked Iranian intellectuals. With all that, I did not feel at ease calling him when his historic article was published. Nor had I ever called such *eminent* figures before. Finally, I got hold of his telephone number, from what source I don't remember. I rang. My hands and voice quavered. A man picked up and quietly said something like, "To what do I owe the pleasure?" I replied, "You don't know me. I used to teach at university." I did not say where. "I wanted to call and say I am in awe of your courage and I salute you." He said thanks. He did not ask my name, out of caution, I believe, and perhaps the certainty that his phone was tapped and outsiders could listen in. "People call all day long to pummel me with insults and threats. My wife feels exhausted. I thought I should answer some calls myself." Our conversation was brief.

I did not tell him that I, too, had published a letter about the approaching danger, though one far less brazen and foreboding, and not even in my name. I had sent the letter to Rahman Hatefi, the de facto editor-in-chief of *Keyhan*. He called me in the evening of the same day he received it. I was playing poker with four other Tehran University professors. "Things are going downhill at *Keyhan* every day," he said. "Don't publish the letter in your name alone; the more impactful and safer thing to do is to have it signed by a group." Asking him to hold the line, I explained the conundrum to my colleagues at the table and asked if they would agree to sign as co-authors, without being named. They all agreed. We were then oblivious to the sweep of the looming menace. A few years later, all of us had emigrated. Rahman published the letter on the front page of *Keyhan*, credited to "Five University of Tehran Professors," though he warned us: "If *Keyhan*'s Hezbollah press me, I will be forced to divulge the names." He never divulged them. Mostafa Rahimi, however, would pay an extremely high price for his insights and valor.

Some time passed after our brief phone call, then one day Rahimi invited me to his house through a friend of his; I believe it was Nasser Katouzian, who after the revolution was appointed dean of the Faculty of Law and Political Science at Tehran University by the faculty and students and was later expelled by a bunch of hooligans deputized to administer the *cultural revolution*. I was also among those expelled. Katouzian wrote a remarkable open letter denouncing *Layehe-ye Qisas*, the Bill of Retribution – the bill was in reality a summary of the "Guardianship of the Islamic Jurist" replacing modern notions of jurisprudence with Shiite Sharia laws. I had signed it, as had about forty of the forty-five members of the faculty. Consequently, the whole group was expelled for a period of between one to four years. In terms of its legal subject matter and historical perspective, our open letter in *Keyhan* had in effect supplemented Rahimi's deeply perceptive letter.

He lived mid-city in a simple, two-story house with a small front yard in an alley lined with similar buildings. Aside from Katouzian, I remember the poet Mohammad-Reza Haqshenas and the translator of French literature Abolhasan Najafi being among the guests. It seemed like a gathering of like-minded people, with me as a young newbie. The chief purpose of such interactions was political gossip and metaphysical discussions that, according to Nietzsche, are worthy pursuits of an inquisitive mind. Nietzsche should have perhaps added that those two pursuits are even more seductive to people whose dream of a democratic revolution has turned into a nightmare. After that evening and a rendezvous a few days later to have tea, my friendship with Mostafa Rahimi gradually deepened, as did my admiration for his searching mind and liberal persuasion. We never spoke about that phone call the day after his letter was published. He liked the articles that Manuchehr Safa and I had co-authored as a critique of Najaf Daryabandari's Stalinism. At the time, Rahimi and I were busy translating books that were critiques of orthodox Marxism. I sometimes asked him for Persian equivalents of philosophical terminology in Kolakovsky's *Main Currents of Marxism*. It was at Rahimi's home or maybe at Kharazmi Publishing that I had the good fortune to meet the lauded translator Ezzattolah Fouladvand. He, too, had tended left in his youth and bemoaned the staying power and longevity of Stalinist dogmatism. His translation of Karl Popper's *The Open Society and Its Enemies* was part of his effort to challenge such enduring dogma. But the price that Rahimi paid for publishing his translation of a critical account of Marxism was, like his letter to *Ayandegan*, very high.

The *comrades* were outraged by the book and boycotted it. Rahami used to complain that some bookstores refrained from distributing it in fear of the comrades. Their outrage dovetailed with the mullahs' vengeance, and thus Rahimi's life, like Iran's fate, was turned upside down.

Rahimi had translated both Sartre and Camus. But his ethos was closest to a rebellious and ingenuous Camus than to a Sartre who was both a political acrobat and performed a thousand disingenuous stunts in his personal relations, especially with his legendary partner Simone de Beauvoir. Rahimi, with his humanity and gentle soul, and his rebel and at times poetic spirit, was in many ways closer to Camus. I learned later that his depression was also closer to Camus's.

The regime published a list of purported SAVAK collaborators with the help of a leftist group that had just returned from the West. My old friend Parviz Shokat heard from Mostafa Chamran whom he had known from his student days at Berkeley, and who had become minister of defense post-revolution, that the Islamic regime had shared the list with the leftist group. He added, "The list has been *politically* manipulated;" they had purged the names of mullahs and *allied comrades* from the list, and out of vengeance and hatred, added the names of individuals like Rahimi. That crass manipulation pushed Rahimi to the brink.

Although he was aware that anyone who knew him would realize that inserting his name in the list was an act of revenge and malice, that he was known to have lived an honorable life, and that the alleged membership in SAVAK contradicted his ethos, still, the heavy weight of that false accusation pressed down upon his distressed soul. It is as if he felt insulted, and it certainly was insulting. A few months later in 1981, they put him behind bars. He served three months in prison. Some speculated it had to do with a certain unpublished work of his. According to Rahimi himself, he was at a garden party when security agents came looking for someone whom they believed had authored *Twenty-Three Years* – the same book that they once thought was written by Ali Dashti, for which they had condemned the old man to death; the same book whose substance was already available in the decades-old writings of German orientalists, and also notably by the English orientalist David Margoliouth; the same book most of whose content was summarized under the entry "Mohammad" in the fourteenth edition of *Encyclopedia Britannica*.

After emigrating to the U.S., I used to hear news of Mostafa Rahimi, usually via friends. Except for occasions when we exchanged messages through a mutual acquaintance, I did not hear from him directly. Until *The Persian Sphinx* came out. Given his learning and my fondness for him, in going through the book reviews I found Rahimi's critique both touching and strange. While treating me with utmost affection, he had slammed the book. He compared *The Persian Sphinx* to an infamous verse that the French poet Paul Eluard, an otherwise lucid human being, had penned in praise of the KGB – an excusable error. Rahimi asked what riddle was there in the life of Amir Abbas Hoveyda that I had spent several years trying to explain or unravel? Given how much I respected him, I responded to his commentary. I wrote that it was hard to understand how an astute exponent and translator of existentialist works could not accept that everyone's life and personality holds riddles. Even before my response was published, he reiterated in a brief article that his take on and critique of my book had been overhasty.

Some time went by. One day, I read somewhere that he had passed. Part of the pain of exile – and perhaps even its definition – lies in the fact that we live in one place and our loved ones often die elsewhere. Rumor had it that Mostafa Rahimi had climbed to the roof of his house to repair a wire or an antenna and had slipped, and that his body was recovered in the yard below. A close relative of his told me once, without offering any details, that perhaps what led to his death was his mounting depression; that during the last few months of his life, he faded more each day. The American writer Saul Bellow wrote in a highly engaging book that in America everyone worries about a heart attack while most in fact die from a broken heart. Whatever triggered Rahimi's demise, the chief cause of his death was likely a heart broken by the times that were mendacious, and a frivolous society that disregarded his warnings and, instead of heeding and deliberating his message, killed the messenger.

Fereydoun Hoveyda

According to the great Historian Beyhaqi, "A seat is enriched by a man, not the man by the seat." That poignant adage applies to Fereydoun Hoveyda. Iran's ambassador to the United Nations for ten years, he was preceded in that post by eminent figures such as Hasan Taqizadeh and Nasrollah Entezam. Hoveyda had graduated from the Sorbonne having studied under a professor who played an important role in shaping the U.N. The professor had also drafted the Universal Declaration of Human Rights, an initiative where he had also involved Fereydoun as one of his star students. While living and working in France, he was recognized as a distinguished intellectual and an artist. When he returned to Iran after years of working at UNESCO and the Iranian embassy in Paris, he was appointed U.N. ambassador. To get a sense of the distorted outlook of Iranian intellectuals of the time, suffice it to say that they put it about that it was his brother's clout that got Fereydoun the post. The Shah's son-in-law and U.N. Ambassador Ardeshir Zahedi used to say it was Ashraf Pahlavi – the Shah's twin sister – who had the biggest hand in Fereydoun's appointment. "Ashraf was in cahoots with Amir Abbas Hoveyda," he declared, "and she pushed for his brother Fereydoun because she had great personal ambitions at the U.N." When I think about the past, I say to myself, lucky the country that should have been represented at the United Nations by someone of the intellectual heft of Fereydoun.

His parentage was Iranian and his education French-international. His mother was a devout Muslim and his father was an even more devout Bahai. Fereydoun was a staunch atheist, by contrast, and proud of his irreligiousness. Nor did he ever try to hide that aspect of his ethos or pretend otherwise during the time I had the good fortune to enjoy his friendship.

In France, he was one of the foundational figures in the renowned journal *Cahiers du Cinéma* where he helped shape the "auteur theory," a critical approach to filmmaking that defined the director as the author, a primary creative force whose work is marked by a personal style and technique and signature. His essays were reprinted in special issues of the journal that singled out the most significant contributions and which were translated into other languages. His assertion that mise-en-scène rather than plot is the most vital element in cinematic aesthetics and language has been published repeatedly in different sources. Not only were Claude Chabrol, François Truffaut, and other directors of that caliber his close friends and colleagues at the journal, but during that time he also collaborated with the Italian master of neorealism Roberto Rossellini in writing the script for his acclaimed *India*. As well as having many friends among French poets, writers, and artists, he engaged in all those fields himself and received major awards for his work. Andy Warhol was not a mere acquaintance but an intimate friend and created a portrait of Fereydoun Hoveyda in his signature style. Even when Hoveyda was U.N. ambassador, Warhol's studio where his parties had enormous cachet was one of his regular hangouts. He used to take some of the distinguished Iranian guests who were in his charge to Warhol's studio. "All those guests," he said, "from Princess Ashraf to Queen Farah Pahlavi, from the SAVAK chief to various ministers, were eager to meet Hollywood celebrities and, in those days, Warhol was of the same stock as Hollywood celebrities." Relatedly, I heard from Ebrahim Golestan that when he returned from the 1961 Venice Film Festival where he had won a prize for his *Yek Atash* (A Fire) and was invited to the court for a screening, the first question the Shah asked was, "So, which stars did you meet?" To which Golestan responded: "Your Majesty, this was a documentary film. That class of guest was not in attendance."

Fereydoun's band of creative friends were not only from the West. He had no shortage of artist or writer friends in Iran either. Golestan always spoke of him as one of the stellar personalities of the times and as one of his dearest friends. It is on Fereydoun's advice that his brother Amir Abbas, who was then prime minister, commissioned a series of small paintings from Sohrab Sepehri to be given as gifts to foreign visitors. "I said to Amir, why not gift artwork by Sepehri to visiting dignitaries instead of pistachio, candy, and carpets?" The first time I visited Fereydoun at his home in the U.S., I noticed one of those small paintings on the wall. A work by Warhol and, if I remember correctly, one by Jasper Johns hung on another wall.

The house was in a new suburban district near a small town called Clifton in Virginia. It sat in a construction site next to large pits dug by heavy machinery to build dream homes for other happy families. Looking at his house from the outside, one would never imagine that inside was a veritable gallery of notable artworks and that the proprietor himself was one of the noted artists and thinkers of our time.

I knew he had always lived in big cities like Tehran and Beirut, Paris and New York. I asked if adjusting to that sparsely populated and newly built suburb had been difficult. "Yes, but we didn't have a choice," he admitted. "New York had become too expensive; we couldn't afford it." I thought he would have the means if only he sold one of those high-priced paintings. But then I guessed each was a piece of him and a token of the life he had lived and that parting with any one of them would have been like losing a limb.

I had gotten his phone number from Ebrahim Golestan, who naturally forewarned him that I would call. I said hello. He responded in a charming Persian tinged at times with a slightly French intonation. "As you may know, I plan to write a book about your brother," I said. He cut me off. "Why?" I was caught off guard. To buy myself some time to think of an appropriate answer, I said, "What do you mean by 'why'?" He replied, "Twenty years have passed since my brother was executed; in that time, they either haven't thought about the tragedy or, if they have, they've tried to somehow justify the grounds for his killing." He went on: "Given such a sour history, isn't it natural that I should ask why you have come looking for him now?" I replied, "I was commissioned to write an article on Amir Abbas Hoveyda for *Encyclopædia Iranica* at Ehsan Yarshater's request and in the process of my research realized that his true character was much more complex than my perception of him – and I believe society's perception of him." I then added, "I believe his life needs to be revisited and reconstructed." He agreed to talk to me. I knew that Golestan's recommendation had played a role in his decision and that he wanted to test me. A little later, he said, "You should talk to Dr. Fereshteh Ensha, his trusty maternal cousin, and Mrs. Marefat, Hoveyda's assistant," and added that he had talked to both and told them to expect my call. I knew I had passed the test.

Either that same time or perhaps the following week when I went to see him again, he brought out his photo albums and very generously said, "Help yourself to any pictures you like." Among the photos I picked was a childhood shot of him and his brother, which had faded and yellowed over time. It became the image on the front cover of the Persian version of *The Persian Sphinx*, which was published abroad. Designing the front cover was not the only thing that would not have been possible without his understanding and spirit; despite all his love for his brother, not once did he try, during my research or afterwards when I asked him to read parts of the book, to impose his views on the narrative. He had respect for other people's writing because he had respect for his own.

What he knew about contemporary history and his own life was like a chest with a thousand drawers. Every now and then, he would open one and astonish me. And when he opened one drawer, you could tell a few more lay concealed below and might stay closed for ever. The riddle of Fereydoun deserves as close and careful a scrutiny as the riddle of Amir Abbas.

His experience and expertise as a novelist meant that he related every event with the clear narrative flow of an absorbing story. I heard from Golestan that when Fereydoun got hooked on writing science fiction, he studied complex theorems in math for a while so he could build his *vision* on firm scientific and mathematical foundations. The fact that he had spent years delving into Freud meant there was always an undertone of psychoanalysis not only in his novels but also his historical studies. In one of the short books that he had written in English after the revolution, he attributed one

of Iran's problems to the nation's historical attachment to
Rostam, the epic hero who kills his child yet deflects criticism.
He said that until such time as we recognize as a national
hero not Rostam but Kay Khosrow who gave up the throne
at the height of his reign, the vicious cycle of dictatorship and
patriarchy will continue to play out.

When relating the story of how he was summoned from
New York to Tehran to meet with the Shah, and how he was
driven directly from the airport to the Niavaran Palace where
the Shah met him in private and said he was looking for a
way to end the Vietnam war and requested that Fereydoun
contact his "leftist friends" in Paris and ask them to put him
in touch with the North Vietnamese embassy, he described
every element of his account – from his treatment by the
airplane staff to the Shah's expression when he reiterated,
"You may not share any of this with your brother" – with the
rigor and sophistication of a brilliant novelist. His readings in
psychoanalysis had convinced him that every word and every
sentence, every move intended or unwitting, was an ingress
into the thousand folds of the subconscious mind.

One day I asked him about Amir Abbas Hoveyda's
tenure at the Iranian embassy in Paris. My curiosity had
been aroused especially by the indictment against him in the
Sadeq Khalkhali *court*, where he was accused of smuggling
during his work as a diplomat at the embassy. In response,
Fereydoun made a reference in passing to his maternal
uncle Abdolhossein Sardari, saying he had saved the lives of
hundreds of French Jews. "Sorry," I said, "would you mind
repeating that name?" He repeated it. He then described the
story in more detail. I did not believe him. Maybe my denial
arose from a false sense of pride? How was it possible that
Iran had a Schindler and I had not even heard of him? Perhaps
it reflected a sense of inferiority among some of us Iranians

who do not defend and champion greatness and the great among us. Whatever the reason for my skepticism, I told him that because this important issue regarding a sensitive time in Hoveyda's life had been brought up by his brother, writing about it without corroborating evidence would almost certainly be seen as an attempt to exonerate Hoveyda. I asked him timidly, "Do you have any evidence to back it up?" He responded genially and sympathetically: "I have not told this story to anyone before, and I never looked for any evidence. But I know it to be true." He promised to try and find some records or living witnesses. A few months later he sent me a photograph of a commemorative plate. After the Jews who had been saved from the Nazis in Paris with Sardari's help returned to their homes and former lives, they had organized a memorial in his honor and inscribed the story, together with statements of gratitude, on a silver plate.

A few months later, I visited the diplomatic archives of the French Ministry of Foreign Affairs, hoping to uncover details of the indictment that Khalkhali's court had issued against Hoveyda for smuggling while at the embassy. I was given access to the extensive file on the subject – even though it was to have remained under seal for seventy-five years. When I finally read reports by the French police and official communiqués between Iran and France associated with the event, Sardari's name cropped up. It made me realize that Sardari was indeed a kind of Iranian Schindler. I also discovered later that my initial skepticism had little to do with my being an Iranian. When the book hit the shelves, the publisher sent a copy to the Holocaust Museum in Washington pointing out the Sardari connection. It took thirty years before the curators finally ascertained the extent of Sardari's role and hosted a commemorative event for him. Sometime before that, just when Mahmoud Ahmadinejad was spewing claptrap in his Holocaust denial, a film director in Iran produced a highly popular television series about the story. I never saw the series. A few years before it was broadcast in Iran, a young man at Berkeley contacted me and said he planned to serialize the story for TV. He asked if I would be willing to collaborate on the screenplay. Naturally, I declined. I had neither expertise nor experience in writing film scripts, nor had I any idea about the quality of his work. I still don't know whether that popular TV series was produced by that young man.

From day one, whenever I spoke with Fereydoun about Hoveyda's life story, he would say, "My only wish is for my brother to be released from the curse of this amnesia," or to borrow from Beyhaqi: "When might justice be done to that history?" The curse of amnesia on Sardari ended with that television series and a documentary and several articles that followed suit; I believe that in *The Persian Sphinx* and other books that were written about him later, Hoveyda was likewise released from the curse of amnesia and that it was Fereydoun Hoveyda who more than anyone else had "done justice to that history."

General Alavi-Kia

At the time I played back his first message, there were no mobile or smart phones around, only the type of devices that connect to the wall with a cable. We were not indentured to cellphones in those days and did not feel compelled to be perennially in touch with the world or eternalizing and socializing every dish we tasted and every scene we saw. The message light was blinking red when I entered the house, indicating a voicemail.

I pressed the button. An unfamiliar but friendly voice said something like, "I am Alavi-Kia. I have read your *Persian Sphinx*. I heard you are writing a book about the Shah." He didn't mention who had given him my number, and of course I never asked. "I have some information about SAVAK that I could share with you if you like." I had certainly heard of *General* Alavi-Kia. He had served as the first deputy director of SAVAK and starting in 1962, led its operations in Europe where the anti-Shah Confederation of Iranian Students had formed some two years earlier. I didn't know anything more, however, and thought he must have died a long time ago. I assumed it was a courtesy call from his son. At any rate, I called back right away.

A woman answered. I introduced myself and said I wanted to talk to Mr. Alavi-Kia. After greeting me with a graciousness that I later found to be very typical of her, she called out in a loud voice, "Hasan, Mr. Milani!"

A moment later, I heard him speak: "This is Alavi-Kia. I am grateful you called." I asked, slipshod: "Are you General Alavi-Kia's son?" "No," he replied. "I am Alavi-Kia himself." He dropped the "General." I was taken aback, somewhat embarrassed, and he noticed. I don't think it was because of his smarts as an intelligence officer, but had to do more with a sense of empathy. He said, "You're not the only one who thinks I died along with the Shah's regime." It did not take long before I realized he was a markedly decent human being, and the opportunity to meet him was among my greatest rewards for writing *The Persian Sphinx*. Between that first call and a few months before his death, I must have spoken to him for at least two hundred hours – at times in person in California and at times by phone. He placed information at my disposal of a kind I had literally never read or heard anywhere else.

The first time I met him, I felt apprehensive, having no idea what kind of a house or set-up I would be stepping into. The city where he lived was famous for its cadre of wealthy California residents and waterfront mansions. The house, however, turned out to be in a district of modest, uniform homes with neat, tree-lined lawns and tidy flowerbeds. The ocean was far away and out of sight. When I knocked, his wife opened the door. The living room I entered was plain, the furniture worse for wear and the walls bare, except for a splendid textile that hung in a frame. I did not inspect it too closely so as not to appear indiscreet. A wedding photo of the general and Jila Alavi-Kia in an inlaid wooden frame sat on a small side table. Persian confections – sundry nuts and dried fruits, sugar-plum candy, and toffee – tantalized on a large table. Mrs. Alavi-Kia showed me to a seat as she called out, "Hassan, come!"

One reason for my anxiety was that I didn't know whether one was supposed to wear a tie when visiting a high-ranking official of the former regime. Since my return to the U.S., I only wear one when attending a formal event or when giving a talk that will be broadcast in Iran. I finally decided on a dark suit and blue shirt – *casual business attire*, as they say in America. The moment he walked in, I regretted skipping the tie. He was wearing a simple and stylish suit with a tie in a handsome color and clean knot. He was not as tall and imposing as I had imagined. Immediately after exchanging greetings, I apologized for not wearing a tie. He said warmly and lightheartedly, "Well, that's our generational habit." I hurriedly pulled out my notebook and tape recorder and thanked him for making time for me. He, too, seemed anxious to get on and forego standard, time-consuming preliminaries. "Are you going to ask questions or should I just talk?" he said. "Please go ahead and talk," I replied. "If I have any questions, I'll interrupt if I may." I reckoned my questions would depend on what he talked about and how transparently. With memories of SAVAK in the back of my mind, I doubted I would dare ask too many. I was wrong on that score, too.

He talked about his friendship with General Hassan Pakravan and how both had landed in the army counterintelligence service. He added, "As you may know, that service was also known as *Rokn-e do* (Second Bureau)." I did not say that I knew this already and that I had also heard a great deal about its infamy. He talked about the direct line between the Shah and Pakravan who headed Rokn-e do and later SAVAK. He said one of his earliest *intelligence* responsibilities

was a weekly secret briefing with someone at the heart of
the Tudeh Party who had been introduced to the Shah by
Mozaffar Baqaie, the statesman who turned against his
former ally Mosaddeq and in 1953 helped restore the Shah
to power. Every week, the contact transmitted the party's
news to Alavi-Kia, who in turn shared it with Pakravan, and
he with the Shah. He promptly added that the Tudeh Party
had infiltrated the army; SAVAK had located and raided one
of the party's printshops where the *Abbasi codebook* – whose
discovery eventually led to identifying and decimating the
Tudeh Party's military network – had fallen into the hands of
one of their agents. However, that fellow was a double agent
and had managed to get the codebook back to his Tudeh
Party minder. It took another two to three years before the
codebook found its way back to the Shah's regime; they broke
the mathematical code that Khosrow Ruzbeh had developed, and almost the entire membership of the network was
arrested.

Finding every word he spoke fascinating, I both recorded
him and took notes. He spoke evenly and deliberately, with
dispassion and precision. It felt as if memories and images
had been stored away in his mind over a lifetime and now
that they were gushing out, he did not want to say anything
unsound by being careless or hyperbolic.

After a while, he said, "You must be tired. Shall we have
some tea?" Moments later, the general's daughter emerged
from her room and set down a pot of tea of just the right
color and aroma before us. Her father said, "I live here with
my wife and daughter. We own a small apartment in Paris."
He offered no details about his daughter's life, and I didn't
ask. I have read somewhere that he had three daughters,
Farnaz, Golnaz, and Tannaz. Which one owned that house,
I do not know. While sipping tea, the general said, "Over

here, we are with our daughters; over there, with old friends."
When heading toward our first meeting, I had thought that
surely an army general and co-founder of SAVAK must live in
a luxurious home. The simplicity of that house and its small
size surprised me. When in the same period I visited General
Manuchehr Hashemi in London – he had helmed SAVAK's
Eighth Bureau for a long time, battling Soviet espionage – I
was equally taken aback both by the humbleness of his flat
and his patriotism. I had heard that Teymour Bakhtiar who
was appointed the first chief of SAVAK in 1956, had lived in
impressive luxury not only in Iran but also later in exile. The
modest lifestyle of these two seasoned officers in contrast with
that opulence is something to chew on.

We were chatting and drinking tea when Alavi-Kia got
up, went to his room, and returned with a small tape recorder.
"I imagine you probably like traditional Iranian music," he
said. I said that I did but that I did not know it well and
was no expert. "I've made this tape for you," he said. "I
doubt if anyone else has a copy. We were in the company of
Nur-Ali Khan Borumand one evening; I taped him with his
permission." He then spoke of the venerable musicologist's
moral integrity; I later learned more about his extraordinary
virtuosity from Shajarian. Alavi-Kia also spoke about other
friends of his who were music buffs. Pakravan, too, counted
a lot of friends among intellectuals and artists. I heard that
from Sadeq Chubak himself who was part of Pakravan's
circle, sometimes even of the same opium demi-monde. Over
the next few years, General Alavi-Kia recorded an exquisite
collection of his favorite music for me on cassette tapes that
were current in those days and boxed in clear plastic so one
could watch the reels turning. Today, one can probably find
cassette players only in thrift stores though most tapes are
now widely available in new formats.

When he started to talk again, he spoke of the founding of SAVAK and the nature of his relationship with Pakravan and Bakhtiar. He described how he and Pakravan had hoped to create a sort of *thought chamber* – I don't remember the exact term he used – meaning a place where one might probe and discuss the country's problems freely and fastidiously and look for solutions. I asked if that was the time they hired Alinaqi Alikhani, then a graduate student in Paris who later rose to be minister of economy and chancellor of Tehran University. He confirmed it was. "In the beginning, I used to personally meet with and interview every candidate who was up for employment." He reiterated many times that Bakhtiar was not an *intelligence officer* but the director; the main work was done by himself and then deputy director Pakravan.

Once I realized that given his directness and honesty I could pose any question I wanted, I asked about torture and the number of informants they hired. Choosing to answer the second question first, perhaps because it was easier, he said, "Contrary to general perceptions, we collected most of our information not so much from agents as from people who volunteered information. One would be nosy, another vengeful, a third an opportunist, while a fourth might have their eye on landing a high post."

On the matter of torture, he began by making the point that from the perspective of *intelligence*, torture is essentially a nonsolution. He said the first group of SAVAK interrogators had mostly come from the Second Bureau where the branding iron was the currency of the day. Sometime later, I came across a file in the British Public Record Office titled "Torture in Iran." The file was dated 1957; the label read that it was under seal for seventy-five years. The archivists said I could submit a request justifying my reasons for wanting access to the file. I sent a letter to the Foreign Office saying I was writing a book about the Shah; that it had been twenty years since the monarchy was toppled and that establishing historical facts at this point in time took precedence over political expediency.

A few months later, they handed me the file in a room where I had been waiting, pencil and paper at the ready. What I found in those few pages was certainly worth the trouble and the wait. It was the transcript of a conversation between Teymour Bakhtiar and a British embassy delegate in which Bakhtiar described varied types of torture. He insisted that its scope was narrower than what the opposition claimed. At the same time, he acknowledged one case in which they had hauled a bear into a Tudeh'i prisoner's cell. The opposition had put it about that a bear had mauled an inmate; Bakhtiar claimed that, contrary to their claim, the bear had not done so. "It was enough to exhibit the bear at the cell door for the inmate to come unglued." That inmate had likened the royal court to a zoo, he said. "We had to punish him." When I read the file, I called Alavi-Kia. I told him about what I had found. He said that, overall, the file rang true, then added that not only does he not remember the details – he was now about ninety – but that Bakhtiar enjoyed notoriety and was not always to be trusted. "I don't know his motive for talking to a delegate from the embassy."

"Details aside, where did you find the bear?" I asked. He laughed. "Yes, the story of the bear is true. It was a cub that the son of General *Hāj* Ali Kia kept as a pet." He didn't mention it, but I knew that was the general who was stuck with the label "Whence your riches?" He enjoyed hunting in the Caspian Sea area. One time, he trapped a bear cub and gave it to his son as a gift. If I had the presence of mind, I would have said Hāj Ali had given a fresh and terrifying meaning to the Persian witticism "a trifle off a miser is a trophy."

Comments by the British embassy personnel on the report were as shocking to me as Bakhtiar's revelations. The first staff member to read it had expressed disgust about the Shah's regime in the margin and said they should tell the Shah as soon as possible to stop such acts. The farther up the ladder the figures who read the report the more muted their fury and the stiffer their pragmatism. I believe it was the foreign secretary who finally decreed that the issue of torture and this report should be brought up only if the Shah himself mentions SAVAK in a meeting. "Furthermore," he added, "what about the way we treat our Irish prisoners? It's not as if we offer them tea and sandwiches!"

I spoke with Alavi-Kia many times over several years. Mostly by phone. I used a notebook for recording our conversations. Sometimes he would remember a point and call, and sometimes I would call him if I had a question, such as about Bakhtiar's tête-a-tête with the embassy. He had no shortage of astonishing stories to tell. One time he talked about the propaganda war between Iran and the USSR. The Shah had invited a Soviet delegation to Tehran to conclude a twenty-five-year agreement. At the last minute, he pulled out of signing it, perhaps mostly under pressure from the U.S. and Britain. Instantly, Radio Moscow launched a barrage of virulent broadsides against Iran. The Shah dispatched Alavi-Kia to Germany to recruit an adviser adept at anti-communist propaganda. According to Alavi-Kia, the moment he presented the issue to the director of the West German "service," he replied, "I have a candidate who suits your needs." Alavi-Kia always referred to intelligence and counterintelligence agencies as "service." In *The Shah*, I wrote at length about that special adviser's visit to Iran. Citing both Alavi-Kia and material that I had found in German newspapers, I found that he had been one of the most notorious antisemitic and anti-communist operatives in Nazi Germany. Like many of his fellow ideologues who had honed their trade fighting communism, he joined the intelligent services in the West when Nazi Germany fell. There was an ongoing competition among such services to identify and recruit German experts not just to build an atom bomb and rockets but equally to enlist anti-communist experts. It was that adviser, by the name of Taubert, who according to Alavi-Kia first broached the idea of an army literacy corps in Iran. I later wrote in *The Shah* that when the USSR and Israel found out about Taubert's presence in Iran, they pressed to have him expelled on the grounds that he was a disgraced Nazi, and the Shah and SAVAK sent him packing. At the time, I tried to contact anyone that might have a clue about where Taubert ended up. No one was willing to talk. He had reportedly lodged at the house of a SAVAK officer the whole time he was working in Iran. Speaking on my behalf, General Alavi-Kia asked that officer who was then living in exile to agree to talk but was turned down.

Ten years after *The Shah* was published, I received an email that described what had happened to Taubert after he was banished from Iran. Sent on 15 May 2021, the message was not signed, though the content was compelling. According to the writer, until the day Taubert was alive, he was on assignment with SAVAK in various capacities and salaried. His last task was to collect and submit a daily report on any publications in Germany that covered Iran. Did people like Sabeti and Alavi-Kia and Hashemi whom I asked about Taubert really not know what had happened to him? Were the statements by the anonymous but evidently well-informed writer of the email to be trusted? I may never find the answer to these questions, but in raising such possibly unanswerable queries lies the charm and the challenge of studying history – a thousand certainties, speculations, cover-ups, and secrets kept and unraveled, that in their complexity make the historian's job of uncovering the truth like Sherlock Holmes's.

Some of the other stories that the general told me were no less astounding than the one about Taubert. He talked about his friendship with Abbas Saberi, who he said was KGB's star spy in Europe and yet close friends with people like Shahdokht Ashraf Pahlavi, Deputy Director of SAVAK Hossein Fardoust, Ebrahim Golestan, and Alavi-Kia himself. He said if it's true that Fardoust was affiliated with the Soviet service, the relationship would most likely have been established by Saberi when Fardoust was exiled to Paris during Mosaddeq's time; Fardoust was poor at the time and Saberi loaned him some money. When he told me about Hossein Yazdi, the son of a Tudeh leader Dr. Morteza Yazdi spying for SAVAK in East Germany, his story did not seem credible. But when the son published his memoir a few years later, his story was even more stupefying than Alavi-Kia's account of his life.

Yet despite his extensive experience, Alavi-Kia was suddenly forced to retire. He returned to Iran and became president of Hashem Naraqi's agribusiness company. Naraqi had come to Iran from the U.S. at the Shah's invitation and, according to both Alavi-Kia and Hashemi, fled Iran to dodge the maneuverings and menace of then SAVAK director Nematollah Nassiri and his deputy Fardoust. Alavi-Kia also spoke over a few sessions about the time an American adviser contacted him when he was deputy director of SAVAK and asked whether, if there was a coup against the Shah, he would agree and go along with it. Alavi-Kia asked for time to think about it. He told the Shah about it right away, who ordered him to say yes to the adviser so the Shah could learn about their plans. But the adviser never followed up. American records make it explicitly clear that the Kennedy administration had contemplated a coup for some time but finally dropped the idea. Did the Americans change their mind because they somehow found out the Shah was in on their plans? Did the Shah lose his trust in Alavi-Kia after that first American contact? A short time after the affair, he was packed off to SAVAK's bureau in Europe and a few years later, as he said with tears in his eyes, "They retired me in two short lines, though I had done nothing wrong."

Hossein Mohri

Editor-in-chief of some of the leading newspapers in the country as a young man, including *Ayandegan*, he was among the first journalists who braved the deluge of the revolution. The article that he addressed to Ayatollah Khomeini did not create such a stir as Mostafa Rahimi's but was just as audacious. After the revolution, he collaborated with Shapur Bakhtiar in Paris and ran his radio channel with Iraj Pezeshkzad for ten years or so. Bakhtiar had an office in Paris at the time and was the champion of national resistance against the Islamic regime in Iran and the institution of *Velayat-e faqih*, Guardianship of the Jurist. Following the assassination of Bakhtiar and with the regime regularly eliminating the opposition in France and elsewhere in Europe, Hossein Mohri was forced to leave – according to him on the advice of the French police – and moved to Los Angeles. After Bakhtiar's demise, it became public that their activities had been partially underwritten by the Iraqis.

To cite Mohri, everyone was up in arms against the new and violent Islamic dictatorship in those days; no one went around asking about their operation's source of funding. From the time he arrived in the U.S. until the final days of his life, he produced radio and television programs in that city and contributed articles to various publications. Making a living was sometimes a struggle, but his perspicacity and self-esteem ruled out complaining and seeking pity or charity. He was a clearsighted, gifted writer, eloquent, charismatic, learned and humble. As a journalist in Iran, he had a wide readership. "One of my most popular works was the series of articles I wrote from the viewpoint of prominent Western writers and thinkers," he said. "I knew their works and my essays were based on them, but the story and style were entirely mine; I adjusted their thinking to the conditions in Iran." It reminded me of Zabihollah Mansouri who was probably the single most popular contemporary Iranian writer. He wrote at least six hundred books, each of which was reprinted multiple times. Those that generated the highest sales were published as "translations" but were entirely the product of his own mind and pen. Just as Western products in Iran were regarded as superior to domestic ones, it appears Western minds enjoyed the same privilege.

Mohri did translations, too, of course, and they had a wide readership, just like his newspaper reports. With each targeted translation, it was as if he anticipated the events that were to unfold in Iran. He would envision what lay on the horizon and translate a book that was apt or necessary for understanding whatever was coming. He had profiled the Guardianship of the Jurist era in his translation of Gabriel García Márquez's *Autumn of the Patriarch* prior to the revolution. By translating the first volume of Simone de Beauvoir's *The Second Sex*, known as a foundational work in the feminist movement, he presaged the reality that in the last thirty years, women and their struggles for justice have been the vanguard and the bastion of democracy in Iran. A Nietzsche aficionado, he had mulled over his work and translated some selections into Persian. I never saw or heard him talk about his rich literary résumé, and any time someone mentioned his accomplishments in admiration, he would either hedge or try to downplay his own role and instead highlight that of others.

The first time I heard his voice on the telephone, the name was familiar but not the man himself.

The aura of many a well-known name diminishes in our mind the more we get to know the person. Mohri was the exact opposite. The more you knew him personally, the brighter the aura of his name. He was then the host of *Chehreh-ha va Gofteh-ha* (Profiles and Precepts), broadcast from Los Angeles, which was one of the most popular programs on the radio. I had heard its praises. The Persian version of *The Persian Sphinx* had come out only a few months earlier. He introduced himself in a kind and courteous manner that he would maintain in all subsequent conversations with me for the next twenty years until a short time before his death, and invited me to talk about the book on Monday at nine o'clock. I accepted on the spot. I had only talked about the book on a couple of programs in Los Angeles at the time, including those of Alireza Meybodi, and of Shohreh Aghdashlou and her husband Houshang Tozi.

He called on Monday, and as best I remember, devoted the entire program to the book. Thanks to his engaging conversation and exceptional skills in creating a relaxed and stimulating atmosphere, time passed so quickly, at least for me, that it didn't feel like we had been talking for some two hours. When wrapping up the program he said, "Well, we haven't finished talking about your book. If you're willing, we could continue our talk next week." I agreed and from then on, and for the next ten years until the radio station closed down, wherever in the world I happened to be, I would tune in every Monday and spend time with him on his show for about an hour. Once, right after telling the audience on the live show that I was talking to him from such and such a city he added that I traveled a lot, and that if he traveled as much, his wife would certainly divorce him. Later on, when he told me more about himself, I understood the extent of the complexities of his private life and the price he paid for an unexpected midlife romance.

When Radio Iran ran into a cash crunch like so many other diaspora media and eventually closed shop, Mohri's life also went downhill. A few months before the complete shutdown, the job of running the radio station changed hands from the father, Asadollah Morrovati who was its founder, to his son. Asadollah Morrovati was once a Majles deputy; he appreciated Mohri's value and had been a witness to his glory years. Morrovati's son did not value Mohri as he deserved. I once heard Mohri say it was a year or so since he had last been paid. He didn't say "salary," but "chicken feed," which without my asking, he said was eleven hundred dollars a month. He was on air five nights a week from nine to eleven-thirty. He could not drive, or perhaps due to various physiological issues, he would not, and instead used a special service that the state government provided for low-income residents. His nightly round trip took an hour each way. In spite of it all, he never mentioned his miserable lot until the very last straw. That moment coincided with the time the *Hovviyat* (Identity) program in the regime's *Keyhan* newspaper published a smear campaign against Mohri as a "mercenary" of imperialism.

In those days, I was on the executive board of the Pars Equality Center, founded by Bita Daryabari, which had just set up a branch in Los Angeles. I proposed they host an event to pay tribute to otherwise unsung exiles who lived in that city, the scope of whose past achievements was unknown to their fellow citizens, and to award each honoree a cash gift. Bita accepted my suggestion. Part of my motivation was that I knew Mohri would not accept assistance under any other circumstance.

In the ceremony, which was attended by many of the city's cultural luminaries, including Iraj Pezeshkzad and Hossein Hejazi, it was my good fortune to converse with Mohri after introducing him. The scene was an example of how the tables can turn. He answered my questions with a degree of humility and at times diffidence, which invariably colored his cheeks, his eyes fixed on the floor as he fidgeted with his hands. Whenever he spoke, his words were profound and often humorous. He had by then moved on to television. A skilled physician had recently helped him overcome a medical crisis induced by heart disease. He invited me to his weekly television program as well, which I proudly accepted. The people who ran the TV channel showered him with affection. They knew his worth and showed him respect. But he was all about talk and voice, not image and studio. The tie he was obliged to wear was always loosely knotted; it likely made it easier to breathe and perhaps unwittingly expressed that his sitting before a camera was involuntary. Nevertheless, given his robust experience conducting historic interviews in the past – more than eleven thousand, including his conversation with the Islamic revolution's infamous hanging judge Sadeq Khalkhali where he grilled him about the details of how he came to be hospitalized at the psychiatric ward at Fakhr-e Razi – each of his programs, despite his ever-debilitating fatigue and deteriorating heart condition, had a fluency and brilliance all its own. Toward the end of that run, he would sometimes drift off on the air. For me, those moments epitomized a disgraceful turn of the times that forced a decent and depleted human being like him to keep on working for a beggarly wage. Perhaps the director was also at fault for not moving the camera away from his face during those lapses. Or perhaps it was better that everyone should see the sad end of a man who had lived honorably, penned sagaciously, and refused to peddle his pen.

Jalal Matini

Three invaluable Persian-language journals dedicated to Iranian studies by the Iranian diaspora have appeared over the last hundred years. Jalal Matini was editor-in-chief of two of those publications. The first such was *Kaveh*, named after the mythical hero who rescues Iran from tyranny in the *Shahnameh* (Book of Kings). Largely funded by Kaiserreich Germany at the outbreak of World War I, the journal lasted for only a few years. Its most active member and principal leader was Hasan Taqizadeh. Many cultural luminaries of the time contributed articles to it, from Foroughi and Qazvini to Jamalzadeh and Kazemzadeh-ye Iranshahr. Notably, the first book on the economic history of Iran *Ganj-e Shayegan* (The Great Treasure) was a supplementary issue of *Kaveh*. Taqizadeh's collection of articles on the *Shahnameh* also appeared in the journal. The other two great scholarly journals, *Iran Nameh* (The Iran Report) and *Iranshenasi* (Iranian Studies) were edited by Jalal Matini whose accomplishments were no less significant. They were in circulation for about thirty years. Throughout that period and in every contingency, he was able to secure the patronage of the Iranian diaspora despite the toll that exile had taken on them at a time when assailing the Persian language and Iranian culture and identity was at the top of the Islamic regime's agenda, and he never abandoned his Iranophilia.

Most such donors did not even want their name to appear in the journals. One day, I was talking to a venerable individual, Ahmad Khayyami who for years was *Iranshenasi*'s main sponsor, having committed to funding the journal on the advice of Ahmad Qoreishi. A native of Mashhad and a well-known businessman, Khayyami was also familiar with the particulars of Matini's academic career at Ferdowsi University. When I asked him about his sponsorship of *Iranshenasi*, his eyes filled with tears. "We should not have ceded the country to those people," he said, then added without pausing: "It's the least I could do."

Although each of the two journals edited by Jalal Matini had the highest circulation among scholarly Persian-language journals, revenue never matched expenses. A constant budget shortfall is the cross that most scholarly journals have to bear, even as Matini ran the journals practically single-handedly. He was not only the chief editor but also the office assistant and subeditor and even the coordinator for distributing the journals to subscribers. He left the printing process in the hands of a few soulmates who appreciated the worth of *Iran Nameh* and *Iranshenasi* and were willing to shoulder type-setting and printing with minimal pay. Nevertheless, each set of the two quarterlies garnered an annual budget shortfall of seventy to a hundred thousand dollars. In the first years of its operation, *Iran Nameh* was subsidized by the Foundation for Iranian Studies, a nonprofit funded by the Shah's sister Ashraf Pahlavi. The foundation's genesis and progress were owing to the leadership and dedication of Mahnaz Afkhami who had served as the first Minister of Women's Affairs in pre-revolution Iran. Once it became clear to Matini that he could not continue as editor-in-chief – he shared the reasons with me, though only he can decide whether to disclose the details – he set up *Iranshenasi* under the auspices of the Kian Foundation and its namesake president, Dr. Kian Motahhari. At the time, in addition to sponsoring *Iranshenasi*, the Kian Foundation had built a large library in Los Angeles with a focus on Sa'di's oeuvre. It also operated a residence for literary guests who traveled to the city. Dr. Motahhari was a practicing physician with a zeal for the Persian language and literature. The first time I saw him was at a tenth-anniversary celebration of Matini's contributions and service to culture. His red jacket ruffled me. Later, I felt bad about being irritated by it. As if a fan of Iranian traditions is not allowed to choose the color of their jacket and must submit to my conventional taste. When the Kian Foundation was no longer able to provide funding due to Dr. Motahhari's unforeseen financial troubles, Ahmad Khayyami and others who had a passion for culture stepped in to ensure the journal's continuity.

The generosity of each of those Iranian patrons – and hundreds more donors to other philanthropic causes – upends the big lie perpetrated by those who harbored ill-will against Iranian émigrés then and even today. Breeding divisiveness and hopelessness, pessimism and mistrust of oneself and one's fellow citizens has been part of the perennial machinery of propaganda by dictatorial regimes. They know that solidarity and belief in the prospects of unity is the antidote to fear and factionalism, and that fear is the chief guarantor of a dictatorship's survival.

The secret of the unprecedented success of *Iran Nameh* and *Iranshenasi* lay both in Matini's scholarly and cultural capital and in his uncompromising commitment to upholding and even elevating standards in operating a first-class academic journal. The editorial board that he

assembled for each journal comprised the veritable elite
of Iranologists in Iran and internationally – from Ehsan
Yarshater and Zabihollah Safa and Jalal Khaleqi-Motlaq to
Mohammad-Jafar Mahjoub, Heshmat Moayyed, and Roger
Savory. Gholam-Hossein Yousefi, whose edition of Saʿdi's
Golestan and *Bustan* is the paragon of scholarship, was
Matini's friend from Ferdowsi University and his lifetime
adviser. They were also related. Each had married a sister
from the same family. Matini's second wife, Parvaneh Bahar,
was the daughter of historian, literary scholar, and "Poet
Laureate" *Malek o-Shoara* Bahar. Each article in *Iran Nameh*
and *Iranshenasi* was reviewed and edited by Matini several
times before it saw the light. He would not touch a single
word without consulting with and obtaining the author's
approval. In my experience, every suggested modification
and correction derived from erudition and deliberation and
close scrutiny. If he felt a submission was beyond his own
expertise and that of the journal's official advisers, he would
consult with others he believed had the requisite knowledge
and skill. Although both journals had an editor to handle
book reviews, he personally managed that feature as well. He
knew to whom to assign which book for reviewing.

By and large, every issue of *Iran Nameh* and *Iranshenasi*
carried one or more articles by Matini himself. In the beginning, his writings were in the main on literature. The more
distressed he grew by the turn of events, the more political
fantasies danced in the minds and on the tongues of fellow
Iranians, the more iconoclastic his approach became. By
sharing his personal experiences or delving into other Persian
sources, he periodically offered a novel interpretation of the
life and works of this or that figure. With a hardy animus
toward endemic superstition, he took every opportunity to

expound on that subject himself or urge a skillful writer to pen a lively piece to debunk sundry gratuitous yarns. For instance, he might ask a scholar to write about the ancient historicity of Iran and Iranian identity and demonstrate the imbecility of the Westmaniac illusion that the notion of Iran was concocted by Western orientalists. His essays on Ali Shariati, the influential Islamist ideologue whose verbal flourish matched his intellectual bombast exposed a veritable plethora of concerns previously unspoken. In 1964, when Shariati began teaching at Ferdowsi University under pressure by savak, Matini was dean of the Faculty of Literature where Shariati taught. The faculty prized Matini's leadership so highly that when the Shah allowed in the final years of his reign that university rectors be elected by the faculty rather than by the Shah or savak – first tested at Ferdowsi University – Matini became the first to be so elected. As expected, though, some students and colleagues were critical of him, saying he was too close to the regime. His fastidiousness about observing rules was well known. It was with that degree of focus and fussiness that he reviewed Shariati's appointment and conduct as a professor, candidly and without mincing any words. He spoke of Shariati's regular absenteeism in the classroom and his lack of discipline in performing his duties as a faculty member. When he thought the legend of Mosaddeq had lodged too firmly in the minds of Iranians without adequate deliberation, he spent months researching contemporary Persian sources and wrote a substantive book on the subject. He also wrote an article about the "nooks and crannies" of the life of Islamic philosopher *Seyyed* Hossein Nasr, a critic of modernity and its empirical rationalism. Throughout, Matini sustained his own lasting contributions to Persian literature, which was his area of specialty. He felt proud saying he was once a

student of the renowned Persianist Badi'ozzaman Forouzanfar
at Tehran University. At times, he also carped that he didn't
have enough time to focus on Persian literature.

After a while, Ahmad Khayyami fell ill and *Iranshenasi*
was suspended for a period. Many fans of the journal looked
for a solution so Matini could continue his work. They all
recognized that the journal was a vital flame whose extinc-
tion would mean a cultural blackout and loss. However,
Matini was not willing to accept any solution without considering what it might entail. He was cognizant of his own and
Iranshenasi's standing, his self-esteem prohibiting an indis-
criminate use of his name. He did not want the journal to
come under the control of individuals who might use it as a
political front or as a tool to satisfy their egos. In the end,
ill-health and fatigue caught up with him and he decided to
close it down.

As regards the impact of the journal's mission, I can only
speak for myself. From the first time I had published an article
in *Iran Nameh* and come to know the function and value
of the work of an editor like Jalal Matini, I grew increasingly eager for my work to be published in *Iranshenasi*. The
drive to have a piece in such a distinguished journal under
the oversight of an editor that erudite and caring, and alongside great authorities in Persian literature, was very powerful.
The closure of *Iranshenasi* left a void without a substitute,
at least for me. All efforts to fill the chasm, though earnest,
have fallen short. An immense undertaking like *Iran Nameh*
or *Iranshenasi* needs an editor like Jalal Matini – wise,
genial, meticulous, discriminating, hardworking, diligent,
and productive – and such editors are a rarity. These days,
he is living in a retirement home near Washington, D.C. His
daughter is his caretaker and closest companion. His thirty

years of nurturing *Iran Nameh* and *Iranshenasi* are as much a source of pride for the Iranian diaspora as the cessation of his work is a source of sorrow for any Iranian with a passion for culture.

Zakaria Hashemi

Zakaria Hashemi is a creative and audacious artist and a humble and unassuming human being. His passion for experimental art and risk-taking is insatiable and his humility outdoes humility itself. He is so free of the need for fame and riches he seems of the essence of Sufi characters such as conjured in Attar's *Tazkarat ol-Olia* (Memorial of the Saints).

I saw him close up only over the period of a few days. I had been planning for some time to invite him to Stanford University. But in the twenty years he had been living in Paris he had never obtained a passport. When he finally got one, he agreed to give a talk about his new book, *Cheshm-e baz, Goush-e Baz* (Open Eyes, Open Ears). The acuity, candor, and daring he displayed in that talk echoed the book's content to the letter. He paints a gut-wrenching and myth-shattering picture of the front lines in the Iran–Iraq war during the 1990s, yet there is not one iota of rage and fury in the book, nor was there in his words during the talk, and there still isn't. He describes the valor of young Iranian fighters with the same precision and dispassion as he does the depravity and corruption of some of the commanders. He does not sloganeer. He does not try, as some *committed* writers do, to force a fully digested thought on the reader (or an audience). He knows

213

that art does not preach and does not pitch. It presents and generates awareness. It makes the reader or audience think. The courage and freshness of his outlook in that book is his signature style as a restless actor, director, and writer and above of all, as an enormously creative and modest and lovable individual.

Before knowing anything about him as a person, I had seen his exceptional performance in *Khesht o Ayneh* (Brick and Mirror). Later on, I repeatedly heard Ebrahim Golestan sing his praises, saying how Hashemi had grasped the essence of the film more than any other cast member and played his role with especial diligence and skill. It was on Golestan's recommendation that I read Hashemi's *Tooti* (The Parrot). I felt bad that I had not read such an important novel before then – I had not even heard of it. After spending a few days with Hashemi himself and seeing and reading his other works, I realized that even Golestan's accolades fell short of capturing the full scope of his qualities and talents. Although his novels and films give away vignettes of his protean life, his modesty and demureness prevent him from readily talking about it. He neither seeks nor accepts pity, feigns neither heroism nor ingenuity. He does not extol martyrs, nor is he interested in putting on a martyr's act.

Born into a poor family in Shahr-e Rey to the southeast of Tehran, he worked as a laborer for a while. He turned up at Golestan's studio to audition for a small role in a production based on a story by Sadeq Chubak.

Golestan had been making a film based on Chubak's *Tangsir*, but then he transferred the rights to the screenwriter and director Amir Naderi. In any event, Golestan stopped shooting and did not make that film, but Zakaria Hashemi stayed on at Golestan's studio. All his life, whatever job he took on to make a living, he still found time to write on the side, whatever the circumstances. Forugh Farrokhzad, who was involved in Golestan's studio when Hashemi joined, read a chapter of one of Zakaria's works and urged Golestan to read it, which he did, and that marked the start of a friendship and collaboration between them that lasted till the end of Golestan's life. When *The Parrot* came out, its prose was so precise and well crafted, and the narrative so engrossing and groundbreaking, that a few "critics" looked for Golestan's hand behind Hashemi's outstanding novel. Perhaps in their narrow-minded and class-based minds, they wondered how someone without a college degree could have created such an original work, explored Tehran's *lower depths* better than Maxim Gorky detailed his wretched Russian enclave, and expressed the shattered lives of the oppressed women of the red-light district so empathetically and in such a wholly original way. There had to be more to it than met the eye! In fact, there was no behind-the-scenes hanky-panky, nothing ersatz to unearth. As Golestan made it clear over and over again, and sometimes with a wry laugh: "I had nothing to do with that novel. Zakaria gave me a draft to read before its publication and I read it and offered a few suggestions; *The Parrot* is entirely Hashemi's work and nobody else's." The episode was perhaps an illustration of the then polluted intellectual climate wherein critics met Golestan's unequivocal role in getting Akhavan Saless's *The End of the Shahnameh* published with silence but, by contrast, greeted his indistinct role in *The Parrot* with tall tales.

Hashemi was also a film director. Before the revolution, he made movies both for cinema and television. His film adaptation of *The Parrot* was never released and Tehran's red-light district, *Shahr-e No*, was set on fire by freshly minted revolutionaries. Seen through the lens of absolutists, a humanitarian view of women who sold their bodies out of

desperation was irrelevant. His greatest box office success was
Se-Qap (Three Crapshots), starring Nasser Malek Motiee and
Bahman Mofid and with a score by Morteza Hannaneh. The
story has a touch of Hedayat's *Dash Akol* and a slim veneer
of the popular movie genre, *Filmfarsi*.

Hashemi stayed in Iran after the revolution, believing
he would be able to continue his artistic and creative work.
When the Iran–Iraq war erupted in late-September 1980, state
TV asked him to make a documentary about it. Naturally,
his film had no appeal for the regime or its trumpeters and
eulogists. Hashemi made films with his eyes and ears open;
the regime preferred to see the battlefield through the cheer-
leading lens of Morteza Avini. In short order, he had no choice
but to emigrate, and left for France.

For at least twenty years, he worked as a chef in a Parisian
restaurant. "I'm not a bad cook either!" he'd say. During that
time, and after retiring from the restaurant business, he not
only wrote *Open Eyes, Open Ears* but several other books as
well. Among these, *The Final Execution* is likewise an original
mix of a historical account and a hypnotic novel. In writing
In Cold Blood, Truman Capote is said to have invented a new
genre of fiction based on facts now known as "faction." *The
Final Execution* is similarly a fictionalized retelling of a series
of murders, based on the taped confessions of an actual serial
killer who lured young men and then raped and murdered
them. He was finally caught and executed. The tapes fell into
Hashemi's hands by accident. Neighborhood kids had forced
their way into an abandoned building where they found the
tapes and passed them on to Hashemi, who resolved to turn
them into a novel someday. His latest work is *Ayyar* (Knight
Errant), also based on a real person, in this case a professional
thief in Iran who later emigrated to Europe and continued to
make a living by practicing his tried-and-true profession. To

understand the nuts and bolts of such an enterprise, Hashemi accompanied the *knight* in question on several burglaries in Paris. One time they were almost caught, he said; after that, he decided not to enter any home but watch the burglary from a distance. He is apparently writing a multi-volume memoir as well, with the first volume already published.

Naturally, he was vexed by the deplorable state of Persian book publishing abroad. When *The Last Execution* came out, a group of *committed* critics and readers raised hell and cried foul. They vilified Hashemi for portraying the life of a murderous sexual predator in detail. Not only did they overlook the novel's originality, but they dismissed its superb narrative structure as well, failing to acknowledge how the book's every phrase and sentence, along with the tapes on which it was based, were a mirror of the hardshisp and privations and shattered hopes of a neglected underclass of Iranian society. Both then and now, Zakaria Hashemi has had the courage and insight and talent and selflessness to describe reality without dressing it up, and nothing – from his family's indigence to the wretchedness of exile, from the myopia of critics to the tyranny of overlords – can stop him from continuing to search and explore and try to illustrate and help elevate the world, fortunately for us and for future generations.

Arshia Tabrizi

Arshia was a poet who became a lawyer. His outlook on the world was delicate and poetic. He approached every event not per se but as a gateway into larger meanings. Nevertheless, he built a career as a computer engineer, then a lawyer specializing in the nascent field of virtual law. But his virtual ideal lay in the domain of the written word. In his world of poetry, and above all in the universe of his sensibilities, each word and every event had symbolic and virtual meanings. The vitality of all literary works, and perhaps speech as well, is contingent on the breadth and interwoven layers of such meanings. In the sphere of law, the more restricted the sense of a word, and the more utilitarian, the more apt it is in a dispute. The computer language Arshia used as an engineer consisted only of ones and zeroes; in his poetics and soul, the breadth of his recall went from zero to eternity and knew no bounds.

But he was "a master of all trades" above all in being and watching and loving. Whenever I spoke with him, I was touched by his genuine warmth and at the same time knew that he was taking note of every particle of my being, every word and move, as if under a magnifying glass. He enjoyed

the good life but was also a lively observer of it. At least
outwardly, he seemed happy with everyday distractions – *la
vie quotidienne*, as they say in French – but was not seduced
by them. A hint of grief permanently lurked at the back of
his eyes. As Attar put it, everything has a price and the price
of reason is immense sorrow. In that sense, Arshia was highly
rational, but his reason, for which he paid a price, was not
merely utilitarian.

The first time I saw him was two or three years after
I returned to the U.S. I had not yet heard of his father and
mother who became my close friends later on. My financial
state in those days was dire. Some friends at Berkeley set up
an independent lecture course on modernity in Iran and the
West, mostly to help me out. The participants paid a registra-
tion fee and I offered them lectures over one academic term.
This was followed up by another course on contemporary
political thought. Arshia and a young woman whom he later
married took both courses. I did not know then that he was a
stellar cyber lawyer and worked in one of the most prestigious
law firms in Silicon Valley, the Mecca of cyberspace.

Arshia never spoke up in class. He did not ask questions. But there was a glimmer in his eyes that betrayed his
familiarity with the topics, the kind of glimmer that excites
teachers and lecturers everywhere. When I got to know him
better, I found out that the glow issued from his extensive
reading of the work of Nietzsche among other thinkers.

The other side of his character became clear to me years
later. In the days when he used to drive a long way to attend
my classes at Berkeley, Silicon Valley was sizzling. Legal firms
and startups were making gobs of money faster than they
could rake it. New wealth and ambition and luxury were
the name of the game. None of that appealed to Arshia,
however. He left everything behind and returned to Toronto.

That his parents were wealthy and he could be comfortable anywhere might have had something to do with his decision. I know children of affluent families whose financial security and freedom from want does not diminish their ambition and drive at all. He opened a law firm in Toronto where he advised startups on legal and technical matters and found a way to merge his passion for culture with his legal and computer-technology expertise. He built a firm that, as he put it, enabled good writing to be more widely disseminated and for users to be able to contact the authors directly to share their views and get feedback – a sort of virtual forum to enhance communication between the public and authors. The firm had just launched when Arshia fell ill.

Since high school, his talent and intellectual prowess had attracted top U.S. universities, which were always on the lookout for the most promising students around the world. He had emigrated from Iran to Spain with his family at age thirteen. He knew Spanish and English like his mother tongue. All his published poetry is in English, but in all those years, he never lost his love for the Persian language. He spoke Persian with his children, who were born in Canada. When he graduated from high school in Spain, Brown University, one of the oldest and most prestigious in the U.S., invited him to apply. Such invitations are normally sent to students whom the college has already decided to admit. It so happened that Brown had at the time surged in the rankings, a rise owed in no small part to the university chancellor Vartan Gregorian – an Iranian of Armenian descent who was among the most distinguished academicians and intellects in the U.S. But Arshia chose to go to Toronto with his family instead where he obtained his master's degree in engineering and then a doctorate in law.

Arshia never took any task lightly. He was not into sham or half-baked ventures. His knowledge and love of football in Spain were as earnest and deep as his passion for cinema. He watched the films that he loved over and over again. I discovered in person that he knew the lines of all his favorite movies by heart. He was a great fan of the Coen Brothers and could parrot all the best one-liners from *The Big Lebowski*. The parade of irony in the movie is spectacular. Perhaps irony was a means for Arshia to ease his inner sorrow.

When *Sea of Snow*, a collection of his English poems, was published, I attended the book launch at a Toronto bookstore at Arshia's invitation. Also at his invitation, I had written a brief foreword to his book. The rigor of his poetry was truly admirable. His cultural presence in the city was plain to discern, considering the number and the diversity of guests at the book launch, including the director of the Toronto Film Festival and his academic colleagues. The first time I came within the purview of his presence and weight was when *The Shah*, the English version of my *Negahi be Shah*, had just come out and the University of Toronto had invited me to give a talk. On that trip, all major TV channels in Canada – an Iranian was the anchor in one of them – signed me up for interviews. I had no doubt that Arshia's prestige had played a role in those invitations. His modesty, however, would not even let him concede he enjoyed such renown.

When at the height of his youthful vigor he was suddenly struck by an advanced stage of cancer, he never quit fighting back nor, as far as I could see, begged or pressed for pity. On the contrary, whenever he noticed the pain in someone's eyes, it was he who offered solace. He went on to live many months longer than his prognosis. His fighting spirit and his family's support were key, as were the doctors, every one of whom grew attached to him, knowing him to be a rare species who had fallen prey to a deadly and ruthless tumor. Or perhaps the real tumor was a reality such as is evoked in the age-old Persian poem: *Alone among a hundred thousand / Without a hundred thousand alone.*

Hasan Milani

Hasan is a born smith and craftsman who became an engineer and a business executive. Enormously gifted and skilled in all four areas, he is also consummately persevering and diligent. Our mother became "heavy with child" eleven times. Five survived the then common fate of child mortality. Hasan was the second child and I the fourth. One of the children – probably my sister Farzaneh – had once asked our mother in a sympathetic tone whether it was difficult to have had so many pregnancies. She had smiled and replied nonchalantly, and perhaps a little testily and teasingly, "No, it wasn't difficult. We'd squat, and the baby would drop." Naturally, if half the children – or half the "burden" carried during pregnancy – were expected to die, no excessive attachment to the fetus or child would set in. Had anyone intuited Hasan's disposition at birth and his survival, they would have predicted the extraordinary arc of accomplishment through the rest of his life.

My memories of childhood with my brothers and sisters are filled with fun and mischief and their occasional if futile efforts to turn me into a better student. My sister who was always first in her class was more my mentor than the rest. One time in sixth grade, after I twice failed to earn a

French-language certificate of the kind issued by the French embassy in Tehran, my younger brother Mohsen perched on my chest teasingly and made me promise I would pass the test the next time. I passed the third time round, with my sister's help and to keep the promise to my brother. But my memories of my brother Hasan in those days are mostly of my wonderment at his paintings and handicrafts and other inventions.

From the earliest memory of him etched in my mind, Hasan painted. He also had elegant handwriting. A work by Kamal ol-Mulk hung on the wall in *Daie* Jalal's home. One day Hasan made a bet he could make an exact copy, and that replica later hung on a wall in our house. I believe he made a couple more copies for other relatives. Later, in exile, we once talked about Parviz Kalantari's original paintings of rural earthen houses. The next time I visited Hasan and his wife Mahvash, a copy of a Kalantari was hanging on their wall. When his talent and skills proved to be unquestionable, he signed up to study under the famous artist Mohsen Soheili. We used to pass by Soheili's studio on our way to school and I would look at the window display with pride knowing one was by Hasan – a painting of a creek with autumnal trees that looked as beautiful as their reflection in the water. His handicrafts were also a marvel to behold – especially for a clumsy person like myself.

When Pepsi-Cola first came to Iran, the factory owners who were well versed in modern marketing, launched a contest for the best original maquette of a Pepsi bottle. Hasan carved one from a piece of wood and masterfully painted its polished surface. His finished model earned him one of the three prizes awarded, which he received in a ceremony broadcast on television. It was the first time I had seen a relative or a familiar face on TV.

Hasan's craftsmanship was not limited to paintings and sculpture. One time, one of the women in the household had bought an expensive dress. I think it was made in France. They pored over the exquisite finesse in its design and stitching; that is why it was so expensive, they said. Hasan made a bet that if he could find a similar fabric, he could make the same dress and nobody would be able to distinguish the domestic from the foreign. As best I remember, he won the bet. One of my most painful childhood memories is also tied to Hasan's talent and abilities as a craftsman.

A common pastime in those days – and a standard class assignment in "handicrafts" at school – was building a model of the Eiffel Tower using plywood and a coping saw. Perhaps the trend rose out of a subliminal foreign hype that had turned the Eiffel Tower into the ideal structure – a concept we wrangled with for weeks on end – in our heads. Perhaps that tower's dominating presence in the painting that Parviz Kalantari drew when I left Iran was a residue of that history. In any event, after weeks of effort, Hasan built a fine and beautiful model of the Eiffel Tower that was about three feet tall. One day, I got a brotherly smacking from Hasan for some reason I don't remember. As a rule, it would have been my fault because I don't remember him smacking me much for no good reason. I ran to my mother weeping and whining. My mother was close to Hasan since our childhood. Their relationship grew twice as close as my mother aged and declined. She was a staunch believer in the power of a parent's damnation and a mother's prayers and, after she fell ill, told me time and again that Hasan would for sure achieve success in the future "because of the love he showers on me and his father." But on that day, seeing me cry, she went out to the yard. She summoned Hasan for a whacking in retribution for having beaten me up. Needless to say, Hasan was not keen to be whacked. My mother chased him around the yard for a bit. There was a large shallow pool in the yard, a "swimming pool" in our lingo, where we used to splash about all summer. Hasan took a position on one side of the pool. My mother chased him around a couple of times but could not catch him. She gave up and went inside, before returning with Hasan's Eiffel Tower. She stood on the opposite side of the pool across from him, the Eiffel Tower standing next to her in all its delicate grandeur. Zizi *Jan* said, "If you don't come forward on your own, I'll smash your tower." Hasan did not budge. I think he, too, like me, assumed our mother was merely bluffing. But she never made empty threats. Hasan did not come forward and my mother, angry and intent, smashed up that product of weeks of toil. I stood watching in disbelief and crying. Even now, whenever I remember that scene and the agonizing sound of the plywood cracking and Hasan's stunned expression and tear-filled eyes, I get a lump in my throat. I feel guilty that I whined about him to my mother.

Of course, Hasan's craftwork was more often a source of joy and entertainment for me and my other brothers and sisters. He was the originator and architect, for instance, of our first experience with "home movies." Having fashioned a makeshift film projector out of some magnifying glasses, light bulbs, and pieces of wood, he then covered the large dining-room table with a blanket and turned the space underneath into a movie theatre. Putting up with the heat and the crammed space was worth watching John Wayne and Rita Hayworth in action. He bought the overused film strips on Shahreza Avenue and Darvazeh Dolat.

Hasan was the only one among us children to have a bicycle. I don't know how he acquired that bike; it certainly wasn't a gift from my father or mother. He sometimes lifted me on the saddle behind him and rode around the yard. He had also learned how to repair and clean the bike. I don't know why, but in those days bicycle makers were reputed to be pedophiles; therefore, interacting with bike peddlers was not only frowned upon in our household but prohibited. Sometimes, I would sit by Hasan and watch him repair his bike full of admiration, and perhaps envy. One time, he was testing the rear wheel by spinning it suspended in the air. Unthinkingly or curious, I pushed my left hand into the spikes and broke my little finger. Sixty years later, that day's insignia is still emblazoned on that jagged nail.

Besides ingenuity and talent and perseverance, the other secret of Hasan's success in every domain of his life is discipline and forward planning. He called one day when I was coming to the U.S. from Iran. "I have a favor to ask," he said. In our life, it was usually I who needed a "favor" from him; this was one of the rare instances where he wanted something from me. "There are two notebooks in storage at our parents' house that I'd like you to bring for me." I knew one large room was filled with boxes where Hasan had left his belongings before leaving Iran. "Of course, dear Hasan," I said. "But you know my flight leaves in two days. How am I going to find anything among all those boxes?" He said, "That's easy, they're in such and such a box." Then he gave me the box number; I realized he had numbered them all. "You'll find the two notebooks in such and such folders in the box." "You know those details by heart?" I asked, stupefied. "I listed the contents of the box when I filled it up and brought the list with me." Knowing him to be a skilled and organized engineer, I had no doubt that his numbering of the box and its contents was accurate. I found the two notebooks exactly where he had indicated. He added that the notebooks were benign. "They're the daily planner of the last two years I lived in Iran." In those days, travelers' luggage used to be scrupulously inspected at the airport; they were looking for gold coins and evidence of being a *taghuti* (idolatrous). I think Hasan's explanation was meant to give me peace of mind.

Once I boarded the plane, I pulled out one of the note-books. Its precision and order and detail were amazing. Each appointment, each meeting, and each task that he had to perform on any day was inscribed and color-coded. There was a mark before each as well. When I saw Hasan, I asked him about the colors and the markings. He said he color-coded each task in accordance with its urgency. Of course, there were also routine daily to-dos, like, "call parents at eight o'clock sharp." Every task was checked once it was done. I later learned he has notated every day of every year of his life in this manner and still does. He still calls members of the family at certain times every day as well as friends, some close to him since childhood, and sometimes colleagues. He still reaches out to them at a specific hour to say hello even if for only a few moments. It is as if every friendship and every family relation is a seedling that needs to be cared for and tended to on a regular basis.

That same attention and exactitude, planning and punc-tuality, applies to all his activities, including his extensive philanthropy. He is deliberate and unrushed. He does not put on an act. Nor does he stand on ceremony. He looks at every organization that he supports in depth, and he cannot be fooled either. While he has devoted most of his first sixty years to commercial and industrial ventures and accumulated a considerable fortune, he plans to donate the major portion of his wealth to various causes during his lifetime, evidently with the agreement of his wife Mahvash. He supports any cause he believes is deserving, from student scholarships to a ship-cum-hospital that sails around the world and treats poor people who need surgery gratis in its well-equipped operating theaters. In terms of the percentage of donations based on wealth, I know hardly any Iranian who has given as much to charitable causes as Hasan. A few years ago, he gave forty percent of his total assets to Stanford to underwrite scholarships for Iranian students, especially those whose studies are focused on Iran.

The arc of the ups and downs, the failures and successes, in Hasan's life mirrors that of other talented Iranians who came to the West to pursue higher education without relying on family or government support, and who after completing their studies returned to Iran filled with hope, and following years of helping advance the country, ran into the dead-end of the revolution and were forced to emigrate. A few weeks after earning his master's degree in engineering in the U.S., having previously gained work experience at Ford with a B.Sc. in engineering, he packed all his belongings, including the LPs of his favorite artist Frank Sinatra – he took me to one of his last concerts – and sailed to Iran on the last voyage of a liner named after the Queen of England. Based on Iran's "Special Plan for Professors," he did his military service in the army and for a time taught at the new Institute of Science and Technology. He was contemplating an academic career but then decided to join the private sector. He became the CEO of Arvandan, a company headquartered in Abadan that built ships for the Iranian navy. When Abadan was occupied by Iraqi forces at the onset of the Iran–Iraq war, Hasan told me how he watched U.S. television coverage of the soldiers dismantling the shipyard and hauling the equipment away to Iraq. "I broke down in tears watching that scene," he said. The first step in dismantling the factory had in fact been taken before the Iraqis ever plundered Arvandan. The Islamic regime had confiscated all the assets of the Fouladi brothers who owned the company. The fate of top management, even the most unimpeachable among them, hung in the balance. Some of them were arrested; others fled abroad out of fear. Hasan was among the latter group. When he arrived in the U.S., he had no qualms about doing what it took to support himself and his family. Just as in his student days, he worked in a restaurant for a while. After some time, he took out a loan and bought a mill for repairing industrial refrigerators from its aged owner. As in his past life, he showed up at work at four o'clock every morning. He worked harder than any of the manual laborers and knew every detail of the operation. With perseverance and diligence and integrity, he grew that small firm into one of the largest manufacturers of industrial refrigerators in the U.S.

Though he has built a successful career and a comfortable life in exile – trials and tribulations notwithstanding – the hold that Iran has over him is still strong and hard to resist. Time and again, I have heard him say, "If the day ever comes when I can return to Iran without fear, free from the pall of anxiety, I won't hesitate for a moment. I'll buy an orchard on the north coast and devote myself to philanthropy and art."

Once, in search of something closer, he told me, "I want to sell my business, buy a spot in Italy, and spend my days painting and sculpting." He had even compiled a list of the master craftsmen he longed to learn from. Long ago, he had drawn up a bucket list of fifty dreams and ambitions. He told me he had achieved all but two. I imagine one of the two was the orchard – a place where he could retire to a life immersed in his creative and philanthropic ventures.

Whenever I think of that orchard and of the dreams it holds for him, I am overcome with an even deeper longing for the Iran he and so many like him yearned to create. But then, the catastrophe that happened, happened.

PART 2

Farzaneh Milani

The earliest and sweetest memory of my childhood is spun out of the empathy and moral support of my big sister Farzaneh. Of all my mother's array of punishments the most terrifying, at least for me, was to be banished to the coal bunker, a cramped space etched in my mind as a spine-chilling cavern. A Persian colloquialism for a coal bunker is a dungeon. The floor and walls of the "dungeon" in our house were blackened with soot. Because it sat under a stairwell, it had a steeply slanting low ceiling. Entering the heart of that darkness obligated a lowered head. If, according to Freud, the womb was akin to paradise to the unborn, in my infantile mind that dungeon was synonymous with purgatory. Our entire load of coal for the year was stored in that bunker, enough to heat the samovar, the kabab grill, and the *korsi,* the coal-heated, blanket-topped low table around which we sat with outstretched legs to keep warm during cold winter nights.

I don't know what I had done to make my mother banish me to the dark side, and my mother's decree was absolute. I headed to the dungeon with a fluttering heart and teary eyes. Once inside, I stuck by the door so the light filtering in through the cracks might allay my fear of the darkness. The soot-blackened wall was right in front of me – standing in that position was considered part of the ordeal. All of a sudden, the door opened and Farzaneh walked in. "I'm here so we can be together," she declared and turned to face me with her back against the wall. As she held my hand in hers, the darkness became bearable. She stayed with me to the end of my sentence. I did not know it then, but that experience was to epitomize the entire arc of my life with Farzaneh.

Half a century later, this time not at my mother's bidding but owing to a medical diagnosis, I was banished to another dungeon, this time at a hospital, the modern purgatory. Thanks to Hamid Moghadam's keen and fortuitous observation of a tremor in my hands, I had been to see a doctor and after tests and imaging in a coffin-like device, a tumor was located in my brain. It required a nine-hour operation that revealed it to be a rare type of tumor that grows in the fetus but does not manifest earlier than age forty or fifty. In all probability, my mother's stroke was caused by a similar tumor. Removing mine required a complex and dangerous operation. Farzaneh was by my side from two days prior to surgery until a few days following my discharge after a week-long stay in the hospital. I learned later that to be there she had canceled a trip to a conference that she had long planned for. Other family and friends, too, extended kindnesses, some traveling long distances to keep me company. But to me, Farzaneh's canceled trip and her presence at my side was a replay of her decision to share my childhood banishment to the coal bunker. It is a stroke of good fortune that in between these two events and throughout my life, a gracious and sophisticated person like Farzaneh should have been my patience stone and backbone and refuge and consoler and companion.

One day, several classmates were beating me up in a hallway at school. Childish animus was all it was about, but someone reported it to Farzaneh. The moment the kids caught sight of her, they stopped immediately and scattered. Our school was small and co-ed and went up to fourth grade. Everyone knew Farzaneh to be the darling of the formidable principal, Madame Marika. They knew that if Farzaneh breathed a word, the perpetrators would be the target of the her terrifying rage. Madame Marika's physique and condition belied her might. She was stocky but stooped and confined to a large wheelchair in which she moved around. Her right arm, crushed and paralyzed, hung in a sling over her chest, close to her heart. Rumor had it that someone who was in love with Madame Marika when she was young had seen her with another man and shot her, and that she had deflected the jealous man's bullet by placing her hand over her heart. An emancipated woman wheelchair-bound for life was the price paid for a deranged lover's selfish sense of honor. That said, Madame Marika, especially when she made the rounds in the yard with her dog, was a force of nature. In all the years we attended her school, Farzaneh was a star pupil. As for me, I failed the very first grade and in the following years needed help from my sister and the private tutors that my mother hired. After every exam, Farzaneh was emphatic that she had done very poorly, but she was proved wrong every time.

In the orthodoxy of literary criticism and political thought in recent decades, a convention took hold to reduce women to irreconcilable polarities. The literary version was the saintly female versus the slut, and the political version was the rebellious, aggressive feminist versus the traditional, docile and servile female. The former of these binary constructs is the product of the mindset and inclination of men who look for myriad causes and culprits to explain historical discrimination against women but who do not recognize or acknowledge patriarchy and men's hunger for power and privilege as responsible and culpable. The latter construct is rooted in the belief among women who maintain that millennia of female oppression and domination can only be reversed through revolt and nonconformism and misandry. Frantz Fanon wrote that Blacks who have been haunted by the curse of racism and have "internalized" the racists' dehumanization can only be liberated by killing their appropriated "Whiteness." By "killing," Fanon meant a notional and psychological act. An even more radical iteration of that view was formulated in the 1960s by a Black American revolutionary named Eldridge Cleaver who held that liberation from the curse of racism required the actual killing of Whites. While he turned into a staunch conservative during Reagan's presidency, the ideas that he promoted in his youth persisted. Along the way, or perhaps because of the resurgence of such thoughts, some radical feminists have advocated that the internalized patriarchy of the female can only be overcome by killing the "male."

Anyway, the apostles of both extreme positions have developed a particular style of comportment and speech, even a dress code, for their "type." Farzaneh, however, does not fit in either bipolar model and does not brook their mandated air and style and judgments. I have never seen her back a woman, per se, either in a relationship between two people or in critiquing a literary text. In fact, she holds that misogyny and forced hijab shackle not only women but men as well. That may seem paradoxical, but her personal yardstick is based not upon theoretical or political doctrines but upon the collective values and code of ethics that she herself upholds. The pillar of these values is equality between men and women and the need for both to free themselves from the stranglehold of patriarchy. Attaining that state entails resistance but not misandry.

She has spent the greater part of her life introducing and analyzing the works of female Iranian writers and poets and photographers from a feminist perspective with due theoretical polish and structure. Whether writing about Qorrat ol-Ayn's poetry or researching Daneshvar's novels, she has never been beholden to conventional niceties or demands. When she was editing an anthology of studies on Simin Daneshvar, she tracked down Daneshvar's professor and adviser from her student days in the U.S. and invited him to record his memories of that trailblazing Iranian writer. To go by the published letters of the likes of Daneshvar and Simin Behbahani, Farzaneh established close relationships with many individuals about whom she wrote in depth. Despite, or alongside, her sterling feminist accomplishments, she also indulges in fashionable clothing, as well as cooking and motherhood and grandmotherhood. She takes and gives no quarter on the basis of her gender. She establishes her voice and makes her mark – in professional and social spheres as well as in personal relationships – not as an angry litigant but in a mixture of assertive scholarship and humanity, fairness and sound leadership.

Part of the secret of her success – aside from her natural empathy, her ability to listen patiently to what others have to say and the balance that results from the combination of those two traits – is her admirable facility in reading people's expressions and in grasping the intricacies of their speech and writing. I witnessed as a child how my mother would make a slight movement with her eyes or eyebrows as she stood amid a group of guests and Farzaneh would instantly know that she wanted her to fetch this fruit on that platter to offer round. When in a group, Farzaneh mostly observes in silence – unless she's had a glass or two, in which case her peals of infectious laughter will light up the room. But even when she is silent, one can tell that she is keenly and meticulously studying every subtle detail in the exchanges around her and as reflected to perfection in her own writing, expresses her views in a delicate and clear manner that is never coarse or harsh. The secret of her success also lies in the fact is that she never looks for a shortcut in any task she undertakes, for they only result in mediocrity. Perhaps mediocrity is what makes people look for shortcuts in the first place.

She approaches every task with deliberation and scrutiny, rigor and constancy. If she is to give a talk for half an hour, not only does she work on it to the point of exhausting the subject but she will read her lecture aloud at least once before-hand to make sure it does not overrun the allotted time. After researching the life of Forugh Farrokhzad for four decades, she finally convinced Ebrahim Golestan who until than had declined to give an interview about his former lover Forugh, to sit down for a chat. Golestan found Farzaneh's incisive and at times tough questioning so gratifying that when the fourteen-hour tape of the interview was bizarrely lost in the British mail system, he agreed to a repeat exchange. I noted how Farzaneh weighed every poem by Forough, and every dialogue and every second of her film *The House is Black,* over forty-odd years. She translated some of Forough's poetry into English. She talked to every character (or crank) who knew or claimed to know something about Forugh. She heard everyone and did not accept any statement wholesale. She fastidiously picked every line and every word in her *Forugh Farrokhzad: A Literary Biography With Unpublished Letters* (2016). She wanted to say what she had to say with economy and precision. At the same time, she worried about being misunderstood and constructed each sentence in such a way as to avert misinterpretation as far as possible. Of course, it wasn't averted and the book ignited a firestorm. True to form, though, Farzaneh did not indulge in controversy. She left the original text, not the critics' and claimants' marginalia, to people's judgment and, ultimately, to history.

Such care and integrity are manifest in all her pronouncements as well, as if she drafts every sentence in her mind first and utters only the finalized version. At the same time, there is not a whiff of ostentation or gratuitous oversight or expedient correctness in her speech. The gentleness of her tone and the clarity of her voice belie their candor and courage. In appearance and manner, she is compliant; to cite Saʻdi, she does not seek confrontation. Nor will she shy away from defending her rights – or if she hears of others' rights being trampled. It does not matter whether such trampling has occurred to a colleague on campus or at a famous restaurant in their university town. Farzaneh appreciates culinary delights. She once took a course in Europe on the history and variety and characteristics of fine wines. One evening, she was having dinner with two likewise epicurean colleagues. But the food did not live up to their expectations and they argued so vigorously with the owner – who also happened to be the chef and who, like many chefs, was not sans affectation – that he bounced the three of them out of the restaurant and told them never to come back again.

I read in Jung that the mark of passage from childhood to adulthood is understanding and accepting the reality that life is not a game, nor instant gratification its purpose. He said the ability to delay gratification today for tomorrow's reward is the definition and exigency of adulthood. Farzaneh has had that ability since childhood. That trait, plus her eschewing of the obsolete polarity of saintly female and unruly slut, has made her enormously endearing as a person.

One time, I woke up to the sound of my phone ringing an hour after midnight. It was a dear friend and gifted poet.

He used to drink a lot. That night, too, I could tell from his undulating speech that he was tipsy. "I'm in love with your sister but she snubs me," he said without preamble. Perhaps the courage to blurt out something like that boldly and spontaneously was prompted by intoxication. I laughed. I was touched by his words for various reasons and liked him all the more. I approved of his taste, for Farzaneh is both beautiful and smart and a free spirit. But Farzaneh's husband was alive at that time and the amorous poet knew that. I liked it that he was not bound by the patriarchal notion of "honor" and had shown me respect by sharing his feelings and recognizing that I too did not abide by such codes. I promised to pass his message along, and I did, and Farzaneh passed it up with a chuckle. She said something like, "O well, Abbas *Jan*, he must have been joking." In our times so full of adversity and mendacity, friendships are either utilitarian or they sooner or later succumb to the altered status or changes in the life of one or the other person. Farzaneh exhibits unconditional loyalty in relationships. Many of her childhood friends who used to visit us at home – and I admired them not always innocently but with infantile fantasies – are still her dearest friends even though their views and lifestyle may have changed and their paths diverged over the rocky course of life. Also, more than any other family member as far as I'm aware, she stays in touch with relatives near and distant.

Sisterhood or brotherhood is not a conscious choice but a natural charge. Having a sister the constancy of whose affection is as solid as her intellect is an immense blessing. For as long as I can remember, I have been blessed thus and felt grateful. That day in the "dungeon" was a part that represents the whole.

Nasser Shadman

Dostoevsky had never met *Daie* Nasser but it is as if he had modeled his great novel, *The Idiot*, about Jesus Christ on my uncle. His madness was above all rooted in his goodness and nobility and guilelessness. There was no room in his soul for aggression and animus. He was as one, both inside and out, his love of an abject prostitute as innocent as his love of God. But of course, Daie Nasser never claimed the mantle of a messiah. Was his madness a means of confronting the lovelessness of the times, or was it its consequence? In any event, for us children who loved him, his presence and persona were a joyful sanctuary removed from the lumbering protocols and mores in force during my childhood.

Daie Nasser had a curious relationship with time and space. He wanted to master time and traverse space. "Taking a ride" was among his cherished pastimes. He would buy a ticket from Tehran to Qazvin, the city where he spent most of his life at Daie Kamal's house, and barely having arrived, return to Tehran, on the same bus. Everyone in the family believed he was blessed and that his prayers would always be answered. He, too, believed in the power of his prayers. At the same time, he wasn't into dispensing them for free. It is said that due to the prophet of Islam's mercantile career, the

243

Quran teems with terminology related to commerce. In that vein, Daie Nasser perceived his prayers not as holy gifts but as transactional commodities. If, for instance, he believed that my passing a school test was a product of his prayer, he would demand instant compensation. If delayed, he would say, "Was I your serf that I should have prayed for you?" There was of course no greed in him. His most cherished reward was a round-trip ticket to Mashhad. His relationship with time was as strange and fixated as his obsession with taking rides. Both were, I believe, corollaries of his disorder, a metaphor of its root cause and how society responded to mental illness.

I never found out the nature of Daie Nasser's illness, perhaps because at the time mental illness was not recognized as a pathology in Iran. When I was a child, my mother and other charitable women in the family would occasionally shop for confectionery and cigarettes and roasted seeds and take them to the "lunatic asylum"; it was sort of a trip to wonderland, not particularly safe either. Dr. Ebrahim Chehrazi had built the first psychiatric hospital in Tehran. I know Daie Nasser was confined there for a while. His tenure was short. After a few days, he made his getaway over a wall. In the Middle Ages where insanity was feared and thought to be diabolic, people who showed signs of "lunacy" were ostracized. They were purportedly dumped in a boat and left to drift around in the water. Daie Nasser drifted himself around in space. Certainly, his big-wheel brothers, while providing him with everything he needed, did not wish to be "dishonored" by his lunacy. Daie Kamal and his family looked after him in Qazvin most affectionately. When Daie Nasser came to Tehran, my grandmother tended to him dotingly while she was alive. Once, when Daie Zia slapped Daie Nasser to lull a frenzied rage, my grandmother forbade him – her youngest child and mayor of Tehran at the time – from visiting her.

The embargo ended a few months later with the mediation of Daie Jalal and my mother and due apologies from Daie Zia. When my grandmother died, my mother stepped into that role and our house became Daie Nasser's sanctuary in Tehran. When in Tehran, he naturally enjoyed visiting Daie Jamal too. Daie Jamal was an army colonel until he had a stroke. Claiming that had been entitled for a promotion to general, a rank he was apparently on the verge of attaining before his stroke, he called himself "General" and dressed as a brigadier general. A charming character, he lived in Sar-Sabil on the west side of town and had a wide assortment of friends. He used to bounce Daie Nasser into his army jeep and drive him around all the time. For me as a child, his house was likewise a Shangri-la, for one of Daie Jamal's daughters was then the love of my life. At any rate, whether over there or in our house, Daie Nasser was always preoccupied with his other obsession.

Daie Nasser's other obsession was time. As far as I recall, it started when I was a child and persisted throughout his life. One day, for reasons best known to himself, he decided to produce a calendar. Perhaps he thought that if he inscribed one in his own hands he would gain control of time; the calendars that were available in those days and carried corporate or banking ads would not do. Not only would he write down each date, but he also cut the paper to fit, making the sheets into small squares for every day of the year, each square about the size of the palm of his hand. Blank paper, along with bus tickets, were the currency he greatly favored in payment for his prayers. He always carried a cloth in which to wrap his belongings when he went on a trip. He would tie his paper stacks carefully with string and wrap them in the cloth together with a pair of scissors.

I was a child when Daie Nasser fell and broke two fingers on his right hand. The accident happened in Qazvin; the operation had not been up to par, however, and he could no longer bend those fingers and his right hand looked like a gun ready to fire. He would cut the sheets with his damaged hand carefully, but slippage of hand and scissors was inevitable. If he didn't cut one piece properly, instead of throwing it away he would cut the rest of the sheets to the same size. Perhaps his objective was the infinite continuum of the act of cutting. Psychologists say cutting paper calms the spirit and is effective in fighting depression and grief. It is as if Daie Nasser knew that intuitively. Perhaps Daie Nasser's obsession with time was a by-product of coming down with an undefined disease at age twelve. He was taken to an Armenian doctor who had recently returned from Russia and who prescribed searing a section of his skull. The cross-shaped sear mark still branded the top of his head, and because he always shaved his head close, that cross was always visible. The fact is, since my childhood, Daie Nasser had the mind of a child in the body of an adult. Perhaps he wanted to stop time from moving on because his mind had stopped developing due to that operation.

Pointing out that cross was one of Daie Nasser's favorite clown acts. There was also a small hole at the tip of his nose, I never discovered why, and when he was in a really jolly mood, he would press the twig of broomstick inside it and make us children laugh. If my mother was nearby, she would chastise him gently and say, "Nasser, you're playing the idiot again," and he would respond, laughing: "Sis, these kids won't leave me be."

More serious chastisements by my mother were saved for moments when Daie Nasser spoke of his love for a woman who lived in Qazvin. He believed the two had been certified for a temporary marriage, *sigheh*. When I was older, I asked my mother about that. With a smirk that meant she did not wish to go into detail, she nailed it with, "The slutty bitch wanted to nab him for moola." In any event, we applauded and enjoyed Daie Nasser's allusions to that romantic affair. In those pre-internet times, such affairs were only mentioned in *Asrar-e Magou* (Unspoken Secrets) an assortment of racy anecdotes collected and published clandestinely by the poet and radio personality Mehdi Soheili in the 1940s. We used every trick of the trade to get Daie Nasser to speak about such topics. If my mother was within earshot, voicing her reproof and Daie Nasser's "Sis, these kids won't let me be" would end the discussion. In the film *Amarcord*, Fellini depicts the kindly figure of Uncle Theo who, overcome by spermatic vapors - to echo Rostam ul-Hukama's 19th century *Rostam ol-Tavarikh* (Histories of Rostam) - climbs a tree and keeps yelling at the top of his lungs, "I want a woman!" No amount of pleading and remonstration can coax him down from the tree until a nun arrives from the mental asylum where he is confined. The moment she appears in her white coif and black habit and medieval figure and form, the uncle dismounts and ditches his visceral craving. For Daie Nasser, too, a snap and a barb from my mother were enough to silence him – until the next time he broke his silence. Like us children, he also enjoyed speaking of unspoken secrets.

Like every child who longs for signs of entry and admission into the world of grownups, Daie Nasser, too, treasured various roles, whether real or imagined, that were assigned to him. He would proudly point out that, per two official orders, he was a "shoe-keeper" at the shrines of Imam Reza and Imamzadeh Davoud. Whenever he insisted on returning to Qazvin despite our pleas to stay in Tehran he would say, "Daie, I can't stay. *Aqa* Kamal needs me." He went on a

trip to Mashhad at least once a year, and on pilgrimages to
Imamzadeh Davoud numerous times. Another of his treasured posts was as "storage officer" at the Iranian Glass
Company. I had not yet been born when my father served
as the company's general manager for a time and assigned
him that position. The only time when Daie Nasser had a
real job, which he took very seriously, was at Daie Kamal's
house during the *rowzeh-khani* nights of lamentation. When
tea was served, Daie Nasser was responsible for organizing
the serving platters and assigning them to those tasked with
carrying tea to the guests. Whenever the elegist reached the
Battle of Karbela and made everyone cry over the martyrdom
of Imam Hossein and his kin, Daie Nasser, too, in his words,
wept for his "ancestor." I don't know why, but nobody's
weeping moved me as much as his did. It was fairly obvious
that most people shed tears over their own personal predicament. Perhaps because I did not know why Daie Nasser wept
nor ever doubted the sincerity of his lamentation, his tears
were that much more touching.

Nothing was a testament to a childlike mind inhabiting a
man's body as Daie Nasser's attire, especially given our fairly
affluent family that as a rule minded its social status. Every
year, he was outfitted in one of Daie Jalal's nice suits from the
previous year. Among all the brothers, Daie Jalal was closest
in height and build to Daie Nasser. Nonetheless, his tailored
jacket looked more like a short overcoat on Daie Nasser and
his trousers came practically up to his neck, so he had to fold
them over at the top and tie a belt around his midriff to stop
them from falling down. Daie Nasser always wore a white
undershirt and a pair of linen underpants that were tailor-
made for him and threaded at the ankle so he could pull the
strings tight and fasten them in a knot. When he was in a
particularly cheerful mood, he'd say – and never shied from

repeating himself – "Daie, you know why I tie the legs of my pants with string?" and if my mother happened to be around, she'd interrupt before Daie Nasser could intone, "crap!" "Nasser, you're playing the idiot again." In all my childhood, the happiest days were those when Daie Nasser stayed at our house. It was as if, to paraphrase Carlo Levi, "Christ had stopped at Malek o-Shoara Avenue."

Parviz Shokat

Parviz Shokat cannot be described in words. He can only be known through experience. Every faithful portrayal of him, even if tempered by the forewarning that such heights of praise are implausible, may appear exaggerated even to a sympathetic reader. Parviz is a rarity and everyday language falls short of illuminating rare phenomena. Difficulties aside, these sketches of the individuals I have been fortunate to know, each of which forms part of a portrait of our generation and times, would be incomplete without the story of Parviz.

For more than half a century, he has been my closest friend and the standard by which I measure fairness and justice. In these dark days whose bleakness and lost dreams and crushed utopias are captured by Golshiri's *Shah-e Siyah-poushan (King of the Benighted)* and its kinship with Nezami's *Black Dome*, uplifting figures like Parviz ought to be invented even if unreal so that a ray of light and hope may, to borrow from Golshiri, "nurture survival" in this twilight of death.

In Berkeley where Parviz has worked and been active since arriving in the U.S. at age fifteen, there is no dearth of post-revolution immigrants who consider themselves "notable" or "revolutionary" or even "legendary." What they share in common is a claim to fame even as they may be struggling to transcend the bitter experience of exile. Parviz's work is the exact opposite of these self-proclaimed celebrities. He shuns fame, brushing off any mention of his service with a self-deprecating "C'mon!" His collected documents of the leftist movement and the Confederation of Iranian Students abroad testifies to his agency in generating those currents. Quietly, and without even asking for his name to be acknowledged, he donated this collection to Stanford University and the Hoover Institution. His fame lies almost exclusively among seasoned activists. Nor have I heard him wish anyone ill or speak ill of anyone. The only "criticism" leveled against him is that no one criticizes him. They say that is probably because he gets along with everyone. Though Parviz is also a first-class cook and an esthete decorator and art connoisseur, people don't realize that his greatest art is his life. Like all great artists and writers, his capacity for empathy and his interest in viewing current and world affairs through the eyes of others is endless. The other feature of his life is his unquenchable thirst for life and the wish to fathom its meaning.

Parviz's hunger for knowledge has turned him into a profoundly erudite person. His grasp of the status of social epistemology, for instance, is as precise and in-depth as his proficiency in Marxism in its varied forms. By contrast with the opinion-based approach of most political activists, the breadth of his curiosity equals the depth of his knowledge and ideation in any field he is drawn to. Yet I have never seen him take to the pulpit and preach or sermonize on any topic. On the contrary, the extent of his expertise only comes to light in the course of a live interchange in which he raises questions following the Platonic dialectic, a method that is open, undulating, and inquisitive in nature (and is akin to Stalin's closed, dogmatic, and repressive "dialectic" in name only). He has engaged with the distinguished thinker John Searle more than any student or academic researcher in recent years, and not only participated creatively in his courses and seminars but acted as that great philosopher's friend and succor in times of duress.

If his pursuit of learning leads to an unassuming and laudable wisdom, Parviz's urge to experience life, by contrast, sometimes exposes him to serious danger. Some years ago, I dropped him off at the railway terminal in Oakland, California. From there, he got himself and his bicycle to Florida on the exact opposite side of this vast continent. He got on his bike in Tampa and from there pedaled across most of the rest of the country without taking any shortcuts along the several-thousand-mile-long route. To visit a friend, he would often go off track. One such time, he arrived in Arizona, which borders California. He was riding along a feeder road at dusk one night when a careless driver hit his bike and knocked him high into the air and onto the desert, where he passed out. In the distance, another driver whose sharp eyes matched his sense of responsibility and kindness noticed the faint blinking light on Parviz's helmet. He got out and walked to the source of the glow, where he found Parviz, clearly in a bad shape. There were no cell phones in those days let alone smartphones, so he drove to the closest emergency phone bank on the roadside where he transmitted news of Parviz's critical state and was told an ambulance would be dispatched. But his humaneness would not let him leave Parviz alone. He explained what was going on and waited, and when help did not arrive, went back to the roadside phone. The location had been miscommunicated. He gave them clearer directions and returned to Parviz's side until the ambulance arrived.

When I visited Parviz in a hospital in Arizona the next day, he had just come to. Despite several broken ribs, he kept laughing and cheered everyone up. He would get back on the road the next day if he were allowed. Or start over in Florida. If I had told the story to my mother, for sure she would have said, "It's people's prayers that saved him." Perhaps the whole thing is as simple as the proverbial story in Sa'di's *Bustan*. Parviz "did good for a lifetime and tossed it in the river, and luck tossed it right back at him in the desert."

Parviz's defiant and adventurous spirit does not stop at biking across a continent. One day, we were out in the yard at Qodsi and Sadeq Chubak's home in northern California. It is no exaggeration to say that they both loved him like a son. One side of the yard abutted a hill covered with massive trees. Chubak said they needed to be pruned and talked about the difficulty of finding people in the know who could do the job for a reasonable fee. He had barely finished speaking when Parviz took off. A few minutes later, when the first branches crashed to the ground from on high we knew where he had gone. He had learned to climb and prune trees from the time he went to prison in place of another student who was a member of the group that had attacked the Iranian consulate; if arrested, the student's legal status would have meant expulsion from the country. That is why Parviz admitted to a crime he had not committed and spent six months in a low-security prison in the middle of a forest by the sea. One of his prison chores had been pruning trees.

Perhaps the root of Parviz's standout traits may be found in his generosity and boundless zeal for justice. In his case, those traits are two sides of the same coin. Contesting injustice is his innate reflex and fundamental ontology. It has nothing to do with Marx's theory of surplus value or other measures of injustice and inequality, but more to do with his character. He was born into an aristocratic family. His father had fallen for another woman and married again and Parviz was brought up by his grandmother whose grandiose lifestyle and the effort to control her children's lives were consistent with the conduct of the modernized Qajar nobility. His childhood photographs speak of a life of prodigious comfort and luxury. It is as if Parviz has spent all his life redressing the injustice that in his mind had been dealt him by that much wealth and opulence. I have repeatedly seen his eyes fill with tears at the sight of a needy soul or a protester being roughed up. He might even head out to the site of a "happening" in order to be confronted with injustice. He had come to America at age fifteen and was as outraged by injustice against Blacks as against Iranians back home. Among life's strange coincidences is that he had attended the same high school that I enrolled in when I came to the U.S. a few years later.

To overturn injustice or inequity, Parviz, by contrast with many *revolutionaries*, does not use others as a tool to advance himself. He is the first to take a step toward whatever action he considers necessary or apt for others. How many times have I seen him give away whatever he had – from the book in his hand to the coat on his back – to someone that he felt needed it more. It is as if there is no room in his mind for what Sufis call worldly "lucre." I saw him give shelter to some homeless strangers in his home for a time. When as a cautionary note I asked if he wasn't concerned for his family's or his own safety, he laughed. "Concerned for what?" he said, with no hint of reproof, only surprise at my strange question.

I never witnessed any jealousy or envy in him either, the hallmark of many Iranian immigrants. Those who profess hatred of their culture or who, conceivably agents of the

Islamic regime, begrudge any signs, or the potential, for camaraderie in the émigré community, invariably chime in with: "Iranians don't lift a finger for each other." They say Iranian immigrants have a "crab" culture, resembling crabs that pull down any fellow crab that tries to edge higher to escape an open water tank. Here, it is instructive to look at Hannah Arndt's reflections on the experiences of intellectual German immigrants who, having escaped the claws of a monstrous regime like the Nazis, were nonetheless mean and jealous and envious in exile. Arndt even holds the meanness of the eminent German philosopher Theodore Adorno partly accountable for the death, or suicide, of the venerable cultural critic Walter Benjamin. In a word, such meanness is neither limited to Iran nor did I see any sign of it in Parviz. On the contrary, he delights in the success of any Iranian and as best he can, helps them rise even higher. I believe supporting Iranians is one of his life's main preoccupations. He once took a two-day trip to Australia to help out a friend. His support takes many forms.

When I returned to the U.S. in 1986, Parviz and his wife Ruth who herself has shown much valor in seeking social justice, owned a successful printing house in northern California. Producing posters for plays, rock bands and operas and specialty art books was the crux of their work. In those same years, he also printed dozens of books and pamphlets for Iranians for free in that same establishment. The distribution of the books was in the hands of the authors themselves. It is amazing that thirty years later, the Iranian diaspora has not built a serviceable book-distribution network. In the same year that I returned to the U.S., the four articles that Manuchehr Safa and Najaf Daryabandari and I had ostensibly written about Arthur Koestler but were in fact about different interpretations of Marxism appeared in a book titled *Topics in Democracy and Socialism* with Parviz's help. It was also with his help that my anthology of articles, *Topics in Totalitarianism*, was published. Indeed, the selection of articles for that book was carried out in consultation with Parviz who helped compare the original Persian text with the English translation with extraordinary patience and attention to detail.

Parviz, along with two of his friends, founded one of the most active Marxist groups in the Confederation of Iranian Students who called themselves the Union of Communists. The moment he discovered that their course had deviated from the goal he had envisaged, he left the organization. Whether in the years before the revolution or as an immigrant, Parviz endeavored to bring about a kind of unity among sometimes hostile political factions. He is that rare breed of person that all contentious political factions agree has goodwill. When the revolution came, he returned to Iran for a time. His old friend from Berkeley Mostafa Chamran was then the new regime's defense minister. When they met up, Chamran told Parviz, "Don't stay here. These people are going to start a bloodbath." Although Parviz was not afraid of the coming carnage, neither was he tempted to join the new power structure and so he returned to the U.S. Now, as then, his self-appointed mission has been neither to seek power nor pretend to fight for justice but to try to live as an exemplary humanist, Iranian patriot, and seeker of social justice. And he has achieved great success in realizing this mission. Perhaps that is why describing him in words is so difficult and experiencing his friendship so delightful.

Faramarz Pakzad

Politics, like wine, "makes the core even more transparent," as they say. I don't mean politics in the broad Aristotelian–Foucauldian sense – that is, a paradigm that encompasses every part of the life of a family, city, or country, and plays a key role in fashioning the identity and character, or "core," of the individual. I mean political activity of the professional or revolutionary sort that many students at the Confederation of Iranian Students and other political organizations were engaged in at the time. In my experience, the activists' visceral ethos and ethical values were not altered by those political activities, only their expression changed. The humble and selfless grew humbler and more selfless, and the arrogant and the crooked grew more arrogant and crooked. At times, arrogance and dishonesty proceeded from ambition for status and wealth and at times same desires masqueraded as revolutionary action and its concurrent moral justifications. Faramarz Pakzad whose friendship I have had the privilege to enjoy for half a century, is a rare exception of someone with integrity and a sense of justice whose ethos before and after the revolution did not change. Generous and honorable, diligent and affable, he is disciplined in his work and flexible in his mindset. He is not easily excitable, and I

have never seen him behave in a distraught manner or lose
control. He has great capacity for hearing other people out
and exercising patience. When in a group, even one he has
personally brought together, he listens more than he speaks.
And when he does speak, it is generally to identify common
denominators among the views expressed. Even at the height
of factionalism at the Confederation, where one camp was
fiercely agitating for a rallying cry to topple the Shah and
labeled all who opposed the move heretic and defeatist, he
argued firmly against such a move while trying to maintain
comity and rapport across the different camps. He refused
to sloganeer. He had the ability to let even his ideological
"enemies" believe that he empathized if not with their views
then at least on a personal level. That posture did not change
in the years since he quit "political" activism. His core grew
"even more transparent." In the underground organization
of which we were both members, following standard practice
in such forums, each had to adopt a pseudonym. "Steel,"
which in Russian translates into "Stalin," was the pseudonym
of that revolutionary who upon becoming the autocratic
leader of USSR commissioned the famous Russian composer
Shostakovich to write an orchestral work based on the newly
built steel mill, hence his Symphony No. 3, subtitled "The
First of May." Faramarz's pseudonym was *Dānāie* (Insight).
Every pseudonym should perhaps be regarded as a window
into the character of the one who adopts it.

When I met him fifty years ago, we were both students.
He was studying architecture and I political science. We
were both political. I was new to the fold and he, without
telling me about his background, was an influential and
key leader in the organization. As someone who worked in
a restaurant that specialized in omelets, he broke eggs all
the time, but not of the kind that, per Mao's fatwa, was the

requisite of every revolution. He had focus and integrity and discipline in everything he did, and never rushed into things. We sometimes used to talk about his brother Bijan, who he said was in the clothing business and whose specialty was designing and tailoring very expensive suits for those who aspired to high (and costly) fashion. The topic of "Bijan" was part of our punditry on the curse of the *bourgeoisie* and its kitsch values. But while Faramarz never espoused such values himself, he did not cut off his relationship with his brother. After the revolution, too, when Bijan became a highly successful couturier in the U.S. with high-profile clients around the world, Faramarz maintained his tie with him as before. He never used Bijan's name to boost his own status nor ever stopped soliciting his support to help other Iranians. *The Shah* had just been published. I was at a bookstore in Los Angeles to participate in the book launch and sign copies for well-wishers who attended the event. At one point a man walked in, slim, with a hat pulled over his brows and wearing dark glasses. He bought a copy quickly and left. His entrance and exit caused a murmuring in the crowd and so I asked who it was. "Didn't you recognize him?" people asked. It was Bijan. I hadn't recognized him. But I did not tell them that I knew about him from his brother Faramarz.

Though Faramarz used to mock the preoccupation of Bijan's clients with fashion, he himself always dressed in fine, classic attire. Perhaps because he had once been a student of architecture. He mostly wore dark, polo-neck sweaters with a matching vest and comfortable pants and shoes. Whether then, as a wild-eyed revolutionary, or today, when he can afford any garment he pleases, he has never heeded the "gospel" of fashion and physical appearance. He never sported a revolutionary mustache and beard; nor did I ever see him in an army overcoat à la Che Guevara. The peace and empathy that graced his countenance in youth is now coupled with a penetrating, sensitive expression – that of someone who has tasted the vicissitudes of life and experienced the ups and downs of politics.

As his wealth accumulated in the years following the revolution, so did his willingness and interest in helping others. As in the saying "the larger the roof, the more the snow [to shovel off]," in his case, with more snow also comes greater responsibility. In helping others, he never makes a promise he cannot deliver and never breaks the promise. Nor does he usually wish to be identified as the source. He appreciates his creative friends. The house he shares with his wife Jaleh Pirnazar who taught Persian language and literature for some forty years at the University of California at Berkeley is akin to what was called a "salon" in France beginning in the seventeenth century, a venue for artistic, cultural, and occasionally political get-togethers. Faramarz and Jaleh may host an eightieth-birthday celebration for Sadreddin Elahi one evening, and on another evening an event to promote Shahrnoush Parsipour's latest book. Faramarz's moderation in all affairs manifests most of all in the compassion he has for errant individuals. He recognizes that to err is human. His world is colored in gray, not in black and white. That is why he shuns passing stern judgments on people's shortcomings.

If political activism allows the core of a seeker of justice endowed with "insight" to become "even more transparent," that same kind of activism exacted a sad fate on one of Faramarz's and my mutual friends. His name was Faramarz Vaziri, and I met him in the U.S. through Pakzad. It had been a few months since I had joined the revolutionary organization. In the rigid hierarchy of such entities, highly military in structure, I was no more than a novice cadet. Pakzad announced to me one day: "The central committee of the organization has decided to conduct an in-depth study of Iranian society and has formed a research committee to undertake the project. The committee leader has read one of your papers and invited you to join the group." In those days, the "toppling" slogan and the question of the nature of Iranian society were subjects of heated debates in the student movement in the U.S. Some held that Iran had become a capitalist system following land reform; others that despite such "reforms," a form of feudalism continued to reign in Iran. Faramarz went on: "Until the project is finished, you will have no other duties than the work you do for the committee."

A few days later, Faramarz and I went to a small house in a poor neighborhood in Oakland where the residents were by and large Black. We entered a dark room with a table in the corner heaped with papers and books. Pakzad introduced us to Vaziri by our organizational names and left the meeting after a brief introduction. Speaking with contagious enthusiasm and language steeped in revolutionary theory and terminology, Vaziri emphasized the "critical" responsibility that the organization had conferred upon us. As if the weight of the world, Atlas-wise, was on our shoulders. Except that Atlas is a figure of myth while we saw ourselves as leaders of the proletariat. It didn't matter either that the proletariat hadn't a clue that we even existed. Though animated and categorical, Vaziri was also bashful and kept looking down at the table. While Pakzad's speech was free of revolutionary fervor and admonition, Vaziri's statements that day – and subsequently – reflected the minutiae of Marxist and Maoist polemic. The plan was for us to both read Mao's writings attentively and also research and assess relevant data and statistics to determine whether the Shah had overturned feudalism as he claimed or whether, in consonance with Mao, a society like Iran could not transition from semi-feudalism without a revolution. In practice, though, our job was to find out how those statistics confirmed Mao's fatwa.

Faramarz Vaziri was very sharp and industrious, but in becoming a *revolutionary*, his slogans had become his wisdom. Being intelligent, he could marinate and cook those slogans in reason and dish them out with the air and credibility of insight. He stayed up most nights and worked, then slept during the day but only for a few hours. Sometimes he claimed not to have slept for two to three days in a row. He knew that Stalin used to stay up until the wee hours of the morning and have dinner and wine with his apostles (such as Khrushchev) and watch Western movies and then fall asleep, at which time his companions would have to leave and go to work. Vaziri did not like Westerns, though, but horror movies. I never found out whether the strange hours he kept for work and sleep were to mimic Stalin or were just by chance. His pseudonym was *Dādgar* (The Just). I had no doubt in the sincerity of his boundless quest for justice. But in his mind, "justice" was defined and summarized in M.L. – Marxism–Leninism – which is why he had absolute faith in the "reality" of Marxism and Maoism. What transpired post-revolution showed that he was prepared to put his life on the line for that faith.

The task of reading Mao's writings and restating the intricacies of his thoughts about semi-colonial, semi-feudal systems was assigned to me. On the side, we began collecting data and statistics and research materials on the economic structure of Iran. The more I read Mao's writings the less theoretical exactitude and attention to detail I found in them. Whenever, tactfully and discreetly, I brought up those issues with Vaziri he would cut me off decisively. "Comrade Mao does not err," he would retort. "Any error is due to the deficit in our understanding." In those days, I had read Karl Popper's theories of epistemology in a course on research methodologies where he posits that unscientific religious theories are invariably framed in such a way as not to be falsifiable; thus, people do not regard any error they may encounter or find in conflict with reality to be a weakness in the theory but in their own understanding or belief. Vaziri who considered himself an irreligious Marxist analyst knew, perhaps unwittingly, that he had turned it into an unfalsifiable religion. After the revolution, I heard from Pakzad that once the organization was essentially dismantled under attack by the Islamic regime, he and a couple of other friends had arranged for Vaziri to leave Iran. They sent him a letter. Rejecting their offer with harsh words, he said he would stay put like Khosrow Ruzbeh and fight. "Don't urge me to 'prostitute' myself," he added. On hearing that, and after reading some of the last reports that Vaziri wrote prior to his arrest and execution, I discovered the extent of his infallible faith in unfalsifiable precepts. To him, individualism was a profanity and democracy a petty bourgeois siren song. He regarded democratic centralism, the absolute power of the party, and Marxism, to be the very definition of freedom. To him, historical wisdom did not go beyond such axioms. In his last report prior to his arrest he had written: "In spite of all challenges, the Party will abide and press on." It did not abide and did not press on.

By contrast, both in his activist days in the past and later in exile, Faramarz took reality with all its messiness to be preferable to pure speculation, doing his best to correct its faults. No longer does he ask, after Lenin, "What is to be done?" Instead, he says, "We have to understand why things happened the way they did. How can we avoid repeating those mistakes? How can we help the victims of those mistakes? How can we take a small step toward fashioning a 'prosperous and free and thriving' Iran?" Faramarz Vaziri dedicated his life with valor to a speculative utopia, while Faramarz Pakzad has spent most of his life dedicated to the Sisyphean labor of always heaving the boulder of justice and equality and freedom in Iran one step, small as it may be, forward.

Farrokh Modabber

Farrokh Modabber is a noble and principled individual and one of the most distinguished Iranian scientists of the past half century. For a time he taught in the School of Public Health at the University of Tehran. In the day, not only that school but the biochemistry and biophysics departments had achieved great international recognition thanks to professors like him, Khashayar Javaherian, and Fereydoun Javadi who was also a friend of the Queen and better able to subsidize the development of that group's scientific agenda. Farrokh had previously taught and pursued research in some of the best universities in the world, including Harvard and UCLA. Before the revolution he served as head of the Pasteur Institute in Tehran – the medical facility that had enabled Reza Shah in the early years of his reign to stamp out a new wave of cholera that had killed hundreds of thousand Iranians in the past.

After leaving Iran, prompted by the rising fear of "Islamic mercy" shown by the likes of the "hanging judge" Sadeq Khalkhali, Farrokh was put in charge of critical areas in some of the most prominent international institutions of public health and medicine. For years, he headed the division dedicated to fighting leishmaniasis, or Aleppo boil,

267

at the World Health Organization and was then engaged by the Gates Foundation whose mission is to eradicate infectious diseases globally. Leishmaniasis, which was for some time endemic in Iran, was Farrokh's specialty. While he has written more than a hundred scientific articles on the subject, I have never heard him boast about his achievements or sing his own praises. And if someone happens to mention his feats, he will shrug it off with a laugh. Most importantly, in all the years he has lived in exile he has remained attached to and concerned about Iran, and taken every opportunity to apply his vast scientific knowledge to help rescue the country from the plague of a regime whose leaders' medical wisdom lies in *moste'an,* supplicating God's mercy. The truth, above all, is that Farrokh is a romantic soul. His love for Iran, for his family and friends, for his work and research, and of course for the women he fell in love with knows no bounds. Farrokh is also very forgetful, a veritable image of the absent-minded genius.

We were once having lunch with some mutual friends a few days before a trip to Europe, unaware that we had booked the same flight. We had talked about the trip but without sharing details. His destination was Tehran, via Vienna. I was going to Montreux and then on to London. Over the forty-some years since the revolution, Farrokh traveled, gypsy-like, between Europe and the U.S. and Iran – and sometimes to other continents. His emotional home was always Iran though, and his cerebral home the world of science. His recreation was books and poetry and history, his residence the whole world. On that trip, neither of us realized he was seated in the row in front of me. I had reached my seat late and in a hurry and didn't take note of those sitting nearby. This being a red-eye flight, the cabin lights were soon dimmed. When the lights turned on close to Zurich, which was the flight's final destination, there was a lot of movement in the next row. A passenger seemed to be searching for a lost object under the seat cushion. When a flight attendant who came by to help gave up, a technician walked up with a large flashlight and a tool bag and after rummaging for a while, recovered the passenger's spectacles. They had slipped off when he fell asleep while reading he explained, and apologetically added that he did not have a spare pair and could not manage without reading glasses. I naturally recognized his voice.

We deplaned together. He had to wait for the next flight to Vienna and I was due to take a train to Montreux. I was happy that I could spend at least another hour with Farrokh. We walked about for ten minutes then stopped at a café. Farrokh who is unconditionally generous insisted on paying for the coffee, but then he realized he had left his wallet on the plane and we said goodbye. He left in search of his wallet and I felt guilty that he must have been distracted by my show of exuberance on seeing him on the flight. This episode put me in mind of a tract I had read about a class taught by Theodor Mommsen, one of the greatest historians of the nineteenth century. The author describes that standing at his desk Mommsen gave a brilliant lecture about Athens during Aristotle's lifetime and drew an accurate map of the city on the blackboard showing Aristotle's residence and its position vis-à-vis Plato's Academy. Once the lecture ended, a student walked up to him and escorted him out of the classroom. The author then adds, "I asked my friends, What is the story about this young man? They said the professor normally gets lost on his way home; his young student helps him stay on track." Mommsen knew how to get from Aristotle's home to the Academy in his mental world, but in the actual world he readily lost the way to his own home. Farrokh Modabber readily loses his glasses and wallet, but his mind is spot on when it comes to navigating the map of human anatomy.

Hormoz Hekmat

The failures and triumphs, the hopes and despair, the heroism and heartbreaks of three generations of Iranians reverberated in the ebb and flow of the singular and little-known life of Hormoz Hekmat. A rare personality, he well understood the mendacities of our times but never succumbed to them. All his life, he tried to surmount them, whatever their nature. Ever righteous in his conduct, he was never beguiled by self-righteousness. His gentleness and affability – despite the shadow of grief that always lurked at the back of his eyes – and his political and everyday ethos were a reflection and an outcome of his mental agility and adaptability. More than anything, he was committed to his high moral standards but would not commit himself to a specific dogma or political utopia. His yardstick for action was invariably the reality on the ground, Iran's best interests, and his own ethical princi-ples. Everything he did seemed to meet alongside those three parallels. He spoke little and selectively, his words measured and judicious. He had a biting, though not wounding, sense of humor, generally spiced with a jab at himself. He would point out the absurdity of the situation but without, as is some-times the case, the humorist's malignant mental jabs. He had

271

turned silence into a vividly eloquent feature of his conversation and discourse. His manner was incisive and keen, and
always kind. His love and loyalty towards friends and family
was boundless. In the last years of his life, he had an incredibly considerate and caring relationship with his niece. Even
before that, I was privy to the great trouble he went to in
order to help a mutual friend.

When Hormoz and I were teaching at Tehran University
in late 1979, a number of our students were among the
self-absorbed, perhaps duped, and injurious "Followers of the
Imam's Line" – a group that modeled its activity and even its
name on Mao's Red Guards, or "Followers of Mao's Line."
The Islamic iteration was involved in the imbecilic hostage-
taking affair at the American embassy in early November
of that year. One day, a group of them came to see Hormoz
and me and a mutual friend. For them, what the three of us
had in common was our "mastery" of English. From day
one, all pretense at anti-Americanism notwithstanding, the
regime was both enamored and intimidated by the U.S.; in
Attar's words, "Who wrecks the ware wants it." Indeed, some
folk who had mastery of English, and who, of course, were
masterful in justifying the regime's crimes, earned ambassa-
dorial and ministerial posts after the revolution.

The Followers of the Imam's Line who came to visit said
they wanted us to translate some American embassy documents into English. As was the regime's custom, a pledge of
"economic rent" was included in that invitation to collaborate. Both Hormoz and I declined the offer: "This venture is
illegal and inadvisable and we will not participate in it." Our
third colleague accepted the students' invitation, however,
not for the "rent" but because of his close relationship with
one of then-current political organizations. It was not long
before he was incarcerated on the charge of collaborating

with that organization and was locked up for a few years. Once released, he fled across the border to Turkey, planning to join his family who had earlier traveled to the U.S. When he showed up at an American embassy in a neighboring country for an interview, they paraded his "case records" before him and, on account of those translations, denied him a visa. On hearing the news, Hormoz took the initiative to help. He wrote them a letter in defense of our colleague describing the conditions in Iran at the time, and persuaded a number of academics to sign it so that our friend was eventually able to join his family.

I have never known whether "a man for all seasons" denotes praise or blame. Does it describe a farsighted person who is made for braving all trials and judiciously prepares for each, or an opportunist who indulges his every whim? Hormoz was loyal to his friends in all seasons but he was not made for any one season. In "every season," while being realistic and sensible and patriotic, he was also an unruly rebel whose nature clashed with what the great fourteenth-century Iranian satirist Obeyd Zakani called the "convenience creed." The sum of those factors had produced in him an odd amalgam of rebellion against oppression, an aversion to histrionics, and in the end, reclusiveness. He always approached every matter with detachment and deliberation. His father may have had some influence in encouraging such detachment. I knew he loved his father very dearly.

Hormoz and I had been collaborating at the university for some time. In years past, I had heard about his ethical standards and impressive scholarship from my friend Khashayar Javaherian. He and Hormoz had been fellow students at Columbia University. Each member of that graduating class went on to become a star in their field, Ahmad Ashraf in sociology, Farhad Ardalan in physics, Javaherian in biochemistry, and Hormoz in political science.

Like all other members of that standout class, Hormoz returned to Iran prior to the revolution. Despite his stellar educational record, despite his important dissertation comparing the policies of the Shah and Mosaddeq during the Cold War, and despite his years of teaching in the U.S., SAVAK barred his appointment at the university. Hormoz's work in the U.S. and his treatment by SAVAK recalls the experience of Parviz Nikkhah, one of the leaders of the Confederation of Iranian Students. After four years in prison in Iran, he concluded that the Shah's reforms, despite their shortcomings, were the best route to achieving an independent and modern Iran and announced his new thinking in a televised interview. His fellow ex-crusaders abandoned him for having caved in, and SAVAK disallowed his rejoining the university on account of his Marxist background. They obliged him to assume the role of a propagandist for the regime. While in the U.S., Hormoz came to the same conclusions that Nikkhah had done. After stopping his political crusading, he taught in the U.S. for some time and then returned to Iran eager to serve his country. "I reckoned the Shah was steering the country in the right direction," he told me. "When I arrived in Iran, I was summoned by SAVAK. They shoved a 'case record' in my face detailing all my political activities as a student." He, too, was eventually barred from a formal appointment at the University of Tehran.

It is curious that someone like Morteza Motahhari, a student of Khomeini and an enemy of the Shah and modernity was then on the faculty at the university, while someone like Hormoz Hekmat was denied that opportunity. Stanger still is how, in the years when he was an anti-Shah activist, while as a leader in the movement that eventually led to the creation of the Confederation he worked alongside people like Sadeq Qotbzadeh, a close aide to Khomeini who was executed on his orders a couple of years after the 1979 revolution, and Mohammad Nakhshab who promoted a form of God-worshiping socialism in the 1950s and early 1960s, and Ebrahim Yazdi who was an Islamist activist at the time and who later became minister of foreign affairs in the Islamic regime, Hekmat himself pursued a path far removed from extremism and affectation. He dreamed of a just and independent Iran under a constitutional monarchy; his disposition was closest to that of Khalil Maleki, Iran's most influential social democrat. At the time Hormoz was active in the U.S., Maleki met with the Shah and Court Minister Asadollah Alam in Iran, contravening the mostly phony puritanism of the *revolutionaries* and their empathy for Khomeini, and openly declared that in the battle between Khomeini and the Shah, one must back progress and modernity – not reaction – and threw his support behind the Shah. But even Hekmat's moderation in the face of the then-rampant radicalism did not, in the eyes of SAVAK, qualify him for an official university appointment.

A few months after the university hired both of us on a "temporary" basis post-revolution, he invited me to his father's home for lunch. It was the first time I had met his father, though I had often heard Hormoz sing his praises before. He owned a modest house, befitting of an honest, senior government functionary and scion of the prominent and affluent Hekmat family in Shiraz. We sat around a small dining table in a pleasant and airy foyer. Aside from the father's quiet bearing and genuine warmth, what I remember from that encounter was what he said to me: "Sir, people are bastards." In none of the four seasons of his life – his youthful rebellion and anti-Shah activism; university teaching; political exile and renewed political aspirations in mid-life; the autumn of his days and editorship of *Iran Nameh* – though he stood out in every domain and, in Beyhaqi's words, was a "master of all trades," did Hormoz Hekmat ever fall under the spell of the masses as did numerous leaders of the National Front and the revolutionaries on the Right and Left; nor did he ever stop trying to bring about a prosperous and free and independent Iran for and alongside his compatriots.

The last time we spoke was in the final weeks of his life in spring 2020. He had stepped down as editor in chief of *Iran Nameh* after fifteen years. I had heard that he mostly stayed at home and was not aching for conversation. But that silence was of a different kind than his natural serenity. It was rooted in a massive grief, not from thinking that "people are bastards" but for knowing, like Borzuyeh the Physician, that "the times were aching for adversity.

Hamid Mohamedi

Hamid Mohamedi was a tragic figure – in the Greek sense, with the seeds of tragedy ineluctably embedded in the depths of one's being. Once established, they cannot be uprooted. Their noxious "sores" are of the kind that "like leprosy" to cite Sadeq Hedayat, "silently scrape at and consume the soul in solitude." And every sedative – from love to political activism or academic work – is only a temporary redress that "after a while rather than relieve, aggravates the pain."

It was the year 1987 and I had just returned to America from Iran. A group of Iranians living in Berkeley had invited me to give a talk. A few weeks earlier, I had lectured at UC Berkeley at the invitation of the Center for Middle Eastern Studies. The subject of my talk was the intellectual orbit in post-revolution Iran. My friend Hamid Mohamedi was in the audience. Hamed Algar, the British born-again Muslim with whom I had worked as an assistant in my student years, was also present. He was a staunch supporter of the Islamic revolution and a bloodhound in countering its critics. I later learned from one of my students who was by then teaching at Tehran University that sometime after my talk, Algar had traveled to Iran to write a biography of Khomeini. My former student had been assigned as his host and guide. Through him, Algar had written a letter to the "authorities" squealing that I was in Berkeley and had been speaking disparagingly of the revolution and had asked them for any information they had on me that could help malign me. After the lecture that day, Hamid and I went to a restaurant near the campus with a few friends and grabbed a bite to eat and some beer, and Hamid, kind as ever, said that by and large he agreed with everything I had said.

The talks I gave in Persian to a group of Iranians a few days later was about Sadeq Hedayat and his tragic vision. I delivered the same talk that had I stayed in Iran and had Azar Nafisi and I finished the book we were co-authoring would have essentially been my contribution to the volume. The lecture took place in a small and intimate venue that was at the disposal of the city's Iranian Theater Group. The hall was packed. A few people had also lined up against the back wall. Hamid Mohamedi was among them too. During my lecture I pointed out in passing that in his stories, Hedayat often exhibits a problem with women; it is as if he is unable to establish an emotional or romantic relationship with them. I said that this facet of the author's character deserved further study. I emphasized that I had not researched the topic in depth and that I was merely sharing what I had deduced from his novels. I added that the only scene where one finds a hint of true love is where the narrator in the *Blind Owl* shoves a cucumber into the mouth of the goodly woman's brother. Years later, when I got to know Sadeq Chubak, himself an acclaimed writer and Hedayat's friend, he told me many stories about that facet of Hedayat's character.

When my talk ended, before inviting anyone else to comment, I pointed to Hamid who had raised his hand to ask a question. This was both out of respect for his position in the city's Iranian community and our long years of friendship. I had known him since my student days at Berkeley in the 1960s. He was then completing his doctoral dissertation on the Pahlavi language and I recall holding him in high esteem for his learning. I knew that he had been politically active in his youth. Back then, he was a supporter of Khalil Maleki and was friends with Hamid Enayat. Hamid Mohamedi did not take any endeavor seriously, however, including political activism, and whenever he failed at something, he held everyone else responsible except himself. He blamed others and the times for his own failures and never accepted that perhaps he lacked the ability and fortitude necessary to apply his talents to the full. Or perhaps the cause of his failure lay in those cankerous "sores."

At the talk, both his question and tone and his reaction before hearing my response, surprised me. Hailing Sadeq Hedayat as one of our literary and cultural icons, he said the point I had made about Hedayat's sexuality – without specifying my passing reference to a possible homosexual bent – was an insult to Hedayat and to our culture: "We will not allow our luminaries to be thus disrespected." Before I could say I had intended no disrespect and that Hedayat's sentiments and sexuality were his business and no one else's, Hamid stormed out of the hall in protest. I knew that his "We" dovetailed with the "We's" that we assumed as part of our revolutionary persona when we were students; the same "We" used by those who still claim the mantle of *revolution* and exploit it by fiat to claim the role of mentor, messiah, and guardian of the people; a claim as false in those days as it is today. Had the aforementioned Hamed Elgar been present and voiced such an objection, I would not have been at all surprised. But coming from Hamid Mohamedi, a one-time follower of Maleki, such an objection was truly astonishing.

His exit naturally drew a lot of attention. But Berkeley in 1987 was no longer the Berkeley of our student days where a few or even just one of the "We" among political activists could not only disrupt a session but cancel it altogether and by dint of conjuring the self-righteous "We" interdict serious discussions. By now, however, all those present at the talk had had a taste of revolution and the bitterness of exile and had thus been freed from the facile certitudes of youth. They stayed and heard my response to the absent Hamid and carried on with insightful questions and criticism.

Hamid's strange behavior that evening did not dent my regard for him. I could not figure out what had upset him. In essence, he was open-minded. I had rarely met with political dogmatism in him. Perhaps because Hedayat had also studied Pahlavi, Hamid's own area of expertise, he didn't want anything less delicate than silky-smooth to be said of him. Needless to say, in my mind I had said nothing less delicate. The fact is, Hamid felt unhappy about his lot in life and held the whole world responsible for it.

When he returned to America from Iran, he applied for an important position at UC Berkeley as curator of the library's Middle East Collection whose holdings on Iran was one of the most important and richest of its kind in America. At the time, Berkeley's Department of Middle Eastern Languages and Cultures employed about ten notable full-time professors. Among them they covered ancient and modern Iranian history as well as Pahlavi and Persian literature. When Hamid submitted his application, the department's Iranian studies division had started losing its credibility and vitality in a most disheartening way. A few of the eminent professors had retired. Hamed Algar, then in charge of the program, was meanwhile rankling Berkeley with his Islamic apologia and ongoing antisemitism. Hamid Mohamedi had taught courses in that same department when he was writing his doctoral dissertation. He later became a leading scholar of Middle Persian. His article on Davān, a village in Kazeroun, and his description of the story of Rostam and Esfandiyar as narrated by a man named Alibaba Sadeqi in the Davāni dialect was brilliant and bespoke the widespread popularity of the *Shahnameh* in every corner of Iran, including rural areas in the south. Hamid had also studied with the venerable Richard Frye, professor of Iranian Studies at Harvard. Crucially, however, he had no expertise in library science.

My friend Parviz Shokat who was hosting Hamid as a houseguest at the time, said that as soon as Hamid applied for the position he started to wallow in gloom. "There is no way they'll offer me the job," he would say. "*So and So* hates me. For sure they'll offer it to a Jew." But the job was offered to him, presumably on the strength of his learning and his erstwhile affiliation with the university. They asked him to take certain courses to acquire the necessary expertise for his new role. But whenever we saw him in the library or in the company of friends in those days, he whined about the job, which he essentially regarded as beneath him. That may be the reason why, as best I know, the scope of the Persian collection narrowed during his tenure as a curator, perhaps it was due to his peculiar selections or lack of interest in the work.

His discontent was not limited to his job. His wife Afsaneh, who could turn her hand to anything, had opened a restaurant in the city where they lived. Hamid used to sometimes help out there as well, but one invariably sensed a hint of belittlement in whatever he said about it. In that regard, Hamid's fate and conduct mirrored that of many other Iranian immigrant men. It was their wives who carried the burden of managing the household and securing it financially; they did not even mind manual labor. Rather than be grateful, however, the men mostly indulged in nagging and whining and held the world accountable for their loss of status.

Sometime later, Hamid and Afsaneh divorced. His other romantic relationships also ended unhappily. At the time, he let the poet Ahmad Shamlou lodge in his home for a while; that "poet of the masses" later described in a travelogue how he had mistreated Hamid and one of his sweethearts.

If the revolution had not happened and Hamid had stayed in Iran and pursued the kind of research he had conducted in the village of Davān, our knowledge of ancient Iran's rich culture would have been much enhanced. But I doubt if he would have been any less discontented, for I believe his grievance was above all rooted in those inborn "sores of the soul."

Parviz Vaez-zadeh

A free-spirited man and a skilled architect, Parviz Vaez-zadeh lived the last half of his life as a devout revolutionary crusader. Had Plato depicted a zealous and stalwart revolutionary in his world of Forms, it would likely not have differed much from Vaez-zadeh in his ethos and conduct. Vaez-zadeh was of the line of nineteenth and twentieth century revolutionaries who perceived their mission to be akin to the fire of Prometheus. On the other hand, their conviction about the soundness of their beliefs and the imperative to impose them onto society was consonant with Plato and his philosopher king. I knew revolutionaries who adopted some prescribed model they had come across somewhere, but I always felt that Parviz's conduct emanated from the core of his being and was not simulated.

Humble and ever optimistic, he was also affectionate and always puckish. Those traits loomed large in the days he and I spent producing a pamphlet on Mao's death in an empty apartment. Fereshteh and I had recently married and rented it unfurnished. We had yet to move in. The building was on a street close to Eisenhower Avenue, the location being a political choice. We did not want to rent a place in a working-class

283

neighborhood, nor did we feel that living uptown was appropriate. The first would look suspicious to the neighbors and SAVAK and the second would be a betrayal of our revolutionary code of honor.

Mao had died a few days before Parviz and I moved into the empty apartment. My sister later recalled that on hearing the death of Mao broadcast on the radio, I had wept. That day, Farzaneh and I both happened to be at our parents' house. For believers such as myself, the death of a "saint" like Mao was calamity personified. Perhaps because I am today more au fait with Mao's unsaintly character and feel ashamed and astounded at my blind faith in him at the time, I had also erased the memory of weeping for him and had to be reminded by my sister. Parviz and I planned to write a pamphlet about Mao and print three hundred copies right there on site. Parviz had supplied the equipment needed for the task.

We worked nonstop. Parviz played pranks all the time. The windows were still bare and he kept saying, "You write, I'll hang the drapes." He claimed to have run a drapery store for a while. I didn't know whether he was joking or not; all I knew was that he had once set up a shop selling knitwear. I later learned that he was among the first Iranians that at the height of the rift within the left over the Soviet Union, had visited China at their invitation and received training in Mao's ideas. Evidently, he had even met Mao at a reception. Yet during the days we worked together, he never so much as hinted at having a greater knowledge and understanding of Mao than me. He laughed all the time, as if a smile dwelt in a niche on his face. In all the time I knew him, only once did I see him without that smile or looking troubled. One felt that his courage and fearlessness were not a mark of a benighted risk-taker but of a seasoned revolutionary and selfless activist.

The time I saw him looking a little rattled and even angry was, unfortunately, our last meeting.

We had driven to Kermanshah together. When I had visited the city alone two weeks earlier, my *liaison* with a group of Marxists in town had asked that "Hamid" also come along the next time. "Hamid" was Parviz's secret organizational name. It is in his honor and out of respect for his memory that when Fereshteh and I had a son, we named him Hamid. By sheer coincidence, Fereshteh's father was also called Hamid, and she and I were conscious that our families believed we had named our son after him. The Kermanshahi *comrade* wanted to meet Parviz because he knew him to be the highest-ranking member of our organization and wished to discuss an important question with him. He had dropped a hint about the subject too: "I have heard from a reliable source that someone in your organization's leadership is a SAVAK collaborator." I knew he meant Cyrus Nahavandi for such a rumor had been going round months earlier. At the time, I had no doubt that it was baseless. Today, I know just how naïve I was. Parviz was even more wide-eyed than me and his naïveté bred disastrous consequences.

For a few months prior to our joint trip, I had been making a biweekly visit to Kermanshah. The liaison who happened to be a famous writer and I used to have theoretical discussions about Marxist topics; he belonged to a study group that were ostensibly sharing their questions with me and Parviz. In reality, they wanted to gauge our revolutionary mettle and to invite us to join them if we passed the test. They were still undecided. Khosrow Saffari, a close friend of Parviz, was in charge for a few months before me. After he was killed – Nahavandi having apparently had a hand in that – their choice fell on me.

I used to start out toward Kermanshah on a Thursday and drive all afternoon and part of the evening. Fearing my own shadow, I would avoid checking into lodgings in the city. We would meet up at our place of rendezvous the next day and walk along sparsely populated streets and chat. Aristotle is known as peripatetic because he used to walk about while conducting philosophical discussions. We were also peripatetic but the only thing we had in common with Aristotle was the walking about. He was given to prudence and inquiry into objective reality. We took pride in insisting on our subjective beliefs and dismissed any suggestion of modification or prudence as "heretical revisionism."

Once, when night fell as I was driving to Kermanshah I started to feel tired and drowsy, so I pulled over and instantly fell asleep. At the crack of dawn, I was roused by a knocking on the car window with what turned out to be a soldier's gun. I rolled down the window tentatively, my hands atremble. The car was surrounded on three sides by armed soldiers. What we called "guerrilla" attacks were rife in those days. I felt anxious about the soldiers' own understandable anxiety. The one who had tapped on my window with the butt of his gun asked in a scared and hurried way, "Why did you park here?" His relatively respectful tone might have had to do with the latest 504 Peugeot that I was driving. My father had paid for it and the Shah had made it lawful for new Iranian graduates of foreign universities, which I was, to import a car without paying a customs fee. "I'm driving to Kermanshah to visit a friend," I said. "I felt tired and decided to take a nap." He asked for an ID card. When he learned that I was a university professor his manner softened somewhat and his anxiety diminished. Speaking with a tinge of sarcasm, he said, "Don't you know you're next to the entrance gate of the Shahrokhi Airbase?" I didn't know. It was that same airbase – later renamed Nojeh – where a coup against the newfangled Islamic regime was plotted in July 1980 when Abolhasan Banisadr was president. It was said that Soviet counterintelligence had alerted the regime to the coup through the Tudeh Party. I told the soldier, "It was dark. I didn't notice where I was." I apologized. I lied about not having noticed it; I did not admit that until that moment, the fact that the entrance to such an important base lay nearby had not caught my attention. When I told Parviz about the incident, he laughed. "They must have thought what a clueless Johnny-come-lately-from-the-West!" I think he must have thought something along the same lines himself.

The day I drove along the same route with Parviz, we were in his car. On the way, we spent the night in Hamedan in a noisy guesthouse. Parviz fell into a deep sleep but I was on tenterhooks for most of the night, beset by anxiety. When we reached Kermanshah, he dropped me off on a street corner. I was to meet up with a young man who had just arrived from the West. He had joined the *comrades* in Germany and they had designated me as his liaison with the organization. Parviz and I decided to meet at one o'clock sharp. My assignment was soon over. In fact, it never started, for the candidate did not show up. I guessed that fear and doubts had made him change his mind, as in my own case on one occasion. The first time I was due to meet Parviz, I went close to where we were to rendezvous, a bus station across from Arya Mehr University, but I chickened out at the last minute. It took a few weeks before I contacted my friends in the U.S. and we rescheduled. When I mentioned the reason for my hesitation to Parviz he shot back with: "That's the imprint of a bourgeois lifestyle; a little revolutionary action will eliminate all doubts." It didn't, though. When I encountered the dogmatism of the circle of our revolutionary comrades, I neither had the courage nor the heart to tell Parviz that *revolutionary activism* had more than doubled my doubts. I didn't tell him that I preferred working at the university to continuously expecting and dreading arrest. Parviz had told me several times that in Iran, those engaged in revolutionary activity survived for four years on average. He also said he was then in his seventh year. I guess he was implicitly trying to reassure me.

That day in Kermanshah, I arrived at my rendezvous with Parviz on the dot. I had idled about the streets for two to three hours and taken tea in a coffee house. We were to meet at a corner of a large square with a patch of greenery in the middle and the standard statue of the Shah. A dizzying number of trucks and buses and cars were rushing around the square. Here and there a cart tied to a man or a haggard horse traipsed through the throng of traffic oblivious to the smoke, tooting horns, and speeding vehicles. If Kermanshah had once had a city gate, this is where it might have stood.

One o'clock came by and there was no sign of "Hamid." Per the rules, I was to wait for four minutes and if he did not turn up, leave. I was to return an hour later more cautiously, assume that either our rendezvous or he himself had been outed, wait another four minutes, and if he didn't show, bolt.

I waited in the designated corner of the square. Two minutes later, I saw Parviz's car. Right in the middle of the square. Stock-still. I thought he must be having technical trouble. I walked toward him. Suddenly, the car sprang forward. It hurled toward me and hit the brakes right there in the middle of the square. I jumped in. He looked distressed. "Why did you walk into the middle of the square?" he snapped. "We were to meet at the corner. I stopped here so you would see me and realize something was wrong. I came to warn you. I think they're on my tail." He had come to save me. Little did he know there was no salvation to be had.

"Let's drive around a while," he said. "We may be able to shake them off." We headed toward Taq-e Bostan, pretending to be tourists. Parviz's attention was fixed on the cars behind us. I, too, was fixated on them, though without turning to look. A Peykan sedan with three passengers seemed suspect. Close to Taq-e Bostan, it disappeared. Parviz said, "I think we've lost them." Perhaps they'd already stopped the pursuit. "If they're chasing the license plate, we'll be flagged down by the highway patrol." We made certain arrangements as to what to say if we were arrested so they would not learn the reason for our visit to Kermanshah. I do not remember the rather elaborate story we concocted. Whatever it was, it would have made the arresting officers laugh. Not long after, I found out that SAVAK had known every detail of our "organization" for a long time; all our past precautions had merely been to lock the stable door after the horse had bolted. We had been inside a trap the entire time without knowing it. The trap was not just a figment of our imagination but a real one, laid by SAVAK.

Once we passed the highway patrol, an illusory calm replaced our actual disquiet. Driving along, we talked at length about Parviz's conversation with that Kermanshahi intellectual. The comrade had been concerned about Cyrus Nahavandi as a suspected SAVAK collaborator and Parviz had replied, with misplaced certitude, "All that stuff is nothing but KGB rumors." He used to say that the USSR in its "social imperialism" – our moniker for the Soviet Union based on a fatwa by Mao – had grown alarmed at "our" rising influence and spread these rumors to curb the influence of revolutionary ideas. His and indeed "our" delusion about the importance of the few dozen who constituted our "organization" was nothing more nor less than SAVAK's delusion. While they were fixated on a small leftist organization like ours, they not only did not crack down on the vast network of religious forces in play but in fact encouraged and urged them on.

Our anxiety surged again when we approached the highway patrol station near Tehran, but once we had passed it we regained our misguided sense of calm. We decided not to meet for a few days. A week later, newspapers reported confrontations with some "terrorist" members of the Liberation Organization. Nine were said to have been killed and eleven arrested. Little did I know at the time that Parviz, who was killed shortly after the announcement, would be included among the list of the nine dead, and that I, though I was not apprehended until two weeks later, would be counted among the eleven arrested. Two or three days after the news broke, Parviz called me at the university. He had never done such a thing before. A feature of the hierarchy of organizations such as ours was that the workplace of the lower-ranking members was known to the higher-ups. He spoke briefly and cryptically. "The situation is dire. Go into hiding or get out of the country." I had neither the option to leave the country nor the courage to hide – or as Saʻdi would say, *neither the legs to walk / nor a place to stay*. Thanks to SAVAK and Nahavandi, fate, too, 'lurked in ambush, and did what it must.' My next sight of Parviz was among the most merciless and painful experiences of my life.

I was arrested about ten days after that phone call. A few hours had passed since my arrival at SAVAK's infamous Joint Committee. I was in the office of an interrogator named Rasuli. He sat behind his Nile-blue metallic desk and I across from him on a small chair. An army cot with a brown blanket stood by the wall. A few years later when a group of us from the university went to the Majles to meet Hashemi Rafsanjani, then Speaker of the Parliament of Iran, terrorist offensives had again grown rampant and fearing the opposition, many regime bigwigs slept in their offices at night. I spotted the exact same army cot in Rafsanjani's office that I had seen in

Rasuli's. It is also possible that both kept a bed in their office to show they were at the service of the cause night and day. A faded black and white photo of the Shah in army uniform hung on the wall in Rasuli's room and a photo of Khomeini in his turban in Rafsanjani's. The sickly light of neon snaked through the air. Was it scary by nature or had my inner terror tainted everything with a shade of fear?

The interrogation sheet lay on top of a small table extension to the armrest of my chair. Rasuli would compose a question and slide the piece of paper toward me and I would write a response. The only questions I answered truthfully were my name and place of work. "Why did you go to Kermanshah three weeks ago?" he asked. "I had a quarrel with my wife," I answered. "I went there for a change of air." He would read my answers with a smirk and compose the next question.

I was busy crafting another lie when he pulled out a small, brown suitcase from under his desk. It was cracked in a few places and dented. He flipped it open and as if by accident, flung a few folded sheets noisily across the table. In a quick peek, I recognized my own handwriting. It was a report I had written for Parviz about a trip to Sistan and Baluchestan. I naturally pretended that I neither knew nor had ever seen the report. Rasuli, the extent of whose mental pathologies I discovered over time in prison and later in exile, watched me carefully. He banged a couple more familiar-looking pieces on the table and after ascertaining the extent of my stupid stubbornness, delivered the coup de grâce. He scattered three photos of Parviz Vaez-zadeh's blood-soaked corpse and bullet-punctured skull on the table, one after another, and with much din. Parviz's battered body and the violence in Rasuli's act brought a lump to my throat but also made me determined not to let him win, at least not in that game. His winnings did not last long, in any case. Two years later, on the eve of the revolution, he fled the Joint Committee and shortly afterwards turned up in Paris. He spent some time in fear and out of sight and finally discovered the hangout of former political prisoners who had emigrated following the mass murders committed by the new regime. On the days the ex-prisoners met up, he too would sit at a table at a little distance alone, and observe his former victims. I had heard about Stockholm syndrome whereby prisoners grow attached to their torturers. Rasuli may have been the first reverse case. I later learned that not only did Parviz not take that Kermanshahi intellectual's words and warnings seriously, but that even after a few people who had learned of Nahavandi's double-dealings were arrested and killed, he still fell into the latter's trap.

What a sublime, fertile, destructive illusion it was that drove a band of educated young people dreaming of justice but oblivious to the reality in Iran, to put their time and thoughts, and in the case of Parviz, life, on the line seeking to build a utopian paradise that was in fact not even a purgatory but Inferno itself. Parviz was one of the most zealous among such ideological pilgrims. Like every wayfaring Sufi, he did not take the stuff of this world, even life itself, seriously. At the same time, nothing, not even reality, could ruffle his sublime illusion. Sohrab Sepehri has said: *If you come seeking me / tread gently and softly lest the fragile glass of my solitude fracture.* If Parviz were a poet, he would say: *If you come seeking me / rush fast and furiously so my steely revolutionary soul may harden.* He knew that critical rationalism could not be reconciled with faith, and he chased his dream of revolution like a faithful pilgrim.

Hossein Montazeri

Saidi Sirjani turned the Sheikh of Sanaan into a powerful symbol of the noxious allure of power. For every Sheikh e Sanaan there is no shortage of sincere Sufis and unfettered individuals who pay no heed to worldly temptations and value the solitary recess of integrity over the glory and prestige of power. Sirjani called Khomeini *Sheikh-e Sanaan* of the times and paid for it with his life. I believe future generations will also see Ayatollah Montazeri, Khomeini's student and designated heir, as a symbol of immunity to the siren call of power and will say that in the last years of his life he, too, paid for his unfettered spirit and for standing up to dictatorship with jail and shackles. He prioritized his moral principles over grabbing or holding on to power at whatever cost. He lost the battle, but that was no surprise. As a rule, in such contests the least moral and the most militant forces and individuals are the victors. According to Saul Bellow, power is dangerous and invariably the most dangerous people seek it. I believe history will blame Montazeri for his role in implanting the theocratic system of *Velayat-e faqih*, Guardianship of the Islamic Jurist in Iran, and praise him in equal measure for his subsequent exertions contesting that dictatorship. He finally concluded that what had been forged in Iran was neither a republic nor

Islamic, at least not "Islamic" in the way he had envisioned. In that context and based on his exemplary bravery and conduct, some are trying (and will try) to reinforce the myth that "true Islam" was not, in fact, implemented in Iran and that had such been the case, a worldly paradise would have been on hand and the otherworldly paradise too would have been within reach. I think Montazeri's fate and experience proves the exact opposite of that myth. It shows that even an individual like him, despite his integrity and courage, and despite the power that he wielded as Khomeini's heir apparent, was unable to stop religious power from turning dictatorial. Every power that claims to rest on absolute "truth" or immutable laws – whether they be the truths of "divine" laws or of the secular and "historical" kind – is doomed to turn despotic.

I was in close contact with Ayatollah Montazeri for only six months, in the mullahs' block at Evin. When I asked him why he had been jailed he said, "I had been authorized by Mr. Khomeini to 'collect funds,' and one of the members of the Mujahedin who later converted to Marxism 'ratted' on me saying that I had previously given him funds to support his family." When, on arriving in that block for the first time, out of respect for his age I carried the tea kettle from the entrance door to the cell he shared with other mullahs, there was pandemonium. I did not know about the mullahs' draconian purity rules. They considered us Marxists "unclean" and thus did not take tea that day as they had seen my unclean hands defile the kettle's handle. I heard that Montazeri and Taleqani were the only two who drank tea from that kettle. At the time, it was clear that among the roster of religious jurisconsults and the hierarchy of theological seminaries, Montazeri surpassed the other gentlemen in rank. When, upon Jimmy Carter becoming president and the opening of "political space" - the Tehran Spring so-called - prisoners were allowed to assemble to pray, Ayatollah Montazeri was chosen to lead the prayers. This came at the insistence of Ayatollahs Taleqani, Rafsanjani, his son-in-law and briefly IRGG Commander Hasan Lahouti, and Mahdavi Kani, a Khomeini appointee to the Revolutionary Council who served as prime minister for a while - all of whom stood in the front row. Among the pious, being elected to lead public prayers is an affirmation of rank and esteem. In those days, they recognized and extolled his integrity.

Whenever we walked together in the prison yard, he answered my questions graciously. Sometimes he would ask me a question about an English work he was reading. One time I said, "I have read that in Saudi Arabia banks pay interest, though they call it something else. Is that objectionable from the perspective of religious law?" With the same laughter that later on became famous and also turned into a cudgel in the hands of his opponents, he replied: "That's nothing but a foolish *taqiyyeh*" – the sanctioned religious practice of lying about or faking one's identity for self-preservation or to promote the faith. "Does God's wisdom and His grasp of human needs not measure up to the muftis' in Saudi Arabia?" He then added: "In God's view, interest by any name is usury." He lived to see the Islamic Republic also resort to the same "religious dissimulation." In the end, his integrity prevented him from keeping silent about the regime's other scams. He knew there was a price to pay for speaking up and chose a clear conscience over power at the cost of a guilty silence.

Soon after the victory of the Islamic revolution and his evolution into one of the topmost leaders in the new regime, there was a surge in the wave of attacks against him. People occasionally spoke of him mockingly as *gorbeh nareh*, "male cat." At the time, I gave little thought to the origin of that moniker and the motivation behind it believing that like other officials, he was being targeted by people who had had enough of the regime's massed shortcomings and tyranny. I also remembered that when walking in the prison yard dressed in the white linen garb exclusive to the mullahs, he always seemed to tread on tiptoe, not unlike a cat that can dexterously prowl about without a sound. Then again, on the rare occasions when he played volleyball, his movements betrayed no dash or dexterity. On the contrary, while Rafsanjani, for instance, leapt nimbly from one spot to another, Montazeri recovered the ball sloppily and could never move fast enough to dodge a smash shot. Prison volleyball was as if the prescient signifier of these two individuals after they assumed power.

Montazeri spoke with a heavy Esfahani, or it may have been Najafabadi, accent. He intoned the difficult English terms he asked me about in the same way. The first time he asked me about a certain phrase, the wording had no resemblance to English syntax. I was baffled. "*Hāj Aqa*, perhaps there's been a mistake?" It turned out there was no mistake. At least it wasn't his mistake. The phrase came from an English translation of the Quran by a devout Pakistani. The translator not only revered the Quran as the Word of God but apparently believed that Arabic syntax and the position of words in a sentence was also part of that divine scripture and therefore immutable. He had thus kept the syntax of the Arabic original in his English translation, and if the result was nonsensical, he left the task of unraveling the incomprehensible text to the piety of the faithful. There was no doubt about the faith and piety of Montazeri except of course in the minds of those who used and understood "faith" to be merely a tool of dictatorship.

Today, when I recall those relentless attacks against Montazeri at a time when a backroom battle royale was under way among the regime's powermongers, and not only the Islamic Revolutionary Guard Corps but also the likes of Ayatollah Beheshti and Rafsanjani and Khamenei were vying for more authority by the day, and Montazeri's honesty and candor did not accord with their designs, I ask myself to what extent were those attacks the work of his rivals or of a population that exasperated by the regime, pounced on everyone, eventually including Montazeri? When a few years later he openly criticized Khomeini and the regime's entire power structure, Ahmad Khomeini, likely at the behest of his father, unleashed a verbal assault against Montazeri employing the same bywords and language that his opponents had originally used against him to cast doubt on the soundness of his mind and judgment.

A slew of Montazeri's precepts in the final years of his life – from his fatwa endorsing the civil rights of Iranian Baha'is to proscribing torture and blowing the whistle on the regime's shadowy dealings with the U.S. and Israel in what came to be known as the Iran–Contra Affair – all underscored the contradiction between his integrity and the iniquitous nature of the regime. Once he came to realize the scope of that contradiction in the realm of reality and action, not dissimulation and illusion, he openly broke away from the regime. To him, faith was not to be used as a tool to gain power and wealth. His faith was neither instrumental nor for sale. When he resolved that his former mentor Khomeini and many of his former confederates were consumed by power, he launched into audacious and candid criticisms. One need not be a Muslim to admire his candor and audacity and nonconformism, nor accept the idea that any Shia cleric – even a free-spirited one like him – should ever monopolize regency.

His role in amending the constitution to incorporate the
theocratic Guardianship of the Jurist, an unprecedented and
peculiar Shia system of governance that crowned a "supreme
leader" for life, will no doubt be part of his historical reckoning. In later years, he went out of his way to insist that his
version of Guardianship differed from what Khomeini had
articulated in his book *Islamic Government*. His efforts to
correct and admit his mistake will, I believe, make up the
mitigating part of that historical reckoning. His memoirs,
Khaterat, along with Rafsanjani's likewise published collected
daily journals *Majmu'eh-ye Khaterat-e Ruzaneh-ye Akbar
Hashemi Rafsanjani* (1981-1993), are among the most vital
and candid records of the Islamic regime's power structure
available to us today. A comparison between the writings
of the two men reveals the character of each in the clearest
fashion possible. Rafsanjani's journals are exact and extensive
and full of stories. But every line appears to have two distinct
interlocutors, which is why they teem with ambiguity and
equivocation and laconism. Its first interlocutor is history and
the future. Its aim, above all, is to acquit Rafsanjani before
the tribunal of history. Its second interlocutor seems to be the
Revolutionary Guard Corps' interrogator. That would explain
why despite the fact that the largest portion of the journals
were written in the period Rafsanjani was at the apex of
power, the entries are geared to making sure that in the event
the inquisitor showed them to *Aqa* – a common moniker for
Ayatollah Khamenei – Rafsanjani would find a way to hold
one or another position within the network. Rafsanjani was
not given to burning bridges that might serve him someday.
By contrast, Montazeri's memoirs have a single interlocutor
and judge, and that is his conscience. He was not anxious to
retain his post and reconcile with Aqa. He therefore had no
fear of him.

It is said that the intellectual's task is to speak truth to power and challenge its follies. When, in penning his memoirs, Montazeri called someone like Ebrahim Raisi a murderer for his role in the massacre of around four thousand people, he was acting as a dauntless and unfettered intellectual. He was aware that the object of his hypercritical commentary was not mere lowlife killing agents. His chief interlocutor, other than his own clear conscience, was that *Sheikh-e Sanaan* and history.

Ehsan Naraqi

Every time we spoke, his catchphrase was: "What have those Americans said about me?" He knew that while researching the life of the Shah and Amir Abbas Hoveyda, I had been exploring U.S. archives. Since then, I had also read a few reports about him. I always sidestepped answering his repeated question as I was sure he would not be happy to hear what I had read. His ceaseless efforts to find out what others said about him, and conversely, his eagerness for others to talk about him no matter what, though preferably in his favor, was part of his social persona and character. Politics was his element; he never tired of it. He loved being at the center of every major development in society, even at the price of a degree of infamy. He had friends and buddies and fellow warriors and enemies in every political sect and clique and social class. From Ali Amini and General Pakravan to Morteza Motahhari and Gholam-Hossein Sadiqi, they were all part of his circle of friends. By definition, then, any description of such a complex personality, especially in a brief report by U.S. embassy staff in Tehran, must be flawed and wanting.

One time when he posed the same question on the phone, I finally gave him a brief rundown of what I had read about him in some reports. "They say he is an ambitious and

high-profile intellectual who self-aggrandizes and has delusions of grandeur. They say he is well intentioned; he wishes
to make peace between the opposition and the Shah's regime.
He is also on friendly terms with SAVAK. Because he wants to
empathize and get along with everyone, he is trusted by no
one. Especially the Shah." I didn't tell him that during those
same months, I had heard from his friend Parviz Sabeti that
Naraqi had long eyed a ministerial post and had Hoveyda's
support, but that the Shah had rejected his appointment every
time. Evidently, the Shah had heard a tape recording of a
meeting where Naraqi had disparaged him and the monarchy.
Before I had finished speaking, Naraqi exclaimed: "The imbecility of the Americans knows no bounds. It's not for nothing
there was a revolution." It is interesting that post-revolution
he was imprisoned in Iran three times, and each time one of
the charges was his "relationship" with America. He himself
contended that in all three cases the charges were political.
He was right, too. Early on, his friendship with President
Banisadr and Ayatollah Motahhari saved him from being
arrested; but after Motahari was assassinated and Banisadr
was impeached, those same friendships ensured his arrest.
After that phone call, he never again asked me what the
"documents" said about him.

Following his time in prison, he eventually went to France
and joined the diaspora. His appearance and even his state of
mind matched Shakespeare's King Lear more and more each
day, recalling especially those scenes on the heath where Lear,
disoriented and insane and half naked, wanders about in a
great thunderstorm peering into his past. The time I went to
Paris to interview several ancien régime politicians and entrepreneurs, Naraqi's Lear-like dishevelment was particularly
noticeable. I had called him before going. "I'll be in Paris on
such and such a day," I said. "My brother Hossein will also
be coming along." He invited us to stay in his apartment. I

thanked him and said we had already arranged lodging. It wasn't true, though, as we planned to look for accommodation after we arrived. Hossein had lived in Paris for years as a student and knew its every nook and cranny. Naraqi had in the past told me about a first-class *chelokababi* close to his apartment. He said it was run by the spouse of a once prominent and presently housebound intellectual. As soon as we arrived, our first move was to go there for dinner. It was a small bistro and the kababs were delicious. We were merrily eating when Naraqi emerged in a pair of slippers with rumpled clothing and disheveled hair. It was cold and he had obviously dashed out impulsively and in haste. "I assumed you would come here," he said. "I'd told the proprietor to let me know when you arrived." After exchanging warm greetings with the woman who ran the eatery he insisted we spend the night at his place. His warmth and insistence left no room for dissent. When dinner was over, we drove up to Naraqi's apartment in my brother's car. There was no room to park, but in Paris double and even triple parking on streets and in alleys is not uncommon. Naraqi knew exactly where to park to avoid being ticketed. Knowing such tips and tricks came with living long years in the city. It also revealed something about his character. In politics, Naraqi always straddled the line between the legal and the unlawful. He was not given to bellicosity and bulldozing, and there were no constraints or limits to what he would do to get along with everyone. In his mind, given that his goal was political reform, any means and any compromise in its pursuit was justified. Intellectuals such as Al-Ahmad outwardly, and others actually, had broken up with the Shah's regime. Naraqi had not. Nor did he set any preconditions on staying in the Shah's good graces, or stop the Islamic Republic's later, or trying to reconcile the intellectuals with either regime.

That night, climbing the stairs even with light suitcases was no easy task. Naraqi led the way and we followed in the dark. With the small motion-sensor bulbs casting a shimmering glow on the steps as we climbed, the whole scene was not unlike something out of a horror movie. Naraqi finally stopped before a door and turned the key, which opened onto a darkened interior. As we walked in, he announced: "My electricity was cut off just today. I'd forgotten to pay the bill and no matter how hard I tried to have it restored on the phone, I got nowhere." I could not tell whether his insistence on hosting us that night was owing to his kindness and hospitality or whether he did not wish to spend the night alone in the dark.

He lit some candles. The apartment was very sparsely furnished. I couldn't tell whether this indicated that he had moved in only recently or he was just a carefree soul. Had he disavowed worldly goods or was there a shortage of goods for the same reason there was no electricity? The heating apparatus was cold and silent, also for lack of electricity. The apartment gradually grew colder. He seemed not to notice it. His curiosity about who I planned to interview was bottomless, even inquisitorial, as if curiosity helped fuel his internal heating system. He went on talking until half an hour past midnight and naturally had a myriad comments and stories about each of the people I was due to meet. Sometimes they were original observations and sometimes pure gossip. He concurrently insisted on highlighting his own recollections. As if there was no tomorrow. Around one in the morning, I finally excused myself and went to the room where my brother had retired two or three hours earlier. It was so cold; I slept with my clothes on.

In the morning, he offered to take us to the UNESCO headquarters for lunch. My first appointment being in the afternoon, we accepted his kind invitation. He spoke with pride about the long years he had worked there. And rightly so, for he had once served as an adviser to the director of UNESCO. More than fifty years before Iran became the country with the highest brain drain, he had conducted a substantial study on that syndrome in Third World countries. He did not stay long enough in Iran to see how the consequent economic damage exceeded even the ruin perpetrated by eight years of war with Iraq. The number of people who exchanged warm greetings with Naraqi along the corridors and in the dining hall at UNESCO showed he was not only well known but popular. He sometimes expounded on the lofty cultural or political stature of someone who had said hello.

In Iran, though Naraqi was mostly in charge of cultural affairs, he always had a foot in the political domain as well. In the ebb and flow of the movement to nationalize oil, he was close to Ayatollah Kashani, a once-powerful Speaker of the Parliament, Majles, and acted as his translator in some of his meetings with foreign visitors. He served as the director of the Institute for Social Studies and Research for twelve years since its founding in 1958. The institute's political star was the Paris-educated professor and former Mosaddeq ally Sadiqi, known as the father of sociology in Iran, but its concept and founding were owed to Naraqi. Being close to the longtime head of SAVAK General Pakravan, Naraqi was also in a position to arrange work permits for a number of young, alternately anti-Shah, social science researchers at the institute and reportedly helped Pakravan design a sort of think-tank for SAVAK. Some of those researchers were highly successful and later recognized for their findings and political acumen. Among them were Ahmad Ashraf, Houshang

Sadr Keshavarz, Bijan Jazani, Abolhasan Banisadr, Jamshid
Behnam, and Firouz Tofiq. Much of the research conducted
at the institute under Sadiqi and Naraqi is, to my mind,
among the most valuable in the fields of sociology, urban
development, agriculture, and tribal and population studies
in Iran. The institute was affiliated with the University of
Tehran and the quality of its work, despite being handicapped
by SAVAK, was comparable to any research center at any of
the top universities in the world. Between 1958 and 1968,
close to three hundred and fifty research projects were under-
taken at the institute. Such success owed itself to Naraqi's
diligence, his being risk-tolerant, and his dedication to corral-
ling proficient young researchers, all in the reflected glow of
Sadiqi's name. Naraqi's closeness to Pakravan and his good
relations with Sabeti and Hoveyda were helpful in achieving
such success. Would it have been better if like many other
intellectuals Naraqi had cut all ties with the Shah's regime
even though as a consequence none of those projects might
have been accomplished? Were Naraqi's compromises, his
efforts to get along with a wide spectrum of militant political
factions – the behavior that per the American reports had
made everyone mistrustful of him – the inevitable price for
achieving so much?

Naraqi's next post was as president of the Iranian Institute
for Scientific and Educational Research and Planning. When
Hoveyda's plan to have him appointed minister of science
failed for the Shah disapproved of giving him a cabinet post,
the presidency of that sizable institute was a sort of consolation prize. Though he was a confidant of the queen, the head
of SAVAK, and the prime minister, Naraqi interacted with the
Shah only toward the end of his reign. In 1994, he published
From Palace to Prison: Inside the Iranian Revolution, an
account his visits with the Shah during the final months before

the revolution. The gist of it is that had the Shah listened to Naraqi sooner, the revolution would not have happened. He also claims that on his last visit, he could read in the Shah's eyes that he regretted not having heeded his advice earlier. Many individuals were meeting with the Shah in those months, including Ali Amini, Abdollah Entezam, Karim Sanjabi, Shapur Bakhtiar, and Sadiqi. All of them, except Sadiqi, came away with the same thoughts as Naraqi. Sadiqi's story was different, for he agreed to serve as prime minister but on the condition that the Shah stayed in Iran. I heard from Majid A'lam, a lifelong friend of the Shah's, how on one occasion during those final weeks the two were playing bridge with a couple of friends. The TV was on and Bakhtiar was giving a press conference. "Look at how eloquent he is!" the Shah said, then added: "Where has he been all these years?" To quote A'lam: "Gingerly but on the spot, I said, 'Seigneur, he was in jail for part of that time.'" Naraqi's criticisms of the Shah never amounted to denying monarchy as the best option for Iran. When the Shah established the Resurrection Party, *Rastakhiz*, Naraqi not only knew that any opposition to or put-down of a one-party system would block his chances of ever becoming minister, but he joined the line-up of individuals who were prepared, on the Shah's orders, to craft a party ideology based on "dialectics."

Naturally, anyone who had had past dealings with any kind of "dialectic" stood to play a higher role in drafting the blueprint. An earnest competition set off among the main power blocs – Hoveyda, Alam, Nahavandi – to identify "dialecticians" who could help delineate the ideology of a "one-party constitutional monarchy." Manuchehr Ganji who still taught at the National University and was then a minister vying for the premiership, had joined other enthusiasts to produce the dialectical philosophy of the Resurrection Party.

One day, he invited me to a meeting in Hoveyda's office.
I agreed to attend after consulting with the "organization"
and Parviz Vaez-zadeh. Aside from Hoveyda and Naraqi
and Ganji, the most animated participants in that meeting
were Ahmad Fardid who spewed Heidegger, and Enayatollah
Reza who was marinated in Stalin's dialectic. Fardid had been
invited by Naraqi. As always, he spoke volubly and disjoint-
edly and even Naraqi could not stop him. He constantly
picked a fight with Reza, each accusing the other's dialectic
of lacking "authenticity." Undeterred, Naraqi dragged
Fardid into television where he expressed his bizarre views
in programs anchored by Alireza Meybodi. At all times – even
in the post-revolutionary years when he turned into a devotee
and champion of the Guardianship of the Jurist – Fardid's
goal was to justify a single point: That a new form of
power – whether *Rastakhiz* or *Velayat-e faqih* was beside the
point – was the sign of the resurgence of "Iran's historical
mission." On television, he also spoke of "Westoxification,"
a pernicious concept that he – and *Seyyed* Fakhreddin
Shadman – had planted in Al-Ahmad's confused mind. As to
the regime's incongruity, suffice it to say that while it was the
harbinger of a kind of modernity, many of the Shah's and the
queen's advisers were anti-modernist. Fardid was not alone.
Naraqi, *Seyyed* Hossein Nasr, Dariush Shayegan, and *Seyyed*
Jalal Tehrani all felt antipathy toward modernity. Whatever
the regime's right arm built, its left arm held up to ridicule
and mockery. As an escape route from modernity Naraqi,
borrowing from Henri Corbin, promoted *fotovvat,* the traditional code of chivalry; Nasr, joining heart and voice with
Motahhari, "pure, Mohammedan Islam"; and Shayegan the
"spiritual heritage of India." I only participated in that one
meeting to advise on the party's "dialectical ideology." Then,
by order of the "organization" and taking my cue from the

history of Germany in the years preceding World War II, I produced an underground tract where I likened the founding of the Resurrection Party to a step toward ushering in a new fascistic power structure. The audience for the pamphlet was no more than three hundred while the viewership of Fardid's TV programs and readership of books by the likes of Nasr and Naraqi and Shayegan was in the thousands. On that cold night in Paris, I asked Naraqi about the party's dialectical meetings. He did not remember that I had attended one, which was not surprising. I said nothing. Reza and Fardid and Naraqi had been running the show while Hoveyda sat back like a mere spectator at a circus or play. Naraqi added: "Like everything else in those days, it ended up in a mess."

I never doubted his sincerity, never doubted that he felt for Iran and that he exerted himself to elevate the country – nor had the American report that had upset him questioned him in that regard. But every time he said something had "ended up in a mess," I could never tell if he truly believed it was a messy job or merely that a job became messy when he was no longer involved in it.

.

Qodsi Khanom

The first time I visited them at their home, Qodsi *Khanom* opened the door. In all the ensuing years, it was almost always Qodsi Khanom who came to the door. I don't remember her husband ever doing so. When she had plans to go out and he was expecting a visitor, she used to leave the door unlocked so he wouldn't have to trouble himself. He disdained conversations as much as he did household chores. Qodsi Khanom, on the other hand, always welcomed visitors warmly and sociably, looking animated and lively. From the first time I saw her, her posture was a little stooped. As time passed, she looked gaunter by the day, her hair thinning, and her back more bent. She always wore loose-fitting and comfortable clothes. Not on that first occasion, but later on I noticed she wore a plain gold cross around her neck.

On crossing the threshold into the house, it was impossible to miss the large black wall hanging painted with scenes, some quite brutal, of the Shia zealot Mukhtar Thaqafi avenging the killing of Hossein, the third Imam and the quintessence of martyrdom for Shiites. The textile painting was by Hossein Zenderoudi. It carried weight not for the novelty of its design nor the originality of its portraiture but for the

311

artist's name, or perhaps because it hung prominently in the
foyer. In the small and unadorned living room, two fairly
large paintings of Qodsi Khanom's husband drew attention. Anyone who had read any of his books would have
recognized one of them for it adorned the cover of every
novel, collection of short stories, or translation that he had
published. In the room, which other than those paintings and
books and chairs had no frills, the relatively wide mantelpiece
above the fireplace caught the eye. Three photographs and
a framed verse rested on it. The poem was written in a fine
script: *Alone with a hundred thousand / Without a hundred
thousand alone* and signed Laedri. I recognized one of the
three photographs right away. It was a sullen but expressive
picture of Forugh Farrokhzad. The familiar face of Sadeq
Hedayat appeared in the second photo, with a young boy
with big eyes standing in front of him. I figured it must be the
son of Qodsi Khanom and her husband. No one could have
predicted the tragic end of that child, the apple of his mother's
eye. Both photos were taken by Qodsi Kanom's husband, the
renowned writer Sadeq Chubak, who was a talented amateur
photographer. He said he used to take snap shots with a Leica
since his youth. The first time he mentioned Leica, I had no
idea what he meant. When he lost his camera two or three
years later, he was dejected for a long time. Qodsi Khanom
was his steadfast patience stone and pushed back against his
misgivings about this or that person.

Among the images on the mantelpiece the most striking
was the third one. It was of an extremely beautiful woman.
She looked like a movie star in a world of dreams more than
a real person in the world of reality. "Who is that?" I asked in
admiration and amazement (and my clumsy ignorance). "She
is extraordinarily beautiful!" I had assumed, and my tone
implied as much, that it could not possibly be a relative or an

acquaintance. "That's me when Sadeq and I had just met," she said without any hint of rancor or reproach. That very first day of our acquaintance, I learned that Qodsi Khanom's love for Chubak was even greater than her patience.

I did not ask her about her life, not even her maiden name, as we had barely met. I simply called her Qodsi Khanom. Perhaps I didn't ask because I was feeling nervous and antsy. But in fact in all the years that we met, though I learned a lot about how she and her husband had met and other details of her life, I never asked about her maiden name. Had I asked and then forgotten, it would have added insult to injury. When I thought of writing this piece, I searched for her last name and asked around. They had met when they were both students at the American College in Tehran and married soon after. None of my friends were any the wiser. Even Ebrahim Golestan who was among the couple's closest friends, only remembered her as Qodsi Khanom. He also knew she was Armenian.

Every source or article about Chubak merely mentions "his spouse" or "Qodsi." Even in the *Encyclopaedia Iranica* entry on Chubak, she is only identified as "Qodsi Khanom." Elsewhere, she is sometimes referred to as "Qodsi Chubak." I finally came across a text by an American girl, Qodsi Khanom's granddaughter – and I well remember how the grandmother treasured her – who had built a website in English and identified her as Qodsi Chubak Masoon. In the end, the most accurate answer to my query was provided by my dear friend Parviz Shokat. I believe that in the last years of her life, besides her son Ruzbeh, Qodsi Khanom had no closer friend than Parviz. He said her last name was Masoon Kahālzadeh and that her father had been an optician in Hamedan.

The injustice against Qodsi Khanom is peculiar from several points of view. In our Iranian culture, many women retain their maiden name even after marriage with pride and perseverance, but in Qodsi Khanom's case marrying a famous writer had in effect effaced a part of her identity. Qodsi Khanom worked from the time they were married and was one of the two breadwinners in the family. But she dedicated her life, with endless patience and infinite selflessness, to ensuring her husband had all the solitude and comforts needed for his creative work in becoming Sadeq Chubak, which he certainly did, but she herself became *Qodsi Khanom* or occasionally *Qodsi Chubak*. When he gradually lost his eyesight, Qodsi Khanom not only ran the household but spent hours every day reading him books or the letter.

In those years, a pilgrimage to visit Sadeq Chubak was considered de rigueur by every Iranian writer or poet who came to northern California. Each visit meant hosting a lunch or dinner party for a small group of people. The entire burden of grocery shopping and cooking and serving the food and wine and clearing the dishes was on Qodsi Khanom's shoulders. She toiled away nonstop. Only if she felt particularly close to someone would she let them help. If you engaged in conversation with her, you would discover that she was not only extremely smart but had highly original takes on the "guests" as well. Anything she had to say about Forough Farrokhzad and Ebrahim Golestan, for instance, or Hedayat's writing and persona or Mahshid Amirshahi's behavior was spot on target. Nevertheless, it seemed no one took her seriously at those gatherings. "They mostly know me as the person who prepares lunch or dinner, or tea and pastries," she used to say.

Besides housework, Qodsi Khanom also played the role of mediator between Chubak and his brother and their children. The elder son, Ruzbeh, had completed a first-class education and was a pioneer in applying computer technology to the medical field. He was close to his mother but his relationship with his father was tense as he believed Chubak made life difficult for his mother. Even there, Qodsi Khanom was always the mediator. Sometimes, she even backed her husband: "Well, that's who Sadeq is." The other son, Babak, had strayed from his family since a young age and lived on the other side of the continent. The emotional burden of it all bent Qodsi Khanom's back a little more every day. She sometimes signaled her discontent with her eyes. Once or twice, she left the house in revolt. Job's proverbial patience is legendary. God inflicts extreme suffering upon him as the result of a bet with Satan while Job, to prove his piety, *taqva* – a Quranic term meaning "dread-inspired faith" – endures it all. Qodsi Khanom's patience likewise legendary, but it had its limits. In her youth, she even cared for the child of Chubak's mistress to give him respite, selfless behavior that was a few steps ahead of (or behind) Jesus's command to take a second slap on the other cheek.

Qodsi Khanom's husband was of a class of people who believe that genius, or a claim to genius, is a license to mistreat or be unkind to friends and relatives. In our times, Picasso more than any other person embodied the ethos of someone who had issued himself such license. I believe Qodsi Khanom had put up with her husband's lopsided behavior not out of piety but out of love. Several times, when she could take it no more she rebelled, but her rebellion was due more to exhaustion than to vengeance. At the end of an unequal relationship, as in Hegel's dialectic of master and slave, the two parties inevitably switch positions. Once when Qodsi Khanom left the house for a few days in anger, and another time when she went to Tehran to sell their house in Darrous – which was next to Ebrahim Golestan's – and stayed a few weeks longer than expected, Chubak's anguish and distress and helplessness epitomized the reaction of a master who has suddenly realized that he is a slave to his own self-assumed role of master. Of course even in those days friends and other individuals would not leave Qodsi Khanom's husband alone, which helped satisfy their urge for what Milan Kundera called 'venereal celebrity,' and his endless desire to be loved. Kundera maintained that some people are gratified with a single paramour and admirer while others have an insatiable appetite for multiple suitors. A curious facet of the relation between Qodsi Masoon and Sadeq Chubak was that for whatever reason, Qodsi who personified someone that is contented with just one lover fell in love with a young man whose thirst to be cherished and idolized was unquenchable. Chubak would have probably become Chubak without Masoon, but I believe he would have evolved into a different Chubak. I don't know what the life of Qodsi Masoon would have been like without that particular spouse, but I doubt that she would have been reduced to a mere "Qodsi Khanom" or "Chubak's spouse."

Cyrus Ghani

Cyrus Ghani had a stutter. Though lawyers are ordinarily required to be silver-tongued and even eloquent, he was one of the most successful lawyers in the last twenty years of the Shah's era. He inherited a trove of rare books, antiquities, exquisite calligraphy, carpets, and prestige from his father Qasem Ghani who with the help of Allameh Qazvini had produced one of the still-authoritative editions of Hafez's lyric canon. Given Cyrus's U.S. law degree and his access to a wide network of powerful Americans, he came to represent some of the topmost corporations at a time when commerce with large American enterprises was at its height in Iran; with the income from these accounts, Cyrus doubled his inherited wealth. None of that affected his devotion to his father's name or fame. One of his first clashes with me was in reaction to what I wrote about Qasem Ghani in *Encyclopædia Iranica*. Living in the shadow of a celebrated and, in this case, also domineering father is in itself challenging even for someone as personally accomplished as Cyrus Ghani. The problem is amplified, like Cyrus, one entertains an exaggerated idea of the glory and stature of one's father.

Cyrus Ghani's wide social and professional network was not limited to American bigwigs and the top brass in Iran. He

was friends with many National Front leaders and a coterie
of intellectuals and writers. Filmmaker Ebrahim Golestan,
banker Mehdi Samii, and British writers John le Carré and
Al Alvarez were all close friends. He had a truly astonishing
memory. It was as if the image and attributes of every person
he had encountered was forever etched on his mind even if he
had met them only once. He was a cinephile and had watched
countless movies. Not only did he remember all the directors
and actors by name but also the cinematographers and screen-
writers. Because he also enjoyed gossip, he was also versed
in the scandalous affairs attached to those productions. One
of the books he published in exile was *My Favorite Films*, a
sweeping selection of movies from every era beginning with
silent classics. Another was called *Iran and the West*, a critical
bibliography of his library collection. Both books were the
outpouring of his passion for art and history unburdened
with scholarly constraints. A similarly driven book was his
Shakespeare, Persia, and the East that established the reason
why favorable references to Persia are found in the dramas of
that sixteenth-century British playwright. He had apartments
in London and New York and, later, in Los Angeles. Evidence
of his kaleidoscopic life could be seen in each. He played a
lot of tennis and loved watching it as well. He vaunted the
fact that he had been traveling to London and New York for
years to watch Wimbledon and the U.S. Open.

I got to know him at the outset of my research on
Amir Abbas Hoveyda. After a few formal and semi-formal
exchanges around that period, our mutual interest in movies
and Shakespeare and sports and contemporary Iranian history
helped solidify our friendship. I visited him in London and
New York and on many occasions in his apartment in Los
Angeles. I also sought his advice on various subjects. He
once gifted me three beautiful works by master calligraphers,

including one by Ahmad Qavam. Like me, he suffered from back pain and a slipped disc. One time when he had come to Berkeley with his wife and daughter and son-in-law, three extremely decent and loving individuals, he turned up at my house unannounced carrying a wooden chair as a present. "It does miracles for back pain," he said. "It's a replica of the chair that John Kennedy used in the While House to soothe his pain." When I began my research for *The Shah*, he did not hold back on anything I asked him about except in one instance. Among others, he provided extremely accurate information on Iran's several-hundred-million-dollar loan from Chase Manhattan Bank. He was one of the lawyers whom the Rockefellers had consulted about the loan. Ghani said he had advised them against it. The Shah's regime, which the previous year had loaned and donated close to one and a half billion dollars to this and that country now needed a loan; the Shah wanted to have the loan secured and processed without the legally required parliamentary approval.

Ghani and a few other lawyers had argued that if something were to happen in Iran, the next regime might not regard the loan as legitimate and refuse to repay it. The Rockefellers were the Shah's personal bankers and handled the Iranian government's major accounts as well. They rejected the lawyers' advice, asserting that the Shah's word sufficed as a guarantee for the loan. In 1976 no one, neither the Rockefellers nor the clergy in Evin's "mullahs' block" nor Khomeini in Najaf, could have imagined that the monarchy would collapse in three years. The loan was processed but was indeed jeopardized when the Shah was toppled in 1979. One of the hotly debated narratives in Iran about the hostage-taking crisis is that the decision to admit the fallen Shah to the U.S., which led to the attack on the U.S. embassy in Tehran, was masterminded by the Rockefellers knowing it would instigate Khomeini's backers to take the diplomats hostage; that would in turn leave the Carter administration no choice but to freeze Iran's assets, at which point the Rockefellers would be able to collect their loan. What we know is that the Rockefellers presented a comprehensive and detailed plan to compel Carter to issue a visa to the Shah and that after the hostage-taking incident, Iran's assets in the U.S. were frozen and their loan was repaid in full before any restrictions were lifted. Hence, the conspiracy theory that spread then and has survived to our day.

In one of our exchanges, Ghani mentioned that in the final weeks of the Shah's rule George Ball, former U.S. diplomat and banker under Kennedy and Johnson, was hand-picked for an Iran mission and that Ghani was among those whom Ball consulted. He also said he had a copy of George Ball's report but he never showed it to me. I finally found a copy at the Princeton University library. Not that his refusal to share that report with me hurt our relationship. I appreci-ated that he might have promised Ball or some other person or institution to keep it private. I knew Ghani was acquainted with many individuals who were close to the Kennedy family and his camp in the Democratic Party. When I solicited a travel grant from the Kennedy Library in Boston to visit the facility, Ghani asked his friend Arthur Schlesinger, one of Kennedy's favored intellectuals, to write a letter endorsing my request, which he did. Ghani's reluctance to show me the Ball report might have also had to do with the fact that having published an excellent study on the rise of Reza Shah based chiefly on British sources, he was now planning to write a book on Mohammad-Reza Shah; he had a right to want to be the first to present such important source material in that book. Whatever the reason, I was not piqued by his rejection. But two other events placed a grave strain on our relationship.

Ehsan Yarshater asked me to write an article on Cyrus's father Qasem Ghani for *Encyclopædia Iranica*, which I accepted enthusiastically. I was an avid reader of the critical edition of the *Divan* (collected poems) of Hafez, co-edited by Qazvini and Qasem Ghani. I had also read parts of the elder Ghani's daily journals, which Cyrus had published in thirteen volumes; the *Iranica* article was an opportunity for me to read them all. I knew that Qasem Ghani was involved in the marriage, in 1939, of then Crown Prince Mohammad-Reza with Princess Fowzieh, and that as Iran's ambassador to Egypt had played a key role in their divorce in 1948. In reexamining Qazvini's introduction to the *Divan* of Hafez and consulting many of Qasem Ghani's letters and notes, I had grown curious as to the nature of the latter's role in shaping that co-edited volume. In the late 1930's, Qasem Ghani had also collaborated with the noted statesman and scholar Mohammad-Ali Foroughi in producing a critical edition of Omar Khayyam's quatrains. In reading some of Ghani's letters and interviewing a number of people who were close to both him and Sadeq Hedayat, I had also unearthed certain aspects of Ghani's personal life, some of which I related within the framework of that 2,500-word article. I wrote that Dr. Ghani – who had studied medicine in Paris – used to call Hedayat "boy" disparagingly; I did not add that this was likely because both he and Hedayat had their eye on Maryam Firouz, a prominent female intellectual of the time. What I did write was that a close scrutiny of Qazvini's introduction and Dr. Ghani's letters – the two friends had first met in Paris in the mid-1920s – would paint a more accurate picture of Qasem Ghani's role in the editorial process. I declined to offer my personal take on that "accurate picture." Was it out of respect for my friendship with Cyrus Ghani? Or was it because the subject could not be broached within the confines of an encyclopedia article?

But I did write that Qasem Ghani's two-volume *Tarikh-e Zaman-e Hafez* (History of Hafez's Times) was shambolic and disorganized though replete with substantive material. Before submitting the article to Yarshater for *Iranica*, I shared a copy with Cyrus Ghani and asked for his opinion. He called a day or two later. He sounded displeased. There was no lashing out, not yet. "This article is ridden with errors top to bottom," he said. "It smacks of hostility toward my father." He added that I must have written what I did because I idolized Hedayat. He also questioned why I had not mentioned his father's communications with some world-famous figures. I responded that a mere 2,500-word biography could not accommodate every topic. "Also, what does it matter that your father sent a letter to such and such a writer who then acknowledged receipt? The letters he exchanged with the likes of Qazvini and the notable painter Kamal ol-Molk Ghaffari are important and have been referenced." We continued discussing the article over the next few days. I corrected any errors I recognized in the text but found most of the points that he raised to be irrelevant. I intuited that the faults he found stemmed more than anything from a son's affection for a powerful and famous father rather than from intellectual curiosity or historical rigor.

I submitted the slightly edited article to *Iranica* and it was published shortly afterward. Many months later, I received a communication from Yarshater in the mail. The envelope was marked "Confidential." I was surprised. Inside, there was a sharply worded and threatening letter from Cyrus Ghani to Yarshater and the latter's response. Ghani had alleged that my article about his father was filled with false and libelous claims and that if *Iranica* refused to amend it, he would pursue the matter through legal channels. In response, Yarshater had basically said, "Do as you wish. The article complies with our editorial standards; there is no need to amend it."

Meanwhile, I was in negotiations with a small group of Iranians headed by Akbar Lari to write *Eminent Persians*. I consulted with Ghani as well, as I did on all such matters. His advice was: "Turn down their proposal. You will not see eye to eye with them." When I told him that I had set a condition that no one other than myself had a right to read the book before I submitted it to the publisher, his tone changed. He said, "Let's write it together," and added: "I don't expect any compensation. I know almost all these people." He went on to say he would be a tremendous asset for the book. I did not know that he had also contacted Lari directly, and without telling me proposed to write the book himself. I replied: "No doubt you are right and what you know about that era is invaluable. I know that many of these one hundred and fifty individuals were your friends." If memory serves me right, I had not yet learned about his threatening letter to Yarshater, but I brought up my *Iranica* article about his father and said, "Remember how different our approach was and how much distress it caused?" He flew into a rage and cut his ties with me. I never got to see or talk to him again. When I learned that he had lost his son, I thought of calling him to offer my condolences. Then I heard from Ebrahim Golestan and others that he had broken up with them as well and spewed vitriol at their continued friendship with me. His hatred was as intense as his love.

Abbas Maroufi

Ifirst learned his name from Houshang Golshiri. On one
of Golshiri's trips abroad post revolution, perhaps the
one whose upshot was his 1991 novel *Ayneha-ye Dar-dar*
(Mirrors with Doors), he said he'd come across a young
and talented novelist with an insatiable passion for literature called Abbas Maroufi. When I then read Maroufi's
Samfoni-ye Mordegan (Symphony of the Dead) and some
issues of his literary magazine *Gardoon* (Heavenly Sphere),
I appreciated, in Beyhaqi's words, "the rich expanse" of his
work. In his novel *Peykar-e Farhad* (Farhad's Body), which
anticipates the emergence of increasingly emancipated women
in Iranian society, he rewrote *The Blind Owl* from the point
of view of the woman who in Hedayat's original meets a
bitter end. When I first heard of him I did not know that
in the inhospitable and stone-hearted cultural landscape of
the Islamic regime our fates would, at least in one instance,
unwittingly intertwine in a knot and that I would eventually
meet him in person.

When leaving Iran on a melancholic rainy night, my
friend Parviz Kalantari drove me to the airport. He came
to fetch me at two o'clock in the morning. A few months

later he graciously sent me the piece that he had painted
after my departure. The canvas is composed of two distinct
parts separated from one another with wavelike lines. In the
lower register a woman lies on her back, clad in what looks
like a chador. Her cheeks are flushed. A young boy sits by
his mother's side looking anguished. Attractive houses and
other structures, voluminous and undulating, are embedded
in that black chador and stand out, conspicuous and inviting,
the pitch-dark night notwithstanding. Many of them feature
ventilation shafts that recall the architecture of towns
bordering the Iranian desert. The aura and ambiance of the
structures intimate Kalantari's famed "earthen canvases."
As in that collection, a mosque appears in their midst. The
crescent moon, slender but eye-catching, lies in a corner of the
sky. Every building and even the moon is painted in a cobalt-
blue chiaroscuro. A faint shadow, perhaps of the dark night
oppressing the houses, envelops that particular impression
of Iran in a shroud of sorrow. The intensity in the son's eyes
might also suggest an enduring spirit and a glimmer of hope
in spite of the harrowing bleakness that blankets Iran and
Iranians. In the upper register of the painting, which takes
up the largest portion of the canvas, a colorful airplane not
unlike a child's toy or drawing is headed toward a seemingly
splendorous West. This section is in the style of Kalantari's
"childlike" collection. A man in a suit and tie, bespecta-
cled and luggage in hand – that's me – is dangling from the
airplane and flying toward some glittering skyscrapers.

As the painting was sparked by my departure from
Iran, it may be said to reflect that particular event. But like
every great work of art, it not only embraces dimensions
and meanings beyond any initial "spark" that might have
inspired it, but its layers of meaning transcend even the artist's
conscious intention. Every painting, like every story and

poem or any text or speech, no matter how simple, embodies a subconscious that is more expressive than the artist's or writer's or speaker's consciousness.

With a smattering of attention, the skyscrapers though colorful, appear unstable, towering but one-dimensional, even crooked. They do not have much of a foundation or footing or depth or integrity. Even his Eiffel Tower while set against a golden backdrop, is flat and rootless. The sun above is large, crimson and terrifying. Perhaps Kalantari meant to visualize Sa'di's: *Neither a place to stay / Nor feet to walk away.*

Before sending me the canvas, Parviz who used to publish articles in *Gardoon,* gave a photo of it to Abbas Maroufi who reproduced it on the cover of *Gardoon* 15–16, Khordad 1370 (May 1991) with the question, "Will our fellow émigré citizens return?" No sooner had the magazine hit the stands than Maroufi and *Gardoon* and Kalantari came under attack by hired gangs of *Basij* thugs, and Maroufi was put on trial. Although the powerful lawyer and former judge and future Nobel Laureate Shirin Ebadi represented him – or perhaps because Shirin Ebadi represented him – he was indicted on charges of "publishing obscenities, interviewing counter-revolutionaries, and colluding in cultural invasion," while Kalantari's cover design was decreed an "insult to the Islamic hijab and sanctity." Parviz was obliged to write a letter to the court saying he had not meant to insult anyone or anything. "I drove a friend to the airport and he left his ailing mother and his son in my care," he said. "That painting reflects nothing else." Did the riffraff who attacked *Gardoon* and Maroufi truly miss the point that Kalantari's image of the "Motherland," even though black-clad, was more alluring and wholesome and grounded than his depiction of the West as depthless, gilded and vacuous? A regime of preachers craves and adulates the milieu of a one-man show. Preaching by definition calls for a single voice and a chorus to watch and wail in surrender. As such, the preachers could not tolerate any other voice – especially one so unruly and literate. They wanted to shut down *Gardoon* and kindred publications; Kalantari's painting served as a handy excuse. In any event, there is no avoiding the question that had they not forced Maroufi to emigrate, would he have suffered the same sad fate and died relatively young from cancer? According to him, Simin Daneshvar had once advised him not to be sorrowful "because sorrow breeds cancer." Exile is invariably coterminous with deep sorrow, and Maroufi's experience in Germany where he fled to was no exception to that rule.

He contacted me from Cologne saying he had started up *Gardoon* again. He had also founded Gardoon Press and was eager to reproduce my writings on modernity. Thanks to him, the first version of my collected essays on modernity and its foes was published in Germany in 1998 (the expanded version *Tajaddod va Tajaddod-Setizi dar Iran* appeared in Iran in 1999). I went to Europe for the book launch and to attend a meeting organized by the Iranian Writers' Association in exile. As I later learned, Gardoon Press published about two hundred books on his watch.

Maroufi lived in a small apartment in town with his wife Akram Ayyubi, a painter, and their children. One of their daughters had an astonishing gift for poetry; in the few days I spent in their home she wrote a poem to her father that was incredibly beautiful and endearing. But beneath the serenity of his family life, Maroufi was always a thorny subject in the political and tribal zeitgeist of the Iranian diaspora in Cologne. At the time, many of the city's taxi drivers were Iranian immigrants – perhaps they still are. In whatever cab you rode, the conversation would always turn to Maroufi when the driver realized you were Iranian. A friend told me later that a German philosopher had dedicated one of his books to Iranian taxi drivers in Cologne stating they were the best philosophers in the world. I don't know if that is true, but in Maroufi's case most of them expressed what Plato calls *doxa*, opinion or belief, no more than an emotional feeling as opposed to *episteme*, knowledge, which is based on reason and is the pillar and touchstone of philosophy.

One of the first things you noticed about Maroufi was his burning attachment to literature, especially Persian literature and its corpus of poetry and storytelling and associated commentary. To him, minding that devotion was worth any price. He was willing to expend his family's and his own capital in its service. Letting his nonconformist literary ventures dent his reputation led his critics, even after his death, to call them "tangential" exercises unbecoming of a writer.

One of the first receptions I attended in Cologne with Maroufi was at the home of the literary editor of Suhrkamp, which was (and still is) unquestionably one of the country's greatest publishing houses with many titles in the German literary and philosophical canon to its name. Maroufi insisted that I meet with that erudite editor and even persuaded him to consider publishing a German edition of *Modernity and Anti-Modernity*. One learns from reading the memoirs of thinkers like Adorno and Arendt and Koestler that avarice and narrow-mindedness and an unhealthy competition for limited resources was a common attribute of the intellectuals who fled from the Nazis and sought refuge in the West. I never observed any such attributes in Maroufi. That night I realized that given the German editor's plaudits and the fact that Suhrkamp had published a number of his works, if Maroufi was simply after fame (if only in the interest of his family) he would have continued working with Suhrkamp, likely guaranteeing his renown and financial security. But his heart was entangled elsewhere. He knew himself first and foremost as a citizen of the republic of Iranian literature; on that premise, he was willing to do whatever necessary, even get a loan for Gardoon Press to publish books by authors he did not even know, which put his own reputation at risk in the event he could not repay the loan. The time I had gone to visit him, his inability to repay debts had spawned whisperings against him in Cologne but as best I could determine from afar, he paid no attention to them. His greatest motivation was writing novels and publishing works by others that he considered valuable. His passion for literature and the role that he had assumed for himself on that stage knew no bounds. He often talked about how each person's life and every passing moment in it is the stuff of a story. His own life would have produced a mesmerizing novel indeed.

One characteristic peculiar to many exiles is their intense efforts to gain financial security and regain the lost standing they enjoyed at home. In Maroufi's case, whatever came to characterize his exilic life generally resulted from his intense focus on creative writing and supporting novice writers and other novelists. He never drank from the well of despotic rulers and spurned the easy living of an Iranian-German writer. He endured the pains and pitfalls of an Iranian immigrant's life to his last breath.

Ardeshir Zahedi

Ardeshir Zahedi was a complex figure etched in history with a social persona shrouded in a one dimensional silhouette that most of his detractors, and at times proponents, painted of him. In the twenty years that I had the privilege of being his friend, I came to know several aspects of that Iran-loving and lovable individual's complex nature. I do not intend to appraise his entire political record here, merely to outline some of his personal traits.

In the years I have been immersed in studying the Shah's era, no one's character and demeanor has turned out to be more different from what I, and perhaps even a vast contingent of people, had imagined than Zahedi's. I was said that he was frivolous and devil-may-care, lazy and servile; that for months prior to August 1953 and the overthrow of Mosaddeq he had grown friendly with the Americans; that his speedy rise to power was due to that friendship and the fact that he was the son of General Fazlollah Zahedi who overthrew Mosaddeq; and that in due course, perhaps owing to both those factors, he became the Shah's son-in-law. It was said that he cursed a lot and had no qualms about confronting his adversaries in their face. The story of his poor handwriting and his botching the spelling of *dayyus* (cuckold) in an official communiqué enjoyed notoriety. Such defects were drawn on by his opponents to brandish his incompetence. From our first encounter, I realized that almost everything I had heard and repeated about him was a mischaracterization, except, of course, his handwriting, and that while given to being proper, he also was at home with profanities.

Perhaps one reason for the Shah's enduring love for and unique relationship with him was his plain talking and habitual off-the-cuff cursing. He used profanity even in the strictly confidential handwritten reports he sent to the Shah in a special portmanteau to which only he and the Shah had a key. Other people treated the Shah not like a person but an institution; in the words of Shahbanou Farah: "They wouldn't even dare bark at the Shah's dog." But Zahedi, while he began and ended each royal report with an ingratiating "Crowned Father" and the "Shadow of God," once he delved into the main subject, adopted the style of a normal dialogue between two people. His opening and closing words followed an Iranian ritual in letter-writing, and Zahedi was attached to rituals in all affairs. He used to tease the Shah in his reports and trash other people. In one instance, he calls the powerful head of SAVAK General Teymour Bakhtiar a bastard and his mother a whore. In my first meeting with him too, when talking about Amir Abbas Hoveyda he used derogatory terms to refer to certain alleged aspects of Hoveyda's behavior, behavior that the great Iranian satirist Obeid Zakani described as "requisite for rising in the sultan's court." In one of our exchanges he talked about one of his meetings with the British foreign secretary. "I called him names" – akin to what he had called Bakhtiar's mother – "and threatened that if British ships sailed close to Iranian islands, I would order our naval forces to hit them." I thought to myself his wording must be exaggerated, but when I searched the British Foreign Office records and found the foreign secretary's version of that exchange, I discovered that Zahedi's version was exact to the letter.

My first meeting with Zahedi harked back to the time I had just started researching Hoveyda's life. I knew that his relationship with Zahedi who was ostensibly a member of his cabinet was strained. I asked Ahmad Qoreishi who had been gracious to me when I was teaching at the National University of Iran (later renamed Shahid Beheshti), to arrange a meeting for me with Zahedi if possible. Zahedi agreed to be interviewed but set a condition. When I came to know him better, I realized that he valued and safeguarded his friendships even at the risk of sustaining personal harm. I witnessed again and again how warmly and respectfully he treated Queen Fowzieh – the Shah's first wife, sister of King Farouk of Egypt, and Zahedi's mother-in-law – as if she were still queen. In all those years, I did not hear him even once speak of his only wife Princess Shahnaz other than well and affectionately. By contrast, I heard him say several times, "Well, I behaved rather badly." He never went into the details of their separation.

The condition set by Zahedi for that first interview was that I send him my questions in advance, which I did – I ran up a two-page list. We were to meet in Montreux in a famous Swiss hotel that was once the playground of kings. In 1921, when *Seyyed* Zia Tabatabaie, prime minister of Iran for less than a hundred eventful days was exiled, he went to Montreux where he sold Persian carpets on a street corner nearby.

I arrived at the hotel on the appointed day and hour feeling incredibly nervous, though I had never felt that way about any other interviews I had conducted during that period. In all the years I knew him, never once did he show up late to an appointment, not even by a few minutes. Perhaps my anxiety stemmed from the fact that as an activist student in the 1970s, I had agitated in the opposing political camp when he was Iran's ambassador to the U.S. I knew him then as a diplomat and in today's Westernized parlance, a "celebrity." In fact, he behaved like a celebrity even before that concept was popularized, and used that cachet to advance his goals as an ambassador. Today, in taking measure of his death, I believe he was the last of the politicians who had a particularly prominent impact on their times; from Mosaddeq, Qavam, and Alam to Princess Ashraf, the queen mother, and Kashani, each despite their political differences was part of that influential contingent. I believe Zahedi was the youngest member of that group.

When I arrived at the hotel, the moment I mentioned Zahedi's name the entire staff knew I was to meet him; he must have alerted them in case I had trouble finding him. I was escorted to a spacious niche in the dining room which had panoramic windows and beautiful views. They said it was known as "Zahedi's nook." Handsome crockery was mounted on the corner walls decorated with a crown motif, as I recall. As I came to know his ways, I realized he paid special attention to the relation between architecture and the projection of power; hence, the importance of staging every meeting. As minister of foreign affairs he appointed glamorous new mansions for numerous Iranian embassies. The Iranian embassy in Washington, D.C., was a notable example of his thinking. Its architect was Iranian and the interior stuccowork was crafted by a master he had brought to Washington for that purpose.

The moment I approached Ardeshir Zahedi, he stood up. An older gentleman seated next to him did the same. Zahedi pointed me to a chair across from him. In all the meetings he hosted, even casual ones, he always assigned seating with great care. He introduced his friend without explaining why he was there, though I could guess. I knew he knew that I had been opposed to the Shah's regime in the past. He must therefore have wanted a witness to our discussion, and rightly so. With his permission, I both taped our conversation and took notes. A pile of paper was stacked by his side. My two-page list of questions lay next to it. He started with the first question almost instantly. Although he was known for his hospitality, he knew ours was a working session and he took work very seriously.

It took about three hours for him to answer all my questions. His companion grew tired after a while. Zahedi who I later learned had a habit of closely monitoring his guests, noticed his friend's unstated fatigue. He said pointing to me, "*So and so* has come from far away; I have to answer all his questions." As long as he could manage physically, even in later years when he had to maneuver himself in a wheelchair, he spent hours working every day. He listened to music all the time, both when he worked and at leisure. I once asked him if he listened to Iranian music. "These days what serves best is Western classical music," he replied. "The blues of exile makes it difficult to listen to Iranian music." He had a longstanding and close friendship with the conductor Zubin Mehta who was of Parsi origin. "With His Majesty's consent, I made him an Iranian citizen," he said. Zahedi was also a sponsor and supporter of the famous Montreux Jazz Festival. He used to answer letters and telephone messages or notecards promptly and with incredible self-discipline, and if anyone failed to reply to him on time he would feel hurt and upset.

For me, those three hours passed as if merely a few minutes. I devoured every word of his candid and at times lengthy answers. He had a peculiar way of describing what he remembered. Each recall was a stream of consciousness in the exact sense of the term. I had no doubt he had not read Proust, but his mental webwork was just as fluid. That day, for instance, he began with a description of his verbal clash with Hoveyda on a flight to Pakistan. He then related that as he and the Shah were being driven from the airport to their residence in Islamabad, the crowds that had been lined up along the route were cheering in Persian, though with a heavy Pakistani accent. When the Shah asked, "Ardeshir, what are these people saying?" he replied, "Sir, they're saying, 'Whorah, the king'!" And the Shah laughed. Zahedi then mentioned that Bhutto was a close friend of his and pointed to his wife's Iranian lineage. Then he went back to the story of Hoveyda on the plane, followed by: "Of course I knew Amir – meaning Amir Abbas Hoveyda – from the time he worked in Switzerland," and added: "I was very fond of his mother." He next described the dish that Hoveyda's mother prepared for him in Switzerland and then switched back again to the finale of his brawl with Hoveyda.

Once he decided to write his memoirs, however – he completed three volumes and hastened to finish the fourth in the last months of his life – he ditched the stream of consciousness and opted for covering the events in a chronological order, duly sourced and referenced. He paid close attention to every element and sentence. Despite very high production costs, he decided to commission a new edition of the supplement to volume three, which comprised several hundred documents. He wanted them reproduced in a larger font size. "They have to be legible," he said. When the *New York Times* declined to publish his articles critiquing the CIA's role in the 1953 coup (and then of Trump's policies), he published the first as an ad that cost him $50,000. His exertions with respect to his memoirs were not in vain, however. The book was very favorably received in Iran. Ebrahim Golestan had high praise for it, especially after reading the third volume; he read the entire tome twice, he said, and called Zahedi to share his thoughts with him. "What Ebrahim said brought me to tears," Zahedi avowed to me later. Over the years, Golestan has told me incredibly interesting stories about how he came to know Zahedi, highlighting the singular import of his memoirs, his patriotism, and the character of his father General Zahedi.

Zahedi spent much of his last forty years organizing the enormous mass of his and his father's archive; Dariush Homayoun who was married to Ardeshir's sister Homa helped him with the process for a time. Once completed, he entrusted the several hundred thousand historical records and images to the Hoover Institute at Stanford University. He found it particularly hard to be separated from that archive as if a beloved child was being taken away. The entire time that the material was being boxed and readied for shipping by a team of experts he never left the small room, which is where he used to have breakfast. Every now and then, the team supervisor would walk in and say, for instance, that they had found a suitcase full of photographs and photo albums and ask, "What should we do with it?" "Take that away too," Ardeshir would answer, his eyes betraying the pain he could not hide. While he wanted the documents to be consigned to a secure location, he was adamant that they also be accessible to young Iranians. To that end, he donated funds to Stanford to begin the process of digitizing them.

The orderliness and discipline that he exhibited in the preservation of that archive and the preparation of the first

three volumes of his memoirs mirror the regulation and ritu-
alistic nature of his daily life. He woke up every morning
between eight and nine o'clock and went to bed every night
between ten and eleven. He watched the news on television
late at night and early in the morning. He would then go
to the small room on the mezzanine level. A long table and
four chairs took up most of its length. "I like this room,"
he used to say, "because here I have memories of my father
and mother, my wife Shahnaz, my daughter Mahnaz, and my
friends." During the last weeks of his life, he decided to go
home against the advice of his doctors rather than stay at the
hospital. Though he was only able to navigate a wheelchair
using special equipment, he wanted in whatever way possible
to return to that roomful of precious memories.

Prior to becoming infirm, he used to walk into the room
at nine o'clock every morning clad in an elegant dressing
gown. A copy of the *Herald Tribune* and a batch of letters and
communiqués would be on the table. Before doing anything
else, he would feed the birds. A bowl full of Indian almonds,
walnuts, and seeds would be at hand. He had mounted a
container on the window's outer ledge in which to place
birdfeed. He spent a few minutes whistling and inviting
the birds over. In no time, hundreds – no exaggeration – of
swallows and pigeons and blackbirds would converge on the
trees near the window. "Almost all these trees are souvenirs of
my father," he said. As soon as he dropped the nuts and seeds
into the container, the birds would rush to the ledge or to the
paved area below the window. He stood by watchfully in case
a blackbird or a bullying pigeon tried to rob the swallows of
their meal. He would survey the scene from behind the glass
holding a small toy water pistol. If he noticed an abusive bird
he would open the window and blast some juicy profanities

at the bird and its sister and mother before putting an end to its abuse with the gun – "my F-16," as he called it.

After eating breakfast – which was always the same and included fresh fruit – and showering, come snow or rain he would walk to Zurcher, one of the oldest restaurants in Montreux. That took about an hour. A table large enough for several diners was always reserved for him from noon to about one-thirty. While en route, he would speak with an astounding number of shopkeepers and resident folk. It seemed that not just me but the entire town knew his daily itinerary. When I took a train on my first visit, I hailed a cab at the terminal. It was around midday. Based on his home address the cab driver knew exactly who I was meeting with. He said, "If you have an appointment with Mr. Zahedi, he's not home; he's at Zurcher every day at this hour," and proceeded to take me there. Every time Zahedi entered the restaurant the staff would rush to welcome him and as best I could tell, not just in anticipation of the tip they expected to receive. He always started with a cup of tea, served in a glass and saucer as closely resembling an Iranian set as possible, with a sugar cube on the side to suck on. Most of the time, a bowl of radishes was also brought to the table once he stepped inside – another memento of his favorite platter of fresh greens in Iran? After lunch, he would walk back. In the evening, he either went to a party at around six or seven, or entertained guests at home.

There is no question that someone active in politics for seventy years would have had opinions, or done things, that not everyone would agree with. In the last years of his life, I particularly disagreed with his sometimes validatory views of the Islamic regime. He held that "nationalism demands that I defend Iran and the rights of the Iranian people." When I objected that this regime disavowed the very idea of nation, *mellat* and recognized only the community of the faithful, *ommat*, and even sacrificed the interests of the "faithful" to the thirst for power by usurpers of power, he disagreed. He likewise objected to many of the views I expressed in my books. But he also said, "I believe in your efforts to unravel the truth." That was enough to make him overlook our disagreements and entrust his remarkable collection of historical documents to the university where I worked. Nor did I doubt in my heart, even for a moment, that whatever sentiment he proffered, even those I was adamantly against, was out of his love for Iran and not tainted by hankerings for personal gain or other ambition. He was the stuff of history, and how history judges him, whether negatively or favorably, will be a measure not of this or that opinion he might have expressed – certainly not as an exile – but of the aggregate of his productive life.

Dariush Homayoun

Dariush Homayoun had a passion for Beyhaqi's *History*.
His own prose was likewise clear and powerful and at
same time precise and well-framed. Similarly to his historic
idol, he devoted a great portion of his time to understanding
and presenting the "facts about this history" that is the life
of our generation and exploring its "corners and crevices,"
so that "none of it may remain obscure." and ensure that
"its properties may not lay buried away." Although in his
youth, outraged by the Anglo-Russian occupation of Iran, he
engaged in armed struggle along with a group of naïve and
extremist individuals who succeeded only in injuring themselves when they attacked an Allied army camp, throughout
most of his politically mature days and his entire time as an
immigrant he chose to apply himself to Iran's national interests and political options rather than to dogma and an illusory
utopia. Despite the seduction of *ghogha* (brouhaha) – "mob"
in Beyhaqi – he defended a deliberative and organic development process and disputed the ethos of agitprop and militant
efforts to transform society by force. His curiosities were
not instrumental; nor was his version of events contrived or
derived from selective "facts." In no phase of his turbulent life
did he limit himself to focusing strictly on political events or

discussions. He knew that society does not grow and change within the confines of neatly segregated social science disciplines but at the intersection of economics and politics and culture and literature even as they twist and turn. He knew that a noted nineteenth-century Russian or English novel was as indispensable for understanding the political upheavals of the twentieth as was Marx's disquisition and the history of capitalism.

He loved Iran; he did not idolize it. He wished greatness for the country but in unraveling and elucidating its greatness he was neither extreme nor did he shy away from critiquing and parsing and presenting its shortcomings, today or in the past. As best I could tell, he did not parade Iran's bygone glories to camouflage the pain and failures of the present. He knew the West and its accomplishments very well. Even in the days when maligning America was something of an "intellectual" must, he openly praised both the U.S. and the West, but without being intimidated by either. He knew their shortfalls as well and duly recounted them. The journey between the extreme nationalism of his youth and the democratic liberalism of his exile days was long; he trod that fraught path with an incessantly probing mind and an earnestness for learning and a richly endowed language in which to express his thoughts. Heeding Beyhaqi, he knew that "nothing remains static; change affects everything."

I met him for the first time in the city of Belmont in California thirty years ago. He had come to visit his confederates in the political party that he had founded. One member was Dr. Heydarqoli Borumand who is among the most decent and patriotic Iranians I know. He was a practicing physician who turned to politics in the last years of the Shah and was elected to parliament from Esfahan. He moved to the U.S. post-revolution and never stopped trying to extricate Iran from the clutches of theocracy. I got a call from him one day. "Mr. Homayoun is here and has asked that we arrange to meet," which we did one morning at Dr. Borumand's home – a small apartment in a high-rise building full of Iranian immigrants. Homayoun had read my Persian translation of *The Master and Margarita* and the articles that I had co-authored with Manuchehr Safa as a critique of Stalinism and to refute Daryabandari's judgment of Arthur Koestler; *The Persian Sphinx* had not yet been published. As in the years I continued to see him, he spoke little and judiciously; each statement was polished and thoughtful and every line and every phrase solidly constructed. After a while Dr. Borumand asked in a gentle but reproachful manner why in such fraught times I was busy writing about Iran's past instead of directly addressing current political issues. I felt a little surprised, both by his tone and the substance of his question. Before I could respond, Homayoun turned to his fellow party member with his habitual smile. "The fact is one cannot pave the path to the future without a keen knowledge of the past." He said acts of resistance against despotism and ignorance unfold on myriad fronts and in different forms; we have to resist with that in mind and not regard any of it insignificant. He has often admitted with remarkable candor to having faced a thousand and one tricks and temptations on his long trek across the political map and that like any pathfinder, had at times gone off track. One time, for example, he and a few other rookie patriotic soulmates thought they could chase Anglo-Russian and American powers from Iran by setting off some explosives. For a while, he had also joined SUMKA, the National Socialist Workers Party of Iran, bullying, clubbing, and roughing up Soviet lackeys on the streets to save Iran from the peril of communism. SUMKA was in fact the Iranian version of the Nazi Party led by a particularly well-educated man named Davoud Monshizadeh. An accomplished linguist, Monshizadeh was known for his celebrated translation of the *Epic of Gilgamesh*. Homayoun described SUMKA as an aggregate of alien and unaligned phenomena, like surreal art. In the end, though, he found the ways and means of language to be superior to bullets and belligerence and by embracing journalism played an enduring role in transforming that vital public estate in Iran.

He had a difficult childhood, nothing less than Dickensian. His eyes filled with tears when he talked about that wretched and lonely period of his life. He said he managed to survive misery and isolation with the help of books. His accounts of his youthful temptations and troubles and his analysis and commentary on their circumstances were rife with humor and warmth and honesty. He talked about how he landed a bottom-rung job at *Ettela'at* newspaper and how fast he climbed the career ladder in journalism. Iran's cultural climate at the time was dominated by two dogmatic blocs, both messianic. On one side was the coterie of mostly Marxist intellectuals who modeled themselves on Prometheus, the Greek Titan who defied the gods and brought knowledge to humanity, and on the other were the self-styled devotees of the Mahdi, the Shia savior figure who is expected to rise from occultation someday. In each case, a kind of utopia or flawless society (communist or Shia) lay at the end of the ideological rainbow. But Homayoun was neither Marxist nor religious. He did not embrace the ideological axioms of either bloc. Moreover, unlike the messianic crowd, he did not feel an irreconcilable animosity toward the U.S. Because he did not belong to any clique or sect, the dogmatic camp suspected ill-will and ambition in his every move. That misgiving was twice as strong among the intellectuals on the left who were apparently aware of Homayoun's erstwhile anti-communist activities. At any rate, he did what he had to do and ignored what Beyhaqi called the "mob."

He obtained a bachelor's degree in law from the University of Tehran, but his greatest talent lay elsewhere. Before long, he won a Nieman Fellowship in journalism and spent a year at Harvard University. On completing his research in the U.S., he wrote an article about political sociology and the ins and outs of public media in Iran. His study made an impression and attracted the attention of a number of statesmen, including Amir Abbas Hoveyda. In time, Homayoun founded the daily *Ayandegan* (Futurists) with government funding. He managed to recruit some of the best journalists, which is why a few years later from just before the revolution until a few months after the fall of the Shah, *Ayandegan* was one of the most influential newspapers in the country with the widest readership. The decade preceding the revolution was marked by major highs and lows. He married Homa Zahedi, then a member of parliament and one of the most influential women in Iran; he was also appointed minister of information and tourism in Jamshid Amuzegar's cabinet. While the Amuzegar administration was short-lived, two pivotal events occurred on Homayoun's watch when he was minister that helped spark the revolution. One was the Cinema Rex fire in Abadan in August 1978 where several hundred people where intentionally locked inside the theatre and burned to death. I remember Homayoun giving an interview after reporting that gruesome tragedy where he accused the "revolutionaries" of being complicit and said it was now up to the people to choose. But surging revolutionary "fervor" and the deftness of the religious establishment's public relations precluded anyone from investigating the crime. People pointed the finger at the Shah's regime and by the time they realized it was indeed religious zealots who had set the theatre ablaze, the anti-Shah uprising was unstoppable.

The second event that catalyzed the revolution was a poor decision made by Homayoun himself. "I made a mistake but I had no choice," he explained, which in my view was not acceptable. When in response to harshly worded attacks by the exiled Khomeini the Shah ordered the publication of a pseudonymous op-ed that disparaged the ayatollah and the "Red and Black reactionaries" – leftist and Islamist militants, respectively – and every newspaper editor declined to publish it, Homayoun played a critical role as minister and arguing that the Shah's decree must be upheld, had it placed in *Ettela'at* on 7 January 1978.

As the flames of revolution surged, the Shah concluded on the advice of several army brass and statesmen that the people's abrupt fury could be allayed by placing a number of high-ranking officials under arrest. Despite Homayoun's kinship with Homa and Ardeshir Zahedi – or perhaps because of it as he would present as a prime "sacrifice" – he was arrested, as were Hoveyda and a number of others. I heard from Zahedi that the only time he met his brother-in-law in prison, Homayoun emphatically forbade him from seeking "favoritism" on his behalf. The day the regime fell, Homayoun and several top officials of the regime managed to break out of the prison. He lived in hiding in Iran for about two years. Had he been cornered by the revolutionaries, he would have no doubt been the object of the sword of Islamic mercy. He said that in that period of dread-filled vagrancy, his main focus and pastime was studying and revisiting history. In an act of extreme courage and honesty, he then decided to offer an account of his own past and the Pahlavi regime for critical evaluation. His *Dirouz-o Farda* (Yesterday and Tomorrow) (2000) demonstrates his keen knowledge of and respect for the Shah's accomplishments without glossing over the regime's failures and shortcomings.

He did not let the distress or loneliness of exile or anyone's tongue-lashing distract him from his studies and intellectual interests. He never stopped thinking about the salvation of Iran. As if to answer Beyhaqi's question "How can anyone who does not know themselves know other things?" he resolved to better understand himself and Iran and the world and the democratic trends of the times, perchance to find a way to deliver Iran from the prevailing terror and benightedness. Did he wallow in sorrow? Blame others? Quite the reverse: he took the fraught path of reconsideration and reassessment and, even more importantly, made a concerted effort to instill solidarity among Iranian immigrants. He truly grasped the value of dialogue and its critical place in a democracy; indeed, he loved listening at least as much as he loved talking. I witnessed this time and again at the home of Ardeshir Zahedi.

Homayoun was needless to say aware of the complex relationship, loving and at times stressful, between his wife Homa and her brother Ardeshir. He also knew that his own views and political outlook did not align with Zahedi's, especially not in the last years of his life. I knew that he had a hand in organizing and classifying the large volume of Zahedi's archival documents. I never saw him become argumentative in Zahedi's home, though he never refrained from defending his position, albeit genially and respectfully. In any discussion, he had an extraordinary capacity to be gentle and civil toward his interlocutor while remaining steadfast and decisive about his own views. He spent the last years of his life in a grinding, though to him effortless work to unite supporters of reason and democracy against the advocates and enforcers of ignorance and despotism. At Zahedi's receptions, he was always deferential toward his wife and wary of putting her or her relationship with her brother under any unnecessary stress.

I came to know the essence and brand of Homayoun's humanity from attending those functions, and also from what I learned about his relationship with Homa Zahedi's children from an earlier marriage. He treated them with such love and respect as though they were his own. I observed from afar how they mourned his death as if they had lost a beloved father. I also used to notice how, at Zahedi's receptions, Homayoun would stand at a distance from the crowd and watch quietly; when he found a soulmate to talk to, he would take them to one side and spend the time listening or sharing. I never met anyone who had a conversation with him who was not awed by Homayoun's insight and wisdom and modesty and learning, whether the topic was Beyhaqi or Shakespeare or the lay of the land in Iran.

Mahshid Amirshahi

I had read some of her work before our first encounter and had heard about the impact she had on the lives of several people. Following that meeting, I also experienced the bitterness of her bite.

In the years before the revolution, I had heard stories about her lifestyle and free spirit from Parviz Kalantari. Had Iran had a Nietzsche or a Max Weber, Mahshid Amirshahi would have been its Lou Andreas-Salomé. In patriarchal societies such as Iran – as had been the case in Salomé's Europe – free-spiritedness signals vulgarity in women and virility in men. The first is condemned and the second feted. One of Mahshid's idiosyncrasies was that her free spirit was rarely cited by anyone as an admonition; it even served to further arouse patriarchal men. That may explain why, when relating vignettes of Amirshahi's life, Parviz added, "Of course, I never dared join the ranks of her suitors for she regarded people like me as bumpkins." He also mentioned that Mahshid's house in Tehran was designed by his brother Iraj; in the frenzy of destruction and profiteering characteristic of post-revolutionary Iran, that storied house has reportedly been razed to the ground and replaced with a tower.

What work of hers I had read had a charming, throbbing prose that combined the rhyme and rhythm of a reporter with the keen eye and sharp tongue of a storyteller. In her writing as in her personal life, she was audacious and authentic, not afraid to be iconoclastic in either domain. In both she knew her self-worth (perhaps overmuch) and challenged anyone who did not. Thus, she had an abundance of former and current devotees. The first time she came to Berkeley to give a talk, and I was only able to listen for a few moments, I knew two of my friends in the audience were enamored of her and that a former admirer, Sadeq Chubak, was breathlessly hoping for a visit as he lay sick in the hospital. When I finally met her I felt she had been cradled by votaries all her life to such an extent that she had forgotten how to have a normal relationship with people who admired her work but were not infatuated with her.

Not only is Mahshid Amirshahi highly educated and erudite but she also comes from a very cultured family. As a young man I had heard praises of her mother Moloud Khanlari who was in the vanguard of the women's movement in Iran and whose home, when she lived in Paris, was the haunt of past and current Iranian political figures, both leftist and centrist, but also visiting and émigré writers. Mahshid's writings were at times overshadowed by the fame of her mother and family. In later years, I heard many stories about her entanglements with Najaf Daryabandari and Sadeq Chubak and her relationship with Ebrahim Golestan. She briefly married the filmmaker of great fame Farrokh Ghaffari and they had a daughter. But none of those red-letter marginalia impaired Amirshahi's standing as a writer.

By the time I called her at her home in Paris to let her know that she had been awarded the Bita Prize for Persian Arts at Stanford University her days of fame and notoriety were behind her. In between, I had read her engaging pair of novels, *Dar Safar* (Itinerant) and *Dar Hazar* (At Home). In both, I found the allure and lucidity of her narrative and her beautiful (and at times cutting) portrayal of the characters extremely appealing. Although fictitious, the characters are based on real people and easy to identify, as in a roman-à-clef. The narrative is also appealing owing to her courage in speaking her mind without reservation. Yet even though typically iconoclastic and radical, her portrait of Shapur Bakhtiar is closer to that of an idol than the protagonist in a novel. Post-revolution, both Mahshid and her mother collaborated with Bakhtiar in his office in Paris before he was assassinated. Some of her portrayals of their fellow activists come across as excessively acerbic and piquant, yet they are always laced with humor and wit. Among them, she labels Mohammad-Jafar Mahjoob *Lāt-e Daneshmand* (Learned Lout). She might have been referring to Mahjoob's studies on chivalry, *fotovvat* – an age-old a code of honor that is upheld by some honor-bound popular louts to this day – or to his demeanor and language. In both novels, as in much of her post-revolution writings, there is a marked sense of disillusionment and resentment against people who had acquiesced to Islamic dictatorship. Alongside intellectuals such as Bakhtiar, Mostafa Rahimi, and Gholam-Hossein Sadiqi, she foretold and blasted the menace of despotism that lurked behind the drumbeat of revolution. She was neither seduced nor intimidated by its populist ardor or shibboleths and resisted the onrush of that calamitous deluge as best she could. Needless to say, Amirshahi was awarded the Bita Prize strictly on account of the literary value of her oeuvre and not her politics.

When I introduced myself on the phone she intimated familiarity, though I don't remember her exact words. I gave her a rundown of the prize and the former awardees and the event schedule. She accepted eagerly. We briefly talked about certain technical details such as which of her books we should print specially for the ceremony and which airport she would be flying from. Before ending the call, she said, "I would like to ask a favor, which is for Mr. Shajarian [acclaimed vocalist and former awardee] to be at the event." I assumed she was merely being playful. I told her I could not make any promises as I did not know whether he would be in the U.S. then and that even if he were, all I could do was extend an invitation to him. She arrived in California a few days ahead of time. Two days before the event, I went to see her at her hotel. We had a pleasant conversation; there was no question that she could be convivial when she wanted to. On hearing that she planned to stay around for a few days I proposed organizing one or two sessions in Persian for her to talk about the art of storytelling. She agreed and we fixed the lecture dates. Alas, to borrow Beyhaqi's words, "Fate lurked in ambush, doing what it must."

On the day of the event, as soon as Mahshid arrived on campus her first question to me was whether Shajarian had come. "He's not in the U.S.," I said, for he wasn't. The award ceremony started with my welcome speech and a description of that year's prizewinner. Bita Daryabari then followed up with a brief talk and handed Mahshid the prize statuette and a check for $10,000. When it was Mahshid's turn she began her talk in her excellent English with: "*So and So* [referring to me] had persuaded me to accept this prize by promising that Mohammad-Reza Shajarian would be here. But he is not." I find it hard to pinpoint exactly why I found her words offensive. I knew she liked to pepper her speeches with humor. Perhaps that is what she intended. Or she wanted to make a point and pay her respects to Shajarian. Or perhaps stage fright compelled her to begin that way; I personally experience a great deal of anxiety before the start of every class or lecture. No matter the reason, what she said upset me. For one thing, it wasn't true; it also discredited a prize that luminaries like Shajarian himself and Simin Behbahani had received in previous years.

As always, when the ceremony was over we moved to a reception hall where the audience was invited to enjoy tea or wine and have a chance to meet the guest of honor and perhaps take photographs. Another tradition is that the prize-winner poses for a photograph with the prize's founder, Bita Daryabari, as well as Hamid Moghadam who with his wife Christina had helped establish the Iranian Studies Program at Stanford. That evening was no different. I introduced each of the three to Mahshid in a few sentences and when the event was over, we all went to dinner with her and one of her friends. As usual on such evenings, my colleague Bahram Beyzaie and his wife Mojdeh Shamsaie, a famed actress, also joined us and helped me look after the guests.

Once we took our seats at the table Beyzaie, meaning to express nothing but admiration, commented, "What polished and fluent English you speak, Madam." Mahshid said nothing but she looked hurt. Moments later I said disapprovingly, "I never promised Shajarian would be here." She scowled and said, "Yes, you did!" The rest of our exchange that evening was similarly ill-tempered. At one point she asked me, "How did you find my telephone number in the first place?" "I don't really remember," I replied. "Finding someone's telephone number is not difficult." I then added: "I might have gotten it from my sister Farzaneh." I knew the two were once friends. She replied in a manner I found slighting: "No. She hasn't had my number for a long time." I believe both she and the other guests were happy the dinner was over early.

The next day one of Mahshid's admirers who had accompanied her to dinner called me. "Mahshid was really upset last night," he said. "If you don't make her come round, she will forgo the lectures and return to Paris the day after tomorrow." I had no doubt he had not called me without first consulting Mahshid or even upon her insistence. I replied, "As far as I'm concerned, nothing was said that could have caused any dismay or grievance that call for her to be 'brought round.' If she wishes to return straight away my associates will make the arrangements." The ticket had been purchased by Stanford and could only be changed through our office. Mahshid returned to Paris two days later.

Some time passed. One night I was at a friend's house. She asked if I had read Mahshid Amirshahi's latest piece. I had not; I then read it on the internet, which is evidently where it was first posted. I was stumped and felt quite upset. She had interpreted Beyzaie's words as disparaging and mocked me for bragging about "wealthy" Californians. Despite being struck by the tone and substance of her piece I did not feel any urge to respond. Nonetheless, when I started writing these "portraits" I did not wish to forego sketching the rich and bold and gutsy story of her life while also telling my version of what happened that night.

I never saw Mahshid again nor had any contact with her. Once or twice, I saw her daughter at Ebrahim Golestan's. When she invited us over to her house, some superb "coffee-house paintings" – a genre that originated in the Qajar era – were hanging on the wall. Her father Farrokh Ghaffari who was a famously erudite authority on art was among the first to champion them; his portrait by Hossein Qollar-Aqassi, the twentieth-century master of the style, was on display. As for Mahshid, the last I heard she had moved to a cozy little village away from the hustle and bustle of Paris and in the words of Voltaire, was "tending her own garden."

Shahrnoush Parsipour

In 1940, while France was under German occupation, the famous Jewish thinker Walter Benjamin fled from Paris over the Pyrenees to the Spanish border to escape the Nazis from where, he hoped to reach the United States. But on the day he arrived, for reasons that are still unknown, the Spanish government closed the border. The closure did not last long but that same night intense anguish and depression drove Benjamin to his death, likely by suicide. Berthold Brecht wrote that had the Nazis committed no other atrocities, what they did to Benjamin was depraved enough to condemn them for eternity. The Islamic regime has likewise committed many atrocities, but what they did to Shahrnoush Parsipour is a stain that alone would be enough to condemn them for all time.

The first time I met her was outside Azar Nafisi's house where we'd both been invited as guests. I had read Parsipour's novel *The Dog and the Long Winter* and was in awe of her innovatory style and intellectual daring. She was dropped off by someone, I don't know who, and we happened to reach the door together. I had heard that she was not only creative and prolific and feisty, but also extremely beautiful. Her beauty was greater than I had imagined, as was her originality and as I discovered, diligence. She stepped out of the car slowly and deliberately, her elegance perhaps more a product of my imagination for she was said to be of aristocratic stock. In later years she herself wrote something to the effect that the only thing she had inherited from the nobility was a genteel poverty.

The second time I saw her she was a broken shadow of that defiant and inquisitive and imaginative writer. She had flown from Tehran with a stopover in Europe. I was waiting for her at the airport. The last passenger to get off the plane, Parsipour looked tired and her face was puffy. She was wearing plastic slippers and chewing gum. She walked right past me without recognizing me, staring into space; I don't know at what. "Shahrnoush *Jan*." She paused, then turned and looked at me before saying, "Forgive me, Abbas *Jan*. I think it's the medication." Clearly embarrassed to be caught chewing gum, she said, "My mouth dries up. It's because of the pills." Then she explained her slippers. I knew she had been in prison for several years. The slippers were a habit from those days, she said. What kept her in jail was her rebellious and free spirit. She had not committed any crime. Of course, in regimes like Iran's everybody is "guilty" until proven innocent. Parsipour's brother had a stack of banned newspapers at home and, fearing the ongoing torrent of arrests had asked his sister and mother to take his "subversive" papers away and burn them someplace. The two ran into the Islamic Revolutionary Guard Corps patrol and mother and daughter were arrested, which is how Parsipour came to be locked up. If she had been willing to acquiesce with their demands and keep quiet, her file might have been closed quickly and she would have been released. But in that regime it is a prime "guilt" to protest injustice and inequity and Shahrnoush could not brook the verbal and physical abuse by the interrogators and the Guard. Instead of spending just days or months in prison, she spent a few years. She once told me, "My extended jailtime was mostly because in defiance of *Haj Aqa*'s orders I empathized with the female inmates who had lost loved ones to execution. I used to stay up all night to hear the firing squad give the coup de grâce to those who had been targeted that night. I once heard up to two hundred and fifty shots." She went on: "One night, they suddenly came into the block and lined up the inmates along a corridor. There was no method or logic to their stunt. Which line people were placed in was totally arbitrary. A mullah then entered the corridor. A member of the regime had been murdered by the opposition he said, and randomly pointing at this or that prisoner declared, 'You will pay the price for that terror!' The tabbed inmates were to be executed in short order. The girl standing before me was so terrified her knees buckled under her and she slumped to the floor. It's the first time I'd seen such a thing happen before my very eyes." I did not tell her that it was only in movies about Nazi atrocities that I had ever seen such a ghastly scene.

The night she got off the plane looking pale, her mouth dry and her feet in crude slippers, her face betrayed a trace of those horrors. But being the quintessential writer, though a wreck in body and soul she went on to pen her prison memoir, which is a masterpiece of its kind. Parsipour lived to write. Of course, to endure that much depravity and abuse demands more than Job's patience. Even to read Parsipour's narrative and "bear witness" to that much pain and suffering demands extreme patience. Job's reward for his sufferings was a deeper faith in his god. Our reward in reading Parsipour's memoir is a deeper understanding of the regime's demonic inhumanity but also hope and pride in the knowledge that free-spirited individuals like Parsipour and her kind are part of humanity too. Along with her other masterpieces – *Touba and the Meaning of Night* and *Women without Men* – Parsipour helped break

the forced silence that is symptomatic of patriarchal dictator-
ships. One of the most shocking scenes in Parsipour's prison
memoir is related to that imposed silence. Hannah Arndt
writes that in totalitarian regimes, the vision and ideal model
for controlling society is to transform it into a vast prison in
which people are reduced to a "mass" of indistinct, isolated
entities stripped of any sense of rights or relationships with
other people and dependent on the prison guard for their
every need. The power of a totalitarian state presses against
the throat of "imprisoned" folk like the sharp point of a spear,
directly and unmediated. Parsipour describes the prisoners
being holed up for days or months in solitary cells as cramped
as the grave. Everyone had to keep quiet. The only sound was
recitations of the Quran and Shia elegies that were forced
upon the prisoners. But damned if Parsipour would cave in
to people who tried to crush and silence her. She survived and
wrote her memoir and to my mind, produced one of the most
inerasable chronicles of the regime's wretched enterprise. No
wonder when she stepped off the plane, her troubled eyes and
puffy face and parched mouth brought tears to my eyes. But
what also flickered behind that distraught appearance was a
fighting spirit and determination and an inquiring mind. It
was those sparks and her tenacity and her friends' support
that eventually helped her rise from the ashes.

Parsipour's behavior and vanguardism even when under
duress amazed me and increased my respect for her. That
same depressing day at the airport, she asked me for someone's telephone number, which I did not have. Right away,
she reached into her purse and pulled out the latest mobile
device that functioned as a calendar, scheduler, and address
book. I had read about such new technology that in those
days was in its infancy. Parsipour located the phone number
with superb deftness. She noticed my astonished eyes as if I'd

just watched her perform a magic trick. "It's very easy to use these," she said. "You should definitely get one."

The second time she walked past without acknowledging me was when she came to Berkeley for the launch of her new novel, *Blue Logos*. A few years had passed since that first encounter at the airport. We often spoke by phone. Once she came from Los Angeles and stayed with us for a few days. A number of the finest contemporary female authors, including the Chilean-American Isabel Allende and Amy Tan, an American of Chinese origin, helped organize a ceremony in her honor. This time, she was to give a book talk at Berkeley. I was standing outside the lecture hall when she walked past me. I said hello. Many fans were milling around. She gestured toward me in a sort of nod typical of celebrities at such events as if to say, "I see you've greeted me but as you see everybody is saying hello, so, please resign yourself to the nod." Suddenly a delayed spark of recognition lit up her eyes. When she had contacted me from Tehran and asked me to write a foreword for her new book, I'd agreed without having read it. Naturally, writing a piece for any of Parsipour's books was an honor. *Blue Logos*, brilliant and a little disjointed but very profound, was in due course published with my foreword. Looking embarrassed at not having recognized me right away, she pulled me into her arms with great tenderness and said, "Forgive me. I'm on medication; it makes me a little dizzy. My mouth is also dry." She was not chewing gum.

The hall was more than half full. Parsipour walked up to the stage and sat behind a table. She was to talk about the book and read from it. "I'm not going to read anything," she said instead. "I don't have anything to say at this moment." Then, speaking with a moving candor and honesty, she added: "Depression and hopelessness have paralyzed me." Psychoanalysis was not a norm among Iranians yet, not even voguish. Admitting to mental illness took guts. She said she had been mulling over a new novel for some time. "I've only written the first page in my mind. A girl leaves her village and sees a vast desert before her. She climbs a rock and contemplates her escape route." The story of Don Quixote leaving his home has been called the beginning of modernity in the West. A brave and thoughtful and hapless girl leaving her village and facing the gravity of the desert ahead is a perfect metaphor for the onerous pursuit of modernity in Iran spearheaded by women like Parsipour.

More than twenty years after that speech Parsipour spoke on tape about her financial straits trying to buy a house to share with her son. From the time she left Iran, Parsipour worried not only about her own livelihood but also that of her family in Tehran. One day she called me, sounding agitated and harassed; her voice is oftentimes quavering and forlorn. She said, "If you're free, come over and bring your tape recorder." I went to where she lived in the basement in the home of one of her supporters. The moment I pressed record, a deluge of thoughts and dreams and hopes and hardships cascaded from her lips in a startling fashion in language that was uninhibited and forceful, as if she were tearing down a dam unfettered by any protocols or constraints. To my mind that private tape recording, her plea for help, and her speech at Berkeley share the same spirit. They all reflect her compulsion to expose and unmask. It is she who from the start and perhaps more than any other female Iranian writer or poet has stood before us openly and unveiled, naked and fearless, and while sharing personal woes and griefs forced us to revisit and question our specious convictions. By lifting her veil when giving a speech a hundred and seventy-five years ago, Qorrat ol-Ayn pioneered the women's movement in Iran. As she bares her thoughts and soul and exposes the challenges and callousness and inequities that a liberated woman faces today, Parsipour also discloses certain views that might feel unpalatable to us and clash with our values. Forugh Farrokhzad said "I sinned, a sin filled with pleasure." Parsipour asks "Why should my pleasure and my sexual desires and my creativity and my defiance be a sin? Why do you men and women sit on the sidelines and keep silent before such unfairness?" She explains how our silence ensnares us just as it traps her; that we can only break free by overcoming the divide born from patriarchy and by breaking our silence and renouncing conformity. She knows that no creed or ideology lets one "break free." Dogmatic norms deride every breach or detour from the status quo as a form of "deviation" or "eclecticism" while Parsipour, in the most constructive way possible, is proud of her eclecticism and she is right.

Critics and belletrists are divided into two camps with regard to creative work, especially literature. One camp believes in instictive and spontaneous writing and disdains fine-tuning and revising a text. Twentieth-century Surrealists in that group held that literature should serve as a bridge between the author's unfettered unconscious and the reader's, bypassing the filter of consciousness and societal norms. Some went so far as to state that the most original creative works were done by patients diagnosed as "mentally ill" and "insane." In the other camp are those who believe in polishing and revising and rewriting the original draft and consider massaging it to be a vital part of the creative process. Parsipour does not believe in polishing either her speech or her writing. She is also emphatically against censorship. I always ask myself: what if she were served by capable editors as were, for instance, Hemingway or T.S. Eliot? Would her work have emerged more impressive and effective? Some critics call "instinctive or automatic" writing lazy and sloppy.

That descriptor does not apply to Parsipour. When her pen flows well it is a burst of creativity. It cannot be dammed. Revising and fine-tuning the text might tarnish its pristine tone. Sometimes though, she rushes to get her work into the hands of publishers so she can earn a pittance, which rules out any alterations at all.

In one of her most sublime lyric poems, Simin Behbahani declares with daring and hope: *I shall rebuild you, my homeland / Even if out of my dead limbs / Raise columns to your crown / Even if out of my dried bones.* With dedication and diligence and genius and defiance, Shahrnoush Parsipour whose life the Islamic regime and patriarchal culture had crushed, rebuilt another Parsipour from the ruins and thrived like a verdant cypress. Every day of her existence has been our gain and the despots' loss.

Houri Mostofi Moghadam

Every sudden political "explosion" is rooted in incremental vibrations through history. Its seeds lie in a thousand and one points of light and darkness, triumphs and failures, resistance and suppression. The explosion is the inevitable outcome of suppressing dissent. Struggling and fighting for a fair cause invariably outlives oppression and despotism. The powerful "Woman, Life, Freedom" movement is of the same breed as those sudden explosions. Its roots lie in myriad strands of contemporary Iranian history and the relatively stronger presence of women in that period. The life of Houri Mostofi Moghadam is a poignant illustration of that history. Many of the highs and lows, dreams and disillusions, achievements and heartbreaks of three generations of Iranian women are reflected in her lifestory. Because of her elevated social status, the struggles and upheavals in the lives of three upper-class Iranians can also be traced in the memoir that Houri left behind.

Houri was among the first girls to be admitted to the University of Tehran. At eighteen, she was translating Balzac into Persian. For years she was a schoolteacher and a college professor. She worked with Farrokhru Parsa, the first female minister in Iranian history, who was later charged by the obscurantist Islamic regime and executed in the most gruesome manner. Several prominent women in Iran today are former students of Houri, including Shirin Ebadi who was her student at high school. "Houri *Khanom* was a diligent and strict teacher, cultured and charismatic. Apart from her academic credentials and humaneness, the other point I remember about her is that she was the only teacher who drove to school in her luxury car and parked it there." In other words, Houri worked as a teacher not because her family and husband could not support her but because she had an independent spirit and a head full of ideas; she wanted to contribute to society in a meaningful way.

She was involved in several women's and philanthropic organizations and made the most of her family's resources and wide network to advance such causes. In the 1950s and 1960s, she collaborated with Farangis Namazi Shadman and others in an alliance of women university graduates who undertook a variety of projects that included building an infirmary for women. Once when I was a guest at Houri's house she showed me, with understandable pride, the exhibition catalogue of a show they had organized about Iranian female costumes in antiquity. Then in a friendly taunt she said, "As you can see, we launched Iranian studies back home long before you did at Stanford!" The exhibition, which was planned impromptu and self-funded, had a similar agenda to the state's 2,500-year anniversary celebrations of the Iranian monarchy, an event that greed, including Asadollah Alam's, and the rancor of the Shah's opponents, turned into a farce. Houri and her colleagues' project, on the other hand, attracted little attention owing to the disinterest of people in my generation whose focus was elsewhere. In her memoir, she brags about her close relations with people in power; she was also willing to confront someone as powerful as Ashraf Pahlavi to secure the independence of any entity she was affiliated with.

Because in a traditional or patriarchal society – or because she lived in Iran, which was both traditional and patriarchal – women's freedom is invariably threatened and at risk, she was equally protective of her personal independence and that of her affiliated organizations. At a time when the model of a "good, obedient, and virtuous" woman was a married housewife, she left her husband and three children for six months and went to the U.S. as a Fulbright scholar to learn about the latest developments in the field of education. A few months prior, a trip by Simin Daneshvar who was childless – her husband carped that the "wife" was not fertile – to Stanford University on the same scholarship has been aptly chronicled as a reflection of her free spirit. Houri's spirit and courage were no less striking than Daneshvar's. In her telling, she paid a price for that trip by having to put up with her family's chidings, yet exercising her freedom and the right to advance her career outweighed such abuse. Her journal entries cover both what she gained professionally from the trip and the scorn it provoked. In her own summary of the diary, written in English, she recalls in particular her husband Mohsen Moghadam's attitude with bitterness, and rightly excoriates him for his taunts. But Houri's estrangement from Moghadam in the last years of his life – he passed at age fifty-three – left its mark on her. She repeatedly points out her husband's presumed infidelities and shortcomings. But her perception of marriage and the imperative to uphold it – at any cost – was part of the traditional mores of that otherwise liberated woman. Another aspect of this dualism is evident in her relationship with Islam. She went about without a hijab all her life, was famously fashionable with a taste for fine and expensive clothing and fought for women's equality. Nor was she afraid of criticizing the Islamic regime after the revolution – even while entangled in the "revolutionary court." But her faith in her own version of Islam – which she held to be the version of "true Islam" – remained intact over the years, even in exile. Houri Mostofi Moghadam was a notably modern woman but also tied to certain traditions. In that context, her life sheds a fascinating light on how three classes in Iran's social structure, aristocrats, bureaucrats, and entrepreneurs, experienced the historical upheavals of modernity.

On her mother's side, Houri was related to the Ardalans, nobility of Kurdish descent. More than anyone else she emulated her mother who had a free, independent and modern persona, and while defying male patronage and patriarchy was boastful of her aristocratic heritage and insisted on using titles that were by then obsolete. Houri's father was Abdollah Mostofi whose profile and course of life tally with those of a tier of Iranian scribes and bureaucrats and statesmen known for their wisdom, patriotism, integrity, and exhalted spirit. By marrying Mohsen Moghadam, Houri became related to the class of progressive entrepreneurs who played a pivotal role in modernizing the Iranian economy. Houri's son Hamid, mean-while, is one of the most successful entrepreneurs in exile. I came to know Houri when Hamid and his wife Christina established the Iranian Studies Program at Stanford and I was appointed its founding director by the university.

Houri attended many conferences at Stanford. She lived in a beautiful apartment in San Francisco at the time. The window opened to a view of the Golden Gate Bridge on one side and of the Alcatraz prison on an island in the middle of San Francisco Bay on the other. Her home was at least a ninety-minute drive from the campus. Though she had driven in Tehran since her youth she had later quit driving but managed to get to the conferences with the help of a friend or relative. She always dressed in an outfit she considered appropriate for a woman of her age and position, with no regard to the dictates of fashion or political correctness. In cold weather, she wore a fur coat. She did not refrain from expressing her candid and decisive opinions about the programs and those whom we should (or should not) invite. Even when I and other colleagues spurned her interjections, she would not stop trying to press her point. She was not overly dogged and never tried to create trouble when her views went unheeded. She knew she could interject in the discussions within limits but also insisted on sharing her ideas, as was her right. My friendship with her began with just such interjections.

She sometimes shared her views in a letter following a conference but more often by phone or in person. One time she invited me to her home so we could have a fuller discussion. "I'll cook something simple and we'll chat." The first time, she made a thick noodle soup, *āsh reshteh*. It was delicious. She told me she was such a good cook that while living in Iran – "before it came down to this" – she had trained a few people and that each had become a great chef. It was during one of those house visits that she read me a few sections of her diary. She had been writing entries in Persian and French and English in mostly the same form and size notebooks. Her notes covered every subject, from what was on her mind and the details of her daily life to literary discussions and family gossip, hotels and restaurants she had visited, the ups and downs of her relationship with Mohsen Moghadam, and her philanthropic, cultural, and behind-the-scenes political activities. From the first time I heard parts of her journal, I knew it to be a precious repository of the life of a lettered and independent Iranian woman whose life straddled the twentieth and the twenty-first century. Thanks to the Moghadam family, those journals are now housed in the Stanford University archives.

As in her past life, Houri was never idle in exile. Dividing her time between France and the U.S., she pursued her intellectual and research interests wherever she was and whatever the circumstances. In Paris, she attended the Sorbonne and obtained a doctorate in literature. She wrote her dissertation not on Persian literature – which would have been easier – but about a French poet and writer whose work she had discovered during her first research trip to the U.S. a quarter of a century earlier. In the last years of her life, she devoted herself to revising and editing a summary of her memoir, then spent a few years producing an English translation of it with the help of her daughter Maryam. A short time after the work was completed Houri passed away at the age of ninety-nine. Maryam recalled that until a few weeks before her death Houri would walk along the streets around her house and, as an exercise, recite some French poems that she remembered. Neighbors taking in the mysterious and unintelligible murmurings of a stylish, ninety-something woman were likely unaware of what a remarkable life she had lived. Maryam made a heroic effort to publish her mother's book even while suffering from cancer in her later years. She passed away a few days after receiving a print mockup of the book and its cover design. The title of the book, *Never Invisible* not only captures Houri Mostofi Moghadam's life but sums up the movement whose motto has become "Woman, Life, Freedom." In any society, enjoying freedom and a good life is contingent upon equality between men and women. Fortunately, women like Houri cannot, nor should ever be invisible.

Iraj Pezeshkzad

I raj Pezeshkzad spent a lifetime hounded by the fame of his iconic book *Daie Jan Napoleon* (1973) and his aristocratic lineage. He was hounded by the proponents of what the Islamists called "valued" art and other revolutionaries "committed" art. It matters little whether value and commitment are deemed to be earthly and historical or heavenly and supernal and whether, as happened in post-revolution Iran, they coalesce into a single dogma that treats literature as a tool of ideology. For advocates of value or commitment in art, humor and joy were the nemesis of "piety" and "revolution." Pezeshkzad was further hounded by those that decreed fame to be a "banality and a sign of collusion with "gold and grudge and guile," *zar o zur o tazvir,* as Ali Shariati put it, except, of course, in the case of men of fame who issued such fatwas. Pezeshkzad was hounded by those who held that suits and ties and government jobs, even in the case of an ethical and competent diplomat, do not square with "intellectualism." He was hounded by critics who considered satire "plebian" and felt it had no place in the republic of literature – revolutionary or "modernist." Finally, he was hounded by those he had lampooned in his *Asmun Rismun* (Heavenly Yarn) as a worthless and "cheeky" bunch

371

some seventy years earlier. Later on, he wrote a new and more political parody of the same "chicks" in his *Internasional-e Bacheh Por-rouha* (International of the cheeky bunch).

The hounders were legion. But the scope of Pezeshkzad's work outmatched their capacity for brouhaha and barbs. My first brush with the richness of his writings dates back to the time when I had completed my studies in the U.S. and returned home. I asked some well-read friends for a list of the best books in varied disciplines that shed light on different facets of modern Iran in a clear and fluid prose. I picked up *Asmun Rismun* on the advice of one of those friends and as I read it, marveled at the elegance of the thinking and the charm of every spoof in the book.

I regret to say, however, that despite being awed, despite my own research into the question of modernity over the next three decades, I never paid his work the attention it deserved. In truth, the answer to the very question of modernity lay at the heart of most of his diverse writings, expressed in the canniest and most incisive way; even the books he chose to translate shared that theme. Perhaps the distance one unwittingly puts between oneself and the past as an immigrant, perhaps even the gut punch delivered by the revolution that at least in my case compelled me to reconsider once-revered dogmas and misguided convictions, and perhaps Dick Davis's brilliant translation of Daie Jan, *My Uncle Napoleon,* and its critical plaudits in English helped me grasp the significance of Pezeshkzad's oeuvre and the recognition that had been denied him, his masterpiece included. I also came to know yet other curious details about the enduring appeal of that novel when I was living in Iran.

The phenomenal popularity of *Daie Jan Napoleon* as a TV series directed by Nasser Taqvaie in 1976 was unmatched in the history of Iranian public broadcasting. One day, I was talking with a well-informed friend who like Daie Jan saw the "hand of the British" in everything, including in the then brewing revolution. "You sound just like Daie Jan," I said. He retorted with a sneer, saying something to the effect that either I was playing dumb or was really dumb. He went on to say that the impetus for producing the series and even prior to that, the very writing of the novel – which was woven around the Allied occupation of Iran in World War II with references to the Iranian Constitutional Revolution – was a premeditated British plot designed to groom the Islamic revolution. He further explained that to prevent anyone from saying the presently ruling mullahs were installed by the British, the novel was plotted such that the "hand of the British" would sound like a joke and lose credibility altogether. "Right now, in doubting my words you have knowingly or unknowingly become an agent of the British." Years later, when I got to know Pezeshkzad I told him about my learned and leery friend. He laughed. "Yes, sir. They threw plenty such garbage at me." I think he also said he had written a short story about it. It goes without saying that like any work of art, *My Uncle Napoleon* had multiple angles and layers. Literary classics are as much a depiction of their own times as a relatable outline of later periods. They are as if always contemporary. These days as Khamenei blows the drumbeat of a "cultural invasion" and a "cultural NATO" being led by the Great Satan and its army of jinns and other nefarious actors, and is hailed as the supreme line of defense and applauded in the newly minted song "Heil Commander," which extols General Qasem Soleimani and Imam Mahdi and most of all, Ali Khamenei, he is as paranoid as Uncle Napoleon and his "hand of the British" and equally delusional about his own battle skills. Like a kitsch copy of Daie Jan, Khamenei symbolizes a class that is a relic of the past and incompatible with the times and props himself up by latching on to his titles and lineage.

My Uncle Napoleon depicts an aristocracy stripped of power whose identity is solely based on delusions about their expired titles and outdated sense of lineage. Their notion of love is also as obsolete as their perception of a hierarchical social order based on heredity. In fact, the otherwise pure, unshackled and democratic "love" in the Daie Jan drama may well be the very source of the "hand of the British."

At the heart of My Uncle Napoleon is a love story analogous to that of Romeo and Juliet; Pezeshkzad was passionate about Shakespeare and also wrote plays. For Daie Jan and his aristocratic line – as for Romeo and Juliet's feuding families – love is a poetic notion and a "courtly" affair within the realm of abstraction and notional pleasure rather than of the real world or sensual pleasure; nor is it tied to marriage. To old-time nobility, marriage was strictly a matter of expediency in support of the clan and proprietorship and land, or else a prerequisite for procreation. With the advent of modernity, love turned physical. It became the impulse and the measure, and a main reason to wed. The old nobility did not indulge that new definition, whether in the Verona of Juliet's time or in "Daie Jan's" Tehran. Given some similarities between Romeo and Juliet and My Uncle Napoleon should we then conclude that the book, because it evokes Shakespeare's tragedy, was a British plot? And wasn't Pezeshkzad himself complicit in that plot by packaging his narrative in such a way as to conjures up Romeo and Juliet? Indeed, some Western critics earnestly contend that promoting Shakespeare and his popularity was part of a plot to advance British imperialism. But if we choose to reject Daie Jan-like conspiracies, I believe we could agree that Shakespeare's plot was, via several intermediaries, inspired by Gorgani's eleventh-century romantic epic *Vis o Ramin* (Vis and Ramin), and that Pezeshkzad whose modernity was Iranian and international was well acquainted with both poets. In that modernity he was neither intimidated by the West nor entranced by the East. The only real "conspiracy" is our deficit in understanding the complexities of Pezeshkzad's ostensibly uncomplicated writings.

Not only was he not interested in and did not abide by the utilitarian "creed of convenience" in his everyday life but in his short stories and novels too, he ignored that creed and expressed whatever plot came to his sharp and seductive mind in a style that some critics have called "beguilingly simple but impossible to emulate." He followed his own path and did what he had to do. In the years following the revolution he felt it was possible to challenge religious dictatorship alongside Shapur Bakhtiar and dived into that work without hesitation and without affectation and without covering it up. He lampooned the sanctimonious mullahs with the same openness that he criticized or derided secular intellectuals. His conversation in private was not much different than it was in public. Of course, every piece of writing – even work as deliberate and honest as Pezeshkzad's – invariably has an unconscious subtext of which even the author is unaware. Pezeshkzad's writings are no exception. Only in the future, after accessing his letters and notes and questioning friends and relatives will it be possible to ascertain the nature of that unconscious. He was open to his writing being criticized, but he also knew the worth of his work and his personal worth, without any feigned humility. He did not mind literary argumentation. Once when he disliked the production of one of his plays he expressed his displeasure on the spot and unceremoniously. He talked to me about it in anger. He objected to the staging and explained why. But even when angry he observed standard courtesy, though he upended myriad protocols in his stories. In everyday conversation he was discreet. Whether in his speech and writing or in his choice of proper and fine clothing, in his focus and forbearance, in his enjoyment of food or single malt whiskey – whose best brands he knew well – his stance was always aesthetic. I heard from Hossein Hejazi, his close and loyal friend to the end, that when Pezeshkzad collapsed and his son called an ambulance to take him to the hospital, he asked to be properly suited for the ride. To him, "propriety," *sharaf*, lay partly in beauty – whether the beauty of Sa'di's poetry or the prolific portraiture of a dying aristocracy.

In the *Dehkhoda* dictionary, *ashrāf* (plural of *sharaf*), a sobriquet of aristocrats, has nuanced meanings: "affluent ... grand ... honorable ... virtuous ... prominent figures [of] pedigree, class, and style." Idiomatically, *ashrāf* is nowadays applied to the wealthy who consider their "bloodline" a license for feeling inherently superior and based on heredity, feel entitled to a comfortable and leisurely life. Pezeshkzad had fallen from a pedigreed class into financial hardship. A recurring element in his tart and incisive humor is the tragicomedy of a vanished class that feels alienated. Another recurring element is the "cheek" of the pompous pontiffs who dispense holy titles and consider themselves the new aristocracy and boast knowledge they do not possess.

Pezeshkzad was hounded for a lifetime because of the fame of his Daie Jan and his hilarious rebellion against the "creed of convenience." As his death drew near, however, the very people who had hounded him fell prey to the vicissitudes of the times. More to the point, he came to be duly recognized not as an obsolete aristocrat but as a "grand . . . honorable . . . virtuous . . . and prominent figure."

Bahram Beyzaie

Bahram Beyzaie is the pride of Iranian arts and wearer of the sometimes-thorny crown of Iranian theater. The Ten Nights of Poetry at the Goethe Institute in Tehran in October 1977 was a kind of *Pol-e Sarat,* a "Bridgeway" for many artists who spoke at the event. Of course, if Beyzaie had made that in his presentation, he would have likely called the crossing by its pre-Islamic Zoroastrian name *Chinvat,* and then in simple and eloquent terms articulated the name change after the Arab conquest of Iran in the seventh century. He would have explained how and why a bridgehead where the departed's good thoughts, good words, and good deeds were originally said to be assessed became a tribunal for judging the degree of "sinfulness" of God's creatures. He might have also teased a reminder that those who exhibited a deficit of goodness at the crossing would fall into an abyss of hellish torment – which makes Chinvat an even more apt metaphor for what transpired during those ten nights.

The packed nightly congregation enjoyed relative security sheltered by the German embassy and the name of Goethe, a leading Enlightenment figure and admirer of Sa'di and Hafez. Yet every evening, the Iranian literary virtuosi used their pulpit to trumpet slogans in verse and prose and odes and anecdotes, holding the "other" – especially "bloodthirsty imperialism" and SAVAK and the Shah's regime – responsible for the state of affairs in the country, and occasionally segueing to the desert of Karbela and finding inspiration in Imam Ali and the martyr Hossein and the "revolutionary heritage" of Islam. In her *Ten Nights: A Review*, Mandana Zandian has examined the thought processes of those luminaries with her characteristic focus and insight. The only person who neither sloganeered that night, nor sought feigned refuge in Islam, nor laid blame for everything at the "other's" door was Bahram Beyzaie. On the contrary, he urged the impassioned speakers to be thoughtful and introspective and to ditch dogmas and idols and historical illiteracy, pouring the water of his Ferdowsi-inspired wisdom on the fire of their Hossein and Che Guevara fury. He had not taken the stand unprepared. Nor did he expect a miracle. He knew that his searching and non-dogmatic soul and creative drive, and his clear, refined, and provocative speech would lead to estrangement or even excommunication by the troops who, like the contentious champion of *committed art* Saeed Soltanpour, thought of a *type of art* – in essence a reformulation of Stalinist theories of art – as a tool for revolution and assumed the mantle of a *mahdi*, a "leader" and savior of the masses. Beyzaie neither saw himself as a leader nor was he awaiting the Mahdi, the Shia Messiah. In fact, enlightenment, rejection of craving or creating saviors, and refined language is found in the very first work he published.

Beyzaie was eighteen when he wrote *Arash*, the first in an amazingly rich and diverse collection of plays, which is centered on the mythological archer who forces Iran's chief enemy to retreat and saves the country. In a tersely poetic prose that resonates with the grandeur of myth, he wrote that there is no Arash, no savior – not today nor on the horizon; it all comes down to us; the only path to salvation is collective effort and deliberation. At the exact time the advocates of *committed* and *proletarian* art were using Arash to identify the Tudeh Party as a Mahdi-like savior, Beyzaie was saying we have to wake up, abandon facile dogmas that promise relief, and accept the burden of our own passions and the responsibility of our own decisions.

Ever since that time, the linguistic depth and form and beauty of Beyzaie's plays – from his folk and heroic drama to passion plays and comedy – and their richness and diversity, originality and innovation, has made him the most Shakespearean playwright in Iran. Beyzaie has gone even further than the Bard. As well as being in the vanguard of writing and directing drama, he was also a dedicated researcher in the history of the dramatic arts almost from the time he wrote *Arash*. Written six decades ago, his *Nemāyesh dar Iran* (Theater in Iran) – published at his own expense – remains the most comprehensive and inquiring work on theater in Persian. Contrary to Eurocentric critics who held that drama had never been an Iranian tradition, Beyzaie was able to unearth and write about the roots of theater in Iran in antiquity. Like an archaeologist, he approached his subject with rare diligence, curiosity, and focus. He was simultaneously interested in traditional Eastern drama. Wherever appropriate he would blend certain aspects of Eastern and Iranian traditions in creative ways or talk about the relationship between the two. In short, Beyzaie represented modernity in the field of theater in Iran and helped bring about its rebirth from the depths of Iran's own past. He also applied his findings, both Eastern and Western, to his own work, whether in research or on the stage and wherever it helped advance theater in Iran.

His efforts to highlight significant features of Iranian traditions is not limited to drama. In any field that interests him, he challenges those who overlook Iran's contributions to global culture. I've often heard him say "Why should we apologize and be afraid of defending Iran's cultural achievements?" I once watched him argue without reservation with one of his close friends who was overpraising the West and denigrating Iran. On the subject of art and philosophy and whatever deserves to be defended in Iranian history, Beyzaie is neither quiet nor discreet. He always articulates his views and criticism in an eloquent and erudite manner, forthrightly and without hesitation. In his *Tarabnameh* (The Book of Merriment), a musical comedy in the tradition of folk theater, he takes on the cheerless ignorami who cannot stand laughter and humor, music and dance, even shadow-plays and art. Another instance is his *Hezar Afsan Kojast?* (Wherefore a Thousand and One Tales?), a critique of blind Eurocentrism – or even Westoxification – where he argues that despite the precedence of *A Thousand and One Nights*, the story was published in translation in the West as the *Arabian Nights* with the protagonists' Persian names changed into manufactured ones. In *Jana and Baladoor*, he revived Iranian shadow puppetry after "seven centuries of silence." The play presents a thought-provoking and arresting new creation myth with two female figures as primal, bountiful progenitors, thus upending the patriarchal notion of a male God and prophets and saviors in the Abrahamic tradition.

He gave his all to every one of his productions, including a tireless search for the historical roots of his ideas and assumptions. In researching the background and examples of shadow-plays, for instance, he was able to find a drawing on a pottery shard in a museum and a reference in the travelogue of a foreign visitor. In preparing *Jana and Baladoor*, he worked on every element of the cut-out figures, how they moved and spoke and sounded, for hours and days, even weeks. All this despite a continuous struggle against time, which he feels limits his opportunity for creation and endless creativity. I can't imagine any other director spending as much time with an actor on the correct hand movement in one particular moment of an act. For all the beauty and richness of the dialogue and themes and symbolism, Beyzaie's plays resemble a ballet, with the actors' movements choreographed limb by limb. The respect he is shown by his Iranian and foreign interlocutors is due as much to the quality of his work as to the respect he pays his readers, audiences, and students, whether they be a few thousand experts or a handful of novices. I have experienced and watched just how carefully and attentively he prepares each of the classes he teaches. Though he offers regular courses on Iranian cinema and theater, I have never seen him walk into a classroom without reviewing and revising his lecture notes beforehand.

Beyzaie's dedication to introducing and demanding a fair assessment of Iran's contribution to civilization is in spite of the unkind way that many Iranians have treated him. For years he was harassed and even attacked because of his family's Baha'i faith, and for refusing to abide by the "creed of convenience" to protect himself. Time and again he told me, at times with tears in his eyes, about the verbal, bureaucratic, and physical abuse that he and his family were subjected to. As best I know, his only religious beliefs lie in the sanctity of art and theater, cinema and ideation. To him, the only path to salvation lies in words and images that enrich reality, and in beauty and empathy and self-realization. His sacred books are the *Shahnameh*, the poetry of Sa'di and Hafez, Shakespeare's tragedies, *A Thousand and One Nights*, and the like. He defends that "sacred domain" openly and honestly without standing on ceremony or retreating into expedient silence.

Rather than submit to dictatorial pressure he chose to live meagerly in a room in the basement of his mother's home, and tried to buoy her spirit, a single woman targeted by her neighbors since the advent of the Islamic regime and its anti-Baha'i sentiments. Overtly, and at times underhandedly, he was also accused of expressing Baha'i tenets in his work. And what if the most damning blather about Beyzaie and his beliefs were true and his work in fact betrays a hint, even a strong dose, of Baha'i teachings? According to which ideology is it a "sin" for an artist to refuse to paint women as either a slut or a saint instead of presenting them as free-spirited and intellectual and liberating as in Beyzaie's plays and films? In which teaching is it a "sin" to blend poetry and prose, collo-quial and literary speech, wholeness and detail, structure and simplicity in the way that Beyzaie does, writing plays that compare to Shakespeare in their variety and freshness and depth of thought, or producing a classic like *Bashu*, a feature film about an encounter between a war-ravaged, Arabic-speaking, Afro-Iranian Khuzestani boy with a Gilaki woman hundreds of miles up north that touches on all of the above? According to which outlook is it a "sin" to release people from self-deluding, elitist, and messianic fantasies and, as Beyzaie has repeatedly urged, concede that there is no Arash and no apocalyptic savior, and acknowledge, as Beyzaie does, that waiting for one leads to nothing but perpetual dictator-ship? Why is it a "sin" to repeat, as he does, that it is by us that life is for or against us and that until we understand that, it will always be against us?

While Beyzaie is preoccupied with his work, he does not use his talent or interests as a license to exploit others. He never bucks household chores, for instance. Mojdeh Shamsaie is not only his spouse but, above all, his collaborator and companion and friend. She is also an acclaimed actress and masterful in theatre management. While pursuing her own career she also recognizes that Bahram Beyzaie is exceptional, which is why she makes every effort to help him achieve his goals even as she maintains her own independence. I have no doubt that she would agree with the playwright Akbar Radi who said, "Dear Bahram, luminous Beyzaei, you stand above the peaks of our culture." Indeed, that luminosity was apparent at the Goethe Institute's Chinvat.

Mohammad-Reza Shajarian

His voice was famous before he was. That resonant and delicate tone, first heard on Radio Khorasan in 1959, was known to belong to a certain Siavash – a name that in the Iranian collective memory is associated with heroism and the *Shahnameh*. Soon, everyone found out that Siavash's voice belonged to one Mohammad-Reza Shajarian. Right from the start, no one could have doubted that Mohammad-Reza was of the patrimony of Ferdowsi and Iran and a free spirit and not of the mold of Zahhak, Arabia, and submission. Whether as Siavash or Mohammad-Reza Shajarian, his name and fame spread across Iran, then crossed beyond the borders. He used to say "Fame is like speeding along a gravel road; the end is hard to reach and easy to lose. The smallest pebble can instantly upend hard-won renown." Temptations along the road to celebrity are plentiful, and a hard earned reputation can quickly be squandered. What preoccupied Shajarian along the way was the perilous wiliness of the clergy. "I'm well acquainted with the mullahs," he used to say. "I grew up among them. They are more devious than the Devil. To crush a rival, they will use every trick in the book." Hardly any artist resisted the tyranny and triteness of the Islamic regime as openly and brazenly as Shajarian in the last twenty years of life. He neither fell for the regime's inducements nor took their threats seriously nor abused his commanding status. His fame was exceptional in another respect as well.

Likr him, some people, gain stardom through earnest and sustained work, others through facile popularity or even demagoguery. Those who as Hannah Arndt has said enjoy both public fame and a good reputation among the cognoscenti are the exception. Shajarian enjoyed both fame and reputation. Fully cognizant and protective of his stature without being obsessed by it, he displayed neither immodest arrogance nor false modesty.

The first time I met him was about thirty years ago when I was teaching at the College of Notre Dame. I had been a huge fan of his for a long time. Shajarian's music was to me a pure distillation of Iran and the Iranian identity and a balm for the agony of exile, as it was for Simin in Asghar Farhadi's *A Separation* when she left Nader. One day the phone rang in my office. A vaguely familiar voice said, "This is Shajarian. I've brought you a package from Hadi Khorsandi," the celebrated satirist, I was taken aback. I thanked him.

He came over to the campus a few days later along with his friend Ali Nasiri who called my office to say they had arrived but could not find a place to park. I rushed out to look for them. I felt very excited to be meeting Shajarian. They say getting close to artists is a risky affair as their personality is typically less palatable than their products. The trajectory of my relationship with Shajarian proved to be the exact opposite. The better I knew him, the more I respected him, for his art and for the nobility of his spirit. His friendship with Nasiri was itself a window into his character and values. Nasiri is a very patriotic and generous man, completely lacking in pretension, though his candor sometimes borders on piquancy. His affection for Shajarian and appreciation of his music are boundless, and he knows an astonishing amount of Persian poetry by heart. Like Shajarian, his byword is: "I'm well acquainted with the mullahs."

Our luck in Shajarian visiting Stanford a few years later was the fortuitous outcome of the short-sightedness of one of those mullahs – Ayatollah Khamenei. For some reason, the supreme leader developed an antipathy to Shajarian and banned him from performing in Iran. In Shajarian's words, "Khamenei's animosity springs from jealousy and a sense of inferiority; he cannot tolerate anyone else's popularity and renown." In the end Shajarian moved to Canada, then to the U.S., and used to visit Iran from time to time. He accepted the Bita Prize for Persian Arts at Stanford. For some, receiving an award is an honor. In some cases, the prize itself is honored when a luminary accepts it. Such was the case of Shajarian and others whom we recognized, including, Simin Behbahani, Bahram Beyzaie, and Marjan Satrapi. He later agreed to offer two workshops at Stanford, one on traditional Iranian music and another on its technical complex of modes, *dastgah*, and melodies, *gusheh*. His work ethic was truly remarkable.

The day he was to receive the Bita Prize he had a slight cold. Knowing the worth of his amazing vocal cords, which he regarded as his most important instrument, he neither consumed nor smoked anything that might damage that precious apparatus. On the day of the ceremony, some friends suggested we ask Shajarian to give a recital. I said I wouldn't dare do such a thing nor thought it appropriate. He had written down his speech in an exquisite script, which we distributed among the audience. When the event was drawing to a close he said, "Though my voice is hoarse, I would like to sing a song as a tribute to this evening." And he did indeed sing. It was one of the most memorable moments of the ceremony.

One day he called and said he wanted to meet privately in my office. We set the date. He showed up on time as usual, dressed in a smart suit and tie. Unlike his habit of bringing along a friend or his wife, he came alone. He walked in with a buff-colored envelope in his hand and made sure the door was shut behind him. After a brief and hurried exchange of greetings he said, "I and a few of my friends in Iran have a *dowreh*, a regular get-together. It's a mixed circle of physicians and lawyers and artists and government functionaries." He did not offer any further detail about the group. Nor did I probe, naturally. Such inquisitiveness was neither apt given the fearsome and oppressive conditions in Iran, nor did Shajarian's reputation and prestige leave any doubt in my mind as to the group's goodwill and patriotism. He had once told me that some leading members of the Revolutionary Guard, the army and government were his fans; that they visited him clandestinely to show their regard and sometimes talked about the state of affairs in Iran. "For a while now, our group has concluded that the status quo cannot hold. Some regime officials who visit me discreetly are of the same opinion." The day he had walked along a street in Tehran and cried out, "Death to the dictator!" loudly and with astonishing courage, his protest had not been triggered by a whim; for years, he had believed the regime to be moribund. Now, standing in my office, he said, "Our group has decided we should be prepared for change; in this envelope is the constitution we have drafted for the transitional period." It had been drafted because they cared about the fate of Iran and wished to think ahead; it was not a presumption of leadership. "The group wishes to leave a copy of it abroad for safekeeping. We have all decided to entrust the document to you at Stanford University. When we feel the time is right we will let you know how to share it publicly." He went on: "If something happens to me you are free to make it public as you see fit." I took the envelope and put it in my desk drawer. I felt strange, proud of their trust and scared of the responsibility. I was in awe of their patriotism and farsightedness and Shajarian's courage. When, after his death, I referred to "Shajarian's Constitution" in an interview with Sima Sabet, the news exploded like a bomb. Naturally people took different positions in the ensuing debate depending on where they stood politically.

From the time it became clear that Shajarian would no longer be performing in Iran – unless by bending to the wishes of the Supreme Leader, a price that our Siavash would never be willing to pay – we had thought of organizing a concert at Stanford that was worthy of him and in keeping with the university's mission. But hosting such an event turned out to be not so easy. In the first place, Shajarian was very strict when it came to music. He was a perfectionist with a depth of knowledge and wisdom and uncompromising standards. He could also capture the mood of the times. The zeitgeist of any era manifests in different ways and modes. It has been said, for example, that the prototypical "villain" in James Bond movies reflects the West's ups and downs and its fears and anxieties over the last thirty years. A cursory look at the lyrics that Shajarian chose to vocalize over the last forty years not only demonstrates his mastery of Persian literature but also shows his ability, at any given moment, to find the right poem and musical mode and melody to echo people's anguish and the despots' depravity. At the same time, they invariably hint at a bright horizon ahead. In short, arranging a fitting concert for him, though not easy, was a much-relished task.

The Stanford Iranian Studies Program had periodically collaborated with the Kronos Quartet, which has been around for some fifty years and is one of the most acclaimed string quartets in the U.S. They had played with master musicians like Shahram Nazeri and Kayhan Kalhor in the past. I talked to their founder and leader David Harrington about arranging a joint concert with Shajarian. He jumped at the idea saying they had been trying to contact him for years. When I ran the idea by Shajarian he looked into Kronos and given their mission and profile, agreed to it. After the preliminary discussions and before starting rehearsals a cancer – what Shajarian called an "unwanted guest" that had nested in his body for a while – turned into a malignant villain. I called David and told him that Shajarian had been hospitalized and suggested we call off the concert. He was deeply affected. "If you feel it might help him even a little bit," he said, "the four of us will go and play for him in his hospital ward." It was a three-hour drive from their studio to the hospital. That Kronos were willing to make that long trip was a testament to their humanity and the regard they had for Shajarian. The esteem he enjoyed was reflected elsewhere too.

Shajarian was listed by NPR, one of the savviest and musically inclusive radio channels in the U.S., as one of the fifty leading vocalists of all time along with the likes of Luciano Pavarotti and Maria Callas. When we tried to organize a novel kind of concert for Shajarian with the help of Stanford's Center for Computer Research in Music and Acoustics and its founding composer Chris Chafe, I witnessed another instance of his international acclaim among fellow musicians. The Center had developed a technology that could simulate the acoustic environment of any concert hall or venue in their studio. The Iranian regime had denied Shajarian's access to acoustically well-designed concert halls. Countering the regime, we wanted to recreate at Stanford the acoustics of Shajarian's favorite venue so he could give a recital in his chosen space. On the appointed day, we went to the Center to try out their system. Shajarian recorded two short songs in an acoustic space that simulated that of Hagia Sophia. Though neither Chafe nor his two associates, all three professors of music, could understand the lyrics, Shajarian's recital brought tears to their eyes overcome as they were by the power and delicacy and vitality of his voice. They were also deeply impressed by his knowledge of the technical intricacies of acoustics. That "unwanted guest" forestalled the concert with the Kronos Quartet, but the two songs that had been performed as if inside Hagia Sophia were played back at a commemorative event we held at Stanford after Shajarian passed.

Shajarian's interests were not just confined to acoustics or to a new technology that could enhance his performance. He was into cooking, too, and a talented carpenter. He cultivated and nurtured flowers and had a green thumb. He was also a skilled calligrapher and master of *nasta'liq* script. He used to say there were interesting parallels between calligraphy and vibrato, a variation in pitch that is also a hallmark of Iranian music. In one of the classes that he taught at Stanford he pointed out the similarity between aspects of Iranian classical music and Western opera. To explain what he meant, he vocalized a snippet of an aria. It was unbelievably moving. He was also a movie buff and would sit up until late into the night and watch films. He loved Westerns in particular; John Wayne was one of his favorite actors. His friend Ali Nasiri told me Shajarian's sign-in name for one of his computers was *johnwayne*. He loved soccer too and kept track of his favorite matches.

His varied hobbies aside, Shajarian's pulse mainly beat to music. He recorded several hundred pieces privately, a collection meant to be published after the mullahs were gone, and composed a "March of the Republic" in connection with his

"Transitional Constitution." He once played back a couple of songs on his cell phone while we were driving. I don't know what has happened to those historical recordings. The lyrics I heard were very radical, even revolutionary. But what stuck in my mind was the voice of Siavash.

While he famously contributed to the preservation and propagation of traditional Iranian music, he also broke new ground. He told his students – as I heard him say on a taped lecture he gave with Iraj Bastami – that you have to know the traditional modes and melodies intimately to be able to reinvent them in new forms. While listening to that tape, I remembered the story of the student who went to Picasso for a masterclass on cubism. The master said, "Draw an apple with great precision." Even as Shajarian familiarized a few generations of young Iranians with the poetic magic of Hafez, Sa'di, Khayyam, and the like, he also included contemporary Persian poetry in his "traditional" repertoire. Innovation was indeed part of his interpretation of the roots of vocal traditions. It is often said that classical Iranian music is derived from Quran recitatals, a theory based on the similarities between its modes and melodies and Islamic eulogy, *maddahi*, and elegy, *rawzeh-khani*. Shajarian believed that all those and related styles were in fact influenced by pre-Islamic Iranian music. To him, the battle between tradition and modernity was never detached from his relentless defense of the larger question of the sanctity of art and the artist.

He took neither worldly temptation nor the fatwas of cunning mullahs seriously. The promise of cashing in on sanctified concerts never persuaded him to play it safe. When women were banned from singing publicly he had more female students than ever before and boldly included his daughter Mojgan in his performances.

The flowering of his free spirit and constancy can be seen in choosing to name his voice Siavash, the legendary hero who endured a trial by fire. The Siavash of our times passed every test with distinction, and in return, his name and voice gained immortal fame side by side with Ferdowsi.

Ali-Akbar Moradi

It has been said that in the beginning art had a sacred aura – every work was authentic and had a unique presence in ritual. Once it began to be reproduced "mechanically" – in other words, when art turned into a commodity – it inevitably lost its sanctity.

The tanbur is said to be one of the world's oldest string instruments and the prototype on which the tar, setar, and the guitar are modeled. It was intimately associated with the Iranian plateau where it originated before spreading to other regions. They say that the plaintive sound of the tanbur resonated above all with the sacred world of the Yarsan, a mystical religious tradition with a primarily Kurdish following also known as *Ahl-e Haqq*. In Ferdowsi's *Shahnameh* (Book of Kings) the Kurds, an Iranian ethnic group, are said to be descended from a handful of men who in mythical times escaped the clutches of the serpent-shouldered Zahhak. The tanbur's connection to the Ahl-e Haqq whose esoteric rites are inextricably linked with ancient Iranian beliefs is such that some adherents consider it sacrilegious to play the instrument other than in ritual ceremonies or even to teach it to outsiders.

The etymology of the word tanbur whose sound rises from the soul and abrades the soul is uncertain. One theory suggested by a romantic Sufi is that it is composed of *tan*, "heart," and *bur*, "scraping." It is also said that the best wood for crafting a tanbur is from a mulberry tree that is thirsty for water, as if to "scrape" the soul the body of the instrument itself should have suffered abrasion. I read somewhere, too, that the earliest historical records of the tanbur and its use relate to recitations of the Avesta.

It has been said that music and the joy it gives are inexorably at odds with Islam. As for Iran, we had minstrels like Barbad in times past, and the classical Persian poetry of Rudaki and Ferdowsi, Rumi and Hafez, Khayyam and Nezami is closely attuned to music; Sufis sing and dance when performing Sama; not to forget Sa'di's warning that *The camel is animated by the Arab's song / If you are unanimated you are a cranky beast.* That backdrop notwithstanding, Khomeini proclaimed with a shocking directness and decisiveness that Islam lives by wailing and that music is an opiate and must be eliminated from radio and television. He loved a universe that overflowed with mournful dirges and tears, void of music or joy.

It is perhaps due to that same killjoy fundamentalism that the term *motreb* (merrymaker) acquired a somewhat negative connotation in Persian. The *Dehkhoda* dictionary defines the word as follows: "singer ... minstrel ... someone who sings and makes another merry ... who generates merriment in others through gleeful song and music ... induces joy." In his play *Tarabnameh* (Book of Merriment), Bahram Beyzaie conjures humor to mock the perverse pedigree of people who have an antipathy to merriment, joy, and music. Ali-Akbar Moradi is the embodiment of a hopeful and merry artist who by dint of his genius and unique character protects the tanbur's sacred domain even as he showcases it in word, song, and movement, even in his attire. In his tanbur recitals, he induces euphoria and joy, both preserving and revitalizing the music of Kurdistan and the Yarsan. He is not seduced by the rewards and the lure of recording and distributing his art "mechanically." His music is heavenly in its beauty and he, earthly in his humility.

The first time I had the good fortune to meet him was when he came to Stanford with Kayhan Kalhor, also a Kurd, to perform and give a talk. Much to my chagrin, I was not familiar with his name until then. Sometime earlier, I had watched a telling documentary produced by the music professor Zahra Houshmand Rad about the mysteries of tanbur music among the Ahl-e Haqq. I had also repeatedly watched a mesmerizing short performance filmed in a village in Kurdistan by an ensemble of more than a hundred tanbur players – young and old, male and female – who in one voice pleaded for wine, singing: "I am that fine merrymaker with a broken heartstring," a sentiment that I felt echoed the whole nation at the time. Still, I had not heard of Ali-Akbar Moradi who was an indisputable master of that musical tradition.

During that first Stanford event Moradi was to talk about the tanbur and the musical system, *maqam*, and Kalhor about the kamancheh, also a string instrument, and its place in the tradition. Moradi was noticeably modest from the start, minimizing his presence on the stage as best he could. The amount of background notes he had prepared for his portion of the one-hour session was also impressive. The depth and detail of his explanations about the complex history of the tanbur reflected his knowledge and esteem for his art, the tradition and earlier performers, as well as his respect for the audience. He did not sulk or complain that his allotted time was too short and responded to questions genially and calmly and clearly, even when they were uninformed or hostile. Conscious of the authenticity of his art and his mastery of the instrument, he displayed neither false modesty nor arrogance and was not easily riled. Rarely was his face without a smile. After the event, he accepted our invitation and went on to give several more recitals and talks. We naturally had to discuss the budget each time he visited, and each time he was genuinely loath to discuss financial matters. His reluctance reflected the fact that for him, the tanbur and music were as he once put it, a kind of "prayer." His genuine humbleness, his musical virtuosity, and his unpretentious speaking style and erudition were more noticeable each time he took the stage.

Offstage and in private he is even more jovial and sagacious and humble. While performing he seems enveloped in a bubble of sound and light, wholly absorbed in the tanbur and his song and the musical ensemble. One might say neither is the tanbur his instrument nor he the instrument of the tanbur. Both have an aura that is at times provocative and at times mellow, sometimes mournful and sometimes mythical. A sort of "communion" forms between instrument and player and out of that extraordinary fusion an extraordinary joy is born.

While Kurdistan looms large in all his lectures, his native devotion is inextricably tied to his love for Iran. In tracing the origins of the tanbur to Kurdistan, for instance, he also talked about and recited excerpts from the Kurdish translation of the *Shahnameh*, the Iranian national epic. Time and again, he said, "I tell my Kurdish friends we could have no better country than Iran." Thanks to a perfect synchrony of heart and mind, there is no sign of any tension between his Kurdish identity and Iranian patriotism.

Moradi's love of Kurdistan and his sacred merrymaking tanbur is such that over the past decade he has put all his effort and a significant portion of his personal capital into building the House of Tanbur in Ban Zelan village in Kermanshah Province where he lives. In addition to housing a collection of historical tanburs, the center offers music instruction and hosts festivals like *Kohan Avazeha-ye Tanbur* (The Ancient Resonances of the Tanbur) to keep the instrument's legacy alive. He built the center despite the many obstacles thrown his way by the killjoy club and invited leading Kurdish musicians like Shahram Nazeri and Kalhor himself to participate in its events.

Moradi periodically travels to the West and indulges in exilic comforts only because his sons live here. But he prefers putting up with the obstructionist short-sightedness of the philistine authorities back home because of his love for Iran and Kurdistan and his daughter who lives in his beloved village. He treasures his sacred tanbur and shares its joy and lyricism and defiance and intimacy without commodifying his art in what Walter Benjamin called the "age of mechanical reproduction" – of digital distribution today. What he yearns for is a prosperous and free Iran inclusively for all. Perhaps that is why some of the Kurdish visitors to our university have said that Master Moradi's place among the people of Kurdistan is on a par with Master Shajarian's ubiquitous place among all Iranians.

Simin Daneshvar

I only saw Simin Daneshvar a few times, on each occasion at her home, which had the sense and substance of a museum even before it became one not so long ago. Other than plants, the main life form in the house was the ever-gracious Daneshvar herself who moved about with a warmth and empathy in her eyes that reflected the acuity and liveliness of her intellect. Her brother, a retired army officer, was also present most of the time. He may even have lived there. He did not speak much. The small yard teemed with flowers and flowerpots. A small pond in the middle stamped the space as wholly Iranian.

I do not remember why I was first invited to her home. I know she had liked my translation of *The Master and Margarita*. I knew she was friends with Manuchehr Safa and an ally of the social democratic politician Khalil Maleki and had read and commended the articles that Safa and I had published to critique Daryabandari and his essay on Arthur Koestler. I knew she had a very close relationship with my sister Farzaneh. I had read Daneshvar's *Savushun* (Requiem for Siavash)(1969); it was the first novel written

by an Iranian woman and had been critically acclaimed and
uniquely successful. Daneshvar herself was held in high respect
as an erudite and liberated woman. Rather than entitlement
and superiority, the public recognition had endowed her
with a great sense of responsibility toward literature, literary
criticism, and the place of women in society, and toward
protecting the reputation of her husband, the prominent writer
Jalal Al-Ahmad. As religious dictatorship became entrenched
in Iran after the 1979 revolution – a road long paved for her
by her *spouse* – the altar that Jalal himself, and in Daneshvar's
words his *apostles,* had erected for him began to crumble by
the day. That gradual and mounting disintegration, combined
with Daneshvar's at once complex and caring relationship
with the spouse placed her in a predicament. Her discretion
and praise for his laurels notwithstanding, a tinge of doubt
and dismay colored her words when she talked to me about
him. When I later read Ebrahim Golestan's *Letter to Simin*, I
discovered other twists in that knotty material relationship and
after reading one of her long-overlooked short stories, I was
finally able to better understand the source of that complexity.
I realized that behind her efforts to protect her husband's *name*
and honor, lay sentiments of a different hue.

At the time of one of my early meetings with Daneshvar,
Shams Al-Ahmad, her late husband's younger brother, had
published Jalal's *Sangi bar Gouri* (A Stone on a Grave) without
Daneshvar's permission. Shams as well as Daneshvar and
Golestan had been named by Jalal as his literary executors.
Golestan declined the responsibility for reasons he explains
in his *Letter to Simin* – or perhaps he knew Shams's type too
well. Given the opportunities that opened up in publishing
after the revolution and Shams's yen to put out a high-grossing
book, and perhaps given his eagerness to ingratiate himself to
a regime whose ideology was in line with *A Stone on a Grave*'s

patriarchal outlook, he decided to publish it. Daneshvar was very upset both because of the book's content and the mercenary way in which it had been published. I repeatedly advised her to express her discontent publicly but she said it would only embarrass her. Of course, for Jalal who was the son of a mullah and who according to Daneshvar used to recite the *Jafar Tayyar* prayer in his youth to help achieve his dreams, the very act of writing about his emotional and even sexual relationship with the *missus* in the book was a positive step forward. Yet the narrative's traditional air clashed with Daneshvar's worldview and life experience.

Before meeting her husband, she had lived in Shiraz and Tehran and experienced the world as an emancipated young woman from a modern, cultured, and firmly secular family. Both Daneshvar's expansive compass and the magnetic pull of the spouse's conventions can be seen in her appearance at the Goethe Poetry Nights in Tehran in the fall of 1977. By virtue of her stature, Daneshvar was designated as the inaugural speaker on the opening night. Though I have only heard the audiotape, one cannot escape the event's pernicious patriarchal gaze. As I listen, Daneshvar walks up to the microphone amid a rousing and extended applause by the audience. "I am not such a big deal!" she calls out in a slight Shirazi accent with a tinge of both humility and fervor, even a touch of formality. Before she starts her speech in the silence that falls, the master of ceremonies restates her name and adds, "She's also a souvenir of Jalal Al-Ahmad." To him, Simin Daneshvar – whose *Savushun* was a most widely-read Iranian novel, who was a professor at the University of Tehran, who had won a Fulbright scholarship and attended Stanford's Center for Creative Writing, who had earned accolades from Wallace Stegner, the American novelist and the center's then director, who was a collaborator and soulmate of Khalil

Maleki, whose talent in translation was far superior to the *spouse*'s – is simply Jalal's "souvenir"! No doubt the burden of such characterization rests on the society's entrenched patriarchal heritage, just as later on, the Islamic regime routinely named this or that seminarian son of Khomeini the "Imam's souvenir." But that night, it was Daneshvar's own conduct in life and in much of her writing that together with the hefty weight of patriarchy led to her being introduced as both Simin Daneshvar and Jalal Al-Ahmad's "souvenir." A case in point is how Daneshvar responded to the legend of Jalal in reaction to the publication of *A Stone on a Grave*.

Her initial response was to publish *Ghorub-e Jalal* (Jalal's Sunset), a memoir comprised of two previously published articles. Despite the fact that in *A Stone on a Grave*, the spouse had true to character, to paraphrase the social historian Fereydoun Adamiyat let everything that occurred to his infirmed patriarchal mind drip from his slovenly pen, Daneshvar lavishes praise on Jalal in every other line. Even the title of her memoir reflects the "luster" of his character. The narrator's disposition recalls that of Zari in *Savushun* who makes a hero out of her egotistical and vainglorious husband. In both stories, the chief protagonist is also occasionally panned as when in *Jalal's Sunset* she talks about her spouse's "apostles" and "devotees." As for his Islamophilia that had helped pave the way for the clergy in the decade prior to the revolution, she not only justifies but applauds it.

Daneshvar began her speech on the opening night of the Goethe poetry readings by reciting a surah from the Quran. The words she used to speak of Khomeini at a Writers' Association meeting were in a similar vein. She wrote in an essay, "I recognize Imam Khomeini as the leader of the people's revolution and the Word of God." At the time, while people like Mahshid Amirshahi and Mostafa Rahimi wrote

clear-eyed op-eds about the "leader of the revolution," a significant quota of intellectuals and writers like Daneshvar still
wallowed in illusions about his thinking and character. What
is astonishing is that as the revolution took shape, Daneshvar
and many other secular and religious advocates of religious
reform turned to defending Khomeini, the foremost partisan
of counter-reformation in contemporary Iranian history.

Daneshvar's excessively discreet reaction to *A Stone on a
Grave* was not her last comment on Al-Ahmad. A few years
later she published a punishing short story, *Boro be Chah
Begou* (Go Tell It to the Well), offering a biting critique of
her late husband. Many of the ideas in the story were those
she had shared with friends in the privacy of her home. To
interpret one story, and a mere four-page tale at that, as
Daneshvar's biography of the *spouse* or her sole judgment of
his character is as wrong as dismissing it out of hand. That
said, the story is in part about the narrator's feelings about
a man she has personally helped turn into a "legend." By
astutely using words common to both *Jalal's Sunset* and "Go
Tell It to the Well," Daneshvar clearly intended the reader
to see the connection between the two ostensibly different
texts. She had written the story in code but was also giving
the reader the key to decoding it.

In "Go Tell It to the Well," which was published in a
collection of her short stories titled *Entekhab* (Selection), the
narrator speaks of an "egotistical husband" who is a "remod-
eled *rawzeh-khan,* elegist." He has "some writing talent" she
says and repeating phrases exactly as they appear in *Jalal's
Sunset* writes that her selfish spouse "coerces his countless
devotees to lavish praise on him in newspapers." His writing
is "slapdash, superficial; he is not profound." He "self-aggrandizes and thinks he's an intellectual."

It was only possible for a refined mind and the powerful pen of the author of *Savushun* – and not from Zari's perspective in that novel – to carve a new stone on the grave of the now outmoded Jalal. Today, the house they lived in bears their names in the rightful order: "Simin and Jalal's Museum."

Simin Behbahani

Simin Behbahani was not only a poet; she was a poem herself, an impetuous and beautiful poem with an unquenchable and unbridled thirst for describing the good, the bad, and the ugly. To her, luxuriating in the good and resisting the bad was not a "sin" but a human right. That right did not discriminate between men and women. Brazenly and unafraid, she challenged people who were averse to beauty and pleasure, both in her poems, and in the poetry of her life.

The language of her poetry, like her ethos, was gracious and dignified, unassuming and iconoclastic. For her stylistic innovations, she has been called the Nima of Persian *ghazal*, a genre of lyric poetry. For the quality and content of her verse, the lucidity of her language and the spectacular humanism of her thinking, she perhaps should be called the Sa'di-like Nima of lyric poetry. Vanity and arrogance, disguise and ostentation did not touch her. She did not think of herself as a singular Joan of Arc but as someone who walked in step with those who shared her sense of pathos and persistence and yearning for beauty and pleasure. The sentiments she expressed in her poetry came from the heart and touched the hearts of others. It was hard to see her up close and not fall for her humility and humor. Artists can sometimes be annoying trumpeters of

407

their own work. Behbahani's character was as charming as her poetry, and as delightful. When she recited her poems, the words assumed tangible forms as in a painting. It was possible to appreciate her even without knowing Persian. I experienced that for myself the first time I had the privilege to meet her.

Simin Behbahani was one of the speakers at the first conference on Iran we organized at Stanford some twenty years ago. In her talk about the post-revolution trajectory of literature in Iran, she spoke of hopes and setbacks, sacrifices and acts of valor. Her speech was a mix of prose and poetry, acute in observation, and soaring in delivery. She read it out with immense resolve and strength. Conference participants who did not know Persian could listen to a simultaneous interpretation on their headphones. When, later on we translated her speech into English with the help of my sister Farzaneh who was instrumental in introducing Behbahani to the English-speaking world, I realized how much of it would have been lost on non-Persian speakers; it would have been like looking at a painting through cloudy spectacles. Yet the richness of that canvas was such that its luster shone through regardless. As soon as the session ended, the former U.S. secretary of state George Shultz who was then a colleague at Stanford, walked up to the table where Behbahani was sitting. He said, reverentially and with his eyes welling up, "I do not know a word of Persian. And I didn't listen to the translator. But your speech was so clear and musical, I felt I understood every word. All that suffering and courage brought tears to my eyes." Shultz, who died not long ago at the age of one hundred, was not known for being sentimental or for standing on ceremony. Once, when Shirin Ebadi came to our university and delivered some harsh words on America, Shultz was again the first to approach the speaker's table. I had been translating Ebadi's speech. Shultz turned to me clearly upset. "Tell her that even if everything the mullahs say about the U.S. were true, they will never have the atom bomb." In the session with Simin Behbahani, Reagan's one-time secretary of state expressed no such self-righteousness. It appeared that Behbahani's tone and the genuineness of her sentiments had placated Shultz and won him over. The next time I saw her was when she came to Stanford to receive the inaugural Bita Prize. The timing of the event coincided with the Islamic regime's concerted attacks against the Iranian Studies Program at Stanford. The award was to be granted to someone who had demonstrated singular achievements in Persian arts and literature, and the preference of its founder Bita Daryabari was for us to aim it primarily at female artists. We also knew that the award's prestige and esteem would be in part determined by the first prizewinner. The moment we began the process of deliberating on Iranian female artists Simin Behbahani emerged as the worthiest candidate.

But in a situation where Stanford was the target of attacks by the Islamic regime, traveling to the campus was not an easy decision for artists living in Iran where the Damoclean sword hung perennially over their head. It was not for everyone. It required guts and a belief in the right of artists to protect their freedom and not buckle under the regime's threats of fire and brimstone. Despite the fact that his international prestige assured him some immunity, the filmmaker Abbas Kiarostami stayed away because Stanford was on the regime's blacklist. But Simin Behbahani was made of sterner stuff. She not only accepted our invitations every time we asked – including for the Bita Prize – but in her attitude, speech, and hijab-less head, and nipping humor showed that she did not give a damn about the regime's truculence and intimidation.

At the award ceremony, she walked onto the stage looking graceful and sat behind the table. I was to place the microphone around her neck. The audience now hushed after riotous applause when she took the stage, was breathlessly waiting for her to speak. Before her on the table lay the notes she would be speaking from, scrawled with her son's help in very large letters on several sheets of paper. After a long career spent reading and writing, she was gradually losing her eyesight to the grind of time. By measure of Rudaki and Homer and Beethoven, eyesight is not of the essence for poets, nor hearing for composers; nor was Simin an ingénue to let one failing faculty make her forsake her art. Poetry was her essence and the stuff of her life.

I bent over to clip the microphone around her neck. If someone had snapped a photo it would have looked like I was trying to kiss the top of her head. Perhaps because she knew I was nervous but more likely because she was playful and mischievous, she said in a loud voice, "Be sure to take a picture of this scene!" The poems she recited and her speech were just as dismissive of the regime's "red lines." A fair number of women artists used to travel abroad in those days and in dread of crossing those red lines, would wear a hijab at such events. Succumbing to such fear depends on the artist's character and resolve. Behbahani was not given to such anxiety and uninterested in genuflection. Part of that grit owed to her disinterest in material things.

We knew that many Iranians who lived near the university were eager to hear her talk about literature and recite her poetry. I asked if she would conduct some sessions with that in mind. As always, she accepted heartily but declined any duly allotted fees saying they should all be allocated instead to student scholarships.

For all these reasons, what we owe to her poetry and the poetry of her life is incalculable. When I was a kid, I was puzzled by the title of a film called *The Singer Not the Song*; it made no sense to me that a singer should be more important than the song. In the case of Simin Behbahani, it is very clear to me that the singer is as indispensable as the song. A recurring motif in her poetry is the gypsy, *koli*, and her free spirit: *That gypsy rode away, did not take you along / What abides is the dark night, oppressing.* Every time I replay Homayoun Shajarian singing "Koli Kenar-e Atash, Raqs-e Shabane-at ku?" (Gypsy by the Fire, Where's Your Nightly Dance?) at Behbahani's funeral, the pain of her loss turns into tears of joy and gratitude knowing that despite all the inhumanity and misogyny that she endured, that free-spirited gypsy never failed to perform her nightly dance and her name and words and whirling would abide for evermore.

Mostafa Nasiri

For years, I called him by his nickname *Abar* (Über). Not just because I knew he admired Nietzsche whose philosophy he had been hashing out for years with a group of kindred souls over a pot of meat and potato broth, *abgousht*, though he himself was a vegetarian. The reason I did not know his last name may be the fact that his partiality to solitude and seclusion precluded one from asking. Because he cherished his privacy he never acquired a smartphone; he did not even have voicemail and evidently still does not use it. He never answers his phone. He is like Kierkegaard who said solitude was his sanctuary; that once in a while he would venture outside to capture a prey in order to dissect and understand it. Anyone who is admitted into Abar's sanctuary most of all stands to discover love and warmth.

Abar is protective of his solitude but unlike Kierkegaard, he is not cloistered. He is constantly touring and traveling. He is an explorer and a mountaineer, a gardener with a green thumb, and a cook with a chef's touch. "One time in Iran, after walking for miles I came upon a village where the whole community was vegan," he said. "Best to avoid the chichi in this sort of thing. I go into rural areas and learn." By then he had been a vegetarian for thirty years. He cultivates a variety of plants in his yard, from tender greens and lettuce and cucumbers to peppers and tomatoes and as he says, is perennially "self-sufficient." Every visit to his house means returning with a week's worth of edibles. He has also planted a sour cherry tree in that yard. He steeps the fruit in vodka and preserves the bottles like fine wine before giving lots of them away to his guests.

Abar has keen financial instincts but has zero interest in material luxury. He retired as an engineer with the California Department of Transportation at the earliest opportunity. There, according to him, not only the director of his unit but half the engineers were Iranian, most of whom would have likely preferred to be building roads in the Iranian country-side. After retiring he once said with a trademark laugh that renders his kindly face even more endearing, "Abbas *Aqa*, they pay us just to survive." His conduct at work and in retirement reveals several aspects of his character.

"At work, I mostly nap in my car and read," he used to say, though I later heard that as the supervising engineer he was in fact diligent and at least when it came to environmental matters, quite strict. He had made a contractor who also happened to be Iranian and who had mistaken Abar's disposition as laxness pay the heftiest fine in the agency's history for not complying with environmental regulations. Many people think of retirement as the beginning of the end of their life. For Abar, it has been merely a new stage in life for enjoying beauty.

Though he tends to keep quiet in a group, he pays careful attention to every word and gesture and will sometimes speak up and give a brief, profound, and honest critique of what he has heard. At other times, he will entertain the group with enchanting tales for hours on end like a skilled orator. His stories might be about the wonders he has encountered on a journey, or the stupidity of the rulers and the naïveté of his fellow militants in his youth, or the quirks of the resistance in his father's generation. His father was Major Nasiri, a Tudeh Party officer who had fought alongside Khosrow Ruzbeh. His "courier" at the time had been a young Tudeh'i called Parviz Kalantari, later on, the famous painter. Abar's stories are generally a special blend of sharp satire and tender criticism. About his father, for instance, he chortled about how Major Nasiri had once told the head of the military tribunal, "My services and sacrifices forestalled the Third World War," and the judge had replied, "Oh my, how the *tovarish* (comrades) must be howling!" When telling that story, it wasn't clear whether Aber was deriding his father or the judge or the noxious times whose egalitarian children had no option but to join a dogmatic party whose dreamworld was Moscow. There is a grayish-yellow portrait of Major Nasiri in a suit, not in military uniform, among Abar's impressive collection of contemporary Iranian paintings. At first blush, one could take the photograph to be part of that collection. I once saw a retrospective of works by a German artist who had moved from East to West Germany. One could see that inspired by "socialist realism" his earliest post-emigration paintings were accurate copies of photographs. Major Nasiri's portrait was unwittingly a true reflection of Abar himself; it was not tinted or retouched by hand, merely turned yellow by time. It fit in perfectly with his store of native masterpieces. Perhaps nothing is as telling of Abar's character, or the relevance of his name, as the superiority of that collection.

I have not seen such a representative selection of contemporary Iranian art anyplace outside Iran. Works by some of the most famous artists – from the modernist pioneer Marco Grigorian to the master of coffee-house paintings Hossein Qollar-Aqassi – hung in every room in the apartment. The

first time I visited, it was hard to assimilate all the works
that packed the walls from ceiling to floor, with more kept
in storage. For a few seconds, I could not get a word out. I
had a psychic stutter. The floors were also covered in several
layers of beautiful Persian carpets and area rugs. He knows
every painting and its artist and provenance. He remembers
how he came to buy each piece. A mutual friend who's a keen
art connoisseur says what Abar's eclectic collection has in
common is a romantic view of early twentieth-century Iran.
The grief of exile and its twin, nostalgia, have merged into
a dreamy paradigm of the homeland and its past. A little
probing around the assemblage reveals Abar's particular
attachment to artists whose lives match his idyllic notion of
their persona. Isaiah Berlin described the Romantic movement
as an influential and profound critique of modernity that in
contrast to conservative and religious anti-modernists, did
not embrace the God-centered medieval world and also questioned the rationalist reduction of humanity into machines
and statistics. The Romantics celebrated instead the complex
layers of subjectivity in every individual and rejected a utilitarian notion of art as a social service and the artist as a
tool. Abar is a true romantic in that sense. He favors painters
who conform to his image of an artist: One of them slept in
a coffee house by night and sold his work to the clientele by
day to make a living; another thought selling artworks to
be beneath art and the artist. What follows is a delightful
symmetry between Abar and the artists whose works he
collected. Many collectors aspire to riches or fame (or both).
Some even purchase artworks by the yard to fill a specific
space or select works whose color complements their furniture and floor covering. Abar does not care about size or
color. He looks for the work's authenticity and the artist's
integrity. Like his favorite artists, he is also willing and even

insists on gifting artworks to friends. He values art but does not care about its price. Oscar Wilde called people who know the price of everything and the value of nothing cynics. Abar is the exact opposite of the price-conscious cynic.

He checks out auctions and every estate sale he suspects may hold Persian art. It is as if by finding and collecting artifacts from his beloved homeland that have crossed the border he hopes to placate the gnawing aches of his exilic grief. One time he found a work attributed to Chagall for a good price and gave it away to a relative as readily as he had found it.

His memory of the late fifties-early sixties Lalehzar of his childhood is colored more than anything by his romantic view of the past. Known as the first "modern" avenue in Tehran, Lalehzar was modeled on Haussmann's designs for Parisian thoroughfares. Abar remembers Lalehzar as a meeting place of people engaged in politics and those interested in fraternizing and bona fide artists and chivalrous flâneurs. His description of that streetscape is a fascinating blend of youthful fantasies, life's triumphs and failures great and small, and finally, the immaturity and goodwill of those who aspiring to revolution, paved the way for a retrograde reaction. Sometimes his diatribe makes one laugh, sometimes it infuriates, and most of the time it forces one to think. Either way, you always know that his words come from a pure heart and a cultivated mind; they therefore appeal. You know that he loves and feels sorry for Iran. The beautiful paintings that cover every inch of his walls are an incarnation of a romance with Iran and the Iranian soul that he had once experienced in the "rump of Lalehzar" and whose thrills and escapades still intrigue his mind and play on his memory today.

Ehsan Yarshater

His arms and legs were shaking. He was leaning on a cane. A relative helped him walk to the stage. On the otherwise bare platform stood a leather armchair from which he was due to deliver his acceptance speech for winning the Bita Prize. To introduce him, Bahram Beyzaie and Bita Daryabari and I had each spoken a little earlier about his background and achievements, Beyzaie describing him as one of his hidden mentors.

He sat down. Leatherbound volumes of *Encyclopædia Iranica* that he had spent a lifetime editing and made available online were the only accessories by his chair. He gazed at a packed audience of admirers. He seemed to be taking a breath but remained in a daze without speaking or moving. His eyes appeared unseeing. Everyone was holding their breath. After one or two minutes that seemed to last an eternity, I asked the relative who had helped him earlier to find out how our still-silent guest was faring. I had in fact started to worry before the start of the program. By way of courtesy, I had walked up to where he was sitting. "Sir, with your permission, we would like to start the ceremony." In his usual polite manner, he said, "Certainly, but ask Dr. Milani first." We had spoken a few minutes prior yet he did not recognize me. To de-stress, I told myself it was travel fatigue.

Yarshater remained seated onstage without speaking. His relative approached him and whispered something in his ear. Suddenly, there was a movement. Holding the cane with trembling hands he thrust his body forward in an effort to rise to his feet. A heavy and epic silence blanketed the hall. Nobody moved a muscle. It even felt as if everyone was breathing softly so as not to disturb the professor's concentration and balance, acting as his aids it seemed, as if conscious that in rising to his feet each and every one of us was rising with him. His initial attempt failed. But Yarshater was not one to be easily defeated. He forced that frail thrust into a spring, shot to his feet, and delivered a brief and eloquent speech.

He had spent his bounteous life introducing Iran to the world. That night, his labored and winning effort to rise was a symbol and another standard along his purposeful journey. The *Encyclopædia Iranica*, the only prop on the stage, represented the land whose bounty and breadth and antiquity he wished to lay before the world. He wanted to make known every stream and sea, every hamlet and town, every world-conquering king and short-sighted visionary ruler, every poet and philosopher and architect and critic and historian and physician who had ever lived on the Iranian plateau – whether at a time when sixty percent of the world's population lived within the boundaries of the Persian Empire or in our days when only the hard core of that realm is still called Iran – or ever been mentioned in Persian or another tongue. Even in the last decade of his life he had told the literary critic Mandana Zandian in an illuminating interview that what had kept him up at night was the search for qualified and capable scholars to elucidate and clarify each of the encyclopedia's thousands of entries. With him at the helm, it was every Iranologist's wish to be invited to write for *Iranica*. It was at Yarshater's request that I wrote the article on Amir

Abbas Hoveyda, and my book *The Persian Sphinx* evolved from that research. Indeed, many other books have grown out of articles initially written for *Iranica* while many of its articles are distillations by authors from their original books. I think the encyclopedia was dearer to Yarshater than a child, over and beyond its value as a digest of the civilization of Greater Iran. He put everything he had into that undertaking, from temporal wealth to enduring thoughts on the nature of language and history. It is surprising that despite his attachment and tenacity and sacrifices for the "apple of his eye," he should have failed in the last years of his life to initiate and institutionalize a succession process to ensure *Iranica*'s continuity and preclude its falling into the hands of upstarts vying for fame and riches. One of the problematics in Iranian history is the reluctance to secure the future of weighty personal missions by structuring them as an institution. Had the seminal agendas and exertions of polymaths like Biruni and Tusi been institutionalized they would have likely led to a scientific revolution such as the West later immortalized in the name of Copernicus. Yarshater erected a monument but for some reason did not take the next step to ensure its durability. Did he presume he could escape the terror of time? Did he believe he could maintain his position for as long as he wished? Is it the case, as some of his close associates claim, that the disheartening state of *Iranica* today is the outcome of his inability to discriminate between peddlers of flattery and erudite Iranophiles?

Yarshater's heavy workload did not distract from his other interests in research, writing, and translation, resulting in a truly remarkable output in both volume and depth across diverse fields. In the cultural domain, he particularly admired Hasan Taqizadeh's scholarship and considered him one of the greatest among Iranians in the twentieth century.

We also know from Fakhreddin Shadman's journals that my colleague Kioumars Ghereghlou and I are currently preparing for publication – the first of six volumes is already out – that Taqizadeh was close to Yarshater and recognized his worth. Like Mohammad Qazvini and Mohammad-Ali Foroughi and Ali-Akbar Dehkhoda and Shadman, Taqizadeh and Yarshater were among intellectuals who were not lured by the siren call of voguish dogma; they never neglected what they felt was their main responsibility – namely, to learn about the world and about Iran and share that knowledge with the world and with Iranians. Yarshater was a prolific writer but he was never verbose. He had an inviting and lucid prose, robust and bereft of turgid turns of phrase. Though he ventured into disparate areas – from linguistics and history to theology and art history – he never did so on a whim. His standard was in-depth research and economy. He was averse to slogans but his writing was at times more poignant than any political manifesto. When called for, his candor bordered on invective. For all those reasons, he was distinctive among Iranologists.

I only attended one conference where he was present; at the time I knew him only by name. Ringed by an aura of fame and scholarship, even when he went out for a walk, which was rare, his admirers never seemed to let him out of their sight. His movements and tempo were slow and deliberate and always efficient. In his every move, even in the form and direction and duration of a glance at someone or something, there was circumspection and vigilance. He worked day and night and was not wasteful. His writing was rarely cutting and his speech was unfaltering and blunt. Even when one disagreed with his position – as with his uncritical praise of Mahmoud Dolatabadi's *Kelidar* or his perplexing scolding of Mohammad-Reza Shajarian – one never sensed it was either personal or cliquish, at least not to my mind.

At that conference, Yarshater's wife and lifetime friend Latifeh Alavieh was almost always by his side. Rumors, or accounts of his susceptibility to feminine charm, circulated among the participants; they even reached me who was not that curious nor a regular at such events. My guess is that whether false or true, they must have weighed heavily on Latifeh. Is the spouse of a famous scholar mandated to carry such a burden? I also guess that if in a relationship it is the wife who is rumored to be similarly disposed, neither the relationship nor the woman will endure people's jeremiads for long, regardless of her scholarly feats. Yarshater had no shortage of enemies but given his stature the most they got out of the hearsay were whisperings. One of Yarshater's most dangerous enemies was the Islamic regime in Iran.

Some believe the Iranian regime's animosity towards Yarshater owed to his being a Baha'i. In the early years of the revolution his sister was charged as such and executed in a most gruesome way. I heard from one of his critics Ebrahim Golestan that Yarshater had renounced his Baha'i faith some twenty years before the revolution. In any event, regardless of his faith or lack thereof, I believe the essence of the Islamic regime's animus toward Yarshater lay in his love of Iran. At the exact time the regime set out to bury a thousand years of pre-Islamic Iranian history Yarshater raised the banner of illuminating the Iranian universe with *Iranica*. Was the grotesque murder of the prodigious historian of ancient Iran Ahmad Tafazzoli incidental or was he targeted for being a key *Iranica* collaborator inside the country? Tafazzoli's fate evokes Hafez's line on the tragic execution of the inspired Sufi Hallaj that his only crime – like Yarshater's – was that he divulged secrets.

In that saddening but gracious night of the Bita Prize, the heroic struggle of that ninety-something old man to rise to his feet, and his unstinting toil in raising *Iranica*, added up to a grand effort to capture the heart of Iran and what it meant to be Iranian. Just as the *Shahnameh* had once restored Iran's trampled heritage at home, *Iranica*, though now in English, has shown that Iran can rise again like a phoenix and flourish in exile.

Dr. Josef Parvizi

He was thirteen when he was incarcerated in Zanjan. He had been twelve when the Marxist-Islamist Mojahedin-e Khalq (MEK) first recruited and sent him as one of a string of raw and idealistic foot soldiers to fight an unequal war with a mighty and brutal enemy. He spent the first few weeks of solitary confinement in a toilet. In Zanjan, the Khomeinist mullahs had rounded up their foes pell-mell and were short of prison cells. They finally moved the thirteen-year-old Josef to an actual cell.

He was locked up for nine months. To scare and coerce him to out his MEK partners they roped him to a scaffold and pretended to begin his execution. Dostoevsky was also once placed in a hangman's noose; the tsar's eleventh-hour pardon saved his life but the horrific psychological wound inflicted by that ordeal burrowed into his soul and never healed. Josef's wound was similar. One time they brought in his MEK handler who had been arrested, tortured, and in the end repented. His job was to persuade Parvizi and other prisoners to follow suit. He had urged them to forget about martyrdom and heroism and focus on saving their own lives. The regime was an expert in eliciting repent; sometimes it even forced the repentant to help execute their confederates by obligating them to deliver the coup de grâce. Aiding and abetting murder was their gauge and measure of genuine repentance. In his superb novella *Shah-e Siah Pushan* (King of the Benighted) that was in part inspired by Nezami's *Haft-Peykar* (Seven Beauties), Houshang Golshiri describes the young man Sarmad who delivers the nightly death blows upon his fellow warriors to survive, even upon his beloved. The Parvizis, though upper-crust Zanjanis, had no way of salvaging their thirteen-year-old boy. Josef's "crime" was "political"; in such a circumstance no one, rich or poor, had any choice but to maintain a mortifying and fearful silence before Islamic "mercy." A few months after Josef was released from prison, his mother suddenly died. When reviewing the profile of despotic regimes, it is customary to underline the number of people killed and imprisoned and tortured and exiled. The number of those who die out of grief for those who get the "ceremonial" execution treatment, or of those who die an untimely death out of the despair, despondency, depression, and disillusionment that is innate to dictatorship, are neither enumerated nor easy to count.

Once released Josef was subjected to the constant and covert aspects of "formal" and overt terror. Though he had been a top student in an elite high school in town, the school principal decided against enrolling him out of caution and political expediency saying, "There's a file on you." In authoritarian societies where power is exerted through fear-mongering, the silent majority's resignation to the authorities' physical, legal, or stealthy abuse turns innocent people into aiders and abettors of crime and effectively helps sustain dictatorship. But Josef did not stop trying. He enrolled in a different high school and when he won fourteenth place in a national contest for university admission among about a million other aspiring students, the local press extolled him and Zanjan in their coverage. Naturally, his imprisonment and "execution" went unmentioned in those complimentary write-ups. But the bureau of "security" at the University of Tehran, whose real job is to purge the campus of dissidents and nonbelievers and whose name incarnates the regime's Orwellian "lie," had not forgotten the "execution" and the "crimes" that had been pinned on Josef and on the "charge" of that same "file," barred his admission to the Faculty of Medicine.

Regardless, Josef was determined to get himself educated. On foot and on horseback he braved the mountainous Iranian countryside and after crossing into Turkey and surviving many perils finally found his way to Norway. "I did everything I could to stay in Iran," he told me, "but in vain." He then added, "I will never forgive MEK for using a twelve-year-old as a political tool, nor a regime that tortured that child as if in the Dark Ages." He completed medical school in Oslo. I once heard two of his Norwegian classmates say in awe and admiration that Josef was a top student in the department from the start. Separation from his country and the challenges of a new language did not disrupt his studies; they might have even strengthened his resolve. He completed his residency in neurology at Harvard and the Mayo Clinic. He then earned a second doctorate in neuroscience under the renowned Antonio Damasio, then chair of neurology at the University of Iowa and author of *In Search of Spinoza: Joy, Sorrow, and the Feeling Brain,* one of the most widely read science books at the intersection of neuroscience, philosophy, and literature.

Josef Parvizi joined the faculty of the Stanford School of Medicine in 2007. His latest invention may well transform brain diagnostics and surgery and make facilities currently in the monopoly of wealthy nations and hospitals universally accessible. It is no exaggeration to say that his presence and influence in that department and his genuine kindness also saved my life.

When I consulted him about a chronic headache and hand tremors he ordered a brain scan and found a tumor nested in a corner. It had to be removed. Not only did he assemble the finest medical team for the purpose but stayed at my side for the nine-hour duration of the operation. Nor did he deny me his care and advice during my recovery. Were it not for him, I would have probably not survived the ordeal. Ever since, I notice that on our weekly walks around town and the nearby hills – an "oxygen therapy in his words – he watches my every move not only like a close friend but as a fastidious physician. Going on walks with a cohort who has saved your life is a haul of good luck and an unparalleled delight.

My first sight of his latest invention was on the day he had invited me to visit his laboratory in the School of Medicine. We had met many times before then. He had just joined the university when we had a cup of coffee together. We each talked a little about our backgrounds. "I want to apply neurology, which is a whole new continent and frontier in science," he said, "to better understand the persistence of superstition and dogmatic prejudices and beliefs." It took several years for his laboratory to accomplish a part of that mission with the support of the Iranian Studies Program. We helped organize a series of forums where leading experts could probe key issues in that field of inquiry. They asked questions such as: To what extent are beliefs and political and religious inclinations rooted in the nervous system? Is ethics an outgrowth of religion or do notions of right and wrong have biological and primal origins? Are goodwill and empathy innate or learned in mammals? Is it true as some hypothesize that all humans inherit a God gene at birth? The scientists' responses to those questions were eye-popping. But it was on a laboratory visit arranged by Dr. Parvizi that I truly felt like Alice in Wonderland.

As we walked around the lab he introduced me to some of the medical professionals and students under his supervision. We finally stopped before a computer. He pressed a few buttons, with me staring at the machine wide-eyed, and he in full control. I heard the device make a noise. "It's the sound of the brain," Dr. Parvizi said. At first, it was peaceful and tranquil. It made me feel as if I was standing on a wide plain blanketed in snow from there to eternity. There was no indication of any movement in the air. Suddenly, I heard something like a howl, which gradually grew louder. As it rose in pitch shattering the silence it also induced fear and became terrifying. My hair was standing on end. Dr. Parvizi's subsequent explanation provoked admiration and awe but also generated an indescribable sense of terror and dread in me, the kind of dread that comes from knowing one is beholden to uninterrupted scientific inquiry and also at the mercy of people whose ambition and greed for power might lead them to exploit and abuse any new findings. He explained the noise as the electric brain waves of an epileptic individual: the quiet sound reflected their normal state, the howl indicated that a seizure was imminent. The brain can detect an attack that is underway earlier than the conscious patient. By monitoring brain activity with the device, doctors can forewarn a patient about a seizure and with the right medication soften its dire effects.

The brain waves had been turned into sound waves thanks to Chris Chafe who headed the Center for Computer Research in Music and Acoustics at Stanford. The same colleague later used their innovative technology to create a soundscape similar to Istanbul's Hagia Sophia so we could record Shajarian – banned from performing in Iran by the same despots who had once roped a thirteen-year-old boy to the scaffold. The Shajarian recording was grand and glorious, but the sound of brain waves was of a materially different order.

That hefty machine has now evolved into a device the size of the palm of one's hand. Designed with the help of some of the world's smartest computer scientists, it records the patient's brain waves and can share the data with any medical facility in real time. So, just like the best-equipped hospital in the richest country, any remote village in Zanjan or anywhere else in the world can now use this break-through technology. The application of the pioneering device has spread rapidly and a publicly traded company is now managing its distribution.

Josef Parvizi's dedication to unlocking the key to the secrets of the brain is compounded by his inexhaustible passion for knowledge and the pursuit of new research and experiments. His demeanor differs widely from the clichéd image of scientists of that caliber who are portrayed as forgetful and clumsy, misanthropic, and averse to worldly temptation and physical pleasure. As hard as he works, Dr. Parvizi does not neglect life and its delights. He spends a lot of time with friends and his family, loves nature, and is a great cyclist. On occasion, he takes his son who loves trains on hours-long outings or on trips away from home. He loves listening to Western classical music as much as to Iranian vocalists and Azeri balladeers. With a sharp and witty sense of humor, he still speaks Persian with a slight Turkish accent. From his home in the U.S., he follows developments in Iran attentively and insightfully.

When I think about the aggregate of Dr. Parvizi's scientific feats, I feel great pride but also sorrow that Iran should have sacrificed so much talent on the altar of obscurantist dogma. I am also reminded of Josef's oft-repeated remarks about how he wishes he could contribute to education in Iran and his dream of building a first-class medical school in his hometown of Zanjan. These days, I assuage my sorrow with Hafez's promise: *Josef, now lost, will come home again . . . do not despair.*

Bita Daryabari

My first meeting with Bita Daryabari was about literature. She had just returned from a trip to Iran with her two children. She was keen for them to learn about her homeland and speak Persian and would not cave in to any resistance on their part. A strict and loving mother both then and now, she puts a lot of effort into their education while allowing them to be free to pursue their own interests. We met at the home of one of her friends two or three years after the founding of the Iranian Studies Program at Stanford. After an exchange of pleasantries that in Attar's words serve to "walk along the talk" and pave the way for real dialogue, Bita spoke of a female poet she had met on her trip to Iran saying she wrote well, and that she was blind. She had one of her books of poems with her. Without her actually saying so, I had the impression that she wanted us to invite the blind poet to give a talk at the university. We read some of the verses together. What stood out for me was the poet's blindness rather than the form or the power or novelty of her compositions. I said: "I like literature, but have no expertise in poetry," and added that the lines we had just read were not compelling enough for us to invite her to Stanford, especially given our limited

433

resources. I explained that we were a fledgling program that was limited to offering a few courses, and then mainly in political science and international relations. The rest of that night passed in talking about literature and the dismal conditions in Iran for poets and other writers.

Sometime later, Bita invited me to lunch. By then she and her husband Omid Kordestani had divorced. Despite his fame, Bita had never given up her maiden name Daryabari; Omid once gave a speech at the university where I heard him describe what an important role she had played in his success. Bita and I met in a Greek restaurant that had recently become popular in town. The table adjacent to ours was set so close that even without being intending to, they could easily hear everything we said. Though we spoke Persian and only sometimes broke into English, it felt like the couple next to us were mostly focused on us while feigning a casual conversation between themselves. We carried on undeterred.

Bita asked about our Iranian Studies Program and seemed disappointed that we did not offer courses in Persian language or literature. Before lunch was over she proposed to endow two faculty positions to teach both subjects. Her offer took me by surprise. That was not the last time I was to be struck by her largesse on behalf of Iranian culture. A couple of years and conversations later, she increased her endowment to a point where we had the capacity to create a third faculty position and launch a prize in literature. Not long after, we welcomed Bahram Beyzaie who had accepted our invitation to teach at the university. What we decided to call the Bita Prize was, as she had stipulated, to be awarded to artists who had made a significant contribution to Persian language and literature and Iranian culture.

Bita's approach to the prize, and to the endowment as a whole, reflects her liberality as well as her keen understanding of the U.S. university system. Many individuals donate to universities in the U.S. and then based on their "investment" try to interfere, even in faculty hiring and curriculum development. Bita never interfered in our processes or in the selection of prizewinners. It is only when the parameters of the prize were being formulated that she reiterated as was her right, that female artists were her priority. The first awardee was Simin Behbahani and the second Goli Tarraqi. Others, listed alphabetically, have included Mahshid Amirshahi, Parisa, Shahrnoush Parsipour, Homa Sarshar, and Marjan Satrapi, and among the male prizewinners, Bahram Beyzaie, Kayhan Kalhor, Shahram Nazeri Houshang Seyhoun, and Mohammad-Reza Shajarian.

If meddling by those who endow university chairs or awards is inappropriate, so is a total lack of interest. It is said that theologically speaking, there are two kinds of "creators" – those who interfere in every aspect of their creation, and those who wash their hands of it after the fact and simply watch what happens from the sidelines. Bita is neither: she does not interfere in our selection of prizewinners, nor does she hold back from helping ensure the award's success. She gives a brief speech at every award ceremony and volunteers in the preparations from two or three weeks ahead. Her additional help at the start included underwriting the design and production of the statuette that is given to the awardee along with a $10,000 prize – now increased to $15,000. She typically hosts a reception for the awardees at her home with a superb humility that reflects her enormous respect for the arts. Some among the nouveau riche believe that if they admit an (ordinarily poor) artist into their home, the artist should thank their lucky stars for being in an intimate setting with their patron. Sa'di called such parvenus "a bunch of arrogant, conceited egotists." Bita always behaves as if she is the one who is fortunate that someone like Simin Behhabani should grace her home. Her behavior is sincere and heartfelt, without a hint of false modesty.

Her attitude is not restricted to the illuminati. She has the same warm approach to members of the public who visit the Pars Equality Center. For years, she contemplated helping newly arrived Iranian exiles who endure emotional and financial hardship. To address the "legal" injustices faced by Iranians, she first thought of creating a civil rights organization similar to the American Civil Liberties Union. She explored the possibilities for a long time as she does not make any decision lightly. In the end she decided to build the Pars Equality Center with a more limited mission. "I feel ashamed knowing that refugees from other countries are invariably met by a dedicated organization or group that helps them settle down; Iran is the exception." Pars's mission was in part to address that deficiency. She has not only donated several million dollars of her personal wealth to that organization, but thoughtfully and diligently supported kindred nonprofits and attracted a larger group of fellow Iranians to support philanthropic causes. Pars currently operates out of three cities in California: San Jose, Fremont, and Los Angeles. They serve newcomers who need support and guidance in their daily lives and also help those in the autumn of their days to take up engaging activities such as classes and lectures and community gatherings. Whenever I've seen her among such newcomers, I've never felt that owing to her "fiscal prestige" to borrow a term from Sa'di, she would position herself at the top and regard herself as superior to others.

Despite being unassuming, Bita is not coy about her substantial wealth. She is not swayed by hectoring, but by her own heart. If people find fault with her lifestyle she does not shy away from defending herself, and should they persist in spreading lies about her may even take legal action. She clarified her stance many years ago and continues to advocate for democratic values and women's equality.

The grief of exile is the grief of loneliness. It's the grief of having to abandon one's homeland and its familiar tongue. It's the grief of lacking economic and social anchorage. For those who have spent the last decades of their exile in America, the grief of exile has also been coupled with a sneaking and chronic legal vulnerability, arising on the one hand from the criminality of the Iranian regime and on the other from an American thoughtlessness that makes exiles who are the prime target of the regime's villainy pay for those crimes. Bita Daryabari has spent much time and capital looking for ways to assuage the grief of the Iranian diaspora in the U.S. Her trailblazing work in this area aligns with the singular resistance of Iranian women on behalf of democracy and equality in Iran. Just as women have emerged as the emotional and even economic anchors of the family in exile, and just as the most successful works of exilic literature are by women, so Bita Daryabari is at the forefront of civil society among Iranians in exile. The reality is that the woeful effects of despotism on Iranians over the past forty or so years has driven even those living in Iran to feel like outsiders. Everything we do and say is part of an effort to understand and overcome that exile-inducing drubbing. In trying to overcome her own chagrin, Bita Daryabari endeavors to take the edge off ours as well.

Hamid Moghadam

Hamid Moghadam is a gem who knows the worth of precious gems. With a wealth of personal and social laurels to his name, he values time as the most precious of them all. I have never met anyone who uses every moment of his life as productively as he does. If he has to travel a long way between two meetings, he will listen to a book or a podcast or attend a meeting by phone. Strangely enough, one never gets a sense that he's pressed for time or wants to quickly wrap up a conversation. Though he must be busy in the extreme, I cannot think of anyone who devotes as much of their time to mentoring others, especially young Iranians. He is equally generous with his wealth. He has endowed several chairs and an Iranian studies center at top U.S. universities. The chairs are in varied disciplines – medicine, engineering, management, economics, and Iranian studies. He earned a Bachelor of Science degree in engineering from MIT and a Master of Business Administration from Stanford where he subsequently served on the board of directors for several years. Although he has spent most of his life abroad – high school in Switzerland, college and thereafter in the U.S. – his love of Iran and his efforts to secure a better future for the country are immeasurable. On a personal level, one indicator of his generous spirit is that in all the years I have known him, there has hardly been a time when he has not reviewed and commented on something I have written before it is published. Nor is his interest in Iran t limited to the academic domain.

Some time ago, the Asia Museum in San Francisco was undergoing renovation. They planned to display their Iranian collection under "Islamic Art," a curatorial tradition that has grown more commonplace as investment by Arabs in such institutions has increased. But Hamid and his wife Christina made such a gracious and generous contribution to the museum that when it reopened, a separate gallery was dedicated to Iran. The couple's philanthropy in other areas is generally unadvertised as well, and as effective.

I met Hamid for the first time about twenty-five years ago at a private luncheon where I and a couple of others were invited to speak. I was then teaching at Notre Dame de Namur, a small college in Belmont, California, and had published *The Persian Sphinx* two or three years earlier. The meeting participants' names appeared on place cards before them. I noted "Hamid Moghadam" next to mine. I had not heard of him but assumed him to be a VIP. In such meetings seats are generally assigned by status and those next to the speakers are reserved for important guests. A few years later, the Iranian Studies Program was created at Stanford – which offered no courses on Iran then, not even in history or politics – thanks to Hamid and Christina. The fact that I hadn't heard of him was not entirely owing to my being out of the loop. It was mostly due to the fact that Hamid has always eschewed being in the limelight or even being talked about. Every chief executive of a publicly traded company routinely avoids being the focus of attention, especially politically. But Hamid's reserve was not out of caution. As the Islamic regime's threats and propaganda against him increased once he established the Stanford Iranian Studies Program in 2005, he showed no fear and did not recoil from speaking his mind about the dictatorial regime. Many of these character traits were evident in that introductory luncheon meeting. He spoke judiciously and briefly, and only when necessary. Everybody paid close attention to what he had to say. But neither that day nor in all the years since have I ever noticed him appear conceited by the attention he receives. He keeps his composure and does nor praise or upbraid anyone hastily. Nor does he stand on ceremony. I once sent him an article that one of my students had published, thinking it was brilliant. It centered on certain affluent Americans who aspired to turning the Moon and Mars and space into private colonies. Hamid read the article on the spot. His response was that the student knew nothing about the real world and was floating in a fairytale bubble.

While he talks and acts without rushing, he nonetheless works at great speed. I have never seen more than a few loose papers and file folders on his desk. Though a co-founder of a large company his office and desk are identical to the rest of his coworkers'. Many high net worth individuals are under the impression that their financial success makes them masters of all trades. I have not seen Hamid express an opinion about a subject that is not his specialty or forte. Both he and Christina who is similarly kind and gracious, love sports and get excited about local and college athletics. He has a passion for everything Iranian. Their home is adorned with Iranian arts and crafts and based on my own experience, they always serve their guests Persian food. Hamid's attachment to Iran is balanced and heartfelt. Whenever he criticizes something even if I disagree, I know he means well. One day he was riding in my car. The voice of Gholam-Hossein Banan issued dolefully from the CD player. He said sarcastically,

"You feel depressed because you listen to these tunes." He is not interested in doctrinaire principles or mundane details but in patterns and trajectories. Some years ago, he said, "The mullahs' regime is tactically sharp and strategically dumb." He does not hesitate to criticize what outrages him or praise what pleases him, character traits that are an important key to his financial success as well.

While I have no expertise in commerce and management, I have often heard experts and those who have worked with Hamid say that his success hinges on three principles. The say that above all, he is smart and thinks long term. Some forty years ago, he (and his two business partners) predicted that a novel paradigm of global commerce would emerge and that the new ventures would need state-of-the-art warehouses near important airport terminals around the world. They began building storage facilities with a small investment and created what is today the largest industrial real estate corporation in the world.

The second secret to his success is said to be his financial integrity. CEOs of companies that have worked with him have told me that you can take his word to the bank; that it's trustier than any contract. From what I have observed he is never ambiguous and never breaks a promise; there is no daylight between his words and deeds. Such transparency is even reflected in the interior design of his company headquarters in San Francisco. There are no forbidding walls and no private versus public spaces in that enormous waterfront building that sits on a former shipping dock.

The third secret to his success is said to be his courage and audacity. A few days after the infamous U.S. stock market crash in 2008 – which has been compared to the crash of 1929 – Hamid bought back his company's devalued stock. That move was so unusual and proved so effective that one

Stanford student devoted his master's thesis in management to analyzing it. The day he defended his thesis I was invited to the session simply because of my title as the Hamid and Christina Moghadam Director of Iranian Studies, and listened to the faculty and students explain and extol Hamid's strategy.

The stock market crash happened to fall on my sixtieth birthday. I had invited a few relatives and close friends, including Hamid and Christina, to dinner at an Iranian restaurant near the campus. It was at least an hour's drive from the Moghadams' home to the restaurant. On hearing the dire news of the crash, I thought there was zero chance they would join us. But they came on the appointed hour and passed the evening enjoying good conversation.

A few years later a Shirin Ebadi event at which Hamid was to give a speech happened to coincide with the funeral of Maryam Safinia, Hamid's sister. To excuse himself from the conference would have been expected and completely understandable. But he did come and not only gave a talk but stayed until the close of the fairly long session.

Hamid took a summer trip to Iran after graduating from MIT in engineering. He might have gone back home for good when he earned an MBA at Stanford in 1980, but the seismic upheaval that brought about the revolution did not yield an Iran with a capacity to absorb someone of his talent and worth. Hamid, like millions of his fellow Iranians, has preferred the "sting of exile" to the venom of the despotic obscurantists. But being a connoisseur of precious gems, he is well aware of the gem that is Iran's cultural heritage and makes a great effort to salvage it.

Fakhreddin Shadman

The first library I saw in my life was at the home of my uncle *Daie* Doctor. It was a handsome and inviting house on Vesal Shirazi Avenue in the days when faux modernity and a reactionary revolution had not yet stripped Tehran of many of its abundant trees and much of its local identity. The library was in a large room with a view of a tree-lined yard. Finely-built wooden shelves lined the walls from floor to ceiling, packed with books. That is also where I first saw a mobile library ladder. I later learned that an elegant library and associated ladder are emblematic of the residences of sophisticated and aristocratic people. My whole life, I have regarded books as the most beautiful adornments of any room, a passion and fascination likely rooted, at least partially, in the impressive grandeur of my uncle's library.

Daie Doctor had a desk on one side of the room and his soulmate and wife Farangis Namazi, on the other. Farangis was a Shakespeare aficionado and scholar. She had translated *Macbeth* and *Julius Caesar* into Persian. She was something close to a women's rights activist. Fakhreddin was a writer, translator, and journalist and a long-serving statesman. Whenever I saw the couple – whether in the library or at family gatherings – their attire was consistent. Farangis always wore a chic two-piece suit and Fakhreddin an elegant suit and tie, often with prayer beads in his hands as an accessory. He picked up the habit as a young seminarian and by late in life had amassed an exquisite collection of assorted styles. His favorite brand was the Shah Maqsud, with small beads of jade hand polished to a perfect sheen. When I came to know his character in greater depth, I thought it shared certain attributes with his favorite prayer beads. Because the Shah Maqsud stone is composed of silicate minerals, the beads grow increasingly attractive with age; the more the loop of beads is rubbed in the palm the smoother and more crystalline they become, and the more they are valued. When Shadman passed away, my mother wanted to give me some of his prayer beads that were in her possession. I declined. The beads' natural home was his hands. I also had no doubt that every time I handled any of them, I would be overcome with the grating thought that the hands that had burnished them were now reduced to dirt and bone.

In family gatherings, Fakhreddin was always seated in the lushest armchair. Most of the time, he sat with his eyes shut. It was hard to tell whether he was somnolent and unhappy to be away from his books and pen or if he was alert and silently following the ongoing chatter. Even as a child, I could see that his presence invested the gathering with a sort of solemnity and formality – perhaps because of how highly my mother revered her brother, *Aqa Dādāsh*. It took several decades for my childish reverence to turn into a recognition of his important role in the intellectual history of Iran.

Several years after his death, it was decided to reprint his *Taskhir-e Tamaddon-e Farangi* (Capturing Western Civilization) at the initiative of my maternal cousin Zahra Shadman. The publisher was a former student from the

Faculty of Law and Political Science where I had once had the pleasure of teaching. I was asked to write a foreword, and I proudly accepted. Earlier on, I had written a couple of articles in Persian and English about Fakhreddin Shadman and the question of modernity. While researching the subject, I had read a note of his saying he was in the process of writing a tract titled *Siyasatnameh* (Governance). His untimely death at sixty from cancer – perhaps induced by his grief at the mendacity of the times – is what likely thwarted his chance to finish it. One day I asked Zahra if she knew about the manuscript. She didn't but said "Uncle kept a diary," and promised to send it to me. It took about fifteen years before a trusty traveler – Hossein Shadman, another of my cousins – brought me that fascinating compendium. Even a quick scan of the notebooks was enough for me to appreciate their significance. They contain not only original accounts of his own life but cover many key events in the first half of the twentieth century in Iran. The diary begins when he was eighteen and a seminarian and continues up to a few days before his death. We plan to publish the entire six-volume collection with the help of my friend Kioumars Ghereghlou, curator of Stanford library's Middle East collection.

As I skimmed through more of the entries in his diary I noticed two words that cropped up repeatedly: "Read Book." He apparently began every day with that command and did not go to bed at night before another "Read Book." He was an inveterate reader all his life, though he also loved theatre and music. Even as a seminarian he spent most days prowling around bookstores and thrift shops, and at times his friends' homes, to buy or borrow books. In some journal entries he writes in a despondent tone: "No book." His prose is simple whatever the subject, but its rich texture betrays his infinite attraction to and curiosity about books. Contrary to

some intellectuals who favor simple and simplistic knowledge derived from what they have heard, Shadman belonged
to the camp of the likes of Mohammad Qazvini and Hasan
Taqizadeh, able to abide the tedium and difficulty and
complexity of knowledge that derives from research and hard
work. The texture of Shadman's prose is shaped by that kind
of knowledge. He was critical of the shallow and presump-
tuous *fokolis* (Persianized *faux col*, a detachable collar) – false
intellectuals who use big words borrowed from some Western
thinker and fashion them into sentences that are hard to pene-
trate, and in doing so try to confer a manufactured gravity on
their prose. Shadman's prose is that of someone whose considerable reading has been absorbed and become part of their
thinking, allowing them to present multiple layers of meaning
in plain and unaffected language. In prose, simplicity is the
ultimate beauty. To express complex ideas plainly is a lot
more difficult than describing simplistic concepts cryptically.

Temperance and sobriety were in fact part of the fabric of
Shadman's thought. One night, when I believe he was minister
of justice – his various ministerial posts, especially in General
Zahedi's cabinet, being the chief reason for pushback by the
intellectual community – his home was burglarized. Farangis
heard the intruder's footsteps. She woke up Fakhreddin who
went to the landing to take a look. In the first volume of his
journal he describes a nightmare in which he sees a burglar.
He freezes and is unable to accost the man. He cries out
in despair. His cries reach his friends who are playing cards
downstairs, and they come up and shake him awake. In
reality, standing on the landing Shadman saw a real burglar
bagging their valuables. He stood still for a few moments
then he said, "Mister, you are a thief." His writing is that
simple and honest and precise. His speech and demeanor were
not aggressive. The burglar in the nightmare that virtually

paralyzed him might be construed as an early metaphor for the regime that grabbed power in Iran in 1979 and has since tried to turn back what Shadman and other Iranian advocates of modernity aspired to achieve.

Bullying, violence, and hypocrisy in prose invariably translate into an analogous ethos in politics and society.

Shadman resented the phony modernism of the throng of *fokoli*s who were infatuated with the West but did not know Iran nor valued Iranian culture. He equally disdained an obscurantist tradition that wished to erase Iranian identity and the Persian language by the force of Islam and the Arabic language. He questioned why Persian and Sa'di was not taught in the seminaries. He mocked the *fokoli*s who, having embraced the West in mere appearance, had forgotten their Persian. He refused to be squeezed in either the intellectual or the political arena. Neither the lure of power nor of fame, neither riches nor family pressure could dent his integrity. Part of his ability to resist corruption may be due to Farangis Namazi's wealth shielding him from financial insecurity, although incorruptibility was an inherent trait of his even before their marriage.

That said, at one point in the Shah's era Shadman fell in line with many others, for a short while at least, and grew decidedly drawn to Khomeini. He had spent a lifetime advocating religious reform yet in 1963, several years after resigning his post as head of the Imam Reza endowed trust, he started listening to Khomeini's covertly distributed audiotapes in which the cleric stormed against the Shah's socio-economic reforms. I once went with my mother to the bazaar in Tehran to pick up a tape from a shopkeeper that Shadman would then discuss with her at home. He also discussed professional wrestling with her, which was then popular on television; you could say both topics were in vogue, though it was only one of them that turned Iran upside down and the whole process of modernization with it.

Though modernity was at the heart of Shadman's work, thinking, and writing, he was never infatuated with the West. He spoke of "capturing" Western civilization, not imitating or surrendering to it. A distorted version of his critique of the pseudo-modernists' crush on the West is articulated in Jalal Al-Ahmad's *Gharbzadegi* (Westoxification). Shadman did not believe that modernity was at odds with or hostile to religion as such. During his time in Mashhad, hardly a day passed that he would not visit the shrine of Imam Reza to worship.

Shadman's spirituality did not stop carpetbaggers whose attempts to sponge from the Imam Reza Trust he had thwarted from writing unsigned letters accusing him of blasphemy, which eventually forced him from his post. He was a believer but he did not have any illusions about Islam being "revolutionary." Nor did he wear his faith on his sleeve or use it to gain favor with those who traded in religion. He never tried to keep Farangis from her wide-ranging social and cultural engagements either, or pressure her to wear the hijab. Perhaps one clear sign of Shadman's modernity is to have married someone who had gone to England alone in 1937 to study, knowing that such an emancipated woman would never submit to an outwardly modern but inwardly patriarchal and hypocritical husband, no matter how hard he tried.

To Shadman, being modern did not mean one could not enjoy friendships with individuals of a different persuasion, religious or otherwise. When he was a young seminarian, he worked with the socialist Farrokhi Yazdi; he was friends with Mary, the wife of the American administrator of Iran's finances Arthur Millspaugh; he spent the eve of Ashura with friends and soulmates at the house of his father, himself a cleric, having fun and listening to music until dawn and occasionally even gambling. His religion was not his trade; it was a source of spiritual security, not a means of climbing the social and political ladder. He kept his religion separate from his politics, something he coveted for Iran as a whole. After resigning from his position in Mashhad he taught in the Faculty of Rational and Received Sciences (now Faculty of Theology), which was established by Reza Shah as part of his effort to segregate state from religion as far as possible.

If the rise of Reza Shah and his success in modernizing Iran may be attributed to the support of individuals like Mohammad-Ali Foroughi and Taqizadeh, Qazvini and Shadman, in my view – at least in cultural and economic terms – the collapse of the Pahlavi era at the peak of modernization was partly due to the fact that in the last two decades of Mohammad-Reza Shah's reign people who knew Iran well and were technocrats besides, and also had the wisdom and tenacity of statesmen were rarely in positions of authority in domestic affairs. The likes of Fakhreddin Shadman were replaced with individuals whose understanding of Iranian culture was secondary to their expertise in their respective fields and who were also less inclined to stand up to the Shah.

In recent years, when the Islamic regime hit a wall and its utilitarian promotion of the likes of Al-Ahmad came to naught, some proposed advocating Shadman's fame and philosophy instead. They had no idea. Al-Ahmad was a simplistic and traditionalist cleric in a suit, whereas Shadman, even when he wore a turban, was a profound and progressive thinker who loved Iran. His library, which was donated to the University of Tehran, is now under the gavel of a regime which is by nature an enemy of learning, modernity, and Iran. Fortunately, every page of his detailed daily journal is now at Stanford and will soon be available for all to read in the digital library of the future.

Glossary

aqa, (pron. āqā), "man," "mister," applied to men regardless of age; depending on the tone, it can mean "sir."

aqayan, (pron. āqāyān), "gentlemen." Post-revolution, it is used as a moniker for the **mullahs,** with snide connotations.

aqazadeh, "son of a man," a polite way of referring to a male child, regardless of age. Post-revolution, the term mockingly refers to the offspring of wealthy and powerful clerics.

ayatollah, "sign of God," honorific title of elect clerics in Twelver Shiism, the highest rank being a Grand Ayatollah. Followers may switch their allegiance among ayatollahs at will.

Baha'i Faith, a universalist religion founded in Iran in the mid-19th century that Islam considers an apostasy.

Basiji, "mobilized," initially groups of voluntary vigilantes that the Islamic regime later institutionalized as a militia army that attacks dissidents violently and with impunity.

bozorg, "great," hence *khanom* bozorg, or "grande dame."

chelokabab, a national Iranian dish of rice served with skewered beef, *kabab* in Persian.

Confederation of Iranian Students, an international body formed from the merger of a European confederation founded in Germany (1960) and the Iranian Students Association in the U.S. (founded 1952). The Confederation organized anti-Shah protests abroad in the 1960s. Some of its more radical groups engaged in underground resistance in Iran in the 1970s.

daie, (pron. dā-ī), maternal uncle, also used as a term of endearment to address a male individual regardless of family relationships. Other kinship terms similarly include: *amou* (paternal uncle), *khaleh* (maternal aunt), *ammeh* (paternal aunt), *madar* (mother,) *pedar* (father,) *pesar* (son), and *dokhtar* (daughter).

dāsh and *dādāsh*, colloquially "bro" or "brother."

dowreh, "circle," a regular private gathering.

fatwa, a non-binding but authoritative ruling issued by a high-ranking Islamic cleric.

Haji, Hāj Aqa, an honorific title for someone who has made the Hajj pilgrimage to Mecca; also used generically to mean "mister."

Howzeh, "area," the term is used for specific religious centers or seminaries, as in *howzeh-ye* Qom. It also applied to the Confederation of Iranian Students meetings, and in this book, an affiliated private meeting to test or prepare new blood, hence, a novitiate cell.

imam, "leader," as in a Friday prayer leader. In Shiism, it is also the title of up to twelve descendants of Mohammad through his son-in-law Ali (as in **Imam** Hossein) who are considered holy and able to intercede on behalf of petitioners. The notion is anathema to orthodox Sunni Islam, which upholds a categorial divide between the divine and the human.

jan, (pron. jān), "dear," and, more informally, *joon.*

khanom, "woman," a term of respect applied to women regardless of marital status, the equivalent of Ms./Miss/Mrs./Madam. See also *bozorg.*

Mahdi, Mehdi in Persian, "guide" or the "guided one," the savior figure in Islam. The Shia identify him as the twelfth **Imam** who is presently in occultation and expected to reappear at the end of time.

Mirza/Miz, shortened form of *Mir-zadeh* (child of an [A]mir, "lord"), a generic term of respect that if applied after a first name, as in Soleiman Mirza, specifies nobility.

Miz-Dādāsh. See *Mirza/Miz* and *dāsh.*

Mullah, (pron. mollā), a Shia cleric in Persian, from Arabic *mawla* (master, guardian). Mullahs wear a white turban, or a black one if they claim descent from the Prophet Mohammad. See *seyyed.*

nejāsat (noun), *najes* (adj.), ritually "unclean" in Islamic laws of purity.

nastaʿliq-e shekasteh, "broken script," an ornamental style of Persian cursive handwriting.

National Front of Iran, *Jebhe-ye Melli-e Iran,* a broad political coalition founded in 1949 by Prime Minister Mohammad Mosaddeq, mobilized to nationalize the Iranian oil industry. The Front splintered in the 1960s; the secular factions championed nationalist liberal democracy while the religious supported Khomeini and Fadaiyan-e Islam.

Patience stone, *Sang-e sabour,* in Persian folklore, a magical object that listens to a person's tales of woe and absorbs the pain. In everyday usage, it refers to someone with a strong capacity for listening and empathy.

rowzeh-khan, reciter of Shia elegies in *rowzeh-khani* ceremonies.

SAVAK, *Sazeman-e Ettela'at va Amniat-e Keshvar*, Iranian intelligence and security agency founded in 1957 under General Teymour Bakhtiar and dissolved by Prime Minister Shapur Bakhtiar on the eve of the 1979 revolution.

Seyyed/Seyyedeh, honorific title of a man/woman who claims descent from the prophet Mohammad.

Shia/Shiite, a multiform branch of Islam that idolizes up to twelve descendants of Mohammad as infallible Imams (see **imam, Mahdi**). The Safavids established Twelver-Shiism as the state religion in the early 16th c. to disentangle Iran from the Sunni caliphate in Baghdad. Islamic orthodoxy considers the Shia heretical.

ta'rof, a civil formality such as the offer of a gift, a discount in a transaction, an invitation, or other privilege that is expected to be cordially declined.

taghuti, "idolatrous," an arcane term applied by Khomeini to members of the ancien régime and generally to affluent people outside the religious establishment.

taqiyyeh, "dissimulation," a Shia doctrine that allows individuals to hide their faith when in jeopardy.

Tudeh Party, *Hezb-e Tudeh*, "Party of the Masses," a communist party founded in 1941 by Prince Soleiman Mirza Eskandari-Qajar that built a secret military wing in the army. By 1946, it became devoutly Stalinist and subjected to the Kremlin, compromising Iran's territorial integrity and political autonomy. Key leaders included Ehsan Tabari and Noureddin Kianouri.

Tudeh'i, a member of the **Tudeh Party.**

Velayat-e faqih, "Guardianship of the [Islamic] Jurist," a peculiar form of Shia theocracy headed by a lifetime "supreme leader." The unprecedented doctrine was formulated by Ayatollah Khomeini and incorporated into the constitution of the Islamic Republic of Iran in 1979.

Acknowledgments

LIKE PERSIAN COOKING, writing requires a long, deliberate, simmering process. The ultimate test of the quality of a dish is how it tastes to those who share it. It is up to the readers of *Simorgh: Portraits on My Mind*, a collection of memories that has simmered in my mind for as long as I have lived, to decide whether it passes the test.

Writing is usually a lonely and tortured process. *Simorgh* was for me the exception. The memories recounted here were full of pain and pathos, tragedy and triumph. Putting them into words was cathartic, joyful and almost effortless.

I originally wrote the book in two volumes in Persian, each titled *Si Chehreh* (Thirty Portraits), and published in Toronto in 2022 and 2023. The translated edition, *Simorgh*, encompasses the originals in a two-part single volume.

Some translators are said to murder the text and the author they translate; more are accused of treason, said to be the endemic or ontological nature of their profession; a handful distort the meaning and intent of the original and reinvent it as a work of their own imagination. Lucky is a text that finds a scholar like Mahasti Afshar who renders the original with precision, economy, erudition, and attention not just to a word's literal sense but its labyrinthine layers of meanings. She is no less attentive to the tempo and texture of the original. For me, one of the greatest rewards in writing *Simorgh* was that she decided to translate it.

And it is no less of a cherished award that the English edition is produced by Mage, refined and erudite publishers of some of the most important books on Iran, and pioneer presenters of the delights of Persian cuisine to the world, no less.

Last but not least, I am grateful to my colleagues at Stanford University Roma Parhad and Franco Errico for their indispensable help at every stage of *Simorgh*'s publication.

Abbas Milani

About the Author

Raised in Iran, Abbas Milani was sent to be educated in California in the 1960s. He became politically active and in 1974 received a PhD in Political Science. He returned to Tehran and taught at the National University but was imprisoned by the Pahlavi regime in 1977. After the revolution he became a professor at Tehran University, but by 1986 his utopian illusions had been shattered and he emigrated to the United States. Dr. Milani is the Hamid and Christina Moghadam Director of Iranian Studies Program at Stanford University and co-director of the Iran Democracy Project at the Hoover Institution. His Mage publications include, *Tales of Two Cities: A Persian Memoir*, *The Persian Sphinx: Amir-Abbas Hoveyda and the Riddle of the Iranian Revolution*, *Lost Wisdom: Rethinking Modernity in Iran*, and a translation of Houshang Golshiri's *King of the Benighted*. His other books include: *The Shah*; *Eminent Persians: The Men and Women Who Made Modern Iran, 1941-1979* (2 Volumes); *The Myth of the Great Satan: A New Look at America's Relations with Iran*; *A Window into Modern Iran: The Ardeshir Zahedi Papers at the Hoover Institution Library & Archives – A Selection*

About the Translator

Mahasti Afshar (Ziai), a Tehran native, studied drama and classical music production for television at the BBC/London and ORTF/Paris and as a member of National Iranian Radio and Television, served as a technical director at the Shiraz Arts Festival. After earning a Ph.D. in Sanskrit and Indo-European Folklore and Mythology (Harvard 1988), she pursued a career as a nonprofit executive at the Getty, Los Angeles Philharmonic, XPRIZE Foundation, and National Geographic Society. At the Getty Conservation Institute, she produced documentaries and museum exhibitions around the world on cultural heritage preservation. Mahasti's publications include *Art and Eternity: Nefertari Wall Paintings*; *The Ecology of Conservation*; and the *Landmarks of a New Generation* series. Her translations include Shahrokh Meskoob's *Notes by a Traveler*; Majid Lashkari's *The Theatre and Cinema of Arby Ovanessian*; Saeed Habashi's *Final Sequence, a biography of Esma'il Kushan*; and more recently, Mesbook's *Lament for Siavash*, which along with her book in Persian, *Jashn-e Honar-e Shiraz 1967-1977*, has been published by Mage.

Also Available from Mage
Abbas Milani Books

The Persian Sphinx: Amir Abbas Hoveyda and the Iranian Revolution
Abbas Milani

King of the Benighted
Houshang Golshiri / Translated by Abbas Milani

Tales of Two Cities: A Persian Memoir
Abbas Milani

Lost Wisdom: Rethinking Modernity in Iran
Abbas Milani

An Encounter with Dylan Thomas
By Ebrahim Golestan • Edited and Translated by Abbas Milani

Lament for Siavash: On Death and Resurrection
By Shahrokh Meskoob • Translated by Mahasti Afshar • Foreword Abbas Milani

Shadman Diaries, 1926–1928, Book 1
Fakhr al-Din Shadman • Abbas Milani and Kioumars Ghereghlou

IRANIAN HISTORY BY WILLEM FLOOR
THE PERSIAN GULF SERIES

A Political and Economic History of 5 Port Cities, 1500–1750

The Rise of the Gulf Arabs, The Politics of Trade on the Persian Littoral,
1747–1792

The Rise and Fall of Bandar-e Lengeh, The Distribution Center for the
Arabian Coast, 1750–1930

Bandar Abbas: The Natural Trade Gateway of Southeast Iran

Links with the Hinterland: Bushehr, Borazjan, Kazerun,
Banu Ka'b, & Bandar Abbas

The Hula Arabs of The Shibkuh Coast of Iran

Dutch-Omani Relations: A Political History, 1651–1806

Muscat: City, Society and Trade

The Persian Gulf: Bushehr: City, Society, & Trade, 1797-1947

The Rebel Bandits of Tangestan

Karkh: The Island's Untold Story
Willem Floor & D.T. Potts

Agriculture in Qajar Iran

Public Health in Qajar Iran

The History of Theater in Iran

A Social History of Sexual Relations in Iran

Guilds, Merchants, and Ulama in Nineteenth-Century Iran

Labor & Industry in Iran 1850 -1941

The Rise and Fall of Nader Shah: Dutch East India Company Reports 1730-1747

Games Persians Play: A History of Games and Pastimes in Iran from Hide-and-Seek to Hunting

History of Bread in Iran

Studies in the History of Medicine in Iran

Salar al-Dowleh: A Delusional Prince and Wannabe Shah

Kermanshah: City and Province, 1800-1945

History of Hospitals in Iran, 550–1950

The Beginnings of Modern Medicine in Iran

History of Glace and Ceramics, 1500–1925

Transportation & Technology in Iran, 1800–1940

History of Paper in Iran, 1501–1925
Willem Floor and Amélie Couvrat Desvergnes

Khorshid Khanom
Willem Floor and Forugh Sajadi

German Sources on Safavid Persia

Russian Sources on Iran: 1719–1748

Exotic Attractions in Persia, 1684–1688: Travels & Observations
Engelbert Kaempfer

A Man of Two Worlds: Pedros Bedik in Iran, 1670–1675
Translated with Colette Ouahes from the Latin

Cookbooks by Najmieh Batmanglij

*Food of Life: Ancient Persian and
Modern Iranian Cooking and Ceremonies*

Joon: Persian Cooking Made Simple

Cooking in Iran: Regional Recipes and Kitchen Secrets

Silk Road Cooking: A Vegetarian Journey

From Persia to Napa: Wine at the Persian Table
With: Dick Davis and Burke Owens

Memoir and History

*Discovering Cyrus: The Persian Conqueror
Astride the Ancient World*
Reza Zarghamee

Tarikh-e Azodi, Life at the Court of the Early Qajar Shahs
Soltan Ahmad Mirza Azod al-Dowleh,
Edited and Translated by Manoutchehr M. Eskandari-Qajar

The Artist and the Shah: Memoirs of Life at the Persian Court
by Dust-Ali Khan Mo`ayyer al-Mamalek,
Edited and Translated by Manoutchehr M. Eskandari-Qajar

*Crowning Anguish: Taj al-Saltana
Memoirs of a Persian Princess*
Introduction by Abbas Amanat / Translated by Anna Vanzan

French Hats in Iran
Heydar Radjavi

Father Takes a Drink and Other Memories of Iran
Heydar Radjavi

The Persian Garden: Echoes of Paradise
Mehdi Khansari / M. R. Moghtader / Minouch Yavari

Closed Circuit History
Ardeshir Mohassess, foreword by Ramsey Clark

Mosaddegh: Ahead of Their Time, Book 1
Nicolas Gorjestani

Poetry

Faces of Love: Hafez and the Poets of Shiraz – Bilingual Edition
Translated by Dick Davis

The Mirror Of My Heart:
A Thousand Years of Persian Poetry by Women – Bilingual Edition
Translated by Dick Davis

Pearls That Soak My Dress: Elegies for a Child
Jahan Malek Khatun/ translated by Dick Davis

Layli and Majnun
Nezami Ganjavi / Translated by Dick Davis

Khosrow and Shirin
Nezami Ganjavi / Translated by Dick Davis

Shahnameh: the Persian Book of Kings
Abolqasem Ferdowsi / Translated by Dick Davis

Rostam: Tales of Love and War from Persia's Book of Kings
Abolqasem Ferdowsi / Translated by Dick Davis

Borrowed Ware: Medieval Persian Epigrams
Introduced and Translated by Dick Davis

At Home and Far from Home
Poems on Iran and Persian Culture
Dick Davis

When They Broke Down the Door: Poems
Fatemeh Shams / Introduction and translations by Dick Davis

The Layered Heart: Essays on Persian Poetry
In Celebration of Dick Davis
Edited by Ali-Asghar Seyyed Ghorab

Another Birth and Other Poems – Bilingual edition
By Forugh Farrokhzad
translated by Hasan Javadi and Susan Sallée

Obeyd-e Zakani: Ethics of Aristocrats and other Satirical Works
translated by Hasan Javadi

Milkvetch and Violets
Bilingual Edition
Mohammad Reza Shafi'i-Kadkani/ translated by Mojdeh Bahar

Song of the Ground Jay: Poems by Iranian Women, 1960–2022
Bilingual Edition
Translated by Mojdeh Bahar

Silence and Lost Words
Bilingual Edition
Rouhangiz Karachi translated by Mojdeh Bahar

Audio Books

Faces of Love: Hafez and the Poets of Shiraz
Translated by Dick Davis / Penguin Audio / Read by
Dick Davis, Tala Ashe and Ramiz Monsef

The Mirror of My Heart:
A Thousand Years of Persian Poetry by Women
Translated by Dick Davis / Penguin Audio / Read by
Dick Davis, Mozhan Marno, Tala Ashe and Serena Manteghi

Layli and Majnun
Nezami Ganjavi / Translated by Dick Davis
Penguin Audio / Read by
Dick Davis, Peter Ganim, Serena Manteghi and Sean Rohani

The Shahnameh
Abolqasem Ferdowsi / Translated by Dick Davis
Penguin / Echo Point Audio / Read by
Dick Davis, Sean Rohani, Nikki Massoud

Vis and Ramin
Fakhraddin Gorgani / Translated by Dick Davis
Mage Audio / Read by
Mary Sarah Agliotta, Dick Davis (introduction)

My Uncle Napoleon
Iraj Pezeshkzad / Translated by Dick Davis
Mage Audio / Read by
Moti Margolin, Dick Davis (Introduction)

Savushun: A Novel about Modern Iran
Simin Daneshvar / Translated by M.R. Ghanoonparvar
Mage Audio / Read by
Mary Sarah Agliotta, Brian Spooner (Introduction)

Crowning Anguish: Taj al-Saltaneh
Memoirs of a Persian Princess
from the Harem to Modernity, 1884– 1914
Introduction by Abbas Amanat / Translated by Anna Vanzan
Mage Audio / Read by
Kathreen Khavari

www.ingramcontent.com/pod-product-compliance
Lightning Source LLC
Chambersburg PA
CBHW030311100426
42812CB00002B/666